Historical Studies in

INDUSTRIAL RELATIONS

No. 41 2020

Edited by

Paul Smith and Dave Lyddon

Liverpool University Press

Editorial Committee
Paul Smith
Dave Lyddon (Keele)
Steve French (Staffordshire)
Keith Gildart (Wolverhampton)
Jean Jenkins (Cardiff)
Jim Phillips (Glasgow)
Roger Seifert (Wolverhampton)

Editorial Advisers
Linda Clarke (Westminster)
Richard Hyman (LSE)
James Jaffe (Wisconsin-Whitewater)
Steve Jefferys (London Metropolitan)
Roger McKenzie (Unison)
Noel Whiteside (Warwick)
Chris Wrigley (Nottingham)

Contents

Commentaries

Reflections

Review Essay

Extended Review

Book Reviews

Important Notice

Liverpool University Press is pleased to announce the migration of all journals to a new bespoke online platform, hosted by Cloud Publish.

www.liverpooluniversitypress.co.uk/journals

Our previous website currently has redirects in place and your access to subscribed journals will not be interrupted.

If you have any questions about the migration please contact Clare Hooper, Head of Journals, at clare.hooper@liverpool.ac.uk.

https://doi.org/10.3828/hsir.2020.41.16

Frank Burchill

Without the support of Frank Burchill (1937–2020), *Historical Studies in Industrial Relations* (*HSIR*) may never have got off the ground. Frank, professor of industrial relations and head of department at Keele University, backed the initiative in 1994, leading to the journal's launch as a bi-annual in 1996, initially published by the short-lived Keele University Press. When the publisher folded in 1997, Frank facilitated the Centre for Industrial Relations publishing it in-house, an arrangement that continued until the University finally withdrew support and we went to Liverpool University Press as an annual, starting with issue 33 (2012). Frank was on the original editorial committee but withdrew soon after retiring from Keele in 2002. He published two articles in the journal. The first was in our 'classics' series, 'Walton and McKersie, *A Behavioral Theory of Labor Negotiations* (1965)', *HSIR* 8 (1999); the second, 'The Pay Review Body System: A Comment and a Consequence', *HSIR* 10 (2000). Frank was, first and foremost, an adult educator, but also a long-standing arbitrator and a trade-union historian. These attributes explained his support for Keele's suite of distance-learning qualifications in industrial relations (launched in 1989, with the last intake taught out in 2019, after a long rearguard action in defence of the courses).

Robert Taylor

While working for *New Society* among other weeklies, then as labour correspondent for the *Observer* and employment editor at the *Financial Times*, Robert Taylor (1943–2020) produced a series of important works on trade-unionism. Among them were *The Fifth Estate. Britain's Unions in the Seventies* (1978 and 1980); *The Trade Union Question in British Politics: Government and Unions since 1945* (1993); and *The TUC: From the General Strike to New Unionism* (2000). Robert then published 'Citrine's Unexpurgated Diaries, 1925–26: "The Mining Crisis and the National Strike"', in *HSIR* 20 (2005). He also alerted us to the existence and location of Walter Milne-Bailey's unpublished 'A Nation on Strike: The Causes, Progress and Results of the British National Strike of 1926' (September 1926); extracts (some 40,000 words) were subsequently published in *HSIR* 29/30 (2010). Robert was probably unique in bringing his long experience of labour reporting into the world of academic seminars and conferences, enlivening them in the process.

HSIR 41 (2020) 1–35

https://doi.org/10.3828/hsir.2020.41.1

'A Great Number of … Women'?: The Changing Involvement of Female Workers in Master and Servant Cases in England, 1685–1860

Madeleine Chartrand

On back-to-back days in March 1727, at his familial estate in south-eastern Kent, a Justice of the Peace, James Brockman, heard the grievances of two servants against their employers. Elizabeth Cashpull complained that her master had turned her away before the end of her term of service, while Elizabeth Mittler accused her mistress Hannah Gillett of beating her.[1] The two Elizabeths were among sixty-two women involved in the employment disputes that Brockman recorded in his notebook of magisterial business between 1725 and 1767.[2] One hundred and twenty-six years later, on 3 June 1853, Nathaniel Chandler and two other magistrates presiding at the Tewkesbury Petty Sessions sentenced Mary Merrick to fourteen days' hard labour in the house of correction.[3] Mary worked in the silk factory that the 'adventurer' Humphrey Brown converted from an old theatre after striking it rich in the 1846 railroad mania.[4] According to the factory manager, Thomas Goodwin, she had embezzled more than a pound of silk thread. She was one of only eight women involved in employment

---

1 'Memorandum-book of business transacted as JPs', 3 and 4 March 1727, p. 38: MSS Add. 42599, British Library, London.
2 James Brockman recorded 148 master and servant cases in total.
3 'Tewkesbury Borough Petty Sessions Division (Magistrate's Court)', 3 June 1853, p. 385, PS/TW/B/M1/1: Gloucestershire Archives, Gloucester (Glos. Archs).
4 H. Jennings, *The Childishness and Brutality of the Time: Some Plain Truths in Plain Language* (Vizetelly and Co.: 1883), pp. 338–9.

disputes recorded at the Tewkesbury Petty Sessions from 1829 to 1853.[5] While women made up 42% of all the workers in employment disputes in Brockman's eighteenth-century notebook, they only accounted for 10% of them in the nineteenth-century Tewkesbury records.

These examples are illustrative of a transformation that occurred in female workers' experience of master and servant law – the body of statutes, judicial doctrine and social practice that regulated English employment relationships for more than half a millennium.[6] Through a quantitative and qualitative analysis of employment conflicts found in the records of summary courts, where magistrates administered master and servant law, this article shows that women accounted for a decreasing share of all workers involved in employment disputes from the early eighteenth to the mid-nineteenth century. However, female textile workers, such as Merrick, constituted a notable exception to this trend. Women workers' changing involvement in employment conflicts heard in summary courts is related to shifts in female labour force participation during England's industrialization. Specifically, I suggest that diminishing employment opportunities for women in arable agriculture contributed to the overall decreasing presence of women workers in master and servant cases. Female textile workers were more involved in employment disputes than women workers in general because manufacturers in the expanding textile industries used prosecutions under master and servant law to discipline a largely female labour force. These women's productivity, which helped fuel the Industrial Revolution, was achieved in part under the compulsion of master and servant law.

I

In response to the shortage of workers and wage inflation brought about in the fourteenth century by the Black Death and the substantial depopulation it wrought, the English state began to regulate labour by means of master and servant law.[7] From its inception, its aim was to make the supply and performance of labour cheaper and more reliable by forcing down wages

---

5 Eighty-three employment disputes are contained in PS/TW/B/M1/1: Glos. Archs.

6 D. Hay and P. Craven, 'Introduction', in D. Hay and P. Craven (eds), *Masters, Servants, and Magistrates in Britain and the Empire, 1562–1955* (University of North Carolina Press, Chapel Hill, NC: 2004), pp. 1–58, at pp. 1–2.

7 D. Hay, 'England', in Hay and Craven (eds), *Masters, Servants, and Magistrates*, pp. 59–116, at pp. 62–6; R. Palmer, *English Law in the Age of the Black Death, 1348–1381: A Transformation of Governance and Law* (University of North Carolina Press, Chapel Hill, NC: 1993).

and increasing employers' disciplinary powers.[8] Statute and case law
constituted the foundation of a legal regime that provided the conceptual
framework within which employment relationships were contracted and
disputed. Parliament passed legislation, such as the Statute of Artificers
(1562), which re-codified medieval ordinances and laid the foundations
of employment law for the next three centuries. The twelve judges of
the central royal courts of common law – particularly the four judges of
King's Bench, led by the Lord Chief Justice of England – interpreted the
meaning of these statutes and created case law through rulings that set legal
precedents.[9]

The day-to-day administration of employment law was left to
magistrates called justices of the peace – amateurs who generally had
no formal legal training. When acting alone, they were endowed with
considerable summary powers, including the adjudication of master and
servant complaints. Two or more magistrates sitting together also enjoyed
extensive administrative authority in their neighbourhoods. The need to
associate with other magistrates in order to exercise these powers of local
government led them to hold regular meetings called 'petty sessions'. In
addition to their administrative work, magistrates also dealt with disputes
at petty sessions, including employment conflicts.[10]

The records left by these magistrates are the main repositories of
employment disputes. This article has utilized twenty-five notebooks kept
by individual magistrates and twenty-nine proceedings of petty sessions.

---

8 Hay and Craven, 'Introduction', pp. 26–8; M. Steinberg, 'Capitalist
Development, the Labor Process, and the Law', *American Journal of Sociology*
109:2 (2003), pp. 445–95, at p. 446; R. Steinfeld, *Coercion, Contract, and
Free Labor in the Nineteenth Century* (Cambridge University Press: 2001),
p. 9; Hay and Craven, 'Introduction', p. 28; M. Steinberg, *England's Great
Transformation: Law, Labor, and the Industrial Revolution* (University of
Chicago Press: 2016), pp. 4, 51–138.

9 Hay and Craven, 'Introduction', pp. 1–2, 6; D. Hay (ed.), *Criminal Cases on the
Crown Side of Kings' Bench: Staffordshire, 1740–1800* (Staffordshire Record
Society: 2010); *idem*, 'The Courts of Westminster Hall in the Eighteenth
Century', in P. Girard, J. Phillips, and B. Cahill (eds), *The Supreme Court
of Nova Scotia, 1754–2004: From Imperial Bastion to Provincial Oracle*
(Osgoode Society for Canadian Legal History and University of Toronto Press:
2004), pp. 20–1; W. Cornish, 'Labour Law, I. From Labouring to Employment:
1820–1867; II. The Roots of Collective Action', in W. Cornish, J. S. Anderson,
R. Cocks, M. Lobban, P. Polden, and K. Smith, *The Oxford History of the Laws
of England: Vol. 13: 1820–1914, Fields of Development* (Oxford University
Press: 2010), part 3, pp. 623–66.

10 G. Smith (ed.), *Summary Justice in the City: A Selection of Cases Heard at the
Guildhall Justice Room, 1752–1781* (London Record Society, Boydell Press,
Woodbridge: 2013), p. xi; N. Landau, *The Justices of the Peace, 1679–1760*
(University of California Press, Berkeley, CA: 1984), pp. 8, 9, 23, 27, 28.

These sources have been supplemented with calendars of two houses of correction – since workers (though generally not employers) could be imprisoned for breaches of contract – and one record of Quarter Sessions. At Quarter Sessions, which took place four times a year, all the magistrates in a county, or those who bothered to attend, sat together in judgment on lesser crimes that could not be tried summarily (with the most serious offences, such as murder, reserved for the biannual Assizes, when the High Court judges travelled in circuits around the counties). Master and servant disputes, which fell under the summary jurisdiction of magistrates, were less likely to be tried at Quarter Sessions but did occasionally appear there. Cases of theft by workers from their employers were also heard at Quarter Sessions, since larceny was technically not supposed to be tried summarily until the mid-nineteenth century (though it often was).[11]

These fifty-seven sources in total span from the late seventeenth to the mid-nineteenth century and are drawn from sixteen English counties. In part, the geographic scope of the project has been dictated by the survival and accessibility of records. It also encompasses a range of economic regions, from principally agricultural areas, such as West Lavington in Wiltshire; to areas of textile manufacture, both domestic and factory, such as Guilsborough, Devizes, and Macclesfield; to more industrial areas, such as Atherstone in Warwickshire.[12] No sources from London have been used because the metropolis was exceptional in its size, level of petty offending, occupational patterns, and system of summary justice.[13]

The cases of employment disputes – 3,485 in total – were transcribed for this research. Most, such as claims for unpaid wages and complaints about workers running away, fell under the purview of master and servant law. Others, such as larcenies and assaults, technically did not. Nevertheless, they represented a breakdown of the employment relationship requiring legal intervention the same way as master and servant infractions. Furthermore, though assaults and thefts were legally distinct from master

---

11 Hay and Craven, 'Introduction', pp. 1–2; J. M. Beattie, *Crime and the Courts in England, 1660–1800* (Clarendon Press, Oxford: 1986), p. 5; Hay, 'England', p. 107.

12 Hay, 'England', pp. 97–8.

13 D. Gray, *Crime, Prosecution and Social Relations: The Summary Courts of the City of London in the Late Eighteenth Century* (Palgrave Macmillan, Basingstoke: 2009), pp. 7–17; J. M. Beattie, *Policing and Punishment in London, 1660–1750: Urban Crime and the Limits of Terror* (Oxford University Press: 2001), pp. 4–6, 77–113; Smith, *Summary Justice*, pp. xi–xxx; R. Shoemaker, *Prosecution and Punishment: Petty Crime and the Law in London and Rural Middlesex, c. 1660–1725* (Cambridge University Press: 1991), pp. 90–1. London also had a legal custom of a monthly hiring for some workers, different from the presumptive yearly hiring; Hay, 'England', pp. 68, 89 n. 112.

and servant breaches, in practice the boundaries between these offences were blurred, porous, and frequently ignored. Such interconnections and ambiguities encourage a more comprehensive view of employment conflicts and the responses to them. A stricter adherence to the legal classification of crimes would distort the reality that they existed together on a continuum of transgressive behaviour contested and negotiated by servants, masters, and magistrates.

As much information as possible from each employment dispute has been encoded in a database.[14] This provides a statistical overview of the involvement and treatment of male and female workers in master and servant disputes. As the database consists of an opportunistic combination of heterogeneous sources of varying degrees of completeness, the disputes are far from random samples. Tests of statistical significance performed on the percentages derived from them would be meaningless. Arguments about the significance of the findings relate to their importance from a social, legal, or historical perspective.[15]

II

One principal finding is that females made up a decreasing share of all workers involved in employment disputes over the period. This, illustrated in Figure 1, could be caused by a falling number of cases involving women or a steady number of female cases with a rising number of male ones. Figure 2 shows the total number of employment disputes involving servants per year. The trend lines reveal that cases involving females remained relatively stable, apart from a small spike in the mid-eighteenth century, whereas male cases rose dramatically in the nineteenth century. The falling share of female cases (Figure 1) therefore appears to be caused by male cases increasing rather than female ones decreasing.

However, Figure 3 shows that there are more sources in the database for the second half of the period than the first. The average number of cases per source is given for each sex in Figure 4. There is a clear decrease in those involving females from the early eighteenth to the mid-nineteenth century.

Table 1 shows that, for females, the average number of cases per source dropped from twenty-five during 1685–1780 to six-and-a-half during

---

14 This includes the date of the case; the names and gender of the servants and employers involved; whether each disputant was the plaintiff or defendant; the type of work that they performed (when mentioned); the specific grievances or charges brought; and the outcome of the hearing.
15 Scholars are also beginning to question the value of using statistical signif-icance at all: V. Amrhein, S. Greenland, and B. McShane, 'Retire Statistical Significance', *Nature* 567 (2019), pp. 305–7.

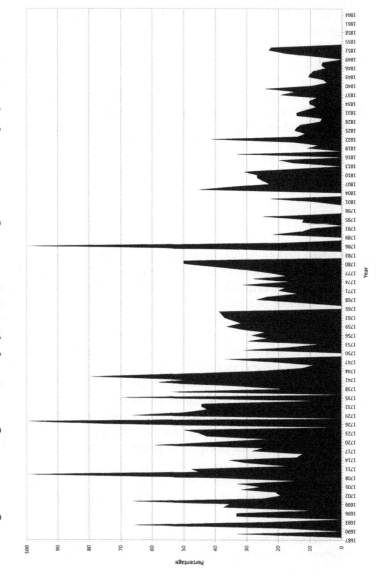

Figure 1: Percentage share of employment cases involving female workers per year, 1685–1860

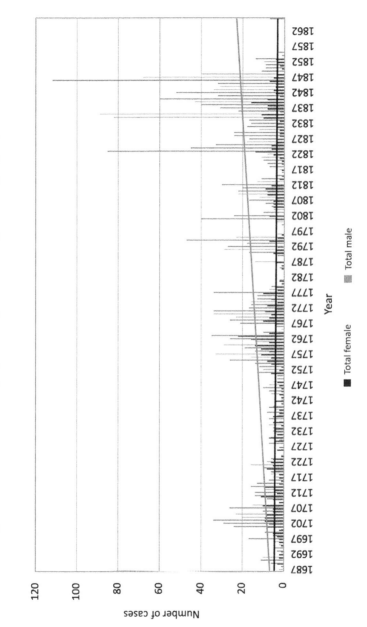

Figure 2: Total number of employment disputes involving servants per year, 1687–1858.

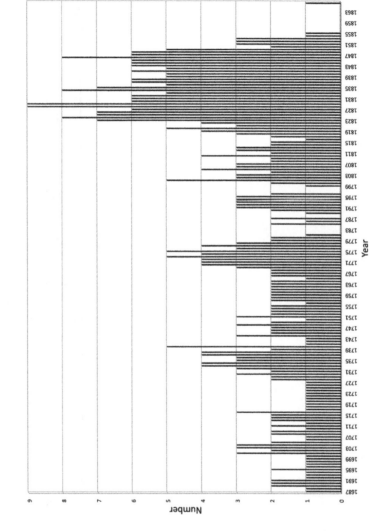

Figure 3: Number of sources per year from which cases were drawn, 1685–1860

Figure 4: Average number of cases involving female and male workers per source per year, 1685–1860

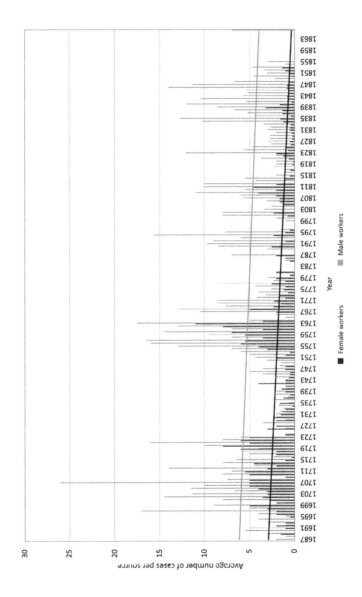

1780–1860, and their average share was halved. The average number of cases (per source) involving males also declined, from sixty-one to forty-one. The trend observed in Figure 1 is not the result of a sharp increase in male cases after all. Females really were less involved in employment disputes in the summary courts from roughly the turn of the nineteenth century.

Table 1: Data from both halves of the period covered by the database, 1685–1860

	1685–1780	1780–1860
Number of sources	17	40
Total number of cases	1,467	2,018
Total number of female workers	420	260
Average number of female workers per source	25	6.5
Total number of male workers	1,033	1,631
Average number of male workers per source	61	41
Share of all cases involving female workers	29%	13%
Average share of female workers per source	26%	13%

III

It is possible that a King's Bench decision of the late eighteenth century paved the way for the declining number of cases involving female workers. There was an ongoing debate about which categories of workers fell under master and servant law. The Statute of Artificers (1562) re-codified medieval labour legislation relating to 'apprentices, servants and labourers, as well in husbandry as in divers other arts, mysteries and occupations'.[16] One stipulation was that every person not 'lawfully retained in household or in any office with any nobleman gentleman or others' could be compelled to serve.[17] The wording of this section was convoluted, but suggested that domestic servants were excluded. Justice Eyre remarked in a rather non-committal way in 1714 that the Statute did not 'seem' to

---

16 5 Eliz. 1 c. 4 (1562), preamble; Hay and Craven, 'Introduction', p. 6; Hay, 'England', p. 63.

17 5 Eliz. 1 c. 4, s. 4 (1562).

give magistrates authority to order the payment of wages to gentlemen's servants, but added that nevertheless they did so 'every day'.[18] This practice was in line with the generally broad interpretation that High Court judges of the eighteenth century adopted on which workers were covered by the Statute – whether labourers in industries not specifically mentioned in its clauses fell within its purview. When, early in the eighteenth century, Lord Chief Justices Parker and Pratt argued for a more restrictive reading of the Statute that went against prevailing theory and practice, Parliament intervened and passed several new Acts extending master and servant coverage to many trades hitherto not specified in the Statute of Artificers.[19]

Then a significant doctrinal reversal occurred in 1796, when *R* v. *Inhabitants of Hulcott*, a case of a disputed settlement, came before King's Bench. Under the terms of the Old Poor Law, paupers had a right to relief and maintenance in the parish where they were last 'settled'. One of the most common ways for men and women to acquire settlements was through a year of service in a particular place. These settlements by hiring produced a large amount of litigation, as parochial authorities, anxious to reduce the financial burden on their ratepayers, took to the courts to contest their legality. Many of these cases were sent on appeal to King's Bench, and so entered the annals of the law reports and established legal precedents.[20]

In September 1793, Joseph Scrivener of Potterspury in Northamptonshire hired Elizabeth Lamb to serve him for one year by working in the dairy but not milking the cows. Upon her 'becoming insane' the following May, he took her before a magistrate who determined that she was 'wholly unfit for service' and discharged her. Ten days later, Lamb was removed from Potterspury to the hamlet of Hulcott, where she had previously gained a settlement. Hulcott appealed the order at Quarter Sessions. Her removal was confirmed pending the opinion of King's Bench on the matter. Lord Chief Justice Kenyon and his fellow judges deliberated over whether or not the magistrate who discharged Lamb had the authority to do so. If he lacked jurisdiction, then his discharge order was void and Lamb's service had in fact not been terminated before the fulfilment of her year's term – meaning that she had not lost her settlement by hiring in Potterspury and should not have been removed to Hulcott.[21]

Kenyon delivered the opinion of the court that the magistrate had not had jurisdiction over Lamb because it did not appear on the discharge order

---

18 *R* v. *Dalloe* (1714), Sess. Cas. 16, 93 Eng. Rep. 16.
19 Hay, 'England', pp. 62–6, 87–9; S. Deakin and F. Wilkinson, *The Law of the Labour Market: Industrialization, Employment and Legal Evolution* (Oxford University Press: 2005), p. 63.
20 C. Steedman, 'Lord Mansfield's Women', *Past and Present* 176:1 (2002), pp. 105–43, at pp. 106, 114–15; Hay, 'England', p. 77 n. 60.
21 *R* v. *Inhabitants of Hulcott* (1796), 6 T. R. 583, 101 Eng. Rep. 716.

that she was a servant in husbandry. This ruling effectively excluded any workers – such as domestic servants – whose occupations were not explicitly mentioned in the Statute of Artificers, or subsequent Acts, from summary wage remedies and penal sanctions. Following the decision in *Hulcott*, repeated attempts were made to pass legislation to bring domestic servants under the coverage of master and servant law, as had already been done for other workers not specifically named in the Statute of Artificers, such as colliers, tailors, and silk weavers. None of these attempts succeeded.[22]

If the exclusion of domestic servants established by *Hulcott* influenced the day-to-day implementation of master and servant law, it could help to explain the declining share of female workers in employment disputes. Women accounted for more than three-quarters of the domestic labour force. Moreover, domestic service was their most common work experience in this period.[23] As domestic servants, women could have been dispropor-tionately affected by these rulings. It is arguable that the share of cases involving female workers might decrease after a majority of them were omitted from the provisions of master and servant law. The persuasiveness of this explanation depends on whether this precedent actually made a practical difference to how magistrates dealt with domestic servants in employment disputes. This is not easy to ascertain.

For magistrates to be influenced by High Court rulings, they had to be aware of them. Accounts of precedent-setting cases were published by private court reporters. Yet these compilations were not collected in one location until the first volume of the English Reports appeared in 1900. Nineteenth-century magistrates would therefore have had to comb through a daunting number of competing law reports, the rapid accumulation of which a contemporary observer dubbed a 'growing evil'.[24] While few magistrates read these reports, they did consult the advice manuals written for them, which offered concise, comprehensible summaries of the statutes and the reported cases. These handbooks were in high demand, as the regular appearance of new and revised editions attests.

Richard Burn's *Justice of the Peace, and Parish Officer* was the most influential and authoritative manual, with thirty editions between 1755 and 1869. *Hulcott* was cited – twice – in the first edition published after the verdict, in 1800. It was referred to briefly under the heading 'Servants' in a discussion of whether insanity was a good cause for discharging a servant; and, at greater length, under the heading 'Poor (Settlement by Service)', where the author noted that the discharge order in the original

22 Hay, 'England', pp. 87–91.
23 C. Steedman, *Labours Lost: Domestic Service and the Making of Modern England* (Cambridge University Press: 2010), pp. 13, 38.
24 J. L. High, 'What Shall Be Done with the Reports?', *American Law Review* 16 (1882), p. 429.

case was void because it had not stipulated that the defendant was a servant in husbandry.[25] In subsequent editions, *Hulcott* was cited in the 21st section under the 'Servants' heading as proof that a discharge order must show that the magistrate had jurisdiction in the case.[26] Interestingly, in the 1810 and 1814 editions, the proceedings in *Hulcott* were described in detail, with a marginal gloss explaining that the discharge was void because the magistrate had not said the defendant was a servant in husbandry.[27] In the 1820 edition, there was no detailed case description and the precedent drawn from the ruling was that 'it must appear on the face of the order itself to be a case within the jurisdiction of the magistrate' – with no mention of servants in husbandry.[28] This reference and marginal gloss were gone altogether in the 1825 edition, but *Hulcott* was cited in a footnote at the beginning of the 'Servants' entry clarifying that the power of magistrates under the Statute of Artificers (many provisions of which had since been repealed by 49 Geo. 3 c. 109, 1809) was confined to servants employed in husbandry.[29]

Given these repeated citations of *Hulcott*, most nineteenth-century magistrates would likely have been familiar with it. Burn's manual did not explicitly link the case with domestic servants, so magistrates might not have deduced that these workers were excluded from their jurisdiction – particularly those who only consulted the 1820 edition, which did not imply that this jurisdiction was limited to servants in husbandry. Confusion existed for decades, as *Kitchen v. Shaw* (1837) shows. A gentleman brought his teenage house servant before a magistrate for absenting herself. She was committed to the house of correction under the statute 6 Geo. 3 c. 25 (1766), authorizing a single magistrate to imprison runaway workers for one to three months. The girl brought an action for false imprisonment at the Cumberland Summer Assizes but was non-suited on the grounds that domestic servants were covered under the statute (which applied to a list of trades and 'other persons') and the magistrate was acting within his

---

25 R. Burn, *The Justice of the Peace, and Parish Officer* (19th edn; A. Strahan: 1800), Vol. 3, p. 570; Vol. 4, p. 248. In 1817, another justice's manual cited Hulcott only in reference to insanity not being a cause for a master to discharge a servant on his own authority. T. W. Williams, *The Jurisdiction of Justices of the Peace and Authority of Parish Officers, in All Matters Relating to Parochial Law: with Practical Forms of All Necessary Proceedings, the Adjudged Cases to Michaelmas Term 1815 Inclusive, and the Statutes of the Last Session of Parliament, 56 Geo. III* (W. Clarke: 1817), p. 41.

26 See, for example, Burn, *Justice of the Peace* (21st edn; 1810), Vol. 5, p. 259; (23rd edn; 1820), Vol. 5, p. 163; (24th edn; 1825), Vol. 5, p. 159.

27 Burn, *Justice of the Peace* (21st edn; 1810), Vol. 5, p. 259; (22nd edn; 1814), Vol. 5, p. 147.

28 *Ibid.* (23rd edn; 1820), Vol. 5, p. 163.

29 *Ibid.* (24th edn; 1825), Vol. 5, p. 120 n. (a).

authority to commit her. On appeal to King's Bench, Lord Chief Justice Denman argued that the 'other persons' referred to were only workers 'of the same description as those before enumerated' and the Statute of Artificers 'expressly exclude[d] domestic servants' and if any subsequent statute had 'been designed to do away with this limitation ... this would have been effected by plain words'.[30] *Kitchen* v. *Shaw* was cited in Burn's manual as proof that magistrates did not 'have any peculiar jurisdiction over *domestic* or *menial* servants' and that domestics were 'not within the enactments', thereby putting an end to any ambiguity on that front.[31]

Some nineteenth-century magistrates – those who heard the teenage maid's case, for instance – were unaware that domestic servants were not covered by master and servant legislation. Others were aware – as attested by their creative attempts to continue adjudicating domestic servants' disputes anyway. Carolyn Steedman contends that there is 'abundant evidence' of magistrates believing or pretending to believe the convenient fiction that domestic servants were actually servants in husbandry so that they could exercise jurisdiction over them.[32] Some of the occupational descriptors in the sources seem like attempts to pass off domestic servants as workers covered by the employment statutes. The magistrate Henry Yate heard the complaint of a Herefordshire man that Elizabeth Lord, his 'domestic servant of all work in husbandry', had run away in breach of contract.[33] By comparison, Yate described James Lord, another worker who had run away, as a 'servant of all work in husbandry'.[34] The term 'domestic' was only applied to the female servant.

Similarly, the magistrate Montague Pennington of Kent referred to Sarah Hart as a 'maid servant (in husbandry)' when he ordered her to return to her master with abated wages after she had run away.[35] The parenthetical phrase 'in husbandry' seems like an attempt to justify Pennington's summary action in the case. It was not his customary practice to describe female agricultural workers as 'maid' servants in husbandry. For instance,

---

30	*Kitchen* v. *Shaw* (1837), 6 Ad. & E. 729, 112 Eng. Rep. 280.
31	T. Chitty, *Burn's Justice of the Peace and Parish Officer* (29th edn; Sweet, Maxwell and Son, and Stevens and Norton: 1845), Vol. 5, pp. 844, 877 (emphasis original).
32	Steedman, *Labours Lost*, pp. 178, 217. This fiction could also be applied to male domestic servants. Hay cites the 1797 case of a master convincing the court that his coachman also performed tasks on his hobby farm. Hay, 'England', p. 89.
33	'Examination Book of Rev. Henry Yate, Magistrate', 6 January 1802, p. 30, BB88/1: Herefordshire Archive and Records Centre, Hereford.
34	*Ibid.*, 9 December 1801, p. 26.
35	'Justice Diary of the Rev. Montagu Pennington, JP', 2 January 1812, p. 42, U2639/O1: Kent History and Library Centre, Maidstone (Kent Hist.).

he called Sarah Kemp, who had also run away, a 'servant in husbandry'.[36] In Hart's case, Pennington was probably trying to give himself jurisdiction. He seems to have been aware that domestic servants were not covered by master and servant statutes but wanted to mediate disputes involving them. When Mrs Curling, who kept a small dairy farm, complained to Pennington and three other magistrates in petty sessions that her 'maid, who milked the cows and sold the milk, etc.', had run away, Pennington noted that there was 'doubt' as to 'whether ... [the maid] was a servant in husbandry, but Mr Backhouse and Mr Leith agreed with me (and with Mr Mercer) that she was'.[37]

It would seem that the *Hulcott* ruling did not have much effect on the number of cases involving female workers if, like Pennington, many magistrates were simply reclassifying domestic servants as servants in husbandry and doling out summary justice regardless. Quantitative evidence suggests that *Hulcott* might have had an impact. Seventy-one percent of cases involving domestic servants in the database date from before 1796. Moreover, half of those cases dating from after 1796 were not master and servant offences, but theft or embezzlement. These infractions fell outside the purview of the *Hulcott* ruling, which did not exclude domestic servants from criminal law altogether. After 1796, magistrates only acted summarily in one master and servant case definitely involving a domestic servant: at a meeting of the Wingham Petty Sessions in December 1816, the magistrates ordered a man to take back his 'maid servant', whom he had turned away.[38] In November 1843 – notably, after *Kitchen* v. *Shaw* – the magistrates at the Fareham Petty Sessions in Hampshire even dismissed a complaint for 'refusal of wages as a domestic servant' because they lacked jurisdiction.[39]

On the other hand, there are only twenty-one cases in the database definitively involving domestic servants, who only accounted for 3% of female workers' cases. This is surprising as domestic service was the most common occupational experience of women in the period. It is possible that because of customs relating to their employment, domestic servants were infrequently involved in master and servant disputes in summary courts both before and after *Hulcott*. Despite a magistrate's approval being ostensibly required to terminate a contract in the eighteenth century, the usual practice, especially in large towns, was for masters to give domestic servants one month's warning or one month's wages and dismiss them

36 *Ibid.,* 20 May 1812, p. 49.
37 *Ibid.,* 30 July 1827, p. 177.
38 *Ibid.,* 3 December 1816, p. 114.
39 'Fareham Petty Sessions court register', 1 and 8 November 1843, 27M78/XP1: Hampshire Archives and Local Studies, Winchester (Hants Arch.).

on their own authority.[40] This custom was not just confined to the cities. A Hampshire farmer, James Edwards, noted that he had 'paid off' three maidservants – two who 'would not do for our place', and one who was too ill to work.[41]

It is also possible that there are few domestic servants in the database because women's work often defied easy categorization – for contemporaries and historians alike. Much female labour straddled the divide between indoor and outdoor work. For instance, Mary Hughes agreed with John Hopkins of Woolstone, Shropshire, to 'serve him as a kitchen maid and to feed the pigs for a year'.[42] Mary Ann Castle was hired by Edward Curling, a farmer, to 'milk cows and to do other things in his farm house'.[43] In Warwickshire, Catherine Evans was responsible for the housework, spreading manure in the fields, getting up the potatoes, milking the cows, and 'anything else there was to do'.[44] This ambiguity allowed magistrates such as Yate and Pennington to plausibly describe women as servants in husbandry rather than domestic servants when they wanted to preserve their jurisdiction. It also made it difficult to classify women in the database. The above-mentioned women were not coded in the database as domestic servants, nor were any workers with equally ambiguous job descriptions. This category, reserved for those explicitly called 'maid servants' or 'domestic servants' in the sources, would otherwise have comprised a larger share of female workers.

Ultimately, it is difficult to determine how much *Hulcott* contributed to the declining share of females in employment disputes. It is probable that it did not make a significant difference. While there is evidence that cases involving women clearly identified as domestic servants did decrease after 1796, the numbers before and after the ruling were small. The observed fall could also be a product of magistrates pretending that domestic servants were other kinds of workers.

40 *R* v. *Inhabitants of Brampton* (1777), Cald. 11; B. Hill, *Servants: English Domestics in the Eighteenth Century* (Clarendon Press, Oxford: 1996), p. 101; Hay, 'England', pp. 89 n. 112, 110 n. 185.
41 'Farm Book of James Edwards, 1800–1806', pp. 9, 17, 21, 2M37/341: Hants Arch.
42 'Justice Book of Thomas N. Parker', 9 June 1810, 1060/168: Shropshire Archives, Shrewsbury.
43 'Upper Division of the Lathe of Scray, Depositions', 6 May 1830, PS/US/Sd/1: Kent Hist.
44 'Atherstone Minute Books', 7 July 1846, p. 74, QS 116/2/1/2: Warwickshire County Record Office, Warwick.

IV

Other explanations for women's declining share of employment disputes require exploration. One potential explanation lies in women's changing participation in agriculture. Ivy Pinchbeck, a pioneering scholar of women's work, argued that there was a rapid increase in female agricultural day labourers from the end of the eighteenth century through the Napoleonic Wars. Agrarian and industrial change had reduced rural women's ability to contribute to household income through exploitation of the commons and by-employments such as spinning, while also creating a demand for irregular daily farm work when many male labourers were away fighting. In the post-war agrarian depression, amid a flood of demobilized men overstocking the labour market, women's agricultural day work decreased. With the 1834 New Poor Law abolishing outdoor relief, numbers of female day labourers in agriculture rose again, but after the mid-nineteenth century they entered a prolonged and permanent decline brought on by rising male wages and mechanization.[45]

More recently, Keith Snell's chronology of women's decreasing agricultural employment has emerged as the leading explanation. Snell argues that from the mid- to late-eighteenth century, in the arable south-east of England, demand for female agrarian labour declined as grain production expanded and the scythe, a strength-intensive technology more suited to male workers, came to replace the sickle during harvest time. In the more pastoral north and west of the country, where livestock and dairy farming made greater use of female labour, women's agricultural employment and wage levels held steady or even rose.[46]

Snell's thesis has not gone unchallenged. Historians have argued that he overstates the extent to which a more equal sexual division of labour prevailed in agriculture before the mid-eighteenth century, pointing out that farm work had been gendered for hundreds of years in many locations. They also note that the replacement of sickle by scythe was gradual, raising questions about whether changing agrarian technology was responsible for women's worsening work prospects on grain farms.[47]

---

45 I. Pinchbeck, *Women Workers and the Industrial Revolution, 1750–1850* (F. S. Crofts and Company: 1930), pp. 53–110.

46 K. Snell, *Annals of the Labouring Poor: Social Change and Agrarian England, 1660–1900* (Cambridge University Press: 1985), pp. 15–67; N. Verdon, *Rural Women Workers in Nineteenth-Century England* (Boydell Press, Woodbridge: 2002), p. 24.

47 Verdon, *Rural Women Workers*, pp. 26–7; A. Hassell-Smith, 'Labourers in Late Sixteenth-Century England: A Case Study From North Norfolk, Parts I and II', *Continuity and Change* 4 (1989), pp. 11–52, 367–94; P. Sharpe, *Adapting to Capitalism: Working Women in the English Economy, 1700–1850* (Macmillan, Basingstoke: 1996), pp. 74–99; P. Sharpe, 'The Female Labour

Nevertheless, while important to note regional variation, the evidence seems to suggest that women made up a diminishing share of agricultural workers in the arable south-east. Although the marginalization of female day labourers outside the south-eastern corn lands was not complete by 1850, farm accounts show their participation falling and becoming increasingly seasonal and casual over the first half of the century. Moreover, farm service – the practice whereby workers were hired for the year and boarded in the farmhouse – was declining in the south-east, at least after 1815 and possibly earlier. Since women were much more likely to be farm servants than day labourers, this development especially disadvantaged them.[48] It is arguable that as women were increasingly driven out of agricultural employment in arable areas, their involvement in master and servant disputes also declined.

The county of Kent, which has a comparatively large number of surviving records of petty sessions and individual magistrates, offers a test case for this hypothesis. Agriculture in northern Kent, an important grain supplier to London, centred on cereal production and the cultivation of hops and fruit.[49] The region was also the scene of substantial agrarian unrest due to increasing immiseration, unemployment, and underemployment of agricultural workers in the face of unprecedented population growth, the disbanding of military forces after the Napoleonic Wars, and soaring poor rates – the taxes levied in parishes to provide poor relief.[50] These mounting tensions are evident in the sources. For instance, in 1830, Pennington noted

Market in English Agriculture during the Industrial Revolution: Expansion or Contraction?', *Agricultural History Review* 47:2 (1999), pp. 161–81, at pp. 170–1.

48 Verdon, *Rural Women Workers*, pp. 51, 101–2; N. Verdon, 'A Diminishing Force?: Reassessing the Employment of Female Day Labourers in English Agriculture, c. 1790–1850', in P. Lane, N. Raven, and K. D. M. Snell (eds), *Women, Work and Wages in England, 1600–1850* (Boydell Press, Woodbridge: 2004), pp. 201–11; A. Kussmaul, *Servants in Husbandry in Early Modern England* (Cambridge University Press: 1981), pp. 15, 97–134; J. Burnette, 'Labourers at the Oakes: Changes in the Demand for Female Day-Laborers at a Farm near Sheffield during the Agricultural Revolution', *Journal of Economic History (JEH)* 59:1 (1999), pp. 41–67; S. Horrell and J. Humphries, 'Women's Labour Force Participation and the Transition to the Male-Breadwinner Family, 1790–1865', *Economic History Review (EcHR)* 48:1 (1995), pp. 89–117, at pp. 105–6, 112.

49 G. Mingay, 'Agriculture', in A. Armstrong (ed.), *The Economy of Kent, 1690–1914* (Boydell Press, Woodbridge: 1995), p. 58.

50 M. Dobson, 'Population: 1640–1831', in Armstrong (ed.), *The Economy of Kent, 1690–1914*, pp. 14–15; P. Hastings, 'The Old Poor Law, 1640–1834', in N. Yates, R. Hume, and P. Hastings (eds), *Religion and Society in Kent, 1640–1914* (Boydell Press, Woodbridge: 1994), pp. 114–16; K. Snell, 'Agricultural Seasonal Unemployment, the Standard of Living, and Women's

that the East Kent magistrates met at Canterbury to divide up their districts and swear in special constables because of recent 'Fires & disturbances' and machine-breaking.[51] In 1832, Zachariah Gardler complained at the Lathe of Scray Petty Sessions that he and his family had been asleep in bed when a group of plough servants had burst through his front door, punched him, and ransacked the house.[52]

These areas – arable regions in south-eastern England where grain production was emphasized over pastoral agriculture, where men's real wages were falling, and increasing impoverishment of labourers in husbandry contributed to unprecedented unrest – were the types of places where women were being driven out of agricultural employment.[53] In some ways, though, Kent was exceptional. At 89%, Kent's reported incidence of women's and children's involvement in harvest work was among the highest of counties responding to the 1834 Poor Law Report questionnaire. Confusion over whether gleaning constituted harvest work might account for such returns.[54] Notably, in the 1851 census, women made up just 4% of enumerated agricultural labourers and farm servants in Kent, compared to 13%, 15%, and 19% respectively in the more pastoral Gloucestershire, Somersetshire, and Wiltshire.[55]

There are problems relying on nineteenth-century censuses for information about women's work.[56] Married women's occupational designations were frequently omitted. They were often classified by marital status even when other sources such as wage books prove that they were employed outside the home.[57] The numerous occupations listed under the 'Agriculture' heading of the census include 'farm servant (in-door)'. For men, this comprised all agricultural labourers living in the farmhouse,

---

Work in the South and East, 1690–1860', *EcHR* 34:3 (1981), pp. 407–37, at p. 420.

51 'Montagu Pennington', 30 October 1830, p. 195, U2639/O1, Kent Hist. On incendiarism and machine-breaking in East Kent in the autumn of 1830, see E. J. Hobsbawm and G. Rudé, *Captain Swing* (Verso: 2014 [1969]), pp. 98–102.

52 'Lathe of Scray', 22 March 1832, PS/US/Sd/1: Kent Hist.

53 Snell, 'Agricultural Seasonal Unemployment', *EcHR*, pp. 407–36.

54 Verdon, *Rural Women Workers*, pp. 56–7.

55 'Population Tables, 1851, Part II, Ages and Occupations. Vol. 1: Report, England and Wales, I–VI, Appendix', 1691-I, *Parliamentary Papers* (*PP*) (1852–53) 88, pp. 65, 68, 345, 348, 369, 372, 445, 448; Snell, 'Agricultural Seasonal Unemployment', *EcHR*, p. 421. I have excluded land proprietors, farmers, graziers, and relatives of farmers, such as wives, children, grandchildren, and nieces and nephews when calculating these percentages.

56 Verdon, *Rural Women Workers*, pp. 16, 31–5.

57 E. Higgs, 'Women, Occupations and Work in the Nineteenth Century Censuses', *History Workshop Journal* (*HWJ*) 23:1 (1987), pp. 59–80, at pp. 63–4.

such as waggoners, carters, grooms and 'general servant[s]'. For women, it comprised dairymaids and all 'Female Servants living in farmhouses, except those employed in domestic duties as cooks, housemaids, nurses, &c.'[58] There were no specific instructions distinguishing domestic service and farm work.[59] Women's duties often blurred the line. A woman might cook or clean the house but also help to make cheese or feed the pigs. It is possible that women who did agricultural labour were returned as domestic servants by householders and enumerators who might have believed that any domestic duties outweighed any work done on the farm. Cross-referencing with wage books and oral histories indicates under-counting of female labour in agriculture.[60]

Furthermore, nineteenth-century censuses were taken in March or April to avoid distortions caused by summer migrations. Since householders and enumerators generally limited themselves to recording occupations that household members held at the time, seasonal labour, such as in the Kent hop fields, was omitted.[61] Female and juvenile labour continued to be very important in the cultivation of fruit and hops in that county. Indeed, women were considered to be better pickers than men.[62] It is probable that women made up a larger share of the agricultural workforce in Kent than census data indicates, at least at certain times of the year.

The agricultural work which women did undertake in Kent, such as in hop fields, might not have been likely to generate master and servant disputes before magistrates. Notably, no employment dispute in the Kent sources involved hop workers. Hop picking, paid by the bushel, and hop tying, done by the acre and almost exclusively performed by women, were both examples of piecework.[63] In *Hardy* v. *Ryle* (1829), the King's Bench determined that for workers to fall under the jurisdiction of master and servant laws, not only did their occupations have to be mentioned specifically in the Statute of Artificers or subsequent Acts, but they must also have 'contracted to serve', meaning that all work done by the job, piece, or task was effectively excluded from coverage.[64] Hence, female hop pickers did not come under master and servant legislation, since they did not have yearly contracts.

---

58 'Population Tables, 1851', *PP*, pp. 59, 62.
59 Higgs, 'Women, Occupations and Work', *HWJ*, p. 69.
60 Horrell and Humphries, 'Women's Labour Force Participation', *EcHR*, p. 95.
61 Higgs, 'Women, Occupations and Work', *HWJ*, pp. 67–8.
62 B. Reay, *Microhistories: Demography, Society and Culture in Rural England, 1800–1930* (Cambridge University Press: 1996), pp. 109–10; T. Richardson, 'Labour', in Armstrong (ed.), *The Economy of Kent, 1690–1914*, pp. 231–2.
63 Reay, *Microhistories*, pp. 109–10.
64 *Hardy* v. *Ryle* (1829), 9 B. & C. 603, 109 Eng. Rep. 224; C. Frank, 'Britain: The Defeat of the 1844 Master and Servant Bill', in Hay and Craven, *Masters, Servants, and Magistrates*, pp. 404–5.

The social context of women's work in hop fields also made it unlikely that they would initiate or be prosecuted in any employment disputes in the summary courts. A nineteenth-century observer in eastern Kent remarked that "'it is made a condition of letting cottages that the family shall go out to work" in the market gardens'.[65] If women's housing situation depended upon them picking hops and fruit, farmers might not have needed to resort to magistrates to compel them to work. The women themselves might also have refrained from bringing any grievances, for fear of losing their homes. Moreover, women tended to work in the hop fields as part of a family group. In many cases, women were not working for their own daily rates, but rather as assistants to their husbands, who had contracted with the farmer on behalf of the whole family.[66] Any employment disputes that came before the magistrates would likely have involved the male labourer and not his wife.

Eleven of the sources in the database come from Kent, containing 696 total employment disputes. With the exception of a gap around the turn of the nineteenth century, these sources cover roughly the whole period under discussion. Figure 5 shows that the nineteenth-century Kent sources contain smaller shares of cases involving female servants than ones from the eighteenth century. It is plausible that the changing economic and agricultural conditions in Kent contributed to this decreasing share. With fewer women working, especially in occupations indisputably within the jurisdiction of master and servant legislation, it is not surprising that female workers made up a declining share of disputants in employment cases.

The effect of women's decreasing employment in arable agriculture on their participation in master and servant disputes is further highlighted by contrasting sources drawn from arable and pastoral regions. Table 2 compares Bicester with the Home Division of the Lathe of St Augustine. At the turn of the nineteenth century, Bicester, a town and civil parish in Oxfordshire, boasted arable and dairy farms. The former collapsed after the Napoleonic Wars so, by the 1860s, Bicester had become a predominantly grazing parish, noted for butter sent to London in waggons.[67] The Lathe of St Augustine was an administrative subdivision of Kent, comprising about 260 square miles in the county's arable north-east. Table 2 shows that, in the 1851 census, women accounted for 9% of agricultural labourers and farm servants in Bicester, but only 3% in the districts of Blean, Bridge, Dover, Eastry, and Thanet, which made up the Lathe of St Augustine.

---

65 Richardson, 'Labour', p. 242.
66 Verdon, *Rural Women Workers*, p. 66; Pinchbeck, *Women Workers and the Industrial Revolution*, p. 91.
67 'The Market Town of Bicester', in M. Lobel (ed.), *A History of the County of Oxford, Vol. 6* (Victoria County History: 1959), pp. 14–56: *British History Online*.

Figure 5: Share of female workers in employment disputes in Kent, 1685–1860

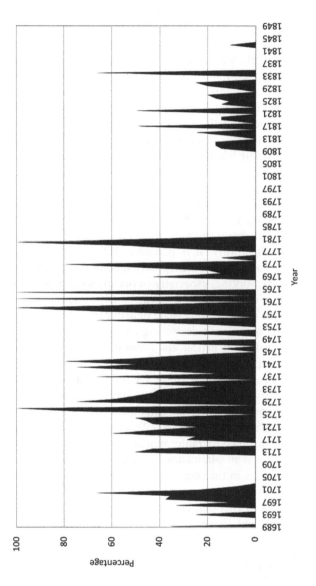

Table 2: Comparing Bicester and Lathe of St Augustine Petty Sessions

	Bicester	St Augustine
Period	1834–52	1843–49
Total cases	201	64
Number (and share) of cases involving female workers	38 (19%)	1 (2%)
Number (and share) of cases involving agricultural workers	101 (50%)	33 (52%)
Number (and share) of agricultural cases involving female workers	23 (23%)	0 (–)
Number (and share) of female agricultural labourers and farm servants in 1851 census	203 (9%)	209 (3%)

Note: 1851 census information for Bicester comprises the sub-districts of Bletch-ington and Bicester. Census information for the Lathe of St Augustine comprises Blean (sub-districts: Sturry, Herne, and Whitstable), Bridge (sub-districts: Chartham, Barham), Dover (sub-districts: St James, St Mary, Hougham), Eastry (sub-districts: Sandwich, Wingham, Eythorn, and Deal), and Thanet (sub-districts: Minster, Margate, Ramsgate). The total of women and their share of agricultural workers uses all the categories under Class IX, 'Agriculture', except for 'Land Proprietor', 'Farmer', 'Grazier', 'Farmer's Wife', and the relatives (daughters, sons, sisters, nieces, nephews, grandchildren) of Farmers and Graziers.
Source: *Parliamentary Papers* 88 (1852–1853), 'Population Tables, 1851, Part II, Ages and Occupations: Volume 1. Report, England and Wales, I–VI, Appendix'.

A comparison of the Bicester Petty Sessions records for 1834–52 (by when the region had become primarily pastoral), and the records of the Home Division of the Lathe of St Augustine Petty Sessions during 1843–49 (Table 2) shows that agricultural workers made up approximately half of all servants involved in employment disputes in each. While 23% of these agricultural workers were women in the Bicester cases, none were in St Augustine. Female workers accounted for 19% of all master and servant cases in the Bicester records. Only 9% of cases in the complete database, for 1830–60, involve female workers. In the St Augustine records, the share was just 2%, the result one dispute: Sophia Wanstall complained that her master had refused to return her clothing and kicked her in the hand 'with vengeance' when she went to retrieve it.[68]

It is possible that women were involved in an above-average share of employment disputes at Bicester because they then constituted a larger

---

68 'Lathe of St. Augustine Petty Sessions Proceedings', 13 May 1843, PS/SA/ Sr/1: Kent Hist.

share of the district's agricultural labour force than in arable areas. Indeed, 61% of all females in Bicester employment disputes worked in agriculture; of these, 65% were dairymaids.[69] Arguably, women would continue to comprise a larger share of master and servant cases in areas such as Bicester, where they worked as agricultural servants, than in areas such as the Lathe of St Augustine, where they were being driven out of agricultural work – at least the type that fell under the summary jurisdiction of magistrates.

V

While women's employment was falling in arable agriculture, it was different in textiles. For centuries, hand spinning had been a customary, even archetypal, female employment. Although poorly paid, it occupied one million or more women by the mid-eighteenth century and could be an important source of supplementary household earnings.[70] At the end of the eighteenth century, as spinning was mechanized it began moving into factories, where, within one generation, men monopolized the new, strength-intensive mules.[71] This increased production of thread spurred a demand for weavers; this trade, primarily undertaken by men in the eighteenth century, was soon flooded with female outworkers. From the mid-1820s the mechanization of weaving brought women in droves into the factories, where they had already been employed on preparatory and subsidiary processes (and, in a minority of cases, spinning). In the eighteenth and early nineteenth centuries, women and children worked in cotton factories in higher proportions than men. They were employed even more extensively in silk mills than in cotton mills. High shares of women also worked in the putting-out lacemaking and stocking-knitting industries. Indeed, women were prominent throughout textile manufacturing.[72]

<hr>

69 There were 23 female agricultural workers, 15 of whom were classified as dairymaids, in the Bicester Petty Sessions records.
70 C. Muldrew, '"Th'ancient Distaff" and "Whirling Spindle": Measuring the Contribution of Spinning to Household Earnings and the National Economy in England, 1550–1770', *EcHR* 65:2 (2012), pp. 498–526, at p. 498; D. Valenze, *The First Industrial Woman* (Oxford University Press: 1995), pp. 68–9; J. Humphries and B. Schneider, 'Spinning the Industrial Revolution', *EcHR* 72:1 (2019), pp. 126–55, at pp. 139 n. 59, 143, 148–50.
71 K. Honeyman, *Women, Gender and Industrialisation in England, 1700–1870* (Macmillan, Basingstoke: 2000), pp. 58–9; W. Lazonick, 'Industrial Relations and Technical Change: The Case of the Self-Acting Mule', *Cambridge Journal of Economics* 3:3 (1979), pp. 231–62.
72 J. Rendall, *Women in an Industrializing Society: England, 1750–1880* (Blackwell, Oxford: 1990), pp. 19–25, 58–9; J. Burnette, Gender, Work and Wages in Industrial Revolution Britain (Cambridge University Press: 2008),

Table 3: Sources with workers in textile industry and agriculture, 1780–1860

Number of sources	Textiles	Agriculture
with workers in these categories	8	30
with ≥10% of all workers in these categories	4	24
with ≥10% of workers in these categories	3	11
(and share of female servants ≥ average)	(75%)	(46%)

Note: The total number of sources used is 57. The percentage in parentheses is the share of sources containing 10% or more of workers in each of the two occupational categories (textiles and agriculture) that also contain shares of employment disputes involving female servants at 13% or higher.

Given this widespread engagement, the relative number of employment disputes involving women did not decline in areas where textiles predominated. The proportion of workers appearing in employment disputes who can be conclusively identified as working in agriculture or textiles can be taken as a rough guide for regional comparisons. Sources drawn from areas with higher shares of agricultural workers had a lower proportion of employment disputes involving women, and the opposite was true for sources with higher shares of textile workers. Table 3 shows that three of the four sources, where textile workers comprised 10% or more of employment disputants during 1780–1860, also contained a share of total female cases equal to or above the overall average (13%) in this period. By comparison, where agricultural workers comprised at least 10% of employment disputants, less than half of the sources (eleven out of twenty-four) also showed an average or above-average share of female cases.

Female textile workers figured exceptionally as defendants: in the database, female workers were defendants in 45% of their cases,[73] whereas female textile workers were defendants in 92%.[74] Forty-nine percent of the accusations made against them were for embezzlement.[75] This encompassed a range of behaviours criminalized by eighteenth-century statutes, such as retaining materials or reeling short yarn. In

p. 28; M. Berg, 'What Difference Did Women's Work Make to the Industrial Revolution?', *HWJ* 35:1 (1993), pp. 22–44, at pp. 27–9; *idem*, 'Women's Work, Mechanization and the Early Phases of Industrialization in England', in R. E. Pahl (ed.), *On Work: Historical, Comparative and Theoretical Approaches* (Blackwell, Oxford: 1988), pp. 61–94, at pp. 68–9; Pinchbeck, *Women Workers and the Industrial Revolution*, pp. 156–86.

73 Female workers were defendants in 307 of 680 cases involving them in the database.

74 There were 51 female textile workers in the database, and 47 were defendants.

75 There were 23 cases of embezzlement.

the latter, spinners would use reels with shorter circumferences than the customary standard to have more leftover raw material, which they could then appropriate.[76] The next most frequent accusation (38% of charges) was running away or absenting themselves.[77] For instance, 75% of female textile workers in employment disputes at the Devizes Petty Sessions between 1834 and 1840 (see below) were charged with leaving their service.[78]

Magistrates and their clerks often did not record which statutes they were acting under, so prosecutions using the embezzlement Acts and those using master and servant legislation can look identical in the sources. Beginning with 12 Geo. 1 c. 34 (1725), some of the anti-embezzlement statutes could be used to charge workers who left their employment before the end of their terms.[79] Provisions like these helped to broaden the legal basis for the control and subjugation of labour at a time of confusion about whether industrial workers and outworkers were covered by master and servant laws.[80] These anti-embezzlement statutes were part of the same project as master and servant legislation – the subordination of labour. As Richard Soderlund argues, anti-embezzlement statutes and master and servant law together defined disobedience and appropriations by workers as crimes and provided for their increasingly severe punishment. The two bodies of law were complementary and overlapping.[81] Their use against female textile workers was a concerted attempt to impose industrial discipline.[82]

---

76 R. Soderlund, 'Law, Crime and Labor in the Worsted Industry of the West Riding of Yorkshire, 1750–1850' (Ph.D., University of Maryland College Park: 1992), pp. 257–61; J. Styles, 'Embezzlement, Industry and the Law in England, 1500–1800', in M. Berg, P. Hudson, and M. Sonenscher (eds), *Manufacture in Town and Country before the Factory* (Cambridge University Press: 1983), pp. 173–210, at p. 176.

77 There were 18 cases of workers running away.

78 'Devizes Minute Books', 16 September 1834, B13/100/2: Wiltshire and Swindon History Centre, Chippenham (Wilts Hist.).

79 Soderlund, 'Law, Crime and Labor', pp. 257–64; *idem*, '"Intended as a Terror to the Idle and Profligate": Embezzlement and the Origins of Policing the Yorkshire Worsted Industry, c. 1750–1777', *Journal of Social History (JSH)* 31:3 (1998), pp. 647–69, at p. 651.

80 Deakin and Wilkinson, *Law of the Labour Market*, p. 63; Hay, 'England', pp. 87–8.

81 Soderlund, 'Intended as a Terror', *JSH*, p. 651; *idem*, Law, Crime and Labor, pp. 262–4.

82 See *idem*, 'Resistance from the Margins: The Yorkshire Worsted Spinners, Policing, and the Transformation of Work in the Early Industrial Revolution', *International Review of Social History (IRSH)* 51:2 (2006), pp. 217–42; and S. Moore, 'Gender and Class Formation: Women's Mobilization in the Industrialization of the Bradford Worsted Industry, 1780–1845', *Historical Studies in Industrial Relations (HSIR)* 35 (2014), pp. 1–31, for examples of female textile

Whether they were putting-out workers accused of embezzlement or mill workers charged with leaving their service, women in textiles were treated harshly. They were dealt with more severely than female workers overall and compared to male counterparts in textiles. In the database, female textile workers were imprisoned in 23% of cases as defendants and male textile workers in only 11% of cases.[83] Overall in the database, female servants were incarcerated in 12% of cases when defendants, and male servants in 19%.[84] Male textile workers were treated more leniently than male defendants overall; the opposite applied for females. In fact, women were 61% of all imprisoned textile workers but only 12% of total imprisoned workers. Textile workers represented 31% of all female servants sentenced to the house of correction in the database, but only 3% of all incarcerated male servants.

The severe treatment of female textile workers is exemplified in the records of the Devizes Petty Sessions kept between 1834 and 1840. Devizes was a Wiltshire market town where silk-throwing had emerged by the end of the Napoleonic Wars.[85] From at least 1823, Peter Walker owned the Belvedere silk-throwing mill, where he employed a 'great number of persons' – 'particularly women and children, who are unable to gain employment in any other branch of trade or agriculture'.[86] In 1855, by when his son Frederick had taken over, the mill still employed 100 people (according to the Devizes Post Office Directory), though it closed four years later.[87] Peter and Frederick Walker's disputes with their workers accounted for 24% of the employment conflicts with which the Devizes magistrates dealt in the petty sessions record.

The Walkers were the plaintiffs in 92% of the twenty-five cases in which they were involved. The Belvedere mill's workforce was largely female, and women were defendants in 70% of these disputes.[88] The Walkers

workers resisting the imposition of industrial discipline and class interest by manufacturers.

83 Female textile workers were imprisoned in 11 cases and male textile workers in 7 cases.

84 In the database, 36 cases involving female servants and 253 cases involving male servants ended with imprisonment.

85 A. Baggs, D. Crowley, R. Pugh, J. Stevenson, and M. Tomlinson, 'The Borough of Devizes: Trade, Agriculture and Local Government', in E. Crittall (ed.), *A History of the County of Wiltshire, Vol. 10* (Victoria County History: 1975), pp. 252–85: *British History Online.*

86 'Journals of the House of Commons', 10 February 1826, *PP* (1826) 81, p. 31; Baggs *et al.*, 'The Borough of Devizes', pp. 252–85.

87 Baggs *et al.*, 'Devizes', pp. 252–85; R. W. H. Willoughby, 'Water-Mills in West Wiltshire', *Wiltshire Archaeological and Natural History Magazine* (*WANHM*) 64 (1969), p. 99 n. 14.

88 Female textile workers were the defendants in 16 of the 25 cases.

prosecuted twenty-two individual women (three cases involved multiple defendants). For instance, Margaret Oakford, Jane Goldberry, Jane James, and Elizabeth Mullins stood accused together of leaving Walker's service without permission on 20 November 1838.[89] Altogether, individual women comprised 76% of the defendants in the Walkers' cases. Not only did the Walkers prosecute more women than men, but the Devizes magistrates treated them more harshly. Female defendants were imprisoned in 50% of these cases, and male defendants in 43%. All three cases with multiple female defendants ended in incarceration of the accused. Thus, fourteen women were imprisoned. The Walkers used master and servant law against their workers – especially women – because it was a successful strategy for them.

Their prosecutions of a mainly female workforce served several related purposes. Foremost, these prosecutions bound mill operatives to the Walkers even when it seems that there was no immediate employment for them. By the nineteenth century, the implied mutuality of obligation in the master and servant relationship had become merely notional. Workers were still bound to their masters for the length of the agreed-upon term, but the High Court refused to uphold the master's reciprocal duty to furnish employment or wages during this time.[90] The Devizes magistrates seemed to have subscribed to this unequal doctrine. Peter Walker was only a defendant at the petty sessions twice, in two cases in 1839. Henry Winter, under contract for twelve months, complained that Walker refused to employ him or permit him to be employed by any other person. The magistrates dismissed his grievance. Walker then brought a charge against Winter, alleging that he had absented himself without consent. Winter was sentenced to one month's imprisonment with hard labour.[91]

The second plaintiff was Mary Ann Wheeler, quite possibly the same Mary Ann Wheeler whom Walker had charged five years previously with leaving her service. On that occasion, the magistrates present, including Thomas Estcourt, sentenced her to twenty days' imprisonment but 'privately recommended' that Walker should discharge her at the end of the period.[92] When Wheeler complained in 1839 that Walker had discharged her 'several months' before and prevented her obtaining work elsewhere, the magistrates dismissed her grievance, as they had Winter's. Walker alleged again that Wheeler had absented herself before the term of her contract was over. The magistrates ordered her to return and perform her work, though based on her complaint it does not seem there was much for her to

89 'Devizes Minute Books', 20 November 1838, B13/100/2: Wilts Hist.
90 Deakin and Wilkinson, *Law of the Labour Market*, pp. 65–6; R. Steinfeld, *Coercion, Contract, and Free Labor in the Nineteenth Century* (Cambridge University Press: 2001), p. 122.
91 'Devizes Minute Books', 19 February 1839, B13/100/2: Wilts Hist.
92 *Ibid.*, 16 September 1834.

do.[93] Three months later, Walker charged Wheeler with absenting herself yet again. This time, Estcourt and another magistrate committed her to the house of correction for seven days and ordered Walker to discharge her at the end of her imprisonment. He 'promised' to do so.[94]

It is possible that the magistrates were being sympathetic to Wheeler in recommending that Walker discharge her. Estcourt seemed to be some sort of paternalist who was, or thought himself, compassionate towards the plight of the poor. A borough magistrate from age 27, he has been described as a popular gentleman enamoured of 'quiet service' to his county and well known for 'unvarying kindness and courtesy of manner'. He was celebrated as a founder of the Wiltshire Friendly Society, through which he strove to raise the 'material [and] ... moral tone of the working classes'. According to his friend Earl Nelson, his own labourers 'looked up' to him 'as a very father'.[95] He was present on both occasions when the magistrates suggested, and finally insisted, that Walker release Wheeler from her contract – something she clearly wanted. As female silk workers were paid piece rates (whereas males received flat rates), Wheeler would not have had an income during periods when she did not receive any work.[96] Walker had to 'promise' to discharge her, the way that recalcitrant servants often had to promise to behave better, or defaulting masters had to promise to pay wages by a certain date, suggesting that it was not a course of action he would have pursued willingly. Indeed, he apparently refused to discharge her the first time the magistrates so recommended.

Peter Walker's history at the Devizes Petty Sessions shows that he used master and servant law as a way of binding his workers to him, whether he actively needed their labour or not, by prosecuting them for absence even if he was not providing them with work. Whether or not Estcourt and

---

93 *Ibid.*, 19 February 1839.

94 *Ibid.*, 14 May 1839.

95 H. M. Stephens, 'Estcourt, Thomas Henry Sutton Sotheron (1801–1876)', in Rev. H. C. G. Matthew (ed.), *Oxford Dictionary of National Biography* (Oxford University Press: 2004); S. Farrell, 'Bucknall Estcourt, Thomas Henry Sutton (1801–1876)', in D. Fisher (ed.), *The House of Commons, 1820–1832, Vol. 4* (Cambridge University Press: 2009): http://www.historyofparliamentonline.org/volume/1820–1832/member/bucknall-estcourt-thomas-1801-1876; J. Stratford, *Wiltshire and Its Worthies: Notes Topographical and Biographical* (Simpkin Marshall: 1882), pp. 9–11; T. Ward, *Men of the Reign: A Biographical Dictionary of Eminent Persons of British and Colonial Birth Who Have Died during the Reign of Queen Victoria* (Routledge and Sons: 1885), p. 303; 'Memoir of Mr. Sotheron Estcourt and Mr. Poulett Sorope', *WANHM* 16 (1876), p. 341.

96 J. Lown, *Women and Industrialization: Gender at Work in Nineteenth-Century England* (Polity Press, Cambridge: 1990), pp. 45, 49; Valenze, *The First Industrial Woman*, p. 91.

the other magistrates sympathized with Wheeler, they enabled Walker's exploitation of his workforce by routinely punishing workers (often with imprisonment) who left his service and by dismissing their grievances.

Not only did Walker use master and servant law to keep his mill workers bound even in slack periods, it possibly served to prevent labour organization and unionization. As well as the three cases with multiple defendants, there were petty sessions where Walker brought multiple cases. For example, Kitty Brewer, Elizabeth Glass, Margaret Oakford, Jane Goldberry, Jane James, and Elizabeth Mullins were all charged in November 1838, the first two for refusing to perform work required of them, and the others for leaving without permission. All six were sentenced to the house of correction.[97] Although there is no definite indication in the court records, it is possible that the workers had been on strike. Douglas Hay notes that employers often prosecuted for offences such as leaving work unfinished rather than striking, since it was easier to secure such convictions under master and servant law than under the Combination Acts. Multiple master and servant charges on the same day for the same offence sometimes indicated a strike.[98]

Finally, Peter Walker might have used employment law in conjunction with another legal device to extract obedience. Hay has shown that mill owners in the late eighteenth and early nineteenth centuries were increasingly using written contracts to grant themselves disciplinary powers over operatives. For instance, the standard contract at Cooper & Company's cotton mill in Ashbourne, Derbyshire, specified that if the female signatory absented herself, the company reserved the right to abate her wages or discharge her.[99] In 1823, George White claimed that the use of such contracts, along with traditional summary penal sanctions, had rendered master and servant law even more inequitable. He argued that illiterate workers came to verbal agreements with masters and then signed written contracts that did not match these terms. When masters enforced the more exploitative terms of the written contracts, the workers objected that they had not agreed and attempted to leave. Then their masters threatened to 'take [them] before a magistrate, and send [them] to the house of correction ... [to] dance upon the tread-mill' if they did not return. These were not empty threats. When workers were brought before magistrates, the latter consulted the written contracts and declared: 'I have it here in black and white, that you agreed to work for so much per week, and you must go to work, or go to the house of correction.'[100]

97 'Devizes Minute Books', 20 November 1838, B13/100/2: Wilts Hist.
98 Hay, 'England', p. 101.
99 *Ibid.*, pp. 102–3.
100 G. White, *A Digest of All the Laws at Present in Existence Respecting Masters and Work People: With Observations Thereon* (I. Onwhyn: 1824), pp. 96–7; Hay, 'England', pp. 103–4.

As White asserted, masters availed themselves of magistrates' summary powers while binding their workers with written contracts. Hay found that Cooper & Co. continued approaching magistrates to enforce penal sanctions, such as imprisonment, on misbehaving workers, despite their contracts stipulating that they could, on their own authority, discharge or abate the wages of absent workers. Written contracts gave employers the double advantage of being able to discipline their workforces with or without recourse to magistrates.[101]

Although there are no examples of written contracts by manufacturers involved in employment disputes in the sources here, many likely used such contracts. Sometimes the exception helps prove the rule. Thomas Allen was a magistrate in Macclesfield, Cheshire, where more than 10,000 were employed in silk mills in the 1820s.[102] His notebook, covering 1823 and 1824, contains many disputes involving silk workers. Several masters recorded as plaintiffs in the notebook, including Nathaniel Davenport and Samuel Wardle, were among the forty-three Macclesfield silk manufacturers and silk throwsters who signed a resolution in March 1824 that 'the servants employed in [their] respective factories, who are not already under written hirings, shall in future be hired for us, in the same manner as the servants are hired in the neighbouring manufacturing towns'. The Macclesfield silk workers opposed this so strenuously – even starting a subscription to fund a strike – that the manufacturers were forced to withdraw it, declaring peevishly that it was 'deeply to be regretted, that the orderly, quiet, and peaceable working classes of this town and neighbourhood, should so far have lost sight of their true interest … as to reject the proposition … which if rightly considered, is fraught with greater advantages to them than to their employers'.[103] This failure to impose written contracts on their workers nevertheless highlights that most other mill owners did so. The use of written contracts in industrial concerns with large workforces was no doubt extensive.[104]

---

101 *Ibid.*, pp. 102–3.

102 C. Davis (ed.), *A History of Macclesfield* (Morten, Didsbury: 1976), pp. 124–34, 196.

103 'Thomas Allen of Macclesfield Justice of the Peace Notebook', 12 and 28 April 1823, D4655: Cheshire Archives and Local Studies; Fifth Report from the Select Committee on Artizans and Machinery P.P. 1824 (51), Vol. 5, pp. 582–5.

104 Hay, 'England', p. 103. For instance, Sarah Peers notes that Samuel Greg used contracts of 364 days for his cotton mill workers, and that these contracts stipulated penalties such as the forfeiture of double wages for absence. Third parties were sometimes bound in £5 to ensure the completion of the contract. S. A. Peers, 'Power, Paternalism, Panopticism and Protest: Geographies of Power and Resistance in a Cotton Mill Community, Quarry Bank Mill, Styal, Cheshire, 1784–1860' (D. Phil., University of Oxford: 2008), p. 195. I am grateful to Douglas Hay for this reference.

Indeed, it is likely that the workers at Belvedere mill in Devizes had contracts. Both Winter and Wheeler, who complained that Peter Walker was not employing them, were described as being under 'contract' to him for twelve months.[105] Brewer and Glass were charged with 'refusing to perform work required of them according to their agreement'.[106] Since 64% of female textile workers prosecuted by Walker were imprisoned, it is likely that he used master and servant law as an alternative to his own power of dismissal through contracts. Walker did not want the magistrates to discharge his workers or abate their wages, which he could probably have done himself. He seems to have preferred incarceration of recalcitrant workers and, in many cases, the magistrates obliged.

VI

In England, women workers' involvement in employment disputes adjudicated in summary courts changed from the early eighteenth to the mid-nineteenth century. This occurred contemporaneously with the momentous social and economic transformations of the Industrial Revolution and was closely related. Women's shrinking labour force participation, especially in arable agriculture, contributed to a downward trend in female workers' involvement in master and servant cases – though female textile workers represented a significant exception. This is because women made up a sizeable proportion of the textiles labour force and manufacturers relied in part on master and servant law to discipline and exploit their workers.

These findings add to our understanding of how the Industrial Revolution affected women's work. Since the trailblazing scholarship of Pinchbeck and Alice Clark in the early twentieth century, the historiography has ballooned. The growth in empirical and theoretical studies in the field has engendered lively debates, including over whether industrialization improved or worsened women's economic position. 'Optimists' argue that industrialization ultimately paved the way for better working conditions, enhanced status and independence, and a happier, healthier domestic life.[107] 'Pessimists' contend

---

105 'Devizes Minute Books', 19 February 1839, B13/100/2: Wilts Hist. These contracts might not necessarily have been written. Oral agreements were also valid contracts.

106 *Ibid.*, 20 November 1838.

107 Pinchbeck, *Women Workers and the Industrial Revolution*, pp. 1–4; N. McKendrick, 'Home Demand and Economic Growth: A New View of the Role of Women and Children in the Industrial Revolution', in *idem* (ed.), *Historical Perspectives in English Thought and Society in Honour of J. H. Plumb* (Europa Publications: 1974), pp. 152–210; R. M. Hartwell, *The*

that it decreased women's productive capacity and opportunities relative to their position in the pre-industrial family economy and relegated them to poorly paid, unskilled, monotonous waged work or to unpaid housework that had previously been more equally shared.[108] Another 'pessimistic' strand of scholarship rejects the idea of a pre-industrial 'golden age' of women's work in the family economy, acknowledging that women's economic opportunities were always more limited than men's, while suggesting that industrialization still led to a reduction in their employment prospects and a deepening gendered division of labour.[109] Related to this debate is another concerning the causes of women's economic marginalization, with scholars variously blaming capitalism, patriarchy, a combination of both, or biology and market forces.[110]

In these discussions, the role of law in subordinating women workers is frequently analysed, but most often the effect that protective legislation of

---

Industrial Revolution and Economic Growth (Routledge, New York: 2017 [1971]), p. 343; E. Shorter, *The Making of the Modern Family* (Basic Books, New York: 1975).

108 A. Clark, *Working Life of Women in the Seventeenth Century* (Cass: 1968 [1919]); B. Hill, *Women, Work, and Sexual Politics in Eighteenth-Century England* (Blackwell, Oxford: 1989).

109 H. Bradley, *Men's Work, Women's Work: A Sociological History of the Sexual Division of Labour in Employment* (University of Minnesota Press, Minneapolis, MN: 1989); Valenze, *The First Industrial Woman*, pp. 3–4; Honeyman, *Women, Gender and Industrialisation in England, 1700–1870*.

110 See H. Hartmann, 'The Unhappy Marriage of Marxism and Feminism: Towards a More Progressive Union', *Capital and Class* 3:2 (1979), pp. 1–33; *idem*, 'The Family as the Locus of Gender, Class, and Political Struggle: The Example of Housework', *Signs* 6:3 (1981), pp. 366–94; S. Walby, *Patriarchy at Work: Patriarchal and Capitalist Relations in Employment* (University of Minnesota Press, Minneapolis, MN: 1986); S. Rose, 'Gender Antagonism and Class Conflict: Exclusionary Strategies of Male Trade Unionists in Nineteenth-Century Britain', *Social History* 13:2 (1988), pp. 191–208; S. Alexander, 'Women's Work in 19th Century London: A Study of the Years 1820–1850', in *idem*, *Becoming a Woman, and Other Essays in 19th and 20th Century Feminist History* (New York University Press: 1995), pp. 3–56; W. Seccombe, *Weathering the Storm: Working-Class Families from the Industrial Revolution to the Fertility Decline* (Verso: 1993); A. Clark, *The Struggle for the Breeches: Gender and the Making of the British Working Class* (University of California Press, Berkeley, CA: 1995). For a review of the field see C. Creighton, 'The Rise of the Male Breadwinner Family: A Reappraisal', *Comparative Studies in Society and History* 38:2 (1996), pp. 310–37. For the debate about the role of ideology versus market forces in explaining women's low wages, see J. Burnette, *Gender, Work and Wages in Industrial Revolution Britain* (Cambridge University Press: 2008) and A. Froide, C. Goldin, J. Humphries, P. Sharp, and J. Burnette, 'Special Section: Debating Gender, Work, and Wages: A Roundtable Discussion', *Social Science History* 33:4 (2009), pp. 459–504.

the nineteenth century had on female employment.[111] This article highlights a different way in which law could affect women. Magistrates administering master and servant law helped to exploit female textile workers by convicting them of embezzlement and punishing them when they left work before the end of their contracts, thus ensuring that manufacturers had access to their labour without any reciprocal obligation to provide work or wages.

This exploitation could well have been a key factor driving the Industrial Revolution. Many scholars now subscribe to the view that an 'industrious revolution' of increased labour inputs helped to fuel Britain's industrial take-off.[112] Jan de Vries argues that this work intensification was the result of family members choosing to work more hours to obtain desirable new consumer goods.[113] Hay suggests that much of this intensification may have resulted from more coercive master and servant law – statute, case law, and greater use of imprisonment.[114]

This article emphasizes the gendered dimension of that labour compulsion. Magistrates treated female textile workers more harshly than male ones. This was a feminized workforce deliberately targeted for exploitation through legal mechanisms.[115] The textile industries were at the forefront of the Industrial Revolution. Even the large sectors that remained unmechanized contributed to the growth and dynamism of the

---

111 See Bradley, *Men's Work, Women's Work*, pp. 46–7; J. Humphries, 'Protective Legislation, the Capitalist State and Working-Class Men: The Case of the 1842 Mines Regulation Act', in Pahl, *On Work*, pp. 95–124; Walby, *Patriarchy at Work*, pp. 100–34; Burnette, *Gender, Work and Wages*, pp. 228–30.

112 J. de Vries, 'The Industrial Revolution and the Industrious Revolution', *JEH* 54:2 (1994), pp. 249–70; *idem, The Industrious Revolution: Consumer Behaviour and the Household Economy, 1650 to the Present* (Cambridge University Press, 2008); H.-J. Voth, *Time and Work in England, 1750–1830* (Clarendon Press, Oxford: 2000); R. Allen and J. Weisdorf, 'Was There an "Industrious Revolution" before the Industrial Revolution? An Empirical Exercise for England, c. 1300–1830', *EcHR* 64:3 (2011), pp. 715–29.

113 De Vries, 'Industrial Revolution', *JEH*, pp. 260–2.

114 D. Hay, 'Working Time, Dinner Time, Serving Time: Labour and Law in Industrialization', *University of Oxford: Discussion Papers in Economic and Social History* 164 (2018), pp. 1–18; Hay, 'England', pp. 82–3, 106–7, 109; Hay, 'Master and Servant in England: Using the Law in the 18th and 19th Centuries', in W. Steinmetz (ed.), *Private Law and Social Inequality* (Oxford University Press: 2000), pp. 231, 247; W. Steinmetz, 'Was there a De-juridification of Individual Employment Relations in Britain?', in *idem, Private Law and Social Inequality, pp. 265, 276*; Deakin and Wilkinson, *Law of the Labour Market*, pp. 65–71.

115 Soderlund, 'Resistance from the Margins', *IRSH*, pp. 224–30; *idem*, 'Intended as a Terror', *JSH*, pp. 658–9; Moore, 'Gender and Class Formation', *HSIR*, p. 30.

more modern factory sector.[116] Thus women, as outworkers and as mill operatives, contributed enormously to the productivity of the nation. It was not only innovative labour practices and new machinery that elicited this productivity. The law played a role. Prosecutions under master and servant law were a key component in the creation and compulsion of an industrious female labour force.

Research Affiliate
Department of History
Georgetown University
3700 O Street NW
Washington DC 20057
United States

---

116 M. Berg and P. Hudson, 'Rehabilitating the Industrial Revolution', *EcHR* 45:1 (1992), pp. 25–50, at pp. 26–7, 30–2.

Important Notice

Liverpool University Press' subscriptions order processing and
distribution is now managed by us and not by Turpin Distribution.

This means that all subscriptions related queries should be sent to LUP
directly using the contact details below:

Email: subscriptions@liverpool.ac.uk
Tel: 0151 795 1080 (Monday to Friday, 9am-5pm UK time)

We are working hard to ensure that the transition between the systems
is as smooth as possible but if you find anything that requires correction
or if you have any questions please do not hesitate to contact LUP.

https://doi.org/10.3828/hsir.2020.41.2

Time, Tea Breaks, and the Frontier of Control in UK Workplaces

Martin Upchurch

Oh, the factories may be roaring
With a boom-a-lacka, zoom-a-lacka, wee
But there isn't any roar when the clock strikes four
Everything stops for tea[1]

One of the by-products of the intensification and reorganization of work over the last four decades has been a squeeze and sometimes elimination of paid rest breaks for lunch, tea (or coffee), and individual 'comfort' breaks. This paper explores the history of such breaks, covering whims, fads and changes in ·management ideologies and practices as they apply to time discipline, as well as patterns of resistance seen through the lens of the 'frontier of control'.[2] More recent developments have seen a partial return to the 'paid break', running against the dominant trend of cutbacks in such breaks or conversion from paid to unpaid breaks.

For employers the squeeze on rest breaks represents a significant increase in their ability to decrease the porosity of working time. Unpaid breaks, or no breaks at all, are now increasingly common in the United Kingdom. A survey in 2008 of 800 workers in the UK by *ukactive* found that the average lunchtime break has fallen since 2012 from thirty-three to twenty-two minutes.[3] A similar survey of just over 2,000 workers in 2017 by *Workthere* recorded that many now skip their lunch break altogether, to eat at their

---

1 'Everything Stops for Tea' (Al Goodhart/Al Hoffman/Maurice Sigler), sung by Jack Buchanan, featured in the 1935 comedy film, *Come Out of the Pantry.*
2 C. Goodrich, *The Frontier of Control: A Study in British Workshop Politics* (Harcourt Brace, New York: 1920), p. 31.
3 L. Donnelly, 'Average lunch-break now last just 22 minutes, down a third on six years ago, survey reveals', *Daily Telegraph*, 21 October 2008.

desk while continuing to work.[4] World Toilet Day is on 19 November each year. The issues raised by its proponents and organizers are serious: lack of toilet facilities (4.5 billion people worldwide do not have access to a safe toilet), as well as time to take a toilet break. For example, in the UK, Unite the Union has reported that

> staff at branches of big high-street banks being required to urinate in buckets, and construction sites failing to provide any female toilets. Bus drivers had been denied toilet breaks for up to five hours, and workers in call centres for big financial institutions were told to log in and out to take a toilet break.[5]

Unpaid work is a major issue. The British Trades Union Congress (TUC) estimates in 2018 that a total of five-million workers put in an average of 7.4 extra unpaid hours per week, missing out on an average of £6,265 pay per working year. For the UK economy, over a full year, this amounts to two-billion unpaid hours of overtime, from which employers collectively benefit to the tune of £31.2 billion of unpaid labour.[6] According to *Unpaid Britain* this is an example of 'employer delinquency', where the search for profits through super-exploitation of the workforce outweighs the risks of being caught and fined by regulatory authorities.[7]

Compounding this 'delinquency' is the employers' offensive on temporal and contractual flexibility, whereby 'risk' within the employment relationship is shifted from employer to 'employee' through the use of part-time, short-hours and zero-hours contracts. Working remotely from home has been increasing and is now at its highest ever level since records were first collected in 1998: 13.9% of British workers now spend at least half their time working in detached fashion at home,[8] with an ever-increasing proportion using Internet-based communication.[9] By the end of the twentieth century the labour market had polarized between workers on

---

4 *Work There*, 'How can the office save the lunch break?', online.
5 G. Topham, 'Thousands of UK workers denied toilet access, says Unite', *Guardian*, 19 November 2018.
6 P. Sellers, 'Work Your Proper Hours Day: Tackling the Culture of Unpaid Overtime' (Trades Union Congress: 2018).
7 N. Clark and E. Herman, *Unpaid Britain: Wage Default in the British Labour Market* (Middlesex University: 2017).
8 Office for National Statistics, *Characteristics of Homeworkers, 2014* (Office for National Statistics, Newport: 2014).
9 A. Felstead and G. Henseke, 'Assessing the Growth of Remote Working and Its Consequences for Effort, Well-being and Work-Life Balance', *New Technology, Work and Employment* 32:3 (2017), pp. 195–212.

very long hours and those, often new groups, on short hours.[10] Added to this trend has been a compression of time at work imposed by intensified monitoring, surveillance and control of the workforce. The range of tools available to the human resources manager in contemporary workplaces is growing from simple recording of tasks and task times by computer through to electronic tagging of workers that measures not only time but also location (by Global Positioning System, GPS; and radio frequency identification, RFID), and even body movements and body language (by gyroscope). This is achieved with the use of wearable accessories or implants to create what has been described as the 'quantified self'.[11]

Rest breaks are symptomatic features of management–worker conflict within the wider arena of time discipline. Changes imposed or bargained are substantive indicators not only of management attempts to intensify or extend working time but also of deeper social forces (state policies, market relations) at work in the political economy of labour markets. To assess the significance of rest breaks as an indicator of time discipline this paper first examines theoretical aspects of time at work within the valorization process, before discussing the history of rest breaks, and contemporary employer efforts to reformulate their place within working time. Recognizing the role of workers' agency in shaping these forces, patterns of resistance by workers to the dilution of the paid break are assessed. The conclusion situates the issue of paid breaks in the light of labour process debates.

Time discipline and the 'frontier of control'

Time is a central feature of the 'pay–effort' and the 'work–effort' bargain between employer and worker and its contestation.[12] The 'pay–effort bargain' involves payment for the job, but can also embrace 'working arrangements, rules and discipline', where disputes 'involve attempts to submit managerial discretion and authority to agreed – or failing that, customary rules'.[13] There is an 'indeterminacy' about the pay–effort bargain

10 F. Green, 'It's Been a Hard Day's Night: The Concentration and Intensification of Life in Late Twentieth-Century Britain', *British Journal of Industrial Relations (BJIR)* 39:1 (2001), pp. 53–80.
11 P. V. Moore, M. Upchurch, and X. Whittaker (eds), *Humans and Machines at Work: Monitoring, Surveillance and Automation in Contemporary Capitalism* (Palgrave Macmillan: 2018).
12 W. G. Baldamus, *Efficiency and Effort: An Analysis of Industrial Administration* (Tavistock: 1961); J. Eldridge, 'A Benchmark in Industrial Sociology: W. G. Baldamus on *Efficiency and Effort* (1961)', *Historical Studies in Industrial Relations (HSIR)* 6 (1998), pp. 133–61; T. Elger, 'The Legacy of Baldamus: A Critical Appreciation', *HSIR* 34 (2013), pp. 229–61.
13 H. A. Turner, *The Trend of Strikes* (Leeds University Press: 1963), p. 18.

in which 'the contract to sell labour power is open-ended, subject to the discretion of employers (or supervisory labour) to enforce or create through consent, a definite measure of output from workers over a definite period of time'.[14] Within this rubric, an employer views time objectively as a linear construct within the day, with possibilities for time 'wasted' or misspent, whereas workers experience time at work subjectively, often experienced as a repetitive cycle.[15] They impose 'norms' and 'rules' through custom-and-practice that challenges management power over time.

Eric Hobsbawm described how workers passed through stages of learning the 'rules of the game' in which they moved collectively from a position of subservience and subsistence payment to one in which they pressed hard for what 'the traffic would bear'.[16] Such struggles over working time may also contain their own inherent tensions and contradictions. For example, the institutionalization of time discipline may be transmuted by labour into demands for overtime pay (double time, time-and-a-half) for work outside 'normal' hours. Such struggles may sit side by side with those that seek to limit or shorten the length of the working day. For Edward Thompson, workers 'had accepted the categories of their employers and learned to fight back within them. They had learned that time is money, only too well.'[17]

Workers' ability to restrain employer attempts to close down on work-time 'porosity' will depend on relative bargaining strength. For example 'high-flyers', those who have high skill levels and are in demand, will be more able to control their time than low-wage, low-skill workers who can more easily be replaced.[18] For contemporary employers, the tension

---

14 C. Smith, 'The Double Indeterminacy of Labour Power: Labour Effort and Labour Mobility', *Work, Employment and Society* (*WES*) 20:2 (2006), pp. 389–402.

15 M. Noon and P. Blyton, *The Realities of Work* (Palgrave, Basingstoke: 2002), p. 113.

16 E. J. Hobsbawm, 'Custom, Wages and Work-load in Nineteenth-century Industry', in *Labouring Men: Studies in the History of Labour* (Weidenfeld and Nicolson: 1968), pp. 344–70, at p. 345.

17 E. P. Thompson, 'Time, Work Discipline, and Industrial Capitalism', *Past and Present* 38:1 (1967), pp. 56–97; also in *idem, Customs in Common* (Merlin Press: 1991), pp. 352–403, at p. 390.

18 See P. Thompson and E. Bannon, *Working the System: The Shop Floor and New Technology* (Pluto Press: 1985) for a description of such differences in the Plessey factory in Liverpool between 1970 and 1984. The author also advised trade-union branches of the Civil and Public Services Association (CPSA, the trade union for clerical and allied grades in the UK civil service) on how to resist and negotiate forms of clerical work measurement. Clerks had to self-record their work output in work diaries which were already matched with photograph banks of timed movements for standard clerical duties (filing, lifting biro, etc.). The temptation for staff was always to record work at the greatest speed (to impress management) but the trade-union advice was to

between output and workers' resistance is an added incentive to increase the degree of temporal and contract flexibility by using part-time workers or zero-hours contracts. For workers in new occupations linked to new industries in the 'gig' economy, for example, this may mean a time-lapse before the 'rules of the game' are learnt to the workers' advantage.[19]

Karl Marx wrote of 'personified labour time', where labour power becomes homogenized and is distinguished only by the quantity of hours expended:

> labour has been equalized by the subordination of man to the machine or by the extreme division of labour; that men are effaced by their labour; that the pendulum of the clock has become as accurate a measure of the relative activity of two workers as it is of the speed of two locomotives. ... Time is everything, man is nothing; he is, at the most, time's carcase. Quality no longer matters. Quantity alone decides everything; hour for hour, day for day.[20]

As William Booth argues, the outcome is 'such a levelling of skills that the movements of the clock's pendulum, marking out its identical passing moments, are an accurate measure of the relative activity of different labour powers'.[21] It is a different form of expropriation than under feudalism, where the peasant's time was divided between producing food for the family and producing for the landlord or church. In the feudal system of expropriation, time was nature bounded, either by the pulse of daylight hours, the turn of the tides, or the season of the year. 'Social intercourse and labour are intermingled – the working-day lengthens or contracts according to the task – and there is no great sense of conflict between labour and "passing the time of day"'.[22]

By contrast, under capitalism, work is constructed around time within a disciplinary frame. The clock and the timesheet, together with the piece and hourly rate, determine the terms of work. Most importantly, the logic of capital accumulation and competition between capitals leads to an inescapable pressure on individual employers to lower unit costs either by reorganizing work patterns or intensifying the effort of the individual

---

record work at slow speeds, so as not to 'normalize' the higher speed. See *Clerical Work Measurement* (CPSA: 1985) available from the TUC Library collection in London.

19 For the emerging organization of Deliveroo couriers see C. Cant, *Riding for Deliveroo: Resistance in the New Economy* (Polity Press, Cambridge: 2020).

20 K. Marx, *The Poverty of Philosophy*, in K. Marx and F. Engels, *Collected Works, Vol. 6* (1847; InternationalPublishers, New York: 1976), pp. 124, 127.

21 W. Booth, 'Economies of Time: On the Idea of Time in Marx's Political Economy', *Political Theory* 19:1 (1991), pp. 7–27, at p. 9.

22 Thompson, 'Time, Work-Discipline, and Industrial Capitalism', *Past and Present*, p. 60; *Customs in Common*, p. 356.

worker. The outcome of this process is not straightforward. Workers may resist intensification and conflict ensue. If so, the co-operation of the workforce needed by the employer to ensure smooth running and workplace innovation will be disrupted or halted. Tinkering with rest breaks must be seen in this light. Something which may appear trivial or slight in the overall pulse of the working day may nevertheless be symbolic of management attempts to disrupt expectations and patterns of behaviour as a precursor to more fundamental change.

In the 1970s, Harry Braverman's *Labor and Monopoly Capital* opened up new debates within the (Marxist) labour process tradition on the degrading effects of time discipline on workers' lives within the factory and office.[23] Taylorism appeared to be successful in subjugating workers to managerial authority in the use of time. With digitalization, time becomes ever more compressed, with further possibilities for multitasking and juggling of tasks *within* time – *temporal density*.[24] Increasing temporal density has the effect of 'broadening' time within allocated working hours rather than necessarily extending the working day or blurring work and non-work time. This is particularly so with the advent of computerization and digitalization at the workstation, whereby more than one task can be undertaken at one moment in time. This is because snatches of time can be used to look at mobile messages (or the computer screen) and respond to them while working on something else (such as reading a document or working a machine) at the same 'time'.[25] As a result, porosity of time within the working day is squeezed. Too much pressure to conform to temporal density may even lead to 'Cognitive Overflow Syndrome' (COS), a newly identifiable term to assess the resultant sense of being overwhelmed and stressed.[26]

Thompson argued that time discipline was tempered by a cultural shift in attitudes, taking years to achieve through ideological and managerial coercion (with the aid of church and schooling) so that in the aftermath of the Industrial Revolution, western industrial cultures were markedly more time conscious than others.[27] Yet precisely because time is central to the dynamic of capitalism, so too is it a source of tension and contestation

---

23 H. Braverman, *Labor and Monopoly Capital: The Degradation of Work in the Twentieth Century* (Monthly Review Press, New York: 1974).

24 J. Wajcman, *Pressed for Time* (University of Chicago Press: 2016), p. 78.

25 K. Mullan and J. Wajcman, 'Have Mobile Devices Changed Working Patterns in the 21st Century? A Time-diary Analysis of Work Extension in the UK', *WES* 3:1 (2019), pp. 3–20.

26 CMS Legal, 'Switching on to Switching Off: Disconnecting Employees in Europe?' (2018), online.

27 Thompson, 'Time, Work-Discipline, and Industrial Capitalism', *Past and Present*, p. 93; *Customs in Common*, p. 399.

between employers and workers. The 'frontier of control', described by Carter Goodrich in 1920 in the mine, factory or office, represented a concrete expression of shifts in the balance of class forces at the point of production or service delivery. A fightback against the employers' control of time could occur when the balance of class forces tipped towards the powers wielded by workers collectively. Goodrich cited 'the case of the Scottish miners who refuse to work while the overman is in their stall, [and] of the Clyde blacksmiths who would not let their managing director watch their fires'.[28] Formal paid breaks also included a subversive element, as workers were given the space within the working day to talk to each other free from management interference, providing a social space for potential collective organization against the same.

Paternalism, the frontier of control, and workers' playtime

Struggles over many decades have been central to the growth and development of trade-union campaigns for the eight-hour day, the weekend, and paid holidays. This created a chemistry of trade-union agitation, social reform and government legislation. The movement for the eight-hour working day proved especially significant. As Sidney Webb and Harold Cox observed, the 'Eight Hours dream has certainly been in the minds of Trade Unionists in England ever since the repeal of the Combination Laws in 1824, and has recurred at every season of reviving industrial prosperity since that Time'.[29] Indeed, as early as 1817 the social reformer and paternalist employer Robert Owen had proposed an eight-hour working day, and after much agitation the Ten Hour Act 1847 imposed a ten-hour working day for women and children. The 1848 revolutionary movements across the European continent also raised a widespread demand for a shorter working day, leading to the introduction of the twelve-hour day in France.[30] The workers' movement embodied in Marx's First International (International Workingmen's Association) in 1864 included the demand for an eight-hour day in the programme adopted at its 1866 Congress in Vienna, while the demand gathered additional pace in Britain with the growth of the Chartist movement. It found a new voice with the creation of the Eight Hour League which in 1886 published an influential pamphlet.[31] The TUC adopted the demand. A long strike by workers at the Beckton gas works

28 Goodrich, *The Frontier of Control*, p. 31.
29 S. Webb and H. Cox, *The Eight Hours Day* (Walter Scott: 1891), p. 15.
30 K. Marx, *Capital: The Process of Capitalist Production* (H. Kerr: 1915 [1867]), p. 328.
31 T. Mann, *What a Compulsory Eight-Hour Means to the Workers* (Modern Press: 1886).

in east London in 1889 ended with a union-negotiated agreement: three shifts of eight hours over a 24-hour period as an alternative to management proposals to introduce compulsory eighteen-hour shifts (itself an increase from twelve-hour shifts). The Gas Workers and General Labourers Union emerged from the strike.[32]

The revolutionary years of 1917–18 brought with them a rash of workers' victories in forcing implementation of the eight-hour day. It was introduced formally in Russia by decree in 1917, Germany in 1918, and France and Catalonia in 1919. Furthermore, the campaign for shorter working hours gained wider legitimacy as a central feature of the first Convention of the International Labour Organization in 1919.[33] Beyond Europe, the first country to introduce the eight-hour day by legislation was Uruguay in 1915. In the United States of America, strikes and agitation for the eight-hour day occurred from 1835 onwards, leading eventually to victories in the most strongly organized sections of workers.

Further reductions in the average working week appeared to be governed primarily by the pulse of trade-union agitation, and the growth and consoli-dation of national and sectoral collective agreements. James Arrowsmith has argued that there were four major waves in which the length of the average working week was cut in Britain: first, from 1872 to 1874, from sixty to fifty-four hours; second, during the unrest after the First World War, an 11% cut to forty-eight hours; third, immediately after the Second World War, to forty-four hours; and fourth, again in the period of heightened trade-union activity and social reform from 1960 to 1966, when average hours worked fell by a further 9% to forty hours per week.[34] The decade between 1980 and 1990, however, marked the beginning of a tentative reversal in some members of the Organisation for Economic Co-operation and Development (OECD). Thus, in the UK, average hours worked per week grew, as they did in Denmark, Sweden, Australia and the US, reflecting a shift in the balance of power towards employers and the widespread introduction of new forms of employment contracts.[35]

The 'weekend' has a more sedate but nevertheless colourful past. Its origins are located in workers' behaviour in industrializing Britain of the late seventeenth century, when the practice of taking Monday off was an ironic version of a Saint's day holiday (in this case Saint Monday). Work time in the

---

32 H. A. Clegg, *General Union* (Blackwell, Oxford: 1954), pp. 11–23.
33 See 'C001 – Hours of Work (Industry) Convention, 1919 (No. 1)', Geneva, International Labour Organization.
34 J. Arrowsmith, 'The Struggle over Working Time in Nineteenth- and Twentieth-Century Britain', *HSIR* 13 (2002), pp. 83–117, at p. 83.
35 M. Huberman and C. Minns, 'The Times They Are Not Changin': Days and Hours of Work in Old and New Worlds, 1870–2000', *Explorations in Economic History* 44 (2007), pp. 538–67.

early factories of Britain usually finished on Saturday, when workers were paid their wages. With cash in their pockets, food could be purchased and visits could be made to the public houses. Sunday was Sabbath, so Monday became the unofficial rest day, with little that the employers could do to prevent it.[36] Saint Monday was not confined to Britain. Thompson notes the practice also existed in France in the nineteenth century, whereby 'Monday was the day set aside for marketing and personal business'.[37] During the nineteenth century, in many workplaces the end of the working week gradually shifted to midday on Saturday; this legitimized leisure time and paved the way for the more substantial 'weekend' of Saturday afternoon and Sunday to become embedded.[38] The consolidation of the principle of workers' rest on Sunday was promoted by such bodies as the Pleasant Sunday Afternoon Movement, which organized one-hour Sunday afternoon sessions for the working man [sic], with religious songs and a sermon as an alternative to the longer and more dismal ceremonies of the established churches.[39] As for holidays, these were based on the traditions of fairs and saints' days (although many were eliminated by the rise of Protestantism), converting later in Britain to 'official' bank holidays and extended beyond by collective agreements and national legislation in 1938 to include paid holiday breaks.[40] The Holidays with Pay Act (1938) provided for one week's paid holiday per year for workers whose minimum rates of wages were fixed by trade boards. The TUC had called for two weeks' holiday for all workers and expressed disappointment at the outcome of the government inquiry leading to the legislation.[41]

Workers also fought for time off *within* the working day. Old traditions of the rest break for tea, beer, bread and the 'piece' (in Scotland) from agricultural times were carried over into the factory.[42] In the late eighteenth

---

36 T. Wright, *Some Habits and Customs of the Working Classes* (London, Tinsley Brothers: 1867).

37 Thompson, 'Time, Work-Discipline, and Industrial Capitalism', *Past and Present*, p. 74; *Customs in Common*, p. 370.

38 D. Reid, 'The Decline of Saint Monday, 1766–1876', in P. Thane and A. Sutcliffe (eds), *Essays in Social History, Vol. 2* (Clarendon Press, Oxford: 1986), pp. 98–125.

39 D. Killingray, 'The Pleasant Sunday Afternoon Movement: Revival in the West Midlands 1875–90?', *Revival and Resurgence in Christian History*, *Vol. 44* (2008), pp. 262–74.

40 In France the link with social unrest, trade-union agitation and reform was strongest during the Popular Front period which in 1936 led to the Matignon agreements that included the first legislation for a two-week paid holiday. See A. Rossiter, 'Popular Front Economic Policy and the Matignon Negotiations', *Historical Journal* 30:3 (1987), pp. 663–84.

41 See https://blogs.londonmet.ac.uk/tuc-library/2015/07/03/holidays-with-pay/.

42 Many local words described the substance of the snack or meal taken into the workplace, harbouring back to work in the fields. In Hertfordshire and in neighbouring Bedfordshire it was a 'clanger' made from suet with an internal

century, as the factory system boomed, employers began giving workers sugary tea. Replacing 'small' or watered-down beer as a refreshment (water was often polluted and too dangerous to drink), this was meant to revive the workforce from their gruelling tasks, so as to work ever harder. As the nineteenth century progressed, rest breaks were consolidated within the factory in part by the emergence of a more benevolent approach to workers' welfare constructed around a paternalist business model, sometimes inspired by religious values.[43] While not a dominant practice, this was designed as an alternative to the predominant drudgery of the Victorian workplace and sought to create a spirit of collaboration, rather than conflict between employer and employee, that went outside the normal boundaries of employment relations.[44] In its 'sophisticated' form the model adopted a unitary ideology to integrate the workforce and obstruct independent, collective worker organization. For example, a lack of any formal procedures (grievance, discipline) frustrated the development of a 'them and us' consciousness between worker and employer. This approach was manifest in a strong element of authoritarianism in the model, described by Roderick Martin and Robert Fryer as 'authoritarianism tempered with generosity' and 'deference, tinged with resentment, on the part of the employed', and by Reinhard Bendix as a continuation of the traditional master–servant relationship tinged with benevolent despotism.[45]

Labour militancy gathered pace in Britain from 1910 onwards, continuing throughout the First World War. Within the workplace, the maintenance and defence of 'custom-and-practice' was driven by rank-and-file workers and embraced new waves of workers in war production. For example, in 1917 women workers at Armstrong-Whitworth in Newcastle struck for the 'tea break'; this escalated to become a strike for wider representation of female workers.[46] Goodrich's research in British industry took place in this period of rank-and-file struggle. The new militancy became identified with the shop stewards' movement, Red Clydeside and demands for workers' control of industry in the immediate post-war years.[47] The struggles of the period included the creation of a defensive Triple Alliance embracing

---

filling. Cornwall, of course, is famous for its pasty (*aka* tatty oggy or knob end).

43 P. Ackers, 'On Paternalism: Seven Observations on the Uses and Abuses of the Concept in Industrial Relations, Past and Present', *HSIR* 5 (1998), pp. 173–93.

44 D. Wray, 'Paternalism and its Discontents: A Case Study', *WES* 10:4 (1996), pp. 701–15.

45 R. Martin and R. H. Fryer, *Redundancy and Paternalist Capitalism* (Allen and Unwin: 1973), p. 26; R. Bendix, *Work and Authority in Industry* (Transaction Publishers, New Brunswick, NJ: 2001 [1956]), pp. 48–50.

46 D. Thom, *Nice Girls and Rude Girls: Women Workers in World War 1* (I. B. Tauris: 2000), p. 39.

47 J. Hinton, *The First Shop Stewards' Movement* (Allen and Unwin: 1973).

one-and-a-half million workers between the miners', transport workers', and rail workers' unions.

Trade unions and workplace organization retreated in the aftermath of the 1921 recession and the General Strike, May 1926. Taylorist and Fordist methods of technocratic management – the assembly line, strict division of labour to discrete tasks, and time and motion study – began to take hold. The nineteenth-century paternalist model was marginalized as employers either victimized activists or began to look to alternative forms of 'negotiated control', seeking to contain trade unions within new institutional practices agreed with union leaders. In many cases, however, rather than abandon paternalism completely, employers sought to 'sweeten the pill' of Taylorism and Fordism by maintaining aspects of welfarism in their employee-relations strategies. As Arthur McIvor and Christopher Wright record:

> The Singer Corporation … introduced a range of welfarist schemes, including sports facilities and a social club, in the decade after the 1911 strike in an attempt to divert workers from the attractions of industrial unionism. Similarly, ICI sweetened the pill of scientific management by an extensive programme of welfare benefits between the wars.[48]

From the other direction, the Quaker-owned companies of Cadbury and Rowntree added Taylorist aspects of scientific management to their paternalistic practices.[49] It is also the case that the introduction of scientific management in British workplaces was tempered and restrained by a mixture of employer concerns at delegating power over industrial relations to the workshop, workers' resistance, and variegated product markets impervious to standardization.[50] Despite these caveats it was through the processes of negotiated agreement and welfarism that rest breaks, where they occurred, became embedded (at least for the better organized workers). They often formed part of collective agreements struck between employers and unions at national or sectoral level covering the whole range of pay and conditions at work.

Labour militancy in Britain did not begin to recover until the late 1930s, most notably in the newly emerging light-engineering aerospace

---

48 A. J. McIvor and C. Wright, 'Managing Labour: UK and Australian Employers in Comparative Perspective, 1900–50', *Labour History Review* 88 (2005), pp. 45–62, at p. 52.

49 M. Rowlinson, 'Quaker Employers', *HSIR* 6 (1998), pp. 163–98.

50 See I. Clark, 'The Productivity Race: British Manufacturing in Historical Perspective, 1850–1990', *HSIR* 9 (2000), pp. 133–46.

and automobile sectors.[51] The recovery was aided by arms production, as well as a renewed rank-and-file combativity (which included women and apprentices) often inspired by Communist Party activists.[52] Strike action in key war-production sectors became a challenge. During the Second World War, this was countered by the Coalition government through a mixture of carrot and stick. Labour's Ernest Bevin, Minister for Labour and National Service (supported by the future Labour prime minister, Clement Attlee) sought to restrict and avoid industrial unrest through issuing Order 1305 in 1940 and enacting a 'Procedure for the Avoidance of Disputes'.[53] This was both a carrot and a stick as it extended recognized terms (collective agreements) to similar industries and strikes were declared illegal, but even here there were few prosecutions.[54] Indeed, Geoffrey Field has suggested that rather than workers becoming bound to a 'national interest' during the period of wartime government measures the net effect was instead to 're-make' and solidify 'class' interests.[55]

This goal of 'managed' industrial co-operation between employer and workers was the context in 1941 for Bevin to launch an hour-long BBC programme, *Workers' Playtime*, which was broadcast from factories and offices during the lunch hour to boost worker and domestic morale. The Ministry of Labour even chose the factories and offices from where the programme would be broadcast 'somewhere in Britain'.[56] Running for three days each week (until 1964), it included among its guests such icons of British entertainment as Tony Hancock, Elsie and Doris Waters (Gert and Daisy), Eric Morecambe and Ernie Wise, Peter Sellers, and Julie Andrews. The lunch 'hour', most often taken in the works canteen at a set time (although with different levels of table service and seating area according to rank), became embedded in working practice, alongside the tea break. The hour-long break was long enough for workers living close by to go home for lunch if they so wished.

In the post-war boom of the 1950s and through to the 1960s, this structured regime of work, rest and play morphed into a partial revival of the paternalistic business practices where many large enterprises would host a range of clubs and societies (for example, drama and sports) for 'their'

---

51 H. A. Clegg, *A History of British Trade Unions since 1889: Vol. 2, 1911–1933* (Clarendon Press, Oxford: 1988).
52 R. Croucher, *Engineers at War* (Merlin: 1982).
53 *Ibid.*, ch. 2. Order 1305 was not rescinded until 1951.
54 See N. Fishman, '"A Vital Element in British Industrial Relations": A Reassessment of Order 1305, 1940–51', *HSIR* 8 (1999), pp. 43–86.
55 G. F. Field, *Blood, Sweat and Toil: Remaking the British Working Class, 1939–1945* (Oxford University Press: 2011).
56 See http://andywalmsley.blogspot.com/2015/08/on-light-part-7-from-factory-somewhere.html.

workers. Such initiatives were validated by the new-found enthusiasm for the 'human relations' school of management theory, originating in interwar America. This took cognisance of workers' needs and desires for social relationships and self-esteem at the workplace, linking these to prospects for increased individual productivity.[57] No doubt inspired by fears of workplace union organization, human relations attempted to ameliorate aspects of the alienating nature of Taylorism but this time through socio-psychological means.[58] Efforts by employers to incorporate the everyday life of their employees into the corporation seemed almost absolute in some cases. For example, the large ladies' lingerie manufacturer, Kayser Bondor, in Baldock, Hertfordshire, went so far as to provide a swimming pool, tennis courts and a ballroom for staff.[59]

The ensuing combination of Taylorist mass production and management theories of motivation allowed the space for new techniques of job 'enrichment', such as job rotation and job enlargement, to take hold, and for rest breaks to be sanctified in workplace practice and culture.[60] Many workplaces were subject to job evaluation and work measurement to establish output 'norms' around which a rate for the job would be agreed and paid. However, the 'scientific' methods employed by such studies were always capable of being undermined or manipulated by workers able to utilize sufficient bargaining strength to their advantage, sometimes by halting work, taking 'leisure time' in work, or even going home once their agreed targets for the week had been met.[61] Tea breaks took their part, centre stage, often with the 'tea lady' doing the rounds with the trolley twice a day, at set times in the office or factory. As automatic vending machines became more widespread, the tea 'lady' began to disappear, but tea and coffee, and the custom-and-practice of taking a break while drinking persisted, often because vending machines (and later the microwave oven) were located in the works or office canteen.

---

57 G. E. Mayo, *The Human Problems of an Industrial Civilization* (Routledge: 2003 [1933]).

58 K. Bruce and C. Nyland, 'Elton Mayo and the Deification of Human Relations', *Organization Studies* 32:3 (2011), pp. 383–405.

59 C. Rose, 'Bondor in Baldock: A Brief History of an Iconic Building', in *The Annual Guide to Baldock and Ashwell* (3rd edn; 2014). An earlier example of such lavish staff facilities was the Quaker-owned Fry's chocolate factory in Greenbank, Bristol, which in the 1920s had a swimming pool, tennis courts and bowling green attached to the factory. See J. Penny, *A Short History of the Greenbank Chocolate Factory* (undated): https://web.archive. org/web/20160303184920/http://www.chocolatememories.org/greenbank_ history.pdf.

60 T. Nichols and H. Beynon, *Living with Capitalism: Class Relations and the Modern Factory* (Routledge and Kegan Paul: 1977).

61 Thompson and Bannon, *Working the System*, ch. 3.

Within schools, colleges and universities its equivalent was time in the common room or playground, as the school bell sounded in rhythm with the factory hooter.

The employers' offensive against rest breaks

Beginning in the late 1960s, intensified global competition and falling rates of profitability ushered in a new regime of capital accumulation (otherwise labelled the neoliberal era of capitalism) which expanded both labour and product markets from the global North to the global South.[62] By the 1980s, labour could be 'sourced' beyond the nation state in a globalizing economy. Employers in the UK sought to abolish the agreed 'rate for the job' designed to standardize reward for skills in national labour markets and consequently eschewed long held national collective agreements in a manner which John Purcell described apocalyptically in his article as 'The End of Institutional Industrial Relations'.[63] The decline of collective bargaining in the UK was indeed significant, and the associated decline in workers' bargaining power 'after the long boom' is recorded by Huw Beynon as he revisits the workplace scenarios of his case study of class relations in the British workplace written with Theo Nichols more than four decades ago.[64] Between 1984 and 2004 the percentage of all workplaces covered by collective bargaining in the workplace fell from two-thirds to one-third. The decline was most severe in the private (and trading) sector where coverage fell from 47% to just 16%.[65]

While struggles over the length of the working day or week have been recorded and celebrated, struggles over time within the working day have been less so, mostly restricted to case-study analyses or ethnographies of the frontier of control in the mine, factory or office. Some classic studies in British industrial relations were conducted through participant observation when the authors worked the 'line' themselves. Workers were studied as subjects rather

---

62 B. Harrison, *Lean and Mean: The Changing Landscape of Corporate Power in the Age of Flexibility* (Basic Books, New York: 1994); R. Brenner, 'The Economics of Global Turbulence: A Special Report on the World Economy, 1950–98', *New Left Review* 229 (1998).

63 J. Purcell, 'The End of Institutional Industrial Relations', *Political Quarterly* 64:1 (1993), pp. 6–23.

64 T. Nichols and H. Beynon, *Living with Capitalism: Class Relations and the Modern Factory* (Routledge and Kegan Paul: 1977), and H. Beynon 'After the Long Boom: Living with Capitalism in the Twenty-First Century', *HSIR* 40 (2019), pp. 187–221.

65 W. Brown, A. Bryson, and J. Forth, 'Competition and the Retreat from Collective Bargaining', *NIESR Discussion Paper No. 318* (National Institute of Economic and Social Research: 2008), p. 5.

than objects. Such studies, towards the end of a 'high point' of trade-union advance in the UK in the 1970s and early 1980s, illustrated the skirmishes over the 'frontier of control' in which the locus of power could swing from employer to collectively organized workers and back again.

Workers' autonomy within the labour process raises important issues. Braverman focused on the degree to which workers subject to scientific management became accustomed to new ways of working through processes of manipulation and coercion by employers. He suggested that while workers are habituated by external forces to the degenerated work they experience, hostility persists as a 'subterranean stream' that may emerge if employers overstep the 'bounds of physical or mental capacity' or if employment conditions permit.[66] The degree to which hostility and resistance exists and persists, according to Tony Elger among others, may have been underplayed by Braverman due to his particular focus on the 'monopoly' aspects of contemporary capitalism and his lack of attention to wider political forces, workers' agency and class consciousness.[67]

Case studies from the 1970s assessed the limits of managerial omnipotence within the context of the Braverman debates. Goodrich's original study was supplemented by Huw Beynon's *Working for Ford* which depicted life in the factory and the struggle between shop-floor worker, the foreman and the boss. Anna Pollert's *Girls, Wives, Factory Lives* studied female tobacco workers in Bristol and explored their struggle in maintaining life both inside and outside paid work.[68] Miriam Glucksmann's (Ruth Cavendish) participant-observation study, *Women on the Line*, described the travails of women in a London car-components factory, and gave an account of struggles over the use of time.[69] Her personal experience of time discipline within the factory was so intense that she reflected, 'For many years afterwards I would always seek the quickest route between *a* and *b*, attempting to eliminate unnecessary movements in completing a task, even if this was in the kitchen, between fridge and cooker. It was as if I'd internalised time and motion study!'[70] In a popular account the journalist Madeleine Bunting recorded evidence from a female worker of the shift in management policy in the 'Saltfillas' (not its real name) factory in the Midlands in 2003:

When I first started we'd go on a line and after a couple of hours, we'd stop the line and all go off for a toilet break. Then we'd be back to work

---

66 Braverman, *Labor and Monopoly Capital*, p. 151.
67 See T. Elger, 'Valorisation and "Deskilling"': A Critique of Braverman', *Capital and Class* 3:1 (1979), pp. 59–99.
68 H. Beynon, *Working for Ford* (Allen Lane: 1973); A. Pollert, *Girls, Wives, Factory Lives* (Macmillan: 1981).
69 M. Glucksmann (R. Cavendish), *Women on the Line* (Routledge: 2009 [1982]).
70 *Ibid.*, p. xxi.

for a while before it was another break, and then the same thing happened in the afternoons. Between 8 and 4.35 we'd stop the line two or three times on top of the two breaks we were allowed. Sometime in the early eighties, they offered us a bribe – a pay rise in return for stopping that.[71]

There have been ingenious ways in which workers have wrested partial control over time, often by processes of time 'fiddling' or 'making out' whereby work schedules are manipulated in the workers' favour,[72] by accumulating time 'off' by over-recording time necessary to complete the job,[73] or even by sabotaging machinery to stop the line.[74] In one example, from the struggle for workers' control in the Italian 'hot autumn' of 1969, a Fiat worker, Pasquale di Stefano, defiantly challenged existing norms:

I decided to get out of my subordinate condition. To make this clear to everyone, every morning, around eight o'clock, I would stop working for about twenty minutes and eat a sandwich. This may sound silly, but no one had ever done it before, certainly no one had done it so openly, right before the supervisors.[75]

Breaks in working time obstruct employers' control of time at the workplace. Employers began to pursue new avenues to raising productivity as a supplement to, or a replacement for, their 'human relations', socio-psychological focus. Rest breaks fell foul of a new rubric of productivity deals constructed to lower unit-labour costs by intensifying work and attacking 'porosities' within the working day.[76] For the tea break, at least, the consequent managerial 'solipsism' ensured its decline.[77]

---

71 M. Bunting, *Willing Slaves: How the Overwork Culture Is Ruling Our Lives* (HarperCollins: 2004), p. 34.
72 M. Burawoy, *Manufacturing Consent: Changes in the Labour Process under Monopoly Capitalism* (University of Chicago Press: 1979); P. K. Edwards and C. Whitson, 'Workers Are Working Harder: Effort and Shop Floor Relations in the 1980s', *BJIR* 29:4 (1991), pp. 593–601.
73 G. Mars, *Cheats at Work: An Anthology of Workplace Crime* (Allen and Unwin: 1982).
74 L. Taylor and P. Walton, 'Industrial Sabotage: Motives and Meanings', in S. Cohen (ed.), *Images of Deviance* (Penguin, Harmondsworth: 1971), pp. 219–44.
75 Cited in R. Franzosi, *The Puzzle of Strikes: Class and State Strategies in Postwar Italy* (Cambridge University Press: 1995), p. 281.
76 For critical accounts see T. Nichols, *The British Worker Question: A New Look at Workers and Productivity in Manufacturing* (Routledge and Kegan Paul: 1986); and R. Brown (ed.), *The Changing Shape of Work* (Macmillan, Basingstoke: 1997).
77 J. Stewart, *The Decline of the Tea Lady: Management for Dissidents* (Wakefield Press, Kent Town, Australia: 2004).

During the initial skirmishes in the 1970s and 1980s, in the better organized union workplaces, workers opposed the creeping encroachment of management authority. This was the case in the car industry where unions had established a base in the late 1950s and 1960s period of mass production; workers often expressed their power by unofficial strikes and unconstitutional action outside procedural agreements. Symbolic struggles set the scene for change. In 1977 Michael Edwardes was appointed as head of British Leyland to restructure the company. His management methods challenged workplace union organization, and in 1979 he confronted the power of the shop stewards at the companies' plants by sacking Derek Robinson, a Communist Party member and the unions' convenor at the Austin factory, Longbridge, Birmingham. A long dispute followed, which finally ended in February 1980 when Robinson's dismissal was confirmed. The remainder of the year saw an offensive against the workers as jobs were shed wholesale. Edwardes also introduced a plan to reduce the company's 'relaxation allowances', part of which was to shorten and stagger across the day the twice daily tea breaks. In response, 100 paint sprayers struck at Longbridge, bringing production of the Mini and Allegro cars to a halt. The tea breaks stayed but in a shortened form. The mainstream press vilified the strikes in an atmosphere where union 'bosses and barons' were blamed for Britain's economic problems in the new era of Margaret Thatcher as prime minister.[78]

Employers' attempts to restrict and reduce rest breaks of all kinds peaked as the rise of new and more aggressive management techniques gathered pace. The piece-rate system of payment had allowed space for workers to negotiate top-up payments and for localized 'wage drift' to take place. Employers reacted by forcing through programmes of measured-day work, wresting back control of time and pay. By the end of the 1980s, new working methods such as lean production, just-in-time, total quality management, and team-working – 'Japanization' – replaced just-in-case and the culture of the stockroom. Within both manufacturing and services new forms of work organization emphasized team-working, which had the effect of deconstructing the custom-and-practice of rest allowances established by shop stewards at enterprise level into more fractured and dissipated forms of labour processes. Andrew Danford, Anthony Richardson and Martin Upchurch, in their study of establishments in south-west England, record the changes voiced by a union steward:

It's made a hell of a difference to how we influence working practices. Whereas before, the management always used to come to the works

---

78 T. Claydon, 'Tales of Disorder: The Press and the Narrative Construction of Industrial Relations in the British Motor Industry, 1950–79', *HSIR* 9 (2000), pp. 1–36.

committee to discuss issues, changes in hours, changes in practices, labour deployment and those types of issues. Now they don't. Now they try to get it through the back door by enticing one or two teams into accepting certain changes without involving the union at all.[79]

For Peter Titherington, the former convener of Vauxhall Ellesmere Port, the result of this shift was that 'Under the piece-rate system we directly sold the fruits of our labour. Under Measured Day Work we sold our time. Under lean, management determine our labour input and time with a vengeance'.[80]

Tensions over tea breaks within the motor industry resurfaced again in 2012 when workers on the Mini's production line at Cowley, Oxford (by then owned by BMW), voted by 97% to reject a pay deal which would have also trimmed the tea break time by eleven minutes per day, and time away from the assembly line would be reduced to just forty-two minutes in an eleven-hour shift, plus an unpaid lunch break. (In contrast, BMW workers in Germany had fifty minutes every eight hours.)[81] Cutting payment for tea breaks or financing pay rises by cuts occurred sporadically across other areas of manufacturing and services. A report commissioned by the Scottish Trades Union Congress cited the example of a merger between Royal Bank of Scotland and Halifax Bank of Scotland (HBOS), which led to the abolition of tea breaks. One national union officer recalled how it had been common practice in Bank of Scotland branches, prior to the merger that brought HBOS into being, for staff to have coffee and scones at 10.00 am every morning. When she visited branches she would be invited to these sessions, which enabled her to talk to staff and thus play an important role in employee–manager communications. After the merger, such breaks became a thing of the past.[82]

During the 2000s other discrete disputes over tea breaks broke out. Examples include a series of one-day strikes at Raven Manufacturing near Burnley in 2002, a strike by both manual and white-collar workers at Falkirk Council in 2007, and a strike ballot by catering and cleaning staff at Addenbrooke's Hospital in Cambridge in 2012.[83] In an unusual inversion

79 A. Danford, M. Richardson, and M. Upchurch, *New Unions, New Workplaces: A study of Union Resilience in the Restructured Workplace* (Routledge, 2003) p. 55.
80 P. Stewart, K. Murphy, A. Danford, T. Richardson, M. Richardson, and V. Wass, *We Sell Our Time No More: Workers' Struggles against Lean Production in the British Car Industry* (Pluto: 2010), p. 16.
81 S. Hawkes, 'Mini workers threaten strike over cut teabreak', *Sun*, 12 April 2019.
82 P. Taylor, *Performance Management and the New Workplace Tyranny: A Report for the Scottish Trades Union Congress* (undated).
83 See reports at https://www.google.com/search?q=tea+breaks&sitesearch=soci alistworker.co.uk.

of the repertoire of industrial action, refuse collectors in Birmingham in dispute against changes in working practices in 2017 voted to work-to-rule by returning to their depots each day for tea breaks, thus enforcing an effective 'strike' by other means.[84]

In summary, it can be argued that neoliberalism as the ideology and practice of free markets in a globalizing economy provided the space to tip the balance of social forces to the employer. 'New Right' values were promoted, characterized in Britain after 1979 by an 'ongoing reform project to remodel society' with a 'particular focus on the deregulation of capital and the re-regulation of labour'.[85] Collective bargaining and collective agreements at the workplace became a casualty in many instances, replaced by individual performance measurement and supplemented by a new target culture, aided and abetted by new technical forms of monitoring, surveillance and control. Downtime within work and the associated 'porosity' of the working day contracted. The evidence of such processes are clear. Paul Blyton in 1992 recorded the increase in employer use of *temporal flexibility*, especially in the manufacturing sector, between 1983 and 1991. The period was marked by the Engineering Employers' Federation (EEF) withdrawal from national collective agreements after a long-running dispute with Confederation of Shipbuilding and Engineering Unions (CSEU) over working hours: 'in October 1989 the CSEU set in motion a year-long campaign of selective strike ballots and strike action, backed by a national strike levy, to achieve an improved offer. *En route* this action precipitated the EEF to abandon its long-established role as industry negotiator on all substantive issues'.[86] The withdrawal of the EEF appeared to be a result of its diminished role from the 1960s as a national negotiator in the face of increasing tendencies for factory-level negotiations.[87] A survey by Industrial Relations Services found that in the ensuing disputes: 'References to cuts in, or elimination of, tea breaks were made in 18 of the 50 settlements, cuts/elimination of washing time in 13 cases and the introduction of "bell to bell" working practices in ten cases'.[88]

---

84 N. Elkes, 'Birmingham bin strike extended through till September after talks break down', *Birmingham Mail*, 18 July 2017.

85 P. Smith, 'Labour under the Law: A New Law of Combination, and Master and Servant, in 21st-century Britain?', *IRJ* 46:5–6 (2015), pp. 345–64, at p. 351. See also W. Brown and D. Marsden, 'Individualisation and Growing Diversity of Employment Relationships', in D. Marsden (ed.), *Employment in the Lean Years: Policy and Prospects for the Next Decade* (Oxford University Press: 2011), pp. 73–86.

86 P. Blyton, 'Flexible Times? Developments in Recent Flexibility', *IRJ* 23:1 (1992), pp. 26–36, at p. 31.

87 A. McKinlay, 'The Paradoxes of British Employer Organization, c. 1897–2000', *HSIR* 31/32 (2011), pp. 89–113.

88 Blyton, 'Flexible Times?', *IRJ*, p. 33.

Temporal density meets temporal flexibility

Regulation on working hours and holidays in the UK has traditionally been left to collective bargaining or, in the absence of trade unions, employer unilateral regulation. Since 1993, however, workplaces in the UK have been governed by European Union (EU) Working Time Regulations, stipulating a rest break where the working day is six hours or longer, but the nature, form and content of such rest breaks is ambiguous and 'escape options' from the regulations are built in.[89] The ambiguities came to prominence in 2009 as part of the unofficial strikes at an oil refinery at Lindsey, north Lincolnshire, where the company awarded the work, the Italy-based IREM, had proposed shift patterns that did not include paid tea breaks, giving it a small but cumulatively significant cost advantage. In contrast, British-based firms bidding for the work had included paid tea breaks in the costing. EU Regulations were complied with as the minimum, legally required rest periods were specified in the proposed contract. The contested issue remained the abolition of the 'custom-and-practice' paid tea break, strongly defended by the workers. The dispute spread to the nuclear site at Sellafield and other oil refineries in the UK. An inquiry by the Advisory, Conciliation and Arbitration Service (ACAS) supported IREM's interpretation of the legislation.[90] Derek Simpson, Unite the Union's then joint general secretary, responded tartly: 'The law wasn't broken – the law was wrong. Unless European governments start to put working people first with protective legislation that applies across the whole of the EU, then protests like the ones we have seen in the construction industry will go on until they do'.[91]

The ambiguity of paid as opposed to unpaid breaks was exploited by the supermarket, Sainsbury, in 2018, when it offered an above-inflation pay rise financed partly by the removal both of a half-hour paid break every eight-hour shift and also a fifteen-minute paid break for seven-hour shifts. After negative reaction from unions and some MPs, Sainsbury revised its offer, but paid breaks remained abolished.[92] Asda in 2019 proposed a new agreement which would remove payment for lunch breaks in return for a

---

89 D. Goss and D. Adam-Smith, 'Pragmatism and Compliance: Employer Responses to the Working Time Regulations', *IRJ* 32:3 (2003), pp. 195–208.

90 ACAS, *Report of an Inquiry into the Circumstances surrounding the Lindsey Oil Refinery Dispute* (ACAS: 2009).

91 Cited in D. Henke, 'Tea breaks helped lose British workers jobs at Lindsey, report finds', *Guardian*, 16 February 2009.

92 S. Butler, 'Sainsbury's increases staff pay, but axes paid breaks and bonuses', *Guardian*, 6 March 2018.

new pay deal. Despite opposition by the GMB, it successfully imposed the change on an individual basis (via a new contract of employment).[93]

South Asian female workers in Southall, west London, producing in-flight meals for British Airways, had also fallen victim to outsourcing in 2005 when their employment contracts were transferred to Gate Gourmet. The new employer sought to cut back on rest breaks, reducing the lunch break from thirty to fifteen minutes and the tea break to ten minutes. One of the women workers records:

> they were trying to squeeze work out of us, like you squeeze blood out of meat. They wanted to change the conditions at work. Like the breaks. It was just a 10-minute break, not even enough to drink a cup of tea properly. Just enough time to go to the toilet, relax for a few minutes. Look at the women today, so many of them have arthritis and pain in their joints and back. That's what you needed the break for, to stretch yourself, ease your aching muscles.[94]

In response the women went on unofficial strike; baggage handlers struck in solidarity, closing Heathrow airport for forty-eight hours. This action came up against Conservative government legislation restricting immunities to unions taking strike action (Employment Acts of 1980 and 1990). The Transport and General Workers' Union (TGWU), after initially supporting the action, distanced itself and then withdrew support and sought financial compensation for the 700 workers who had been dismissed.[95]

Within public services, private contractors have undercut the pay and working conditions of workers transferred from National Health Service (NHS) and local government care services in a variety of ways. Nowhere is this more apparent than in the case of home-care workers. A study by Sian Moore and Lydia Hayes in 2018 tracked the process whereby workers' downtime and rest time was all but eliminated by electronic control mechanisms (through mobile phones). A rest break could often only be achieved by cutting visits to clients short, thus reducing the quality of service: 'For care workers back-to-back visits ('call-cramming') and insufficient travel time between them drives them to cut visits short to

---

93 S. Farrell, 'We won't ask people to do shifts they can't do', *Grocer*, 5 November 2019.

94 'The Gourmet Dispute', *Striking Women Org*, online. See also A. Tuckman, 'Then and Now: Vulnerable Workers, Industrial Action, and the Law in the 1970s and Today', *HSIR* 41 (2020), pp. 251–60, at pp. 258–60.

95 J. Hendy and G. Gall, 'British Trade Union Rights Today and the Trade Union Freedom Bill', in K. D. Ewing (ed.), *The Right to Strike: From the Trade Disputes Act 1906 to a Trade Union Freedom Bill* (Institute of Employment Rights, Liverpool: 2006), pp. 247–77.

58   HISTORICAL STUDIES IN INDUSTRIAL RELATIONS 41

ensure they get to the next service user. ... travel time is not paid in order to maximise the extent of unpaid labour'.[96]

In July 2017 one of the biggest strikes within the NHS took place as workers across Whipps Cross, Mile End, Royal London and St Bartholomew's hospitals in London were transferred to the private Serco corporation in a contract worth £600 million. Three days after taking over the contract, Serco proposed to abolish the ten-minute morning tea break. One hundred and twenty workers struck immediately until the tea breaks were reinstated.[97] A wider strike over pay and 'dignity within the workplace' followed; this resulted in an agreement struck between Unite and Serco for a pay rise of 1%, and an uplifting of all affected staff from the statutory minimum to the London Living Wage.[98]

The conjuncture of time flexibility and time density is a potentially explosive mix. A recent example is in education where a teacher launched a petition over the time allowed for planning and preparation (PPA) which is now restricted to six minutes per lesson.[99] It followed from action over other time allowances and excessive monitoring within schools, leading to a campaign by the National Education Union (NEU) against punitive regimes of workload monitoring and surveillance.[100]

Managerial belligerence towards toilet breaks has been evident in the last two decades with digitalization at the workplace. Contemporary applications of electronic tags and implants empower employers to time workers' toilet breaks. A Norwegian company has been reported as requiring women to wear red bracelets to 'allow' them extra time for toilet breaks.[101] New forms of resistance are beginning to emerge, based on disputes over data ownership and use, or through manipulations of the peculiarities of the app in the gig economy. For example, in September 2019, cycle and motor-scooter couriers working for Deliveroo across sixteen 'zones' in various parts of the UK struck against the discipline of the app

96 S. Moore and L. Hayes, 'The Electronic Monitoring of Care Work: The Redefinition of Paid Working Time', in P. V. Moore, M. Upchurch, and X. Whittaker (eds), *Humans and Machines at Work: Monitoring, Surveillance and Automation in Contemporary Capitalism* (Palgrave Macmillan: 2018), pp. 101–24, at p. 114.
97 S. Whitehead, '"Some days I feel like I'll drop dead": Britain's biggest cleaners' strike', *Guardian*, 1 August 2017.
98 NHS Support Federation, '"NHS For Sale?" Serco', online.
99 https://petition.parliament.uk/petitions/246255.
100 M. Upchurch, P. Moore, and A. Kunter, 'Marketisation, Commodification and the Implications for Teachers' Autonomy in England', *Research in Political Economy* 29 (2018), pp. 133–53. See also the NEU campaign at https://neu.org.uk/campaigns/workload.
101 Z. Drewett, 'Employers time toilet breaks and make women wear bracelets if they are on their period', *Metro*, 13 November 2018.

and its inbuilt non-recognition of payment for 'waiting time'.[102] Assembling at the prime locations for picking up new orders has provided an arena for collective organization and industrial action. In some circumstances the state may be pressured by trade unions and other agencies to introduce legislation to protect workers' health and safety in the new stress-ridden workplace or to protect data privacy.[103] In other cases, trade unions may act to limit exposure to emails and other forms of electronic communication outside work hours. The French trade unions, for example, were successful in gaining a new section of the Labour Code in 2016 which enforced the 'right to disconnect' from IT-devices during holidays and rest periods in companies with more than fifty employees.[104]

Well-being and a 'new' paternalism?

The scenario of an employer removing rest breaks through contractual or other means is not the whole picture. In a new initiative, the Chartered Institute of Personnel and Development (CIPD) has collaborated with the mental health campaigner, MIND to promote 'wellness' and 'well-being' programmes to deal with workplace stress. The CIPD warns that 'Poor workplace wellbeing has been found to cause a decrease in productivity for 63% of employees in the UK, while 21% of workers leave their jobs because they feel that the company culture does not align with their personal values.'[105] However, the 'solution' proffered by the CIPD and other agencies does not focus on the benefits of breaks, rest and recuperation. Rather, 'wellness' and 'well-being' programmes prepared by management consultants are considered the way forward, emphasizing the need for worker 'resilience'.[106] Thus the responsibility for the symptoms of stress is placed on the individual.[107] 'Wellness' and mindfulness programmes are focused at the point of production and, to relieve stress, include such

---

102 C. Cant, 'Deliveroo workers launch new strike wave', *Notes From Below*, 28 September 2019, online.

103 See Moore *et al.*, *Humans and Machines at Work*, ch. 2.

104 CMS, Legal *Switching on to Switching off: Disconnecting Employees in Europe?* (2018), online.

105 CIPD/MIND, *Supporting Staff Wellbeing in the Workplace* (2019), online..

106 N. Aschoff, *The New Prophets of Capital* (Verso: 2015). Nicole Aschoff argues that these new techniques are manifest whereby the super-rich, such as Oprah Winfrey and Melinda Gates, suggest we must examine our inner self or promote charity to alleviate poverty and inequality: https://www.dissent-magazine.org/blog/oprah-is-not-your-friend-a-qa-with-nicole-aschoff.

107 See R. Purcer, *McMindfulness: How Mindfulness Became the New Capitalist Spirituality* (Repeater Books: 2019).

activities as 'desk massage' and 'desk yoga'.[108] Not all mental health charities take the same view. The Mental Health Foundation, for example, continues to offer the advice that employees should 'Take proper breaks at work, for example by taking at least half an hour for lunch and getting out of the workplace if you can.'[109]

New forms of work organization are now promoted by employers, reviving a form of paternalism but without the *formal* tea or lunch break. For example, the 'gig' corporations, otherwise known as the FANGs (Facebook, Amazon, Netflix, and Google), are at the forefront of increasing temporal density. They take the 'resilience' approach one stage further in their prestige head offices, in ways that are reminiscent of the old paternalism, while at the same time exercising extreme temporal flexibility in their outsourced service operations such as Amazon Mechanical Turk.[110] At Google's headquarters, Mountain View, California, employees are never 150 feet away from a micro-kitchen. There is free transport to work where you find an on-site massage parlour, games room, swings, and ball pits where staff may take their laptops to work, a micro-swimming pool which flows the water in the opposite direction to your strokes so you get the impression of swimming a lap, and the right to take your dog to work (cats are not allowed as it would be too 'stressful' for them). Employees who wish to avoid walking down the stairs can slide down a chute instead. Induction of new employees consists of a 'New Employee Orientation and Arranged Virginity-Loss Night'.[111] Facebook's engineering headquarters in London, with 1,000 employees, has sleep pods if you wish to snooze, artistic workshops with a resident artist, games room (billiards, table tennis, football tables), micro-kitchens, and a canteen with free food to which you can bring friends and family.[112]

This new high-tech or cloud version of paternalism shares with the old paternalism an employer strategy which assumes that spending money on staff benefits will buy employee loyalty (and help to keep workers' collective organization at bay). It also repeats the practice of allowing creative and highly skilled workers a degree of 'responsible autonomy' identified in the 1970s as a managerial strategy fit for purpose within large-scale, monopoly

---

108 Stress Management Society, *Corporate Wellbeing Solutions* (undated), online.
109 'Work-life Balance', *Mental Health Foundation*, online.
110 K. Hara, A. Adams, K. Milland, S. Savage, C. Callison-Burch, and J. Bigham, 'A Data-Driven Analysis of Workers' Earnings on Amazon Mechanical Turk', paper to the 2018 ACM Conference on Human Factors in Computing Systems, Montreal, Canada; A. Semuels, 'The Internet Is Enabling a New Kind of Poorly Paid Hell', *Next Economy, The Atlantic*, 23 January 2018.
111 'Inside Google Office: 15 coolest things you get as a Google Employee' , LetsIntern.com (2014), online.
112 D. Ibekwe, 'Facebook's Engineering Office, London', *Business Insider*, 16 November 2018, online.

capitalism. In this model 'managerial authority' is maintained 'by getting workers to identify with the competitive aims of the enterprise so that they will act "responsibly" without supervision'.[113] This blurring of work and non-work life may partly be related to an effect of the Internet (email) and mobile phones, as well as new flexible working arrangements.[114] The FANG approach appears to *embrace* non-working-life aspirations by incorporating them into the working day. The modern, sophisticated paternalist employer socially constructs the workplace so that life becomes work and work becomes life. It uses fun, games and good food in its attempt to bind the company 'associate' to corporate objectives.[115] However, even this world of digital artisans, self-conscious, super-rich and creative entrepreneurs is not immune from resistance as 'colleagues' within the high-tech, high-profile FANGs begin to self-identify as 'workers', rejecting the corporate goals of the giant companies and even making common cause 'with the cleaners and baristas that serve them'.[116] There are also limits to the phenomenon of acting without supervision. Yahoo! (now part of Google) announced in 2013 its intention to stop working from home because, as Jackie Reses, human resources director, explained: 'Speed and quality are often sacrificed when we work from home. ... We need to be one Yahoo!, and that starts with physically being together'.[117]

Outside the FANGs, new forms of paternalism are less common, but employers' efforts to overcome the deleterious effects of work-related stress are in evidence. Some employers are utilizing the mantra and practice of temporal flexibility in new ways in order to combat the stress caused by temporal density. Most notable is the emerging practice of allowing employees to schedule their own hours to complete set tasks, which may involve working a four-day week, or working more often from home. The accountancy firm PwC now offers employees contracts lasting a set number of days to complete specific tasks, rather than contracts which have the expectation of a 9–5 job.[118] In recognition of the positive correlations between rest, recuperation and productivity the Wellcome Trust agreed to trial a four-day working week, only to abandon the idea as 'too operationally

---

113 A. Friedman, 'Responsible Autonomy versus Direct Control over the Labour Process', *Capital and Class* 1:1 (1977), pp. 43–57, at p. 48.
114 N. Chesley, 'Blurring Boundaries? Linking Technology Use, Spillover, Individual Distress, and Family Satisfaction', *Journal of Marriage and Family* 67:5 (2005) pp. 1237–48.
115 A further example is perhaps the new headquarters of Huawei in China, which is designed to look like a European fairy-tale capital.
116 H. O'Brien, 'How Silicon Valley is being reshaped by trade unions', *New Statesman*, 13 March 2019.
117 H. McRae, 'When even Yahoo!'s Marissa Mayer wants workers in the office, is the homeworking revolution over?', *Independent*, 26 February 2013.
118 *BBC News*, 30 August 2018, online.

complex to implement'.[119] Smaller companies, mostly in the creative and design sector, are now offering the same, hoping to overcome, it seems, the negative effect of 'Friday fatigue'.[120] Perhaps most revealing of all is a new trend to introduce 'Swedish-style' *fika* coffee breaks into the modern British workplace. In promoting the idea of fixed breaks away from the desk to drink coffee with workmates, Karen Adams from the Public Relations agency, HatTrick, commented:

> We introduced fika as a way of having a moment to relax and talk to your workmates. If people were having external problems, or just stress, someone might pick that up. ... With fika, you can have a break, come back refreshed and look at things from a different perspective. ... Work talk is prohibited in fika. It forces you away from our work so you can re-evaluate things and prioritise tasks when you do return.[121]

This example of the return of the coffee/tea break, while rare, is not unprecedented. The *New York Times* reported in 2014 the cases of the Bank of America call centre and a pharmaceutical centre: the former introduced a fifteen-minute coffee break while the latter replaced coffee-makers with a larger cafe area.[122] The newspaper records: 'The result? Increased sales and less turnover'.[123] As Winifred Poster remarks, in the case of the call centre, the employers had noticed that 'workers who communicate more closely when off the desk, are more effective when they return'.[124]

Conclusion: the degradation of work

This paper has examined tensions over rest breaks and the control of work time as they have been experienced over many decades. It has argued that breaks – for the weekend, and for tea (or coffee), lunch, and to visit the toilet while at work – have always been a contentious issue, from the Industrial Revolution to the contemporary factory, office, and shop. The tension is a product of the desire of employers to reduce the porosity of working time

119 *Guardian*, 12 April 2019.
120 R. Booth and M. Holmes, 'String of British firms switch over to four-day working week', *Guardian*, 12 March 2019.
121 R. Monks, 'Fika: why more companies are introducing Swedish-style coffee breaks', *I News*, 30 January 2017.
122 Coffee companies are particularly keen to promote coffee breaks, often claiming that the caffeine in coffee will help boost productivity.
123 S. Lohr, 'Unblinking Eyes Track Employees', *New York Times*, 24 June 2014.
124 W. R. Poster, 'Socially Benevolent Workplace Surveillance?', *Work in Progress* blog, 30 April 2015.

and the concomitant resistance of workers to the degradation of work and dispossession of dignity. Debates within labour process theory flourished in the 1970s, initiated by Braverman's study of scientific management and the subordination of workers it described. Braverman has been criticized for paying too little attention to wider political forces and workers' conscious resistance, and such a perspective aids an analysis of employer offensives against rest breaks and increased temporal flexibility and density.

The space for workers to contest and subvert the time discipline imposed by employers has become more restricted as the intensification of global competition has led employers to seek ever greater transparency of the value-added by individual workers and the marginalization of collective bargaining and the 'rate for the job'. Temporal flexibility has marched hand in hand with wage flexibility, disrupting workers' collective organization in the process. In the UK at least, the ability of trade unions to organize has also been restricted by the state as legislation took effect under governments of the 'New Right'. The tightening of time discipline has been aided by new forms of monitoring, surveillance and control which have not only promoted the intensification of work, but also created the phenomenon of increased time density. In a minority of cases, mostly in the 'creative' and high-tech industries, it appears the limits of mental capacity (at least) may have been reached, as employers (ever conscious of the need to raise productivity) return to sophisticated paternalist strategies of ensuring worker commitment to the job by fun and games, mindfulness and resilience training.[125]

For the pressure on time at work to be released on a permanent basis a conscious collective response by workers is required. This would be necessary to overcome Braverman's pessimistic prognosis of 'habituation' to a new normal. There are many examples where this has happened, from the struggles focused in the automobile and engineering industries in the 1970s and 1980s, through to skirmishes in the public sector and the newly emerging 'gig' economy in the twenty-first century. It is not the case, however, that workers instinctively dispute time to move to establish forms and dimensions of workers' control over the means of production. Consciousness is complex, and sometimes contradictory, and will vary from across locations as workers develop cultures of solidarity and different propensities for strikes and control within the workplace.[126] There is a scale of demands focused on time discipline. Struggles over the 'frontier of control' will break out wherever workers are located, as employers intensify

---

125 Braverman, *Labor and Monopoly Capital*, p. 151, referred to the 'bounds of physical and mental capacity' as a reason for employers to relax time discipline.

126 See R. Hyman, *Strikes* (Fontana: 1972), ch. 3; R. Fantasia, *Cultures of Solidarity: Consciousness, Action and Contemporary American Workers* (University of California Press, Oakland: 1989).

pressure to increase both temporal flexibility and density. Such skirmishes can be part of a wider struggle. As a minimum, the struggle by workers to control time at and within work reflects a demand for dignity and respect. As Goodrich observed, 'all this is merely a negative resentment against control and not specifically a demand for control. ... The desire to be let alone, to be free from the irksomeness of control by others, is not identical with the desire to co-operate actively in the work of controlling.'[127] We can appreciate how something so seemingly trivial as toilet and tea breaks are symbolic of a potentially wider struggle.

Business School
University of Middlesex
The Burroughs
London NW4 4BT

---

127 Goodrich, *Frontier of Control*, p. 34.

HSIR 41 (2020) 65–84

https://doi.org/10.3828/hsir.2020.41.3

After the 1910 Eight-Week Lockout: 'Flächentarifvertrag' in the German Construction Industry

Jörn Janssen

The greatest industrial dispute in Germany before the First World War, a national lockout in the construction industry, lasting eight weeks and involving up to 245,000 workers, ended with a defeat of the German Construction Employers' Federation – Deutscher Arbeitgeberbund für das Baugewerbe – on 18 June 1910 after a tripartite process of arbitration. This industrial dispute about a new national framework contract – *Flächentarifvertrag* – on collective employment relations and bargaining in the construction industry heralded a new stage in labour–capital relations. It led to a substantial unification and concentration of workers' organizations and divided the employer's organization, benefiting, on the one hand, the sectoral labour unions to the detriment of local unions, and, on the other, the joint-stock corporations to the detriment of smaller, individually owned companies.

This new stage of labour–capital or employment relations in Germany represents the maturation of the *Flächentarifvertrag*, which had a single predecessor in the printing trade since 1873.[1] This development implied also a change in the meaning of the word: *Flächentarifvertrag* had been a mandatory standard work contract at national level for all printers; the new model contract of 1910 was generally binding for all employers and employees of the central organizations. *Flächentarifvertrag* has no

I would like to express my thanks to Paul Smith. This article has greatly benefited from his critical comments at various stages of writing as well as its final editing. Quotations are the author's translations.

1 H. Lesch und D. Byrski, *Flächentarifvertrag und Tarifpartnerschaft in Deutschland, ein historischer Rückblick* (Institut der deutschen Wirtschaft, Cologne: 2016), pp. 8ff.

corresponding term in English probably because in Britain the dominant form of labour organization and collective 'agreement', not 'contract', was determined by trades and workplaces.[2] Gregor Asshoff, a member of the management board of the supplementary social protection funds – *Zusatzversorgungskassen* – of the construction industry, published an article about the celebrations by the social partners of the hundredth anniversary of the first *Flächentarifvertrag* in the construction industry in 2010:

> The first *Flächentarifvertrag* in the construction industry was a matter of fierce fighting. Unlike as one might assume nowadays, it was not in the spring of 1910 the then still autonomous four organizations of construction workers who demanded the introduction of a *Flächen-tarifvertrag*, but the *employers*, who wanted and enforced by all possible means up to an almost two months' lockout the introduction of a *Flächentarifvertrag*.[3]

There is a further momentum in this collective contract relation specific for Germany. In the 1910 lockout the state played a significant role, almost anticipating a tripartite relationship. The arbitration committee, which was instrumental in bringing about an agreement by both opposing parties, consisted of delegates of the four national labour unions, the employers' federation and three high-ranking government officers: the imperial Home Office official, Otto Wiedfeldt; the Mayor of Dresden, Otto G. Beutler; and the director of the Court of Commerce in Munich, Dr Hans Prenner. Significantly, the final arbitration proceedings of 27–31 May 1910 took place in the palace of the Imperial Parliament, the 'Reichstag'.

This dispute is also a pioneering case in the emergence of sectoral bargaining and binding agreements under the state government regime and hence a cornerstone in the development of wage-labour relations at international level. The following article seeks also to allocate this episode within the context of the political upheavals marked by war and revolution due to the change in the transnational balance of power in Europe related to the sudden rise of German industry by the turn of the twentieth century.

---

2 W. J. Mommsen and H.-G. Husung, *Auf dem Wege zur Massengewerkschaft. Die Entwicklung der Gewerkschaften in Deutschland und Großbritannien, 1880–1914* (Klett-Cotta Verlag, Stuttgart: 1984), pp. 12ff.

3 G. Asshoff, *Sozial- und tarifpolitische Bedeutung der Allgemeinverbindli-cherklärung von Tarifverträgen im Baugewerbe*, WSI Mitteilungen: Zeitschrift des Wirtschafts- und Sozialwissenschaftlichen Instituts in der Hans-Böckler-Stiftung 7 (Bund-Verlag, Cologne: 2012), p. 541.

Though the 1910 lockout stands out as a key event in the transformation of industrial relations in Germany, it was also a component of the wider industrial unrest throughout Europe and the United States of America at the time, and the political advance of labour in the transnational alliance of the 'Second International'.[4]

Capital–labour relations in the German construction industry, 1890–1914

Whereas by 1910 Britain was still by far the largest colonial power in the world, from 1870, Germany, driven by its scientific achievements and Otto von Bismarck's social labour policies, had become the centre of productive innovation and industrial growth in Europe. The structure of German capitalism was in a process of transformation. Rudolf Hilferding's *Finanzkapital: Eine Studie über die jüngste Entwicklung des Kapitalismus* (*Finance Capital: A Study in the Latest Phase of Capitalist Development*), published in 1910, traced the transformation of capital from direct ownership of productive assets to shareholding and other forms of participation by banking capital, 'the liberation of the industrial capitalist from the function of the industrial entrepreneur'.[5]

The accumulation and concentration of industrial capital, instrumental in the formation of large corporations, was not merely a quantitative process. It transformed the very nature of property relations in industry. Its clearest expression was the rise of the joint-stock company – *Aktiengesellschaft* – and other forms of divided ownership. One major aspect of this transformation was also highlighted by Hilferding in 1910: 'the development of joint-stock holding … separates executive leadership from property and makes executive function a special function of higher paid wage earners and employees'.[6] Through this separation, 'a concentration process of property, independent from the concentration process in the industry, also takes place at the stock exchange'.[7] In other words,

---

4 The so-called 'Second International', successor of the 'First International' or 'International Workingmen's Association', 1864–76, was the international organization of socialist or labour parties promoting and co-ordinating politics through nine congresses between 1889 and 1912. At its initial congress, 20 countries were represented. In 1900 its 'International Socialist Bureau' was set up in Brussels. The 'Third International', the Comintern or Communist International, was founded by V. I. Lenin in 1919.

5 R. Hilferding, *Das Finanzkapital: Eine Studie über die jüngste Entwicklung des Kapitalismus* (Verlag der Wiener Volksbuchhandlung Ignaz Brand und Co., Vienna: 1910; edn Dietz Verlag, Berlin: 1947), p. 120.

6 *Ibid.* (1947), p. 483.

7 *Ibid.*, p. 177.

the most advanced process of property concentration became dissociated from direct managerial control. According to Werner Sombart,[8] 'The significant feature of the joint-stock company ... is this, that in the joint-stock company the entrepreneur of things, the "capitalist", is detached from the enterprise'.[9]

This transformation of capital was shaped in part by the rise of the statutory regulation of labour relations. Hugo Sinzheimer's 1907 programmatic publication, *Der korporative Arbeitsnormenvertrag. Eine privatrechtliche Untersuchung* (*The Collective Agreement: A Private Law Investigation*) was already a testimony to the advanced debate on the role of self-government in labour relations.[10] Across the board, labour and capital were about to become components of a tripartite system of industrial democracy.

After the protracted economic depression of 1873–96, the growth in the number of joint-stock companies became a distinctive feature of corporate development. In the German construction industry this transformation peaked with an average annual creation of four joint-stock companies per year between 1906 and 1909, as compared to an annual average of no more than 1.4 between 1891 and 1900, and two between 1901 and 1905 (Table 1).

---

8 Werner Sombart, 1863–1941, was the author of a noted history of capitalism: W. Sombart, *Der moderne Kapitalismus, Bd. II, Das europäische Wirtschaftsleben im Zeitalter des Frühkapitalismus, Erster Halbband* (Duncker und Humblot, Munich und Leipzig: 1916; Unveränderter Nachdruck, Deutscher Taschenbuchverlag, Munich: 1987).

9 *Ibid.* (1987), p. 151.

10 H. Sinzheimer, *Der korporative Arbeitsnormenvertrag. Eine privatrechtliche Untersuchung* (Duncker und Humblot, Leipzig: 1908 [1907]). Sinzheimer was one of the first academics specializing in labour law. He was a member of the Weimar National Assembly, which promulgated the Weimar Constitution. A major influence on the drafting of the labour law section of the constitution, he is considered to be 'the father of labour law' in Germany. As a lawyer, he frequently represented political and union-related groups. He joined the Social Democratic Party of Germany in 1914. From 1920 onward, he was professor of labour law and sociology of law at Frankfurt University. In 1933, Sinzheimer, who was Jewish, was forced to emigrate to the Netherlands. In 1940 he was captured and taken to the Theresienstadt concentration camp for four months. He managed to secure release, and had to return to hiding in the attic of friends in the Netherlands. After the liberation of the Netherlands in May 1945 he did not recover from his poor health and died several months later in September 1945: https://en.wikipedia.org/wiki/Hugo_Sinzheimer. He was a major influence on Otto Kahn-Freund. See also R. Dukes, *The Labour Constitution: The Enduring Idea of Labour Law* (Oxford University Press: 2014), ch5, 2, 3.

Table 1: Foundation of joint-stock companies in the construction industry

1851–60	2
1861–70	1
1871–80	4
1881–90	2
1891–1900	14
1901–05	10
1906–09	16

Source: Statistisches Jahrbuch für das Deutsche Reich, 1911.

Philipp Holzmann, Grün und Bilfinger, Beton- und Monierbau, Julius Berger, Hochtief, Wayss und Freytag, and Dyckerhoff und Widmann, became leading companies in the global development of reinforced concrete, 'Eisenbeton' (Table 2).

Table 2: Formation of joint-stock companies

1880	Grün und Bilfinger
1889	Beton- und Monierbau
1890	Julius Berger Tiefbau
1896	Hochtief
1900	Wayss und Freytag
1907	Dyckerhoff und Widmann

Simultaneous with the rising power of capital, during the twenty years before 1910, labour developed under the auspices of the Second International. From 1890 the membership of the German Social Democratic Party – Sozialdemokratische Partei Deutschlands (SPD) – exploded to almost one million in 1912, while its representation in the Reichstag Parliament expanded from 19% in 1890 to 34.8% in 1912 (Table 3).

Inspired by the politics of the SPD, the development of strike action in the German construction industry epitomizes the surge of labour union power in the decade before 1910. In this process of amalgamation and concentration, labour unions built up their membership and became increasingly active in 'class struggle' as reflected in the rising frequency of strikes and lockouts (Table 4).

Table 3: SPD Reichstag members and party membership

Year	Reichstag members	%	SPD membership
1890	35	19	
1893	44	23	
1898	56	27	
1900			250,000
1903	81	32	
1906			384,327
1907	43	29	530,466
1908			587,336
1909			633,309
1910			720,038
1911			836,500
1912	110	35	970,000

Source: *Statistisches Jahrbuch für das Deutsche Reich*, 1911

Table 4: Strikes and lockouts in the construction industry

Year	Strikes	Lockouts
1901	378	8
1902	467	15
1903	520	28
1904	742	54
1905	865	89
1906	1,079	91
1907	704	84
1908	429	76
1909	605	51
1910	506	1,016

Source: K.-G. Werner, *Organisation und Politik der Gewerkschaften und Arbeitgeberverbände in der deutschen Bauwirtschaft* (Duncker und Humblot, Berlin: 1968), p. 80.

The collectivization of labour in union organization with the development of strikes and lockouts proceeded in step with the industrial concentration and anonymity of capital, as the most dynamic form of industrial property. Most significant, however, was the historical transformation of the relationship between labour organization and employers' federations, summarized by Hilferding: 'As is well known, the fight about the labour contract proceeds in three stages. In the first stage the individual manufacturer faces the individual workers. In the second, the individual manufacturer fights against the organization of workers. In the third, the employers' organizations are united in confronting the workers' organizations'.[11] This assessment had already been anticipated for the construction industry by Franz Habersbrunner in 1903: 'The most effective incentive for the reorganization of the construction employers ... was the lively labour movement starting in the sixties'.[12]

The succession of employees and employers in founding their central organizations was exemplary in the construction industry:

1891 Verband der Bauarbeitsleute und Berufsgenossen (Federation of Construction Labourers and Workmates)

1891 Zentralverband der Maurer Deutschlands (Central Federation of Bricklayers of Germany)

1893 Verband deutscher Zimmerleute (Federation of German Carpenters)

1899 Deutscher Arbeitgeberbund für das Baugewerbe (German Employers' Federation for the Construction Industry)

It was not until eight years after the national Federation of Construction Labourers and Workmates had been founded in 1891 that the German Employers' Federation for the Construction Industry was formed in Berlin, in 1899, to defend employers' interests against the rising power of labour organization. After its foundation the membership of the employers federation increased rapidly from 2,850 in 1901 to 20,930 companies in 1909 (Table 5).

This growth in the membership of the construction employers' federation reflected the consolidation of its role as a body for negotiating and settling collective contracts on employment conditions. It was 'by far on top' of all employers' organizations,[13] with the largest percentage of workers covered by its collective contract, 'Tarifvertrag' (Table 6).

---

11 Hilferding, *Das Finanzkapital*, p. 87.
12 F. Habersbrunner, *Die Lohn- Arbeits-und Organisations-Verhältnisse im deutschen Baugewerbe mit besonderer Berücksichtigung der Arbeitgeber-Organisation* (Deichert'sche Verlagsbuchhandlung, Leipzig: 1903).
13 H.-P. Ullmann, *Unternehmerschaft, Arbeitgeberverbände und Streikbewegung, 1890–1914*, in K. Tenfelde and H. Volkmann (eds), *Streik: Zur Geschichte des Arbeitskampfes in Deutschland während der Industrialisierung* (Beck, Munich: 1981), pp. 194–208, at p. 197.

Table 5: Deutscher Arbeitgeberbund des Baugewerbes

Year	Local organizations	Members
1901	67	2,850
1902	82	3,500
1903	124	5,700
1904	147	7,758
1905	159	8,465
1906	168	13,814
1907	388	18,300
1908	469	20,222
1909	521	20,930

Source: A. Winning, *Der grosse Kampf im deutschen Baugewerbe 1910* (Deutscher Bauarbeiterverband, Hamburg: 1911), p. 23.

Table 6: Percentage of workers under collective agreements in 1912

Sector	%
Textile industry	1.6
Engineering and metalwork	9.7
Polygraphic trades	38.6
Construction industry	39.6
Woodworking	25.1
Food and beverage	10.5
Clothing and cleaning	16.9

Source: H. Volkmann, *Organisation und Konflikt, Gewerkschaften, Arbeitgeberverbände und die Entwicklung des Arbeitskonflikts im späten Kaiserreich*, in W. Conze and U. Engelhardt (eds), *Arbeiter im Industrialisierungsprozeß Herkunft, Lage und Verhalten* (Klett-Cotta, Stuttgart: 1979), p. 428.

The construction and print industries became those with not only the highest percentage of workers under collective contracts, but also the highest level of strike activity. According to the General Committee of Labour Unions in Germany, the eight-week lockout in the construction industry of 1910 was 'the greatest fight that has ever been carried out between the organizations of employers and workers in Germany',[14] involving 245,017 out of 306,613 workers, about 80%, of those employed in the industry in that

---

14 *Correspondenzblatt der Generalkommission der Gewerkschaften Deutschlands* (Carl Legien, Hamburg: 22 April 1910), p. 251.

year.[15] The construction industry, rapidly expanding with the production of housing and infrastructure, was chronically short of labour and already dependent on foreign workers, predominantly from Italy, and, to a lesser extent, Poland, Croatia, and Bohemia.[16]

Construction labour organization in Germany, 1890–1914

1890–1914 is a period well demarcated in Germany, beginning with the expiration of the law that prohibited socialist party organization between 1878 and 1890, and ending in 1914 with the First World War. From 1890 both the SPD[17] and the labour unions expanded rapidly and consolidated their organizational structures. This was a process of centralization and amalgamation, a shift from craft to a broader form of union organization based on sectors and industries. In 1890 the labour unions also set up their Freie Generalkommission der Gewerkschaften Deutschlands (Free General Committee of Labour Unions in Germany) as the national umbrella organization of labour unions.[18]

A major aim of the construction unions was the establishment of collective contracts, *Tarifverträge*.[19] And they were successful: 'At the beginning of 1907 almost 50% of all existing collective agreements and 40% of all workers under collective agreements in Germany were attributable to the various sectors of the construction industry'.[20]

This development was part of a united movement based on the common programme of both the socialist party and the labour unions for 'the protection of the working classes', passed by the SPD at its Erfurt Congress in 1891.[21] As a result, the SPD multiplied its representation in the imperial parliament, the Reichstag, as well as in party membership (see Table 3 above), underpinning and promoting the rising power of labour unions. Significantly, Theodor Bömelburg, trained as a bricklayer and chairman of the Central Federation of Bricklayers of Germany between 1894 and

---

15 *Statistisches Jahrbuch des deutschen Reiches*, 1911, p. 86.
16 M. Pohl, *Philipp Holzmann, Geschichte eines Bauunternehmens, 1899–1999* (Verlag C. H. Beck, Munich: 1999), p. 91.
17 Unfortunately, because of legal restrictions up to 1906, figures of party membership are missing: G. A. Ritter, *Die Arbeiterbewegung im Wilhelminischen Reich* (Colloquium Verlag, Berlin-Dahlem: 1963), p. 46f. The most important body of the SPD was the annual congress of about 200 delegates. The central body of the party was the parliamentary group: *ibid.*, pp. 51, 55.
18 Mommsen und Husung, *Auf dem Wege zur Massengewerkschaft*, p. 288.
19 P. Ullmann, *Tarifverträge und Tarifpolitik in Deutschland bis 1914* (Peter Lang, Frankfurt am Main: 1977), p. 82.
20 *Ibid.*, p. 81.
21 https://www.marxists.org/deutsch/geschichte/deutsch/spd/1891/erfurt.htm.

Table 7: Membership of construction labour unions

Year	Bricklayers	Carpenters	Labourers	Total Construction workers
1891	12,523			
1892	12,928		2,563	
1893	12,073			
1894	12,187	8,862	1,793	
1895	15,360			
1896	26,600	13,701		
1897	42,652		3,840	
1898	60,175	22,104		
1899	74,534		11,149	
1900	82,964	24,149		
1901	80,869	23,246	16,350	
1902	82,223	23,377		
1903	101,155	28,953		
1904	128,850	86,243		
1905	155,911	42,249	39,000	
1906	183,537	50,438		
1907	192,582	54,395	84,612	
1908	175,019	51,315		
1909	171,337	53,077		
1910	169,645	54,550	72,203	241,848
1911				290,313
1912				344,725

Source: A. Tischer, *Der Kampf im deutschen Baugewerbe 1910* (Duncker und Humblot, Leipzig: 1912); K. Anders, *Stein für Stein. Die Leute von Bau-Steine-Erden und ihre Gewerkschaften 1869 bis 1969* (Büchergilde Gutenberg, Frankfurt am Main: 1969), p. 119. Figures in the total column are derived from the sources, not the columns to the left.

1910, was also a member of the SPD in the German imperial parliament. Heribert Kohl summarized this position of construction workers in the first decade of the twentieth century: 'We may rightly say that in this phase the construction workers represented the spearhead of the whole

German labour movement and, moreover, also of its political pillar, Social Democracy.'[22]

The main subjects of the great lockout in 1910 in the construction industry were wage rates, working time, the abolition of piece rates, employment agencies, and the rights of trade unions. The German construction industry was the exemplary sector, exhibiting the power of labour after the lockout through an explosive rise in union membership from 241,848 in 1910 to 344,725 in 1912 (Table 7). Between 1891 and 1910 membership of the Bricklayers' union grew faster than in any other union.[23] Among the construction trades, over this twenty-year period the bricklayers grew by a factor of fifteen as compared to the carpenters by a factor of only six. In the ten years between 1899 and 1910, the fastest growing membership was that of the construction labourers, almost sevenfold, while between 1900 and 1910 the bricklayers and carpenters more than doubled their memberships.

The combined, staggering increase in union and SPD organization, associated with the rapid rise of real wages, was exceptional as compared to that in Britain. And it is significant that the rise in wages coincided with a similar rise in productivity.[24] This unprecedented development of labour power, in politics, civil status and industrial production, well explains the fierce reaction of the construction employers with a national lockout as a desperate effort to defend their supremacy in production relations.

The great lockout[25]

The 1910 lockout was on the agenda of the German Employers' Federation for the Construction Industry from its founding meeting in 1899. The wording in its initial action programme was unmistakably militant:

22 H. Kohl, *Auf Vertrauen bauen, 125 Jahre Baugewerkschaft* (Herausgeber: Bruno Köbele/Industriegewerkschaft Bau-Steine-Erden, Bund-Verlag, Cologne: 1993), p. 33.

23 F. Paeplow, *Zur Geschichte der deutschen Bauarbeiterbewegung.Werden des Deutschen Baugewerksbundes* (Berlin: 1932).

24 H. Phelps Brown and S. V. Hopkins, *A Perspective of Wages and Prices* (Methuen: 1981), pp. 192, 196. Between 1893 and 1913 wage rates were virtually stagnant in Britain at about 75–80 pence per day: *ibid.*, p. 12. In Germany, between 1890 and 1910, bricklayers' hourly rates grew by about 80%: Kohl, *Auf Vertrauen bauen*, p. 35 – not enough, though, to reach the level of their British counterparts.

25 The course of the dispute has been described from the side of the employees by A. Winning, *Der grosse Kampf im deutschen Baugewerbe 1910* (Deutscher Bauarbeiterverband, Hamburg: 1911); from the employers, Deutscher

Before we have been victorious in a great trial of strength, we shall not achieve rest and peace; such a trial of strength has to be carried out. We have to come to a point when we can lock out the workers in large enterprises, if not in the whole of Germany, in order to put an end to the unjustified demands.[26]

Given the dispersed organization of its diverse membership, this project took some time to be put into practice. It was not until its general assembly in 1907 in Cologne that the construction employers' federation took the decisive step with the preparation for a national confrontation to defeat the labour unions in their campaigns for the improvement of pay and working conditions. The employers decided that reductions in working time had to be rejected and no agreements were to be concluded before 31 March 1908 in order to be able to lock out the workers across the whole country. A model contract of the employers contained the following conditions:

1.   All collective contracts have to be concluded as a united whole.

2.   The contractually fixed hourly rate is to be paid only to qualified, skilled, and proficient workers, that is introducing differential wages. The level of achievement is to be decided by a local organization. Also, workers have to reject higher wages with unorganized employers.

3.   Labour unions are prohibited from opposing piece work and exerting their influence on employers' setting piece rates.

4.   Force the labour unions to recognize employers' non-paritarian reference documents for employment (*Arbeitsnachweise*).

5.   Cancel existing collective agreements for civil engineering and leave its wages to the arbitrariness of the individual employers.

6.   Force the labour unions to renounce a reduction in working time of less than ten hours for the whole country ('Reich') and at all times.

7.   Any agitation on the building site is forbidden.

Arbeitgeberbund für das Baugewerbe, *Die Erneuerung der baugewerblichen Tarifverträge im Jahre 1910* (Berlin: 1911); and from an academic perspective, A. Tischer, *Der Kampf im deutschen Baugewerbe 1910* (Duncker und Humblot, Leipzig: 1912). Only a summary is given here.

26 M. Kittner, *Arbeitskampf, Geschichte, Recht, Gegenwart* (Beck, Munich: 2005), p. 80.

8. The chairman of the court of arbitration to be set up is to be appointed by the director (remunerated by employers) of the Technical University of Charlottenburg.

9. The contract is valid for five years.

Furthermore, the Federal Board repeatedly declared that a general rise in wages is beyond consideration.[27]

The construction employers' federation's draft model contract became public and the subject of negotiation for a renewal of the existing national framework agreement with the four construction labour unions of bricklayers, carpenters, labourers, and Christian construction workers, assisted by three arbitrators,[28] 25–26 March 1908, Berlin. As the arbitral award was not accepted by the Central Union of German Bricklayers,[29] another meeting with the same arbitrators was held on 27 April to negotiate a new model contract, *Vertragsmuster*. On this occasion, the arbitral award was accepted by both the employers' federation and the central unions of the construction industry, to be binding for all local agreements until 31 May 1910.[30]

As the existing national framework agreement for the construction industry was due to expire on 1 April 1910, negotiations on changes and amendments began on 11 November 1909.[31] The unions of construction workers resisted all attempts by the employers' federation to revise and amend the existing framework agreement in line with its policy, including, for example, to allow for differentials between more or less proficient workers, to scrap limitations on overtime, a minimum ten-hour day, and work at piece rates.[32] Hence, the employers eventually decided at their assembly on 8 April 1910 that 'All enterprises will be closed down on 15 April'.[33] This lockout, a historically unprecedented event, was to be the

---

27 Zentralverband der Maurer Deutschlands, Zweigverein Breslau, *Bericht und spezialisierte Abrechnung über die Aussprerrung 1910* (Otto Bachmann, Breslau: 1910), p. 1.

28 Max von Schulze, Hans Prenner and Otto Wiedfeldt. Arbitration in labour disputes was a major matter of industrial regulation and jurisdiction at the turn of the twentieth century. For an analysis of its development in France and Germany and the negotiations before the 1910 lockout see S. Rudischhauser, *Geregelte Verhältnisse. Eine Geschichte des Tarifvertragsrechts in Deutschland und Frankreich, 1890–1918/19* (Böhlau Verlag, Cologne, Weimar and Vienna: 2017).

29 Tischer, *Der Kampf im deutschen Baugewerbe 1910*, p. 31f.

30 Rudischhauser, *Geregelte Verhältnisse*, pp. 590–8.

31 Winning, *Der grosse Kampf im deutschen Baugewerbe 1910*, p. 38.

32 Ullmann, *Tarifverträge und Tarifpolitik in Deutschland bis 1914*, p. 87.

33 Winning, *Der grosse Kampf im deutschen Baugewerbe 1910*, p. 108.

first industrial dispute in Germany at central national level and was to last more than eight weeks until 20 June 1910.

From the start, the employers had not been entirely united. The regional federation in Berlin fiercely opposed a lockout.[34] The regional organizations of Hamburg and Bremen also refused to take part. Berlin signed an independent three-year collective agreement for a 9 pfennig (pf) hourly rate increase. Hamburg maintained the still existing collective agreement. Nor did Bremen give way to the pressure of the Federation.[35] Some individual companies, for example the internationally active Philipp Holzmann und Co., declined to join in.[36] Generally, larger companies were prepared to resume negotiations and make concessions and in smaller towns many companies did not take part in the lockout.[37]

The four central construction unions of bricklayers, carpenters, labourers, and Christian construction workers responded with a 'Memorandum',[38] published before the lockout. They pointed to the deterioration in their living conditions as the rise in food prices was coupled with wage stagnation and winter unemployment, particularly in January–February 1909. At the same time, they demanded collective agreements to be negotiated at local and regional rather than central level.

Kohl described the public response to this extraordinarily fierce industrial dispute:

> Given this all-out confrontation, for the first time public opinion in the empire tilted in favour of the locked-out construction workers. The press criticized the disproportionate brutal course of action of the employers. Public collections by professors, intellectuals and artists took place for the support of construction workers whose existence was under assault.[39]

But most financial support was raised by the labour unions. Workers who were not locked out paid between 0,20 pf and one mark per day into a relief fund,[40] while union employees waived half their salaries for the relief of their colleagues. In this lockout, the unions also extended to fourteen days the usual three days until the beginning of support for unemployed workers. In

34 Verband der Baugeschäfte von Berlin und den Vororten (ed.), *Die Stellung Berlins zu dem Tarifkampf im Jahre 1910* (Berlin: 1910), p. 3.

35 K. Anders, *Stein für Stein. Die Leute von Bau-Steine-Erden und ihre Gewerkschaften 1869 bis 1969* (Büchergilde Gutenberg, Frankfurt am Main: 1969), p. 170.

36 Winning, *Der grosse Kampf im deutschen Baugewerbe 1910*, p. 143.

37 Anders, *Stein für Stein*, p. 170.

38 Denkschrift über die Tarifbewegungen im deutschen Baugewerbe im Jahre 1910.

39 Kohl, *Auf Vertrauen bauen*, p. 37.

40 Anders, *Stein für Stein*, p. 168.

all, the collections amounted to 1,233,371 marks,[41] and the overall support by construction unions amounted to 6.6 million marks,[42] paid to 130,000 construction workers.[43]

The number of locked-out workers varies according to the sources of information and over the course of the industrial action. Initially only 130,000 workers were locked out. According to the employers' federation, typically exaggerating the success of the lockout, this figure rose to an alleged final maximum of 197,000 by 25 May.

Over the time of the lockout the resistance of the construction workers intensified and came to a head in the middle of May. The bricklayers' weekly periodical, *Der Grundstein*, expressed the workers' unshakable determination not to give in:

If its leaders [of the construction employers' federation] are sufficiently deluded to perceive their position such as being able to dictate the foundations of a new contract relationship, well, then they may take another six or eight weeks' time for respite; we are strong enough to allow it to them. ... Hence, we are facing the future with relaxation; it will require great sacrifices of us, but it will give us also the victory.[44]

Given the deadlock in the lockout, the Home Office of the Imperial government took the initiative on 12 May to invite both parties to a meeting on 21 May. As this meeting failed to produce any convergence, the Home Office invited the parties again to negotiations for 27 May at the Reichstag in Berlin.[45] Large construction companies were also pressing for negotiations. As a result, proposals for a compromise were eventually achieved on 31 May, with most of the conditions in the standard framework contract of 1908 maintained, that is most of the employers' new demands were rejected. Agreement was reached on these issues:

- Central organization to be accepted by the industrial parties;

- Ten hours' maximum daily working time, further reductions to be negotiated: overtime admitted only under special conditions;

- No wage differentials according to proficiency;

- Wages to be raised variably according to region by on average about 10% and generally binding for all employers;

---

41 *Ibid.*, p. 171.
42 Kohl, *Auf Vertrauen bauen*, p. 37.
43 Kittner, *Arbeitskampf, Geschichte, Recht, Gegenwart*, p. 341.
44 *Der Grundstein* 23, 28 May 1910, p. 254.
45 Winning, *Der grosse Kampf im deutschen Baugewerbe 1910*, pp. 152, 155.

- Agitation of workers' unions to be allowed on construction sites.

Conversely, three of the employers' demands protecting their control over labour were conceded:

- Employers' reference letters remained uncontrolled;
- Workers' sympathy campaigning became forbidden;
- Piecework by individual agreement was permitted.[46]

This framework agreement was to be valid until 1913 and work to be resumed by 20 June 1910. The partners to this compromise contract had to declare their consent by 6 June. After three days of final negotiations, from 14 to 16 June, a national standard contract, binding until 1 April 1913, was finally accepted by the employers' federation. The lockout was called off from 18 June and work resumed on Monday 20 June 1910.

The chair of the carpenters' union summarized the outcome as an outright victory for the workers: 'We have achieved about everything we wanted, but the employers have clearly been defeated.'[47] Even more enthusiastically, the Breslau branch of the Central Federation of Bricklayers celebrated their success: 'Yes, we can assert with pride that this is the first great economic struggle … which was won for us. Thus, the German construction workers' unions have shown that they have become a power, which also entrepreneurship has to reckon with.'[48] The disregard of the three concessions should not be a surprise. Given the increasing stabilization of employment, in particular in larger companies, the dependence on reference letters was anyway on the decline.[49] The abolition of piecework had been a major issue of dispute not only with the employers but also within the Federation of Bricklayers since 1890. As a result, this mode of pay was already marginalized at the time of the lockout.[50] It is difficult to assess the relevance of sympathy campaigning, but the positive enthusiasm of the unions in response to the agreement is unmistakable.

---

46 *Ibid.*, p. 164f.
47 Anders, *Stein für Stein*, p. 172.
48 Zentralverband der Maurer Deutschlands, Zweigverein Breslau, *Bericht und spezialisierte Abrechnung über die Aussprerrung 1910*, p. 5.
49 E. Lederer, *Sozialpolitiasche Chronik: Die Unternehmerorganisationen im Jahre 1910/11*, in *Archiv für Sozialwissenschaften und Sozialpolitik*, Band 33 (1911), pp. 249–303, at pp. 256ff.
50 J. Janssen, '"Bauhüttenbewegung": The Movement for the Socialisation of Construction Companies after the German Revolution 1918' (Unpublished paper: 2017).

What is more important than these direct results are, however, the wider consequences. On the union side the dispute, unprecedented in its scope, duration and the number of workers involved, triggered a process of unification between the five construction unions of bricklayers, construction labourers, insulators, floor layers, and plasterers. The first to join the Central Union of German Bricklayers and form the new Deutscher Bauarbeiterverband (German Construction Workers' Union) on 1 January 1911 were the construction labourers. The insulators and floor layers followed later in the same year; the plasterers in 1912.[51] Only the carpenters maintained a separate craft union. By 1912 the amalgamated German Construction Workers Union, with a membership of 344,725 workers, was ranked as the most successful German labour union in terms of pay regulation by collective agreements. With a coverage rate of 39.6%, it had overtaken the print workers' 38.6%, and by far exceeded all other sectors (Table 6). The third on the list was woodworking at 25.1%.[52]

In contrast, the Employers' Federation for the Construction Industry became more divided as had been evident by the non-participation in the lockout of the regional organizations of Berlin, Hamburg, and Bremen, and, in particular, the resignation of Berlin from the central federation after the arbitration award.[53] National wage co-ordination and wage increases benefited the competitive position of the large and more capital intensive, typically joint-stock, companies. Thus, the new general collective agreement contributed to the process of capital concentration in the construction industry.[54] This explains also why over time the large companies took a leading role in the employers' federations.[55]

The impact of the great lockout in a wider context

The most important impact of the employers' defeat in the eight-week lockout was that the new national model contract on wages and working conditions – *Flächentarifvertrag* – heralded a more equal and anonymous form of wage relations, in contemporary terms 'The standardization of the labour

---

51 Deutscher Bauarbeiterverband, *Protokoll über die Verhandlungen des ersten Verbandstages, Abgehalten zu Jena im Volkshause vom 13. bis 18. Januar 1913* (Verlag des Deutschen Bauarbeiterverbandes, Hamburg: 1913), p. 19.

52 H. Volkmann, *Organisation und Konflikt, Gewerkschaften, Arbeitgeberverbände und die Entwicklung des Arbeitskonflikts im späten Kaiserreich*, in W. Conze und U. Engelhardt (eds), *Arbeiter im Industrialisierungsprozeß Herkunft, Lage und Verhalten* (Klett-Cotta, Stuttgart: 1979), pp. 422–38.

53 Winning, *Der grosse Kampf im deutschen Baugewerbe 1910*, p. 219.

54 Hilferding, *Das Finanzkapital*, p. 248.

55 Ullmann, *Unternehmerschaft, Arbeitgeberverbände und Streibewegung, 1890–1914*, p. 204.

contract replacing its authoritative determination by the employer'.[56] Under the regime of industrial collective agreements, the wage ceased to represent the price for the use of individual labour power paid by an individual employer at a minimum rate to maintain levels in the reproduction of labour power. Instead it was transformed into a share of the social product, differentiated between workers according to levels of qualification in segments of the production process. This share was to be negotiated between labour and capital at the national collective level of specific industrial sectors. In these negotiations, the increase in productivity became the determinant measure for raising wage rates at, more or less, regular intervals. However, the shares attributed to labour, on the one hand, and to capital, on the other, remained dependent on the power relationship – equal or unequal – between the collective parties. This form of national employment contract under labour–capital agreement was to become a matter of socio-economic policy under the supervision of national civil government and jurisdiction, which had a variety of implications at social, economic and political levels.

The social impact is illustrated by a process that transcends the historical stage represented by the 1910 lockout, namely the long-term transition of wage earning from a labour–capital employment relationship towards a legal civil status or, in other words, the expiration of wage earning as a submission under capitalists' control. But in 1908, two years before the great lockout, Sinzheimer had already identified this development of national collective agreements as an advanced stage in the transformation of labour relations: 'The transformation of the employment contract from a one-sided relation of dependency into a legal relationship under mandatory norms'.[57] Though by 1910 these 'norms' were still far from being firmly established or universally implemented, they nevertheless provided the leading standard for the emerging stage of development.

From an economic point of view, sector-wide standard contracts or generally binding collective agreements, *Flächentarifverträge*, regulated labour costs and conditions as a level playing field for competition between companies based on productive investment. In this sense, the outcome of the great lockout was a victory of capital over labour in that capital investment became the decisive factor in economic development based on competition and profits. Under these regulations, piecework became obsolete while industrialization was promoted through the imposition of respective government regulations. This transformation in the conditions for economic progress was not only to the benefit of capital, but also of labour, as wage rates became related to the increase in productivity and not any more to the maintenance costs of workers and their families. In

56 Sinzheimer, *Der korporative Arbeitsnormenvertrag,* p. 277.
57 *Ibid.*, p. 274.

an international context, this form of competitive capitalism also came to supersede or transform colonial imperialism.

The political aspect of this new form of imperialism was certainly not a matter of dispute in the great lockout. However, in hindsight it is all too evident that German industrial development and rising economic power substantially changed the international balance, in particular in relation to the great colonial nations, above all Britain and France. The First World War is not a subject of this paper, nor is the construction industry more than a subsidiary in the rise of the German electrical, chemical and mechanical engineering industries at transnational level. But it was not accidental that this industrial confrontation preceded the First World War and the revolution of 1918. In Germany, labour organizations were about to become 'social partners' in national industrial relations,[58] participating in the achievements of the national industry and its rising industrial power at transnational level, which were at stake in this war. This explains why labour unions supported the declaration of war in 1914 under the so-called *Burgfrieden* (truce) with their financial resources and a strike waiver.[59] It was only a matter of a few years before the Socialist International, the so-called 'Second International', disintegrated.

This labour dispute was a stage in the development of labour relations leading to the statutory co-determination in capitalist companies by works councils – *Betriebsräte* – introduced after the German Revolution of 1918. Incidentally, construction workers also played an outstanding role after the German Revolution with their initiative to socialize the construction industry including housing development in their *Bauhüttenbewegung* – building guild movement,[60] founding the Verband sozialer Baubetriebe, VsB (Federation of Social Construction Companies) in 1920 and the Deutsche Wohnungsgesellschaft, DEWOG (German Housing Company) in 1924.

Summarizing these various aspects of social, economic and political innovation at work in this major industrial confrontation, it is perhaps worth raising the question, what is at the origin of this dynamic in industrial relations? The victory of labour over capital did not come as a surprise in this particular confrontation. The construction employers' federation

---

58 K. Schönhofen, 'Gewerkschaftliche Streikpolitik und Streikverhalten der Arbeiterschaft vor 1914', in K. Tenfelde und H. Volkmann, *Streik: Zur Geschichte des Arbeitskampfes In Deutschland während der Industrialisierung* (Beck, Munich: 1981), pp. 177–93.

59 R. Krämer, *Burgfrieden? Die Bauarbeitergewerkschaften, 1914 bis 1918*, in A. Klönne, H. Reese, B. Schütt, und I. Weyrather, *Hand in Hand: Bauarbeit und Gewerkschaften, eine Sozialgeschichte* (Büchergilde Gutenberg, Frankfurt am Main: 1989), pp. 92–105.

60 Janssen, 'Bauhüttenbewegung'.

took ten years to prepare its assault which, from the start, sought to defend employers' supremacy in production relations. They were compelled to compromise. Though their supremacy was maintained, it was reduced and became a matter of regulation under civil government. In this wider perspective, German construction workers had taken a pioneering role in the international process of the development of statutory industrial collective wage-labour relations.

HSIR 41 (2020) 85–109

https://doi.org/10.3828/hsir.2020.41.4

Cash Wages, the Truck Acts, and the 1960 Payment of Wages Act

Christopher Frank

From the mid-1950s until the early 1960s there was an ongoing tussle between British employers and the Trades Union Congress (TUC) over whether to repeal the Truck Acts. Advocates of repeal argued that these nineteenth-century laws had historically been ineffective at protecting workers, imposed unnecessary regulatory burdens upon employers, and frustrated the growth of more efficient forms of wage payment. Manual workers, represented nationally by the TUC, insisted these laws' existence guaranteed payment in cash ('coin of the realm'), protected pay packets from arbitrary deductions, and prevented employers from unilaterally imposing unpopular methods of wage payment. This dispute resulted in the minor reform of the 1960 Payment of Wages Act, and the establishment of the Karmel Committee (1959–61), which studied the contemporary operation of the Truck Acts. The TUC, following the strongly expressed desires of its affiliated unions and their members, was able to frustrate repeal; by making minor concessions it was able to preserve and consolidate employee leverage in determining the method of wage payment. The Payment of Wages Act reflected the strength of organized labour when it was near the apex of its power in the twentieth century. This legislation preserved the negotiating power of many manual workers over the right to be paid in cash until Margaret Thatcher's second government repealed, in 1986, all truck legislation and the 1960 Act.

After a brief discussion of the content of the Truck Acts and the argument over their effectiveness, the article is broadly chronological. It outlines the (eventually lawful) use of cheque payment for rural roadmen during the Second World War. From the mid-1950s a series of private member's bills in Parliament over payment by cheque brought the issue into public prominence. It was discussed at the NJAC (National Joint Advisory Council of the Ministry of Labour), which led to the 1960 Act – protecting the right of (most) manual workers to be paid in cash – and an independent inquiry (on which the TUC was represented). Despite the Karmel Committee recommending repeal of truck legislation, though keeping some of the protections, there was significant disagreement about who exactly should be covered and what should be protected. The TUC had proved the efficacy of the law as it stood and, given the inability to reach consensus, the government eventually dropped the subject for a generation.

Truck and the Truck Acts

Truck was the practice of paying employees in goods rather than money, or compelling them to spend their wages at a store the employer either owned or was interested in financially.[1] Although payment in kind continued well into the twentieth century, by the 1890s workers had become more concerned about other practices that prevented them from receiving the full value of their wages. These included employers taking heavy deductions from wages for disciplinary fines, for damaged work, for the rental of tools and materials, and for providing heat, light or standing room in the workplace.

During the nineteenth century, laws were passed to regulate these methods of cheating workers out of the full value of their earnings. The 1831 Truck Act made it illegal to pay certain artificers in anything but the current coin of the realm. The Act allowed workers in specifically listed trades to bring an action before two magistrates, who could award the worker the full monetary value of any wages paid in truck, and fine the offending employer.[2] The 1887 Truck Amendment Act expanded these protections to nearly all manual workers, including those in Ireland, and entrusted their enforcement to the inspectors of mines and factories.[3] The 1896 Truck Act was promoted by a Conservative government as offering protections to workers against arbitrary fines and deductions from wages, but sceptical trade-union leaders believed its primary purpose was to give employers a clear statutory right to take deductions. Section one of that Act applied to manual workers and shop assistants and enacted that disciplinary fines were only legal if they were authorized in a signed contract or a posted notice. The document had to list the specific acts or omissions for which a person could be fined, and the amounts that would be taken for each offence. Fines were only allowed for acts or omissions that harmed

---

1 G. W. Hilton, *The Truck System: Including a History of the British Truck Acts, 1485–1960* (Hefner: 1960), pp. 1, 10, 20–2; R. Church, *The History of the British Coal Industry, Vol. 3: 1830–1913* (Clarendon Press, Oxford: 1986), pp. 262–4.

2 1 and 2 Will. 4 c. 37 (1831).

3 50 and 51 Vict. c. 46 (1887).

the business and had to be 'fair and reasonable'. The remainder of the Act applied only to manual workers. It regulated deductions for damaged or spoiled work, stipulating that they also had to be part of a contract or posted notice, could not exceed the estimated loss to the employer, and had to be 'fair and reasonable having regard to all circumstances of the case'. It also required deductions for materials and services provided by the employer to be part of a contract, and could not exceed the true cost, and had to be fair and reasonable.[4]

Economists and legal scholars have argued that these laws were ineffective in protecting workers' wages. The most prominent was George Hilton, an American economist. His articles and monograph (1957–60) were strongly influenced by the contemporary debate over the Truck Acts, and he in turn made significant contributions to these discussions. His work looms large in the historiography of the truck laws, with his interpretation of these laws persisting into modern times with little qualification. His original article asked: 'First, should the truck system have been prohibited by law? Second, given the fact that the truck system has passed out of existence, do the statutes prohibiting it make any positive contribution to current public policy toward the labour market?'[5] He argued that the primary motivation for the introduction of truck in the Midland nail-making trade was as a means to circumvent standard rates of wages in the industry. In the mining and iron trades, sumptuary control was a factor in employers keeping company stores. Remote locations, deficiencies in the money supply, and the use of shops to raise short-term capital were also discussed as possible reasons for the existence of truck. Government action was insignificant in the decline of truck, as Hilton argued that its gradual disappearance was due to its unpopularity with workers and organized labour, its ineffectiveness in controlling workers' habits, the decline of domestic industries in which it was practised, and the reduction of geographical isolation.

Hilton barely mentioned the Truck Acts of 1887 and 1896 and their protections to workers' pay packets. He wrote: 'The truck acts appear to have played a negligible role in the decline of the truck system. Since … [truck] is no longer in existence, and since the acts were generally powerless to deal with it while it was, there is … reason to question whether there is any point in the retention of this legislation'.[6] His second article argued that 'the role of the Truck Act of 1831 in the extinction of the truck system can only be accounted as negligible'.[7] His monograph expressed frustration with

4 59 and 60 Vict. c. 44 (1896).

5 G. Hilton, 'The British Truck System in the Nineteenth Century', *Journal of Political Economy* 65:3 (1957), pp. 237–58.

6 *Ibid.*, p. 255.

7 *Idem*, 'The Truck Act of 1831', *Economic History Review* 10:3 (1958), pp. 470–9.

labour-friendly politicians who argued that the Truck Acts had historically offered important protections to workers, insisting 'this is an indefensible interpretation ... the Truck Act of 1831 was a virtually total failure'.[8] Such arguments from an academic strengthened the case for repeal.

Yet, as has been argued at length by this author, the Truck Acts were more important in the decline of truck and related abuses than Hilton acknowledges. Truck was not only unpopular with workers and organized labour, but also with the general public. There is evidence – from politicians, government officials, retailers, and even employers – that cheating workers through company stores, or excessive fines and deductions, was seen as a disreputable business practice. The Truck Acts and their enforcement strengthened that sentiment. Legislation, parliamentary inquiries, inspectors' reports, and prosecutions, by publicizing workers' plight, established truck and other underhand means of chiselling away at wages as social problems that needed to be solved. Truck was outside respectable capitalism, and a growing number of manufacturers, encouraged by factory inspectors, also began to think that most fines and deductions for damaged work were not characteristic of modern managements. The law has the power to legitimate or delegitimate practices; the enactment and enforcement of legislation against truck gradually made such practices less acceptable not only to workers but to elites as well, and was a significant factor in their decline. Successful prosecutions are not the only metric by which to measure the effectiveness of these laws, as government inspectors were often able to use them to convince employers to voluntarily abandon exploitative behaviour.[9]

The Truck Acts remained in force for most of the twentieth century, but politicians and employers argued for their repeal throughout the post-1945 era. They claimed that these statutes were anachronistic and ill-suited to modern economic conditions, insisting that truck and taking of arbitrary fines and deductions were things of the past. They also complained that they impeded contractual arrangements that were beneficial to workers, such as payment of wages by cheque or bank transfer. They presented obstacles for employers wanting to provide meals, travel vouchers, profit-sharing schemes, loans for housing, or bonuses in company stock. By removing these ancient regulations, businesses would be more efficient and competitive.[10]

The post-war economic boom and the growing power of trade unions

---

8 *Idem, The Truck System*, p. 154.

9 C. Frank, *Workers, Unions and Payment in Kind: The Fight for Real Wages in Britain, 1820–1914* (Routledge: 2019).

10 British Employers' Confederation, 'The Truck Acts: Note Submitted by the British Employers' Confederation to the Joint Consultative Committee [JCC]', 1959: LAB 10/1658, The National Archives, Kew, London (TNA).

assisted in reducing the abuses that these laws were intended to prevent. Wages councils, for example, safeguarded many low-paid workers from unfair deductions as wage orders had to be paid to workers clear of all deductions. Yet, while it appeared that workers had all the power they needed to prevent unfair forms of wage payment and deductions, the Truck Acts still offered important protections against employers' encroachments on the wages of marginal and precarious workers right up to their repeal in 1986.

On 1 April 1946 administration of the Truck Acts (and the Factory Acts) was permanently transferred from the Home Office to the Ministry of Labour and National Service. The early post-war years saw the number of prosecutions decline significantly. During the 1930s there had been an average of around fifteen per year, but between 100 and 125 instances each year where inspectors notified employers to change practices because of violations of the Truck Acts.[11] Between 1947 and 1958 there were only eight prosecutions under the Truck Acts in total. The expansion of trade-unionism and full employment gave workers greater ability to correct workplace abuses on their own. Even during this period inspectors still responded to 115 complaints that 'had been considered well-founded', by compelling employers to return illegal deductions and alter workplace practices to avoid prosecutions.[12] The TUC claimed that factory inspectors received 280 Truck Acts complaints between 1947 and 1958.[13] So, while prosecutions had fallen, violations were far from unknown. In fact, in 1961 the Karmel Committee, which investigated the modern impact of the Truck Acts, found these numbers a sufficient argument against outright repeal, stating 'in our opinion, this figure cannot be regarded as negligible, especially when it is remembered that Inspectors act only upon complaints'.[14]

---

11 During 1934–36, an inspector contacted a British employer regarding violations of the Truck Act on an average of once every three days: extract from the *Annual Report of the Chief Inspector of Factories*, 1934: 292/192/1/1, Modern Records Centre, University of Warwick (MRC). Ministry of Labour, Committee on the Truck Acts (Karmel), *Report* (HMSO: 1961), p. 5. There were also instances where workers or unions used the Acts on their own initiative to sue employers for unfair deductions or fines: *Pritchard* v. *James Clay (Wellington) Ltd.* (1926), 1 KB 238. *The Times*, 7, 8 and 17 May 1930: 292/190/1/1, MRC. There are no published statistics on prosecutions under the Truck Acts during the First and Second World Wars: LAB 10/1656, TNA.

12 Karmel, *Report*, p. 5.

13 Trades Union Congress (TUC), Committee on the Truck Acts, 26 July 1960: 292/192/1/1, MRC. H. Keast, 'A Commentary on the Truck Acts', *Industrial Law Review* 3 (1949), p. 223.

14 Karmel, *Report*, p. 12.

The Truck Acts and the payment of wages by cheque or bank transfer

For most of the twentieth century, the majority of manual workers in England and Wales received their wages in cash – notes and coins – every week. As late as 1979, 77% of all manual workers still received cash wages weekly. In 1969, even 52% of non-manual workers still received cash wages; of manual workers only 5% were paid by cheque and 6% by bank transfer. Manual workers, individually and through their unions, repeatedly expressed a desire to be paid their wages in cash weekly.[15]

One objective of the framers of the 1831 Truck Act was to stop employers paying workers with cheques redeemable at distant banks or their own company stores located near the workplace. This was a barely disguised form of *payment in kind* (which the 1831 Act sought to outlaw), since the only place it was practicable for the employee to use the cheque was the company store. To prevent this, section eight of the Act allowed an employer to pay wages by cheque with the employee's consent if it was drawn on a real bank 'duly licensed to issue bank notes' and located within fifteen miles of the place of payment.[16] Yet the 1844 Bank Charter Act had made the Bank of England the only bank in England and Wales that could lawfully issue bank notes. A strict reading of section eight meant that most workers covered by its provisions could not be paid by cheque.[17]

Yet during the Second World War nearly all county councils in England and Wales paid at least part of the wages of rural roadmen by cheque. These roadmen (responsible for maintaining and repairing the roads) often worked in remote locations but the employers found paying by cash involved the time, labour, risk and expense of preparing and conveying pay packets over great distances.[18] The National Union of Public Employees (NUPE), representing many county roadmen, had fought against this practice since the late 1930s. Few roadmen, or workers in general, possessed bank accounts. Manual workers were dissuaded by a combination of factors, including their meagre wages and savings, bank fees and rules about minimum balances, inconvenient locations and opening hours of banks, and traditions of banks not servicing the working class. Many workers disliked receiving such cheques because they were sometimes delayed in transit, and it was challenging to find a place to cash them, delaying

---

15 Central Policy Review Staff (CPRS), *Cashless Pay: Alternatives to Cash Payment of Wages* (HMSO: 1981), pp. 6–7.
16 Truck Act 1831, s. 8.
17 E. Suter and P. Long, *Cashless Pay and Deduction: Implications of the Wages Act of 1986* (Institute of Personnel Management: 1987), p. 2; Hilton, *The Truck System*, pp. 149–50.
18 LAB 10/1651, TNA.

access to their own money. This was a great hardship for a working-class family. Often workers had to cash their cheques with a shopkeeper or a publican, with the expectation that they would spend some of their money there. In November 1939, counsel advised NUPE that these payments might be illegal under the Truck Act. After unsuccessful negotiations with the County Councils Association, NUPE secured a High Court injunction against Buckinghamshire County Council in October 1941 to prevent it from paying roadmen by cheque. NUPE planned to bring similar actions against a dozen other county councils.[19]

In April 1942, Labour MP Herbert Morrison, Home Secretary in Winston Churchill's wartime Coalition government, announced that the government would issue an order under Defence Regulation 59A of the Emergency Powers Act 1939, modifying the Truck Acts for the duration of the war to allow county councils to pay roadmen by cheque.[20] The government also thought it desirable to temporarily allow certain employers and government agencies to provide workers with accommodation and food as part of their remuneration, or to take deductions from wages for these items, free from the restrictions of the Truck Acts. The Home Office consulted with the TUC, which, despite NUPE's strenuous opposition, agreed, provided that it or relevant unions were consulted and these alterations were only for the duration of the war.[21]

The National Union of General and Municipal Workers (NUGMW) and the Transport and General Workers' Union (TGWU) supported the County Councils Association in this matter, partly because they were rivals to NUPE. W. W. Craik argues that these two large general unions 'were always ready to take any line that seemed to them calculated to frustrate and weaken the growth and achievements of their increasingly powerful rival in the sphere of public service recruitment'.[22] The NUGMW leadership, particularly Tom Williamson (then a national officer), was irritated by the publicly confrontational approach of NUPE and its general secretary, Bryn Roberts, in this matter. Williamson and his allies had hoped to address this controversy through negotiations conducted in the Joint Industrial Council. He complained at a conference held by the TUC that 'the prospect

---

19 *Buckinghamshire Advertiser and Free Press*, 2 August 1941: 292/192/1/1, MRC. W. W. Craik, *Bryn Roberts and the National Union of Public Employees* (Allen and Unwin: 1955), pp. 76–80.

20 *Parliamentary Debates (Hansard)*, House of Commons (HC) online, 5th Ser., vol. 379, 16 April 1942.

21 'Truck Acts – Proposed New Defence Act Regulation: Report of the Proceedings at the Conference of the Representatives of Certain Unions', 6 and 7 November 1941: 292/192/1/1, MRC. Consultative Committee, 30th Meeting at the Ministry of Labour and National Service, 19 February 1942: LAB 10/1653, TNA.

22 Craik, *Bryn Roberts*, p. 81.

of an agreed settlement had been wrecked by the unilateral action of NUPE taking legal proceedings against the Buckinghamshire County Council'.[23] (When discussions took place years later over reforming the Truck Acts, Williamson would have a seat at the table and Roberts would not.) Many unions and trades councils joined NUPE in fiercely opposing the TUC General Council,[24] but Order 1644 was made official in August 1942.[25]

After two attempts to secure an audience with the Home Secretary, Roberts wrote a scathing public letter, warning him that this order, 'in defiance of the judiciary', would cause him to be known as the man who 'shackled the cheque system upon the poor working man'. The language of independence and tyranny, common in labour opposition to truck, was prominent. Roberts related his union's struggle to win weekly cash wages for roadmen and was sceptical of the county councils' explanations, noting that police officers and civil defence workers were paid in cash. Cheques were 'an instrument of torture' for the roadmen because they had no bank accounts, and often lived great distances from banks. If the cheque were delayed, the roadman's wife could not shop unless she secured credit from the local shopkeeper. If the cheque arrived on Saturday morning, the husband would still be at work, and the wife could not cash it without his endorsement. She would have to travel to his worksite or wait until his shift ended: 'the cheque system makes the harassed housewife's task of balancing her slender budget an impossible one'. This was especially so during wartime, with shortages of goods, when those with ready cash had first access to them.[26]

The inconvenient location of banks meant having cheques cashed by a publican, which, Roberts stressed, wives wanted to avoid because of money lost on drink. Another option was a local shopkeeper, who would expect patronage for this service, and the shopkeeper would 'know his earnings'. Roberts begged Morrison not to subject county roadmen to the 'hellish, barbarous and demoralizing practice' of payment by cheque.[27] Morrison

---

23 'Truck Acts – Proposed New Defence Act Regulation: Report of Proceedings', 6 November 1941: 292/192/1/1, MRC.

24 Kettering Trades Council to Sir Walter Citrine (TUC), 14 April 1942; Sheffield Trades and Labour Council to TUC, 31 March 1942; Banbury and District Trades Council to TUC, 17 March 1942; Hastings and District Trades Council to TUC, 16 June 1942; Sutton and District Trades Council to TUC, 17 February 1942; 'Truck Acts – Proposed New Defence Act Regulation: Report of Proceedings', 6 November 1941: 292/192/1/1, MRC.

25 Statutory Rules and Orders, 1942, No. 1644, Emergency Powers (Defence), County Roadmen (Payment of Wages): LAB 10/1653, TNA.

26 'An Open Letter to Rt Hon Herbert Morrison, Home Secretary, from the National Union of Public Employees, General Secretary Bryn Roberts': 292/192/1/1, MRC.

27 *Ibid.*

replied that he was 'pained and surprised' at the letter, arguing that Roberts had not given him 'fair play'.[28]

Parliamentary efforts to modify the Truck Acts

In 1956, almost a decade after Order 1644 had been withdrawn, the electronics company Pye Radio sought an agreement with its employees' union to pay wages by cheque, but its solicitors warned that this could violate the 1831 Truck Act. In November that year, Conservative MP Graham Page reintroduced a 1954 bill of his to simplify rules for the endorsement of cheques. He included a clause that would amend the Truck Act to permit payment of wages by cheque where the employer and employee consented. It also would enable a worker to withdraw his or her consent, and return to cash payment within seven days. He informed the House of Commons: 'I realise that this is a controversial matter and might not find its way on to the later stages of the bill without very full consultation, but I believe that I can produce a formula which would fully safeguard the interests of those concerned, particularly those of trade unions on behalf of their members and those chambers of trade on behalf of shopkeepers'.[29]

The Ministry of Labour wrote to the TUC in early January 1957 to explain the clause in Page's bill and that it would be on the agenda of the next NJAC (comprising representatives of employers, trade unions, and the Ministry of Labour) on 23 January. One argument in favour was that it 'restores the intention of the 1831 Act, which did, in fact allow payment by cheque subject to certain safeguards'. The Ministry suggested cheques might reduce payroll robberies (which were to escalate in the early 1960s) and ease the burden on pay offices in large firms.[30] It was doubtful whether the clause would 'lead to any appreciable change' in the number of workers paid by cheque, because in Scotland, where there were no legal barriers to payment by cheque, most manual workers were still paid in cash.[31]

On 22 January the TUC leadership discussed its position, recalling 'that the exemption from the Truck Act of 1831 was given during the war and that

---

28 Morrison to Roberts, 21 May 1942: 292/192/1/1, MRC.

29 Hilton, *The Truck System*, pp. 149–50; *Hansard* (HC) online, vol. 561, 27 November 1956, cols 237–9.

30 Ministry of Labour to TUC, 4 January 1957: 292/192/1/1, MRC. Payroll robberies were an important concern. In the London Metropolitan Police District alone in 1959 there were thirty-four such incidents in which £40,079 was stolen; in 1960, thirty-five robberies (with no arrests) netted £47,801; and, in 1961, £129,455 was the haul from sixty-six payroll robberies: *Hansard* (HC) online, vol. 652, 1 February 1962, col. 1280.

31 Ministry of Labour to TUC, 4 January 1957: 292/192/1/1, MRC.

the payment by cheque has caused some annoyance to workers'. Although unionized workers could withstand pressure to accept payment of wages in unwanted forms, 'workers in small concerns or in tied cottages might be in a poor position to exercise free choice'. So it was decided 'to inform the Minister that there was no good reason for the law on the subject to be amended'.[32]

After receiving what he called 'some very forcibly' expressed views from unions, the Minister of Labour and National Service, Iain Macleod, urged Page to withdraw the clause. Frederick Lee, Labour MP from Newton and a former local leader in the Amalgamated Engineering Union, pressed for an assurance from Macleod that no government legislation would be introduced to provide for wage payment by cheque, asking him to 'bear in mind that a very large section of organised labour would not like to see such a development'. Macleod responded that he would postpone such legislation 'until the very fullest consultations had taken place'. Page agreed, even though he could not think of 'any good cause why it should remain a crime, under a statute a century and a quarter old, for employers and employees freely to agree amongst themselves for the payment of wages in any form'.[33] Although the clause was dropped, the government continued to feel pressure from inside and outside Parliament to amend or repeal the Truck Act.

In 1957, for example, the Council of the Chartered Institute of Secretaries (of Joint Stock Companies and other Public Bodies, CIS) recommended that the Truck Acts, 1831–96, be repealed but replaced with a consolidating Act.[34] It concluded that they were no longer relevant. There had been considerable litigation to determine who were manual workers, and therefore covered by the acts, with the courts determining that manual labour had to represent a substantial part of the person's employment and not merely an incidental aspect. This case law created anomalies, such as leaving bus conductors outside the Acts, but bus cleaners within them. Most importantly, the Truck Acts should be extended to all workers except monthly-paid salaried employees.[35]

While the rise of organized labour and the passage of time had rendered many wage deductions regulated by the 1896 Truck Act 'now generally

32 TUC Minutes, 22 January 1957: 292/192/1/1, MRC.
33 *Hansard* (HC) online, vol. 563, 29 January 1957, cols 841–2; Hilton, *The Truck System,* 149–50. For more debate over the Truck Acts, see *The Times,* 10 December 1956. D. Howell, 'Lee, Frederick, Baron Lee of Newton (1906–1984)', *Oxford Dictionary of National Biography* (*ODNB*) online (2004).
34 Chartered Institute of Secretaries (CIS), *Modernization of the Truck Acts* (1957): HD 4928 1957, London Metropolitan University Archives. *The Times,* 2 March 1957.
35 CIS, *Modernization of the Truck Acts,* pp. 2–3.

obsolete', deductions for bad work were still made in some industries. For this reason, the regulations of the 1896 Truck Act 'should be maintained to prevent abuse, or exploitation of workers'.[36] The legality of deductions needed clarifying and modernizing in three areas: deductions from wages for provident or pension schemes, for shares of company stock, and for house purchases assisted by employers. The CIS recommended that if the pension or provident fund met the standards set by the Inland Revenue, and the employee requested to join, it should be legal to take deductions for contributions. After 1945 some employers had assisted workers in buying houses through property companies or housing associations, which was thought beneficial to workers and should also be made legal.[37]

On 28 January 1958, Page introduced another bill 'to amend the law relating to the payment of wages', which permitted an employer, with an employee's consent, to pay wages into the employee's bank account, or by a cheque cashable only at the bank. This was intended to overcome the objections of retail shopkeepers, who feared that payment of wages by open cheque might result in workers cashing them at shops, forcing them to carry more cash and exposing them to greater risk of robberies.[38]

The Ministry of Labour contacted the TUC which opposed these proposals. By meeting shopkeepers' objections, Page's bill would make payment by cheque even more inconvenient for workers.[39] The National Union of Bank Employees (NUBE) opposed the bill because 'the volume of work at the counter and in other ways would seriously impair the speed at which the general banking public were served, and also impair progress toward a five-day working week'.[40] NUBE president Edgar Bell feared it would add to the hours and workload of his members. He later observed that, although 'no one seemed to know who wanted payment by cheque', efforts to modify the Truck Acts persisted.[41] Page and his allies clearly had support from the business community and continued to remind government of the need for action. The initiative for truck reform often came from outside government – the 1831 and 1887 Acts had been the work of private members – as the considerable gulf between capital and labour on this matter made legislating politically unrewarding for governments.

---

36 *Ibid.*, pp. 4–5.
37 *Ibid.*, pp. 5–7.
38 'A Bill to amend the law relating to the payment of wages' [Bill 59], 1957–58. The bill also enabled bonuses in company shares and provided for profit-sharing schemes.
39 Ministry of Labour and National Service to TUC, 13 February 1958; TUC to Ministry of Labour and National Service, 18 February 1958: 292/192/1/1, MRC.
40 National Union of Bank Employees to TUC, 22 and 29 April 1958: 292/192/1/1, MRC.
41 *Guardian*, 9 March 1960.

At the bill's second reading, Page stressed that the employer could only pay wages into a bank account or by cheque with the worker's written agreement. It would save employers time and cost and greatly reduce payroll robberies. If a male breadwinner opened a joint bank account with his wife, she could withdraw money to shop on payday morning rather than wait for him to come home. Labour MPs raised issues with the bill. Arthur Moyle, a former NUPE officer,[42] pointed out that over half a million rural manual workers lived great distances from banks. Labour MP Sir Leslie Plummer asked if any discussion had taken place regarding bank fees for potential working-class customers. Page responded that workers affected by these issues would not have to give their consent to being paid by cheque. Labour MP David Weitzman asked about safeguards to prevent employers coercing consent; Page answered that trade unions could prevent such encroachments. Alfred Robens – former full-time official of a union that became the Union of Shop, Distributive and Allied Workers (USDAW), and Minister of Labour and National Service in 1951 – replied that 'from the experience which many people have had in the trade union movement and in industry generally, we are well aware that we can get coercion of a quiet kind'. Labour MPs John Hynd (formerly of the National Union of Railwaymen) and James Chuter Ede (Home Secretary, 1945–51) linked the payment of wages to the patriarchal control of the family by male breadwinners, arguing that cheques would allow a wife to know her husband's salary, when not every man shared that information.[43]

Many Labour MPs agreed that the laws were outdated, but they believed that reform of the Truck Acts needed to be directed by the government, studied more thoroughly, and discussed with a wider range of parties before proposing legislation. Labour MP and barrister Reginald Paget argued this was not 'the sort of matter we could possibly legislate on the nod'. Robens urged Page to withdraw the bill and appealed to the government to appoint a committee to study the question. The parliamentary secretary to the Minister of Labour, Richard Wood, offered some hopeful words on this front, so Page withdrew his bill.[44] Four months later, Conservative MP Patrick Maitland, supported by Page, introduced a bill similar to the one withdrawn, but by then it was understood that the government was in discussion with the interested parties and planned to take the issue up on its own. Thus the bill, opposed by the TUC and NUBE, as well as many retailing organizations, did not progress beyond second reading.[45] By June 1959, the *Manchester Guardian* was reporting the government's intention

---

42 Craik, *Bryn Roberts*, p. 135.
43 *Hansard* (HC) online, vol. 589, 20 June 1958, cols 1491–528, quote at col. 1524.
44 *Ibid.*; *The Times*, 15 November 1958.
45 'Wages Bill' [Bill 25], 1958–59. Hilton, *The Truck Acts*, p. 151. 292/192/1/1, MRC; *Hansard* (HC) online, vol. 606, 12 June 1959, cols 1368–420.

to remove 'the quaint limitations of the pre-Victorian Truck Act' regarding payment of wages by cheque.[46]

The TUC's involvement

In autumn 1958 the Ministry of Labour suggested that the NJAC establish a subcommittee on the Truck Acts. The TUC did not oppose it, but was 'not favourable to a change in the law'. The NJAC agreed to have the examination carried out by the subcommittee, the Joint Consultative Committee (JCC),[47] which met in December 1958 and February 1959.

The TUC was constrained by the overwhelming opposition of rank-and-file union members to payment other than in cash, but wished to appear forward-looking or, at least, avoid resisting change. TUC representatives were aware that payment by cheque was common for American manual workers. Williamson stated that while the NUGMW 'did not want to appear unco-operative', there were many difficulties, particularly the inconvenience for workers of cashing cheques or maintaining bank accounts. He stressed that it was essential that employees gave consent and that such consent was not obtained under duress. He had always 'preferred negotiation to confrontation', which describes his behaviour in this episode.[48] Sir William Garrett, president of the British Employers' Confederation (BEC, representing employers' associations not individual companies), agreed that consent was essential, as was consultation with the banks, but in the United States of America it had led to more working people with bank accounts.[49] Payment by cheque or bank transfer was later estimated as saving businesses as much as 6–7d. (2.5–2.9p) per pay packet every week, substantial sums for a large firm.[50]

The BEC and the nationalized industries produced papers for the JCC, highlighting anomalies of the Truck Acts and, as a consequence, the benefits denied to workers. The BEC argued, for example, that the legislation made it illegal to provide cashless pay to sick workers away from work on payday. The law on deductions from wages was too 'rigid and formalized': 'failure to comply with appropriate conditions in even a minor or purely technical sense invalidates completely what would otherwise be a perfectly

---

46 *Manchester Guardian*, 13 June 1959.

47 TUC, 21 October 1958: 292/192/1/1, MRC.

48 J. England, 'Williamson, Thomas, Baron Williamson (1897–1983)', *ODNB* online (2004).

49 Ministry of Labour and National Service, JCC, minutes, 19 February 1959: LAB 10/1656, TNA; 292/192/1/1, MRC.

50 'Off Loading the Bother of Paying Wages by Cash', 10 July 1965: 292b/190/3, MRC.

legal deduction'. Yet the history of truck legislation and its enforcement demonstrates that what employers perceived as 'technicalities' in making deductions were often very important safeguards for workers. The employers argued that the Truck Acts complicated agreements for deductions from wages for loans and advances, overpayments, the purchase of shares in company stock, sports and social clubs, and even for safety equipment purchased in bulk by the employer and sold cheaply to the employee.[51] The TUC conceded some of these points, but Williamson thought that 'a more elaborate inquiry' was necessary.[52]

The NJAC considered the JCC recommendations in April 1959, and separated the two main issues. The payment of wages was treated separately because it was 'less complicated than the larger subject'; the 'legal complexities and practical difficulties' of modernizing the Truck Acts required a more thorough examination. The NJAC recommended altering the Truck Acts relating to the payment of wages as follows: (1) an employee might have wages paid directly into his or her bank account if requested and the employer agreed; (2) such a request would be in writing and at least a week before the pay change; (3) when absent for illness or work-related reasons, he or she could be paid with a money or postal order; (4) where a worker requested and an employer agreed, provision should be made for the payment by cheque. Williamson demanded that legislation positively stated that employees had the right to continue receiving wages in cash.[53] The NJAC agreed that the government would introduce legislation that would permit payment of wages based upon the above proposals, and that an independent committee would review the Truck Acts.[54]

For the remainder of 1959 the TUC received numerous letters from trade unions and trades councils expressing hostility to legalizing payment by cheque for manual workers. Opposition from affiliated unions was overwhelming. Roberts of NUPE criticized the TUC's acquiescence: 'in light of my experience of the evils of the cheque system ... I regret this decision';[55] it would divide the union movement, complicate the collection

51 'The Truck Acts: Note Submitted by the British Employers' Confederation to the JCC'; 'The Truck Acts: Note Submitted by the Nationalized Industries to the JCC', LAB 10/1656, TNA. National Dock Labour Board to TUC, 30 January 1964: 292b/190/3, MRC.
52 *The Times*, 17 March 1959. Ministry of Labour and National Service, JCC, minutes, 19 February 1959: LAB 10/1656, TNA.
53 *Manchester Guardian*, 23 April 1959. Ministry of Labour and National Service, National Joint Advisory Council (NJAC), 22 April 1959: LAB 10/1656, TNA. NJAC to the Ministry of Labour, 21 April 1959: 292/192/1/1, MRC.
54 TUC to NUPE, 27 April 1959: 292/192/1/1, MRC. *The Times*, 16 March, 23 April 1959.
55 NUPE to TUC, 1 May 1959: 292/192/1/1, MRC.

of union dues, and lead to employer coercion to accept non-cash wages.[56] The Amalgamated Union of Foundry Workers complained to Prime Minister Harold Macmillan as well.[57] The Association of Engineering and Shipbuilding Draughtsmen, whose members were white-collar, thought permitting payment by cheque 'would undoubtedly result in eventual compulsion in practice irrespective of any ostensible freedom of choice permitted by legislation'.[58] The National Union of Agricultural Workers (NUAW) stressed that many agricultural employees lived great distances from banks, forcing them to cash cheques with retailers or publicans who would then know their earnings.[59] Other trade unions joined in,[60] as did many trades councils (the TUC's local arm).[61] The standard concerns were aired, and some new ones: for example, some companies might take advantage to move to monthly pay, with accompanying hardship.[62]

The TUC sent out reassuring letters. It defended its actions to Roberts and NUPE by stating that while it had opposed the private member's bills on the subject, after consultation with the Ministry of Labour and the NJAC about obvious inconsistencies in the law, 'it would be difficult to maintain the position that the law should proscribe payment methods for some but by no means all manual workers and for no non-manual workers'.[63] Through constructive co-operation the TUC was able to shape the terms for payment by cheque or bank transfer, as the government pledged to consult the TUC during the legislative process.[64] The TUC would insist upon the employee's

---

56 *Guardian*, 12 September 1959.

57 Amalgamated Union of Foundry Workers to Harold Macmillan, 19 June 1959: 292/192/1/1, MRC.

58 Association of Engineering and Shipbuilding Draughtsmen to TUC, 30 June 1959: 292/192/1/1, MRC.

59 National Union of Agricultural Workers to TUC, 25 August 1959: 292/192/1/1, MRC.

60 For example, correspondence to TUC from Plumbing Trade Union, 11 August 1959; Enginemen, Firemen, Medical and Electrical Workers, 17 August 1959; National Union of Hosiery Workers, 27 August 1959: 292/192/1/1, MRC.

61 For example, correspondence to TUC from Isle of Sheppey Trades Council, 13 May 1959; Brighouse Trades and Industrial Council, 18 June 1959; Portsmouth Trades Council, 23 June 1959; Norwich Labour Party and Industrial Council, 2 July 1959; Hastings and District Trades Council, 5 July 1959; Spalding and District Trades Council, 28 July 1959; Leeds Trades Council, 4 August 1959; Kent Federation of Trades Councils, 9 August 1959; Horsham and District Trades Council, 17 September 1959; Redhill, Redgate and District Trades Council, 13 October 1959; Welwyn Garden City and District Trades Council, 5 March 1960: 292/192/1/1, MRC.

62 Stretford and District Trades Council to TUC, 3 June 1959: 292/192/1/1, MRC.

63 TUC to NUPE, 7 May 1959: 292/192/1/1, MRC.

64 Correspondence from TUC to: Spalding and District Trades Council, 28 July 1959; Leeds Trades Council, 6 August 1959; Redhill, Redgate and District

freely given consent, and a strong affirmative statement that workers had the right to cash wages if they desired. It recognized that opposition to payment of wages by cheque or bank transfer was 'widely held'.[65]

The government also consulted with retailers,[66] whose representatives told the Board of Trade that it would mean 'heavy demands will be made upon them [retailers] to cash cheques'. While they could refuse to perform this service, it might mean losing customers. In addition to having to carry extra cash on paydays, they were concerned about the reliability of cheques signed by private firms.[67] The Board of Trade met retail trade representatives to discuss a potential bill. While the Chamber of Commerce and some larger organizations had no objections to amending the Truck Acts, the National Union of Retail Confectioners and National Association of Multiple Grocers found reform 'unwelcome' and of 'profound concern'.[68]

The issue received increased public exposure in July 1959 when the BBC television programme, *Matters of the Moment,* devoted an episode to it. Host Percy Cudlipp moderated between Victor Feather (then TUC assistant secretary), Peter Masefield (an aeronautical engineer and industrialist), and R. G. Thornton, general manager of Barclays Bank. The episode began with 'person on the street' interviews, mostly opposed to cashless pay. One worker said he would consider accepting cheques if the employer paid the bank fees. Another argued that bank accounts made little sense for younger workers 'who tend to live right up to the hilt of their income'. Shopkeepers were not keen either; one thought that carrying additional cash on payday would 'make it easier on the hooligan' planning a robbery. Another thought that workers would object because cheque wages involved a potential loss of privacy: 'I am going to know practically the whole of the wages of my customers'. The shopkeeper thought that some male workers wanted to keep their wages secret not only from retailers, but also from their families, asking: 'How many husbands want their wives to know what they are getting? This is going to be the biggest bugbear'.[69]

When Cudlipp asked Masefield to describe the advantages of payment by cheque, the latter emphasized that any legislation would make the

Trades Council 15 October 1959: 292/192/1/1, MRC.

65 Correspondence from TUC to: NUPE, 7 May 1959; Isle of Sheppey Trades Council, 15 May 1959; Portsmouth Trades Council, 25 June 1959; Kent Federation of Trades Councils, 20 October 1959: 292/192/1/1, MRC.

66 *Daily Telegraph*, 11 May 1959; LAB 10/1655, TNA; *The Times*, 12 May 1959.

67 Multiple Shops Federation to Board of Trade, 15 June 1959; National Federation of Retail Newsagents and Booksellers to Board of Trade, 19 June 1959: LAB 10/1655, TNA.

68 Proposed Amendment to the Truck Acts, Meeting with the Retail Trades Representatives, 23 June 1959, and Licensed Victuallers' Defence League of England and Wales, 29 July 1959, at the Board of Trade: LAB 10/1655, TNA.

69 Transcription, *Matters of the Moment*, 23 July 1959: LAB 10/1655, TNA.

acceptance of wages by cheque entirely voluntary. Masefield personally favoured direct payment into bank accounts, and argued that for large firms this would save considerable costs. Furthermore, in male-breadwinner families with joint accounts the wife could collect money for shopping whenever she needed it rather than ask the husband.[70] Thornton, for the banks, was neutral. Banks wanted new customers to be voluntary, and was optimistic that even in the absence of Truck Act reform his bank would continue to attract new working-class customers, claiming that 16% of new accounts at his bank in October 1958 were for weekly-paid manual workers. He favoured workers gradually obtaining bank accounts and payment by direct transfer. He stated that banks, in consultation with NUBE, would consider altering banking hours but that the transition would be easier if pay periods were fortnightly or monthly – a red flag to most manual workers.[71]

Feather said that no trade union had asked for this change, and none was in favour, but none would oppose such change provided that it was 'purely optional and voluntary' and strongly asserted workers' right to be paid in cash. The alternatives shifted employers' costs to shopkeepers, publicans, and banks, who would inevitably find ways to transfer these to workers. At the end, Cudlipp informed the public that there was still time to make their views known before Parliament acted.[72] A few months later, it was also the subject of a BBC *Money Matters* item titled 'The Demise of the Wage Packet' in which Cudlipp explained proposed government legislation.[73]

The Payment of Wages Act 1960 and the Karmel Committee

On 30 July 1959 Macleod announced that the committee to examine the Truck Acts would be chaired by David Karmel QC, the Recorder of Wigan, an experienced member of the Industrial Disputes Tribunal;[74] R. M. Walker of the Ministry of Labour was secretary. Other members were Williamson (by now Sir Thomas, NUGMW general secretary and a senior TUC General Council member): R. Boyfield, TUC Organisation Department head; N. A. Sloan QC, director of the Shipbuilding Employers' Federation; V. Elwes, staff manager of the restaurant chain and food manufacturer

---

70 *Ibid.*

71 *Ibid.*

72 *Ibid.*

73 *Money Matters: The Demise of the Wage Packet?* by Edward Leader; pre-recorded 26 February 1960, broadcast 28 February 1960: LAB 10/1650, TNA.

74 The Industrial Disputes Tribunal was an arbitration body, set up under Order 1376, the Industrial Disputes Order (1951), to replace the National Arbitration Tribunal (1940–51); it was dissolved on 28 February 1959.

J. Lyons; W. H. G. Cocks, Glamorgan county treasurer; Sir Archibald Harrison, formerly solicitor to the Ministry of Labour;[75] D. H. Haslam, legal adviser and solicitor, National Coal Board; and I. H. Shearer QC, a senior Scottish barrister.[76] It was therefore heavily weighted with legal expertise. The terms of reference were 'to consider in the light of present day conditions the operation of the Truck Acts, 1831–1940, and related legislation, and to make recommendations'.[77] The committee held the first of its seventeen meetings on 12 October 1959 and invited interested individuals and organizations to submit information and comments.[78]

By October 1959 the government already had a draft of the Payment of Wages Bill, and the TUC repeated its demand for an affirmative statement retaining the right to be paid in cash, and that accepting non-cash forms of payment could not be made a condition of employment. It feared after the passage of an Act that 'employers' organizations will have many forms printed which member firms will distribute to employees inviting them to apply to have wages paid other than in cash. There may be an element of duress'.[79] The TUC was also concerned for employees outside the coverage of the Truck Acts, because any new protections would not apply to them.[80]

The Conservative government, re-elected on 8 October 1959, lost no time, Minister of Labour Edward Heath introducing the Payment of Wages Bill on 15 December. Clause one proposed that if an employee requested in writing, and an employer agreed, he or she could have wages paid by bank transfer, postal order, money order or cheque. An employer or employee could cancel the arrangement with fourteen days' notice. Employers could pay workers who were absent on payday for reason of illness, injury or work with a postal order or money order. An affirmative statement was in the bill: 'nothing in this Act shall operate so as to enable an employed person to be required, by any terms or conditions of his employment or otherwise, to make such a request as mentioned

---

75 Solicitor to Ministry of Labour and National Service, 1949–59; secretary, Trade Marks, Patents and Designs Federation, 1959–69: *The Times*, 20 November 1976.
76 *Manchester Guardian*, 22 August 1959.
77 *Hansard* (HC) online, vol. 610, 30 July 1959, col. 175W. *The Times*, 31 July, 22 August 1959. Ministry of Labour press notice, 21 August 1959: 292/192/1/1, MRC.
78 *Manchester Guardian*, 31 July; *Guardian*, 13 October 1959; Karmel, *Report*, p. 3.
79 TUC to Ministry of Labour, 18 November 1959: LAB 10/1655, TNA. TUC to Ministry of Labour, 30 November 1959; TUC to Sir Thomas Williamson, 30 November 1959: 292/192/1/1, MRC.
80 TUC to Ministry of Labour, 30 November 1959; TUC to Williamson, 30 November 1959, Extract from Minutes, TUC, 26 January 1960: 292/192/1/1, MRC.

in section 1 of this Act, or to refrain from cancelling such a request'. The TUC noted this 'with satisfaction'.[81] To meet concerns of banks and retailers, and ensure that facilities were available, payment by cheque would operate from an unspecified later date.[82] Some Labour MPs were still concerned that employers might exert pressure on workers to accept non-cash wages. Others insisted that there was little evidence to suggest that manual workers desired this reform.[83]

The bill passed its second reading on 26 January 1960, and the Standing Committee considered it on 23 February.[84] On 1 March clause five was changed to allow an agent to act on behalf of the employee in making or rescinding requests.[85] The only other significant amendment was to increase, from two to four weeks, the notice for cancellation of a new method of wage payment.[86] The bill passed its third reading on 30 March 1960, the House of Lords on 26 May, and was enacted as the Payment of Wages Act 1960.

It thus became lawful for employers, if requested by a worker, to pay wages by cheque to those workers covered by the Truck Acts. But it was not until 1 March 1963, some three years later, that this was implemented. This delay had been occasioned by the concerns of retailers, and to a lesser extent banks, regarding an increase in demands for cheque cashing.[87] The government was under no illusions that the Act would significantly change how manual workers received their wages in the short term. Given that workers outside the Truck Acts' coverage had shown little inclination to cashless pay, there was no reason to think that those covered by them would be any different. Indeed, the legal reform of March 1963 was met with indifference.[88] C. H. Sisson of the Ministry of Labour insisted that

81 Extract from minutes, NJAC (General Council side), 18 December 1959: 292/192/1/1, MRC.

82 'A Bill to remove certain restrictions imposed by the Truck Acts, 1831 to 1940, and other enactments, with respect to the payment of wages; and for purposes connected therewith' [Bill 49], 1959–60; *Guardian*, 16 December 1959.

83 *Guardian*, 29 January 1960.

84 *House of Commons Official Report: Standing Committee A: Payment of Wages Bill: First Sitting Tuesday 23 February 1960* (HMSO: 1960), cols 3–6, 10, 13–14, 27, 30–1, 33–4, 53–4.

85 *House of Commons Official Report: Standing Committee A: Payment of Wages Bill: Third Sitting Tuesday 1 March 1960* (HMSO: 1960), cols 122–30.

86 *Ibid.*

87 *Guardian*, 24 November 1960. *Hansard* (House of Lords) online, vol. 245, 3 December 1962, col. 1. O. Aikin, 'Payment of Wages Act 1960', *Modern Law Review* (*MLR*) 24:1 (1961), pp. 155–7. On the Effective Date of Payment of Wages by Cheque, see LAB 10/1660, TNA; Ministry of Labour, Press Notice, Payment of Wages by Cheque, 30 November 1962: 292b/190/3, MRC.

88 National Debt Office to HM Treasury, 5 February 1962; Bank of England to HM Treasury, 29 January and 8 March 1962: LAB 10/1660, TNA. CPRS,

'The main purpose of the bill was simply to do away with obsolete legal restrictions on the freedom of workers to take their pay otherwise than in cash if it suited both the worker and his employer'.[89]

Most observers would have agreed with Olga Aiken that 'the stringent provisions ... may well prevent the Act being widely used. The initiative is left in the hands of the employee, who in all probability is quite content with his cash payment'.[90] Even where an employee wanted a change, an employer might be hesitant because of the employee's right to revert to cash. The TUC had been able to ensure strong safeguards to meet workers' preferences.

The Karmel Committee's report was presented to Parliament on 12 July 1961. The committee had considered written submissions and oral testimony from a range of experts and interested parties.[91] It recommended that the Truck Acts, 1831–1940, be repealed and replaced by new legislation. The BEC had urged the repeal of 'all existing truck legislation leaving employers and employees free to negotiate such conditions of the contract of service as they may mutually agree'. Even the nationalized industries argued that repealing the Truck Acts without a replacement should be 'seriously examined'.[92] The TUC did not make a formal submission, but had two members on the committee. One of them, Williamson, argued that legislation to protect wages was still necessary, and should be based upon the following principles: subject to very few exceptions, wages should be paid in cash and not goods; there should be no restrictions on employees' freedom to dispose of their wages; employees should be protected from unreasonable and unfair deductions; and new legislation should cover more workers.[93] The committee found that while truck and related practices had declined, they were 'by no means extinct', so 'we do not think the time has yet come when all protections can safely be withdrawn'.[94]

Karmel recommended that new consolidating legislation – to apply to all employed under a contract of service (excepting merchant seamen) – remove obstacles to employers providing benefits and allowances in kind: 'it is quite common and is increasingly the practice to provide employees

Cashless Pay. 'Five Days to the Pay Packet Revolution': 292b/190/3, MRC.
89 Minutes of Meeting at Board of Trade, 13 November 1959: LAB 10/1655, TNA. British Institute of Management, 'Payment of Wages by Cheque: Report on Meeting held on 19 September 1960'; TUC to Ministry of Labour, 19 April 1962: 292b/190/3, MRC.
90 Aikin, 'Payment of Wages Act 1960', *MLR*, pp. 156.
91 Karmel, *Report*, p. 3; Appendix I: List of Groups Who Provided a Written Submission: LAB 10/1658, TNA; LAB 10/1648, TNA.
92 Karmel, *Report*, pp. 11–12.
93 Committee on the Truck Acts: Matters Suggested for Consideration by Committee: LAB 10/1646, TNA. Karmel, *Report*, p. 12.
94 Karmel, *Report*, pp. 5, 12; *Guardian*, 12 July 1961.

with benefits and advantages of different kinds over and above their cash wages'.[95] Wages should be redefined in the new Act to allow workers to receive these in-kind benefits. The committee also suggested legalizing deductions from wages to which a worker freely consented. If deductions were taken without consent, a worker could go to a newly created local tribunal, with the power to award wages owed and expenses.[96] Fines or deductions for bad work should only be permissible where shown to be an accepted part of the trade or the majority consented to them. Fines and deductions had to be fair and reasonable, with the employer to give ten days' notice so that affected workers could raise the matter with the tribunal. The tribunal could decide whether the fine or deduction was part of the trade, accepted by the workers, and was fair and reasonable.

The committee also proposed allowing deductions for overpayments, provided the worker agreed. Many employers advocated automatic recovery, but the committee disagreed and suggested that deductions for overpayments or cash or stock shortages (for retail workers) should not exceed 10% of wages in any pay period. If the employee did not assent, the employer could appeal to the tribunal. Unions wanted protections and fair procedures for workers who handled cash, with employers having to prove negligence or culpability before recovering a cash shortage, but this was not agreed.[97] The possibility of dishonesty or gross negligence meant that employers should be able to make deductions from wages for cash shortages immediately, provided they were allowed by the conditions of employment. Employees should be able to appeal to the tribunal over whether there was a cash shortage, whether it was their fault, or whether the deduction was excessive.[98] The proposed reforms would decriminalize truck law by entrusting enforcement to local tribunals, which could award lost wages and expenses.[99]

The two TUC members of the committee had been willing to accept expanding the range of deductions from wages in return for extending the new protections to all workers. If these recommendations were enacted, many workers previously outside the Truck Acts' coverage would have to give formal consent to deductions, and would have access to a local tribunal when disputes arose over them.[100] A Ministry of Labour official noted: 'Our consultations … have already made clear that … nationalized industries and private employers alike would prefer to have an unfettered right of

---

95 Karmel, *Report*, p. 8.

96 *Ibid*., pp. 31–2.

97 Committee on the Truck Acts, minutes, 27 February 1961: 292b/190/3, MRC.

98 Karmel, *Report*, pp. 31–2.

99 *Ibid*. Decisions of these tribunals could be appealed to the Court of Appeal or the Court of Session.

100 Practical Implications of Legislation on the Lines Recommended by the Karmel Committee: LAB 10/1661, TNA.

deduction ... and they see special difficulties about any limitation on their right to deduct from the salaries of "managerial workers".[101]

The expansion in the scope of the Truck Acts would bring senior management, professional and technical staff within its terms.[102] Some public employers stressed that applying the recommendations to salaried employees would create administrative difficulties. The Treasury was adamant that the Crown should be excluded;[103] one official noted that 'a good deal of doubt was expressed whether we really need to inflict on ourselves special machinery [local tribunals] to provide for appeals by civil servants against financial penalties'.[104] For example, civil servants were sometimes denied salary increments for inefficiency, mistakes, or for disciplinary reasons, and it was unclear whether this could be interpreted as a fine.[105] The government was concerned that 'any legislation is likely to be controversial and there would be political difficulties in introducing the ... recommendations on workers in private industry if ... Government Departments accept no restrictions whatsoever on the financial penalties they are able to impose on non-industrial civil servants'.[106] This was a political disincentive for action.

Trade unions contacted the TUC General Council with their concerns, some of which were passed to the Ministry of Labour. Some unions disapproved of the entire report, but most focused on single issues. For example, while most unions accepted that employers could take deductions from wages to which employees consented, NUAW objected because 'an unscrupulous employer might bring pressure to bear to obtain the workers' consent'.[107] Deductions to recover overpayments and cash shortages were unacceptable to many unions. Alan Birch of USDAW registered the 'strongest possible objection' to the treatment of cash shortages. Employers should prove negligence or dishonesty before such deductions, rather than acting as prosecutor and judge. Not all cash shortages were employees'

101 Barbara Green, Ministry of Labour to Mr Sisson, Treasury, 4 March 1963: LAB 10/1661, TNA.
102 Practical Implications of Legislation on the Lines Recommended by the Karmel Committee: LAB 10/1661, TNA.
103 The Treasury did recommend separate arrangements should be made to give civil servants 'equivalent protections': *ibid.*
104 A. J. Collier, Treasury, to B. Green, Ministry of Labour, 29 January and 26 March 1963: LAB 10/1661, TNA.
105 Establishment Officers Committee, Implementation of the Report of the Karmel Committee, and Practical Implications of Legislation on the Lines Recommended by the Karmel Committee: LAB 10/1661, TNA.
106 Establishment Officers Meeting, Implementation of Karmel Committee, Note by Ministry of Labour: LAB 10/1661, TNA.
107 Report on the Committee on the Truck Acts, 17 January 1962: 292b/190/3, MRC.

fault; facilitating the recovery of cash or inventory shortfalls from pay packets would reduce incentives to improve security or accounting procedures.[108] The TUC decided in October 1961 to oppose the recommendations on cash shortages.[109] Employers were equally adamant that they be able to immediately recover cash shortages from employees.

In October 1962 the TUC informed the Ministry of Labour of its general support for the recommendations but with reservations, particularly over disciplinary fines and penalties for spoilt work; there should be a time limit for employers to recover overpayments through deductions; and 'expressed disquiet' over the procedure for recovering cash shortages. The TUC hoped that a new consolidating Truck Act and the Payment of Wages Act 1960 would be extended to all workers under a contract of employment.[110] Ministry of Labour officials noted in April 1963 that 'the unions and the employers are approaching this from very different points of view'.[111]

The United Kingdom's international obligations were an obstacle to implementing the Karmel Committee's recommendations, which could breach Articles 3, 4 and 6 of ILO (International Labour Organisation) Convention no. 95. Ratified by the UK in 1951, this addressed the payment of wages, with the Truck Acts an important aspect of UK compliance. According to Article 22, signatory nations could only leave 'within a year following the expiration of ten years from the date in which the Convention first came into force and thereafter similarly in every eleventh year'. Unless the government 'denounced' the convention before 23 September 1963, it would be bound by it for another ten years. Because the BEC and the TUC remained well apart on new truck legislation, and the government undecided, it was recommended that the Convention not be denounced.[112]

However attractive for the Conservative government, the prospect of a modernized and simplified Truck Act would come at the expense of new regulations for wage payment and deductions. Employers wanted to repeal all truck legislation without replacement; failing that, they desired minimal restrictions on employment contracts imposed upon the smallest number of employees. Organized labour wanted more comprehensive protections for all employees. It is hardly surprising that from the end of 1961 the government only committed itself to continued consultations. Ultimately, no action was taken on the Karmel Committee report.

---

108 *Ibid.*
109 *Ibid.*
110 TUC to B. Green, Ministry of Labour, 31 October 1962: 292b/190/3, MRC.
111 Establishment Officers Meeting, Implementation of Karmel Committee, Note by Ministry of Labour: LAB 10/1661, TNA.
112 Mr Slater, 19 August 1963: LAB 10/1661, TNA.

Conclusion: from union voice to union exclusion

The 1960 Payment of Wages Act operated for a quarter of a century. The passage of this law illuminates how organized labour gave working men and women some voice in their workplaces and government. Employers wanting new methods of paying wages would have to win workers' consent, and sometimes this required concessions and incentives.

By contrast, the 1986 Wages Act – which repealed all truck legislation and the Payment of Wages Act – was passed over the strenuous objections of organized labour and those bodies that provided legal advice to the poor. It made it much easier for employers to impose, as conditions of employment, methods of paying wages and the terms for deductions from wages (which no longer had to be 'fair and reasonable').[113] The 1986 Act was part of an onslaught to make it easier for employers to resist union demands and recast the employment relationship as more individual and less collective. In 1960 a Conservative government had considered it necessary to consult and consider (and, in this case, be persuaded by) the views of workers, as represented by trade unions. By the 1980s it was explicit government policy to reduce the political power of trade unions and greatly limit their influence in the formation of public policy.[114]

Many UK workers now accept cashless pay as a fact of life. Although some struggle with access to banking services (as cash machines are shut down or charge fees), many find cashless pay convenient. In 1960, manual workers had many reasons to object to cashless pay or any dilution of the Truck Acts. Because of the strength of trade-union organization, and recognition by the government of its legitimacy, workers then had a voice in possible changes to how they were paid. For example, before imposing cashless pay, employers, the state and banks would have to address concerns about the accessibility of banking. During the debates over the 1960 Payment of Wages Act, workers (through the TUC) were able to determine some of the rules under which they worked, lived and consumed. That was much less the case in 1986, and even less so today.

Department of History
University of Manitoba
Winnipeg, Manitoba
Canada R3T 5V5

---

113 C. Frank, 'Cashless Pay, Deductions from Wages, and the Repeal of the Truck Acts in Great Britain, 1945–1986', *Labor History* (2019).

114 P. Davies and M. Freedland, *Labour Legislation and Public Policy: A Contemporary History* (Clarendon Press, Oxford: 1993), chs 9–10.

HSIR 41 (2020) 109–35

https://doi.org/10.3828/hsir.2020.41.5

Crisis at Work: Gender, Class, and the Dehumanization of Jobs

Harriet Bradley

I preface this discussion with a vignette of two young women academics. June is a working-class woman who has just completed her Ph.D. She holds a part-time job at a Russell Group university, while her husband has worked for many years in sales. The couple were refused a tenancy agreement on the grounds of debt incurred by him while a student and because she is only working part time (as are some 40% of women). Selma is a recent migrant, a mother with three young children. She has a full-time job as a lecturer, while her husband supplements their income with unskilled labour. They, too, were refused a tenancy until I volunteered to be their guarantor. These hard-working, ambitious young women – vulnerable because of June's class, and Selma's ethnicity and migrant status – have overcome considerable obstacles to achieve their academic success, only to struggle to enter a vicious housing market stacked against those who lack economic capital.

This article surveys progress made in opening up labour market opportunities for women in Britain over the last fifty years. It begins in the 1970s, as does Huw Beynon in his paper detailing how working conditions within capitalism have declined since the end of the long boom.[1] It suggests that many of the developments he describes apply equally to women's employment, but with the twist that women have always been positioned differently within capitalist formations. In the nineteenth century they served as a reserve army of labour and were also used strategically to undercut male wages.[2] The twentieth century witnessed attempts to curb these tendencies, but, as Miriam Glucksmann has argued,[3] women enter the

---

1 H. Beynon, 'After the Long Boom: Living with Capitalism in the Twenty-First Century', *Historical Studies in Industrial Relations* (*HSIR*) 40 (2019), pp. 187–22.

2 See H. Bradley, *Men's Work, Women's Work* (Polity, Cambridge: 1989).

3 M. Glucksmann, 'Why "Work"? Gender and the Total Social Organization of Labour', *Gender, Work and Organization* 2:2 (1995), pp. 63–75.

labour market under different conditions from men. Their greater responsibility for managing reproductive work limits, for example, restricts their
capacities to manipulate time and place. Some of these constraints were
mitigated, in part at least, by state welfare and family-friendly policies.
But recent political events have reversed those trends: the attacks on
state welfare, the crisis of social care and the rise of precarious labour.
The ill effects that have arisen are heightened for individual women by
the intersection of gender disadvantage with those of class and ethnicity,
leading to struggles and anxiety for such women as June and Selma. These
deteriorations in women's work are set within the wider constellation of
changes described by Beynon, which I term *the dehumanization of work*.

In the beginning: feminism and the gendered labour process

As an undergraduate student of sociology in the late 1970s, among my
'bibles' were Beynon's *Working for Ford*, Theo Nichols's edited collection,
Capital and Labour, and Nichols and Beynon's *Living with Capitalism*.[4]
From the latter comes one of my favourite quotations about capitalist work:
'But I never feel "enriched" – I just feel knackered'.[5] That comment from a
Chemco worker seemed to me to epitomize the gap in perception between
managers and employees about working conditions, a gap which arguably
has continued to widen in the current phase of capitalist development,
characterized by 'the race to the bottom'.

There were other texts, however, which became equally influential
within sociology, reflecting the spread of gender analysis into academia
as a result of 'second wave' feminism of the 1960s and 1970s. Many of the
young women who entered the profession in the post-war decades had been
part of the various radical student movements of the 1960s and brought their
values into their work. Three influential texts were Anna Pollert's *Girls,
Wives, Factory Lives*, Glucksmann's (writing as Ruth Cavendish) *Women
on the Line*, and Sylvia Walby's *Patriarchy at Work* – two ethnographies and
an account which linked male domination in the workplace to patriarchal
structures in the larger social formation.[6] These, and the many other studies
written at the time, highlighted the patterns of gendered segregation,

---

4 H. Beynon, *Working for Ford* (Penguin: 1973); T. Nichols (ed.), *Capital and
Labour* (Fontana: 1980); T. Nichols and H. Beynon, *Living with Capitalism*
(Routledge: 1979).
5 Nichols and Beynon, *Living with Capitalism*, p. 16.
6 A. Pollert, *Girls, Wives, Factory Lives* (Macmillan: 1981); R. Cavendish,
Women on the Line (Routledge: 1982); S. Walby, *Patriarchy at Work*
(Blackwell, Oxford: 1990).

horizontal and vertical; the view of women's labour as 'secondary'; and the lower valuation placed upon it in terms of status and pay.

In my first book, I defined women's work as being characteristically indoor work, lacking mobility, lighter than 'men's work', often repetitive, dexterous rather than skilled, with associations with domesticity and caring, and sometimes with glamour and physical beauty. By contrast, men's work was visualized as heavy, outdoor, mobile, requiring physicality, often dirty and dangerous, more skilled and technical than 'women's work', and often carrying authority.[7] These are stereotypes, of course, and do not apply to all gendered occupations: male tailors are dexterous, and women agricultural labourers undertake heavy, physical outdoor work. Nonetheless, these ideas and stereotypes have historically underpinned which types of work employers and managers have assigned to women and which to men. This sex-typing of jobs has remained remarkably hard to overturn.

Such cultural stereotypes have underlain the processes of 'gendering' that mark our workplaces. An important contribution was made by the American feminist Joan Acker, who argued that each aspect of capitalist production systems, involving labour markets, workplaces and jobs, was gendered.[8] These processes fostered the emergence and maintenance of hierarchies of reward and power by which male dominance was secured. The gendering of organizations was also displayed in the symbols and imagery that surround workplaces: men in suits are aided by female secretaries in neat feminine attire: men wander around the shop floor, while women sit at desks in the typing pool. Linda McDowell's magisterial study of women in the City of London, *Capital Culture*,[9] showed how, while men were 'at home' in the workplace environment, women's physicality jarred within it; female bodies were marked out as abnormal, with women struggling to present themselves professionally while controlling their sexuality.

Of course the ultimate 'women's work' is that of 'housewife'. The feminist studies on productive work were augmented by the pioneering work of Ann Oakley and Hannah Gavron, which treated housework and domestic labour as a topic for academic study.[10] Their researches confirmed not only the isolating nature of the work (leading to 'the disease without a name' in Betty Friedan's famous phrase)[11] but also its important limiting impact on women's opportunities to take up paid employment.

---

7 Bradley, *Men's Work, Women's Work*, p. 9.
8 J. Acker, 'Hierarchies, Jobs and Bodies: A Theory of Gendered Organizations', *Gender and Society* 4:2 (1990), pp. 139–58.
9 L. McDowell, *Capital Culture: Gender at Work in the City* (Blackwell, Oxford: 1997).
10 A. Oakley, *Housewife* (Penguin: 1974); H. Gavron, *The Captive Wife: Conflicts of Housebound Mothers* (Routledge and Kegan Paul: 1966).
11 B. Friedan, *The Feminine Mystique* (Gollancz: 1963).

As Glucksmann subsequently argued,[12] men and women enter the labour market on different terms; men enter as free agents, with unrestricted time for wage earning (witness the surprising appetite among manual workers for paid overtime and the fondness of male chief executives for 'working breakfast' meetings). Women's participation, by contrast, is framed by the restrictions of their responsibilities for childbearing, child-rearing and domestic duties, which impose restrictions of both time and place. Women with young children tend to seek work near home, and have limited ability to travel (whether as lorry drivers or academics).

Some of the feminist writing of that time highlighted the possibility of newly introduced domestic technologies (such as microwaves, electric cleaning devices, washing and drying machines) lightening what was quickly defined as the 'double burden' of reproductive and production work performed by women. This hopeful scenario was not realized, partly because technology heightened standards and expectations: the weekly wash became a daily chore. There was, as Beynon argues, a rosy-tinged optimism about the 'white heat of technology' in those post-war decades, as espoused by Harold Wilson's Labour government of 1964–70. But Beynon's piece tellingly demonstrates that the liberatory potential of technology has been warped by the profit motive, leading to decline in working conditions and the erosion of skilled industrial work.

This paper will consider how the changes noted by Beynon since the days of these early studies – particularly deindustrialization, the demise of the nine-to-five working day, the march of privatization, and the rise of non-standard contracts – have impacted upon women's current employment situations. Gains made as a result of the feminist highlighting of the inequities of gendered labour and of the development of equality policies and monitoring procedures have been assailed by the political conditions of the twenty-first century.

Breaking through? Ceilings, floors, and pipelines

In the 1980s and 1990s, there was a mood of optimism around the prospects for women's employment. The demand for equality at work from the burgeoning feminist movement had been capped by the passing of the Equal Pay Act (EqPA) 1970, implemented in 1975. The historic strike by the women sewing machinists at Ford's Dagenham plant in 1968, calling for equality with the skilled male production workers, had already signalled increasing militancy among women, who were no longer prepared to accept secondary status. The EqPA also brought Britain into line with the European Economic

---

12 Glucksmann, 'Why "Work"?', *Gender, Work and Organization*, pp. 63–75.

Community (EEC); Article 119 of the Treaty of Rome 1957 stated that 'each Member State shall ensure that the principle of equal pay for male and female workers for equal work or work of equal value is applied'. Thus it helped to support the United Kingdom's entry into the EEC in 1973. The EqPA was quickly followed by the Sex Discrimination Act 1975, which covered direct and indirect discrimination and victimization in employment, as well as in other areas, such as education and financial services. Conformity with European Union (EU) legislation is considered by feminists to have been a mainstay of the fight for gender equality at work. A major fear of those opposed to the current British exit from the EU is that employers freed from its constraints will be quick to shed equality machinery, which they regard as blocks to profit accumulation and the free market.

Politics and the law thus came together to create what I termed 'a climate of equality' in my study of women in trade unions, published as *Gender and Power in the Workplace* in 1999.[13] Women became increasingly confident to challenge gender norms and were increasingly entitled do so. The cause of gender equality became a feature of trade-union activity, with women's structures being set up and women taking a stronger role in forming policy. (When as a researcher I attended my first union conference I was shocked when a great number of the women in the hall suddenly got up and walked out: they had gone to make the tea!) Many larger organizations now had equal opportunities policies, administered by specialist equalities officers. The monitoring body set up to look after the equalities legislation, the now defunct Equal Opportunities Commission (EOC), at first somewhat inactive, had sharpened its teeth when the charismatic Joanna Foster took over as its chair in 1988. This was the optimistic period which I was chronicling. Yet the words of Foster as she ended her tenure should have sounded a warning: 'Equal opportunities is now on the agenda. But recession has pushed it on to the back burner'.[14]

However, at that time the idea that work was undergoing a process of feminization was fairly standard, backed by statistics which showed women's labour market participation levels increasing across Europe. *Myths at Work*, published with colleagues, argued against the idea that this was leading to a position where, in the words of author Fay Weldon, men were finding themselves 'out-earned and outranked' by women.[15] It posited that it was necessary to distinguish between three aspects of feminization: of the labour force, of occupations, and of jobs.

What was clearly happening was the feminization of the labour force. Between 1973 and 1993 the economic activity of women aged 16–60

---

13 H. Bradley, *Gender and Power in the Workplace* (Macmillan: 1999).

14 *Independent*, 15 March 1993.

15 H. Bradley, M. Erickson, C. Stephenson, and S. Williams, *Myths at Work* (Polity, Cambridge: 2000), p. 69.

rose from 51% to 73%, while men's fell from 93% to 86%.[16] Alongside changes in women's attitudes, these innovations were clearly the result of processes of deindustrialization as capitalism in western societies moved to a post-industrial phase. A current increase in service-sector jobs reflected the shift to a more elaborate type of consumerism, emphasizing new diversified and personal forms of service; jobs created were typically considered 'women's work'. These included therapies, beauty routines and other types of 'body work',[17] still proliferating today. There were no nail bars when I was a child.

However, this increase in labour market participation was not accompanied by substantial feminization of occupations. On the one hand there was a definite – and continuing if slow – move of women into the traditional male-dominated professions, such as law and medicine. This arose from the increasing participation of women in higher education and a tendency for them to outperform men in the acquisition of educational accreditations. Rosemary Crompton and Kay Sanderson showed how the 'qualifications lever' was leading women to make inroads into pharmacy and accountancy.[18] However, in the lower layers of the occupational hierarchy, there was little shifting of jobs between women and men, and women continued to be clustered into the 4 Cs of caring, cleaning, catering, and clerical work.

The shift to service work was also a factor in the feminization of jobs. As industrial capitalism gradually gave way to consumerist capitalism, the need for skilled industrial work diminished in the face of increasing proportions of 'customer-facing' service jobs based on interpersonal interactions. It was argued that men would find it difficult to adapt to such jobs requiring 'soft skills', which also characteristically involved what Arlie Hochschild defined as 'emotional labour': the ability to mould one's own personality, appearance and behaviour in order to make clients and customers feel happy and comfortable. Airline hostesses were seen as exemplars of this type of performative labour.[19]

Technological innovation was also implicated as jobs were broken down and deskilled. A classic example appears in *Brothers*, Cynthia Cockburn's study of the print industry.[20] The switch from hot-metal to digital technology allowed women into the industry, challenging the dominance and expertise

---

16 *Ibid.*, p. 74.

17 C. Wolkowitz, *Bodies at Work* (Sage: 2006).

18 R. Crompton and K. Sanderson, *Gendered Jobs and Social Change* (Routledge: 1990).

19 A. R. Hochschild, *The Managed Heart: Commercialization of Human Feeling* (University of California Press, Berkeley: 1983).

20 C. Cockburn, *Brothers: Male Dominance and Technological Change* (Pluto: 1983).

of the male compositors – and incidentally their industrial militancy. Now men seated typing at visual display units felt powerless as they had to wait for technical specialists to fix any faults. This was an exemplary case of the deskilling of labour to tighten managerial control over the labour process, simultaneously disempowering the labourers, as analysed in Harry Braverman's influential text.[21]

Despite these developments, patterns of gender segregation, both vertical and horizontal, have obstinately persisted, and though the gender pay gap has narrowed considerably from its figure of around 40% when the EqPA was passed, it still refuses to go away. A report from The King's Fund ascribes its continuation to four factors that mark out women's continued disadvantage: the undervaluation of the type of work carried out by women; gender-based occupational segregation (accounting for 36% of the gap according to the Office for National Statistics, ONS); the penalty for motherhood, which leads to women falling behind in pay and progression; and the fact that men dominate in top jobs.[22] The data gathered by the government on the gender pay gap in 2018 showed this vertical segregation; 30% of women are in the lowest paid quartile, with 20% in the highest paid, whereas for men these proportions are reversed.

A number of metaphors have been utilized to illustrate the problems faced by women workers. The original one developed in the American business world was the idea of the 'glass ceiling', an invisible barrier which prevented women reaching the top posts in their fields. Newer metaphors include that of the 'glass cliff', the setting up of women to fail by offering them roles which are impossible to fill successfully, or of the 'glass walls' which trap women into what Crompton referred to as 'gendered niches':[23] areas of work into which women are permitted to enter, but which restrict their sideways movement into more prestigious pathways. There is also the concept of the 'leaky pipeline' applied to professional jobs such as medicine, or engineering, whereby women start out equally as well qualified and ambitious as men, but drop out of the pipeline at stages along the way. A recent addition is the idea of the 'labyrinth',[24] which Alice Eagly and Linda Carli use to argue that there is not just one point where women typically come up against a barrier, but a number of setbacks and hurdles which they encounter in their work trajectories, slowing down their progress compared

21 H. Braverman, *Labor and Monopoly Capital: The Degradation of Work in the Twentieth Century* (Monthly Review Press, New York: 1974).

22 D. Ward, *The Gender Pay Gap: What Now?* The King's Fund (14 June 2018), online.

23 R. Crompton, *Women's Work in Modern Britain* (Oxford University Press: 1997).

24 A. H. Eagly and L. L. Carli, 'Women and the Labyrinth of Leadership', *Harvard Business Review* 85:9 (2007), pp. 63–71.

to their male counterparts. I imagine many professional women would identify this as fitting their experience.

These various metaphors, however, all relate to vertical segregation and the workplace trajectories of women in middle-class occupations. Arguably the preoccupation with these barriers has been a recent focus of the feminization debate, which has given less attention to the situation of women from working-class backgrounds or of recent women migrants. Here the relevant metaphors might be that of the 'sticky floor' or the 'brass ceiling', all too visible and impenetrable. Low-level jobs such as cleaning, adult care work, or catering often offer limited progression chances. Gail Hebson, Jill Rubery, and Damian Grimshaw,[25] in their study of domiciliary care workers, point to the fact that most of the women undertaking these jobs face very limited employment options. These forms of work have appeal because the tasks involved are ones with which women are familiar from their domestic and family experiences, so that they feel confident and qualified to undertake them. However, movement into a supervisory role is often the only progression possible, unless women are prepared to retrain.

Much of the work on feminization, then, dealt with the experience of women 'breaking through' the barriers to become top lawyers, politicians, senior managers, professors, and entrepreneurs. Two experts in organizational stress, Marilyn Davidson and Cary Cooper, produced a valuable text based on extensive interviews with women managers at all levels, which also served as a toolkit for women struggling to survive in a man's world.[26] Interestingly it had a foreword from Foster. Their study provides a fascinating picture of the situation at the start of the 1990s. Women made up 44% of the workforce, with 55% working part time. In 1988, women were 11% of managerial staff, an increase from 5% in 1971. However, the posts they held were concentrated in women-dominated sectors (catering and retail) and tended to be in gendered niches such as training and personnel (this was before the days of human resource management). Clustered in middle management rather than senior posts, they constituted less than 1% of chief executives.

Finding that many of the women they interviewed reported symptoms of stress-related illness, Davidson and Cooper explored the problems and barriers faced by women: coping with being the lone or 'token' woman, struggling with work overload and the long-hours culture (given their domestic responsibilities), having to outperform male colleagues to prove they had a right to be there, being excluded from the drinking and sports

---

25 G. Hebson, J. Rubery, and D. Grimshaw, 'Rethinking Job Satisfaction in Care Work: Looking Beyond the Care Debates', *Work, Employment and Society* (*WES*) 29:2 (2015), pp. 314–30.

26 M. Davidson and C. Cooper, *Shattering the Glass Ceiling: The Woman Manager* (Paul Chapman Publishing: 1992).

culture of the 'Old Boys' Network', and facing sexual pestering. Almost all reported some kind of discrimination. Was the way to survive to be more like a man, often at the expense of well-being?: 'I have to be healthy, I can't afford to be sick'.[27]

A recent study by Susan Durbin looks at the contemporary experiences of women who have succeeded in getting 'beyond the glass ceiling'. She shows, sadly, that not much has changed. Her research carried out with forty-two senior women in five organizations illustrates how forty years on from the gender-equality legislation, women are still 'strangers' in the top echelons of large organizations. In a minority, they struggle to progress, in particular faced with the difficulty of reconciling their working and family lives. The option of part-time work proved unsatisfactory as there was a general agreement that a manager's role is unsuitable for a part-timer, especially in the hothouse atmosphere of neoliberal competition with its greed for employees' time. As one woman told Durbin: 'Working part time because you have children doesn't work, you end up working full-time in a part-time role ... a senior role is very difficult to do on a part-time basis.'[28] So, three decades on from the Davidson and Cooper study, women still have to manage like a man!

Turning back the clock: the impact of austerity

Yet such high-earning women are fortunate in that they are largely cushioned from the impacts of the austerity policies adopted by the Chancellor of the Exchequer, George Osborne, in 2010, after the formation of David Cameron's Conservative–Liberal Democrat Coalition. The prime mechanism he employed to reduce the public-spending deficit, inherited from Labour after the financial crash of 2007, was to impose stringent cuts on government grants to local authorities. The Fawcett Society described the effect on women's economic position as a 'triple whammy'. First, the budget cuts led to drastic reduction in public-sector employment, in local government in particular. This had been a source of many secure, reasonably well-paid women's jobs; now their holders were forced into poverty, facing unemployment or being compelled to accept insecure ill-paid work in retail or care. Second, welfare benefits have been held back, with a cruel regime of sanctions and long delays in switching to the Universal Credit scheme, meaning that unemployed women struggled to maintain their families, as signified by the massive increase of food banks and the inexorable rise of rough sleeping in our cities and towns. There are now over 2,000 food

---

27 *Ibid.*, p. 29.
28 S. Durbin, *Women Who Succeed: Strangers in Paradise* (Palgrave Macmillan: 2016), p. 55.

banks in the UK, more than there are McDonald's outlets. The Trussell Trust, which operates many of them, reports a 73% rise in handouts over the past five years, as poverty entrenches itself more deeply. In 2010, as part of the *Ordinary Lives* project with Will Atkinson, I interviewed a young, lone mother, Michelle, working shifts at Tesco, who described to me how she fed her children 'pretend pizza': tomato paste and some grated economy cheddar on bread.[29] It seemed to me that she herself ended the month living on toast in order to save enough money to pay her bills. Third, vulnerable women like Michelle were also hit by the axing or slimming down of schemes, in both the state and voluntary sectors, such as Sure Start and Children's Centres, which had been designed by previous governments to ameliorate the plight of disadvantaged families. This meant that more women's jobs were lost and that the poor were pushed deeper into poverty.

However, although the austerity policies of the successive Coalition and Conservative governments have indubitably heightened inequality and disadvantage, declines in work opportunities and conditions must be located within the broader process, described by Beynon as the end of the long boom of post-war capitalism. This phase had supported the growth of working-class affluence,[30] and a militant trade-union movement fighting for better pay and conditions. Now it began to waver as a result of deindustrialization and the development of the consumer-based, neoliberal brand of capitalism. In Britain, from the 1980s, a switch commenced from state to market provision, with a corresponding ethos of individual responsibility. Simultaneously, technological innovations allowed structures of tightened control over employees – the audit culture very much favoured by New Labour governments – and, as Beynon notes, digital technologies were utilized to transform work processes, allowing the shedding of jobs to heighten profits. The ruthless pursuit of the 'bottom line' and cost-cutting also involved major corporations subcontracting and outsourcing parts of their enterprise to other bodies, almost always leading to deterioration of work conditions and, especially, the development of an array of less favourable contractual conditions – such as part-time, temporary and zero-hours contracts.

The north of England and south Wales suffered the greatest losses, with the decline of the coal, steel, and shipbuilding industries. Long-term unemployment has been the result; and where new jobs were created they were often low-paid and low-skilled service work in retail, leisure,

---

29 Economic and Social Research Council (ESRC), *Ordinary People: Class, Reproduction and Culture* (H. Bradley and W. Atkinson, 2010).

30 J. H. Goldthorpe, D. Lockwood, F. Bechhofer, and J. Platt, *The Affluent Worker: Industrial Attitudes and Behaviour* (Cambridge University Press: 1968); F. Devine, *Affluent Workers Revisited: Privatism and the Working Class* (Edinburgh University Press: 1992).

catering, and call centres. Such jobs were often assigned to women, seen possessed of the right skills and lacking the experience of union militancy. In Durham, miners made redundant often found work as taxi drivers and security guards, jobs which were non-unionized and isolated.

All this change has hit working-class women hard, especially lone mothers, as they continue to shoulder the double burden, but in a climate where managing the family budget is tougher as money gets scarcer. Hence, the rise of food banks, school-holiday-feeding schemes, and other voluntary efforts to offset the effects of profit-hungry capitalism.

The Women's Budget Group (WBG) provides a useful survey of current employment patterns. The vast majority of employed men (87%) are full-time workers, whereas 41% of women work part time. Women now are close to half (47%) of those with jobs, but still much more likely to be in non-standard forms of employment. They make up 74% of part-time workers and 57% of those who indicate their part-time employment is involuntary. They are the greater proportion of those working in temporary employment and in zero-hours contracts (54% in each case). They also account for 69% of low earners (defined as those earning less than 60% of an average weekly full-time wage), a figure that has remained fairly constant since 2011. The WBG also point out that the pay of Pakistani and Bangladeshi women is lower than that of other ethnic groups. Their vulnerability is magnified by the fact that they are concentrated in the public sector and thus more liable to job loss.[31]

This picture partly reflects sectors where women characteristically work, such as retail and catering, where part-time work is prevalent, but it also relates to their continued responsibility for domestic unpaid work. In a study of contemporary gender relations of production, reproduction and consumption,[32] I discuss the rise of 'intensive mothering', which has been described as 'emotionally absorbing, expert-guided, labour-intensive and financially expensive'.[33] While this type of parenting behaviour is more prevalent among the affluent middle class, working-class mothers may be caught up within it because of the increased policing by schools and social workers. Mothers are more and more accountable for all aspects of their children's well-being. The labour-intensive nature of all this is reflected in Table 1, which draws upon data from Beatrix Campbell's study of gender inequality.[34] Women continue to perform the bulk of housework, though men's share has increased over the past fifty years. But the most striking feature is the rise in time given to childcare.

31 Women's Budget Group, *General Election 2019: Towards an Economy which Works for Women* (2019), online.
32 H. Bradley, *Gender* (2nd edn; Polity, Cambridge: 2013).
33 D. Cheal, *The Sociology of Family Life* (Palgrave: 2002), p. 104.
34 B. Campbell, *The End of Equality* (Seagull Books: 2013).

Table 1: Time devoted to domestic labour in two time-periods

Year	Women: Average minutes worked daily	Men: Average minutes worked daily
Housework 1975	197	20
Housework 2004	146	53
Childcare 1970s	26	10
Childcare 2000s	42	17

Despite the gains of the 1990s, statistics show that women remain concentrated in the less well-rewarded sectors. Gender-based occupational segregation remains strong as shown in Table 2. Men dominate in skilled trades and as manufacturing operatives, as well as being a higher proportion of managers. Women are still crowded in traditional female work areas: caring, retail, and clerical work.

Table 2: Percentage share of employment of men and women by occupational categories

	Men	Women
Managers and senior officials	66.9	33.1
Professional occupations	50.3	49.7
Associate professional and technical occupations	57.4	42.6
Administrative and secretarial occupations	23.4	76.6
Skilled trades occupations	90.0	10.0
Caring, leisure and other service occupations	18.0	82.0
Sales and customer service occupations	37.3	62.7
Process, plant and machine operatives	88.6	11.4
Elementary occupations	54.3	45.7

Source: ONS, Labour Force Survey (2013).

While the feminization of the labour force has not been reversed by the decades of neoliberalism, the concentration of women in low-paid work areas means that gendered inequality at work continues, in intersection with ethnic inequality. But worryingly, the features of women's work may set the pattern for the kind of shifts within the organization of labour processes since the end of the long boom which can be seen as *dehumanization*.

Austerity at work: the dehumanization of paid labour

Tim Strangleman's fascinating account of the Guinness Park Royal brewery in London provides a paradigmatic case study of the process of deindustrialization and the deteriorating conditions of work that accompany it.[35] At Park Royal in the post-war decades, Guinness operated a benign paternalistic regime. Alongside secure employment, good pay, and pensions, it offered sports facilities, a theatre, parkland, three-course lunches with waitress service – and free beer! Guinness specifically aimed to build attachment to the brewery by creating a community/family spirit, and, judging by Strangleman's interviews with ex-employees, it succeeded. The experience of working at Park Royal was celebrated by a massive collection of photographs and commissioned paintings, recording the formal and informal aspects of work at the brewery, on which Strangleman was able to draw for his study.

However, this employment idyll ended in the 1980s. Falling profits led the Guinness family to recruit a new non-family director, Ernest Saunders, to modernize the company. Saunders's rationalizing strategies, including the asset-stripping so typical of that era, did indeed bring a rise in profits, but ultimately led to disaster, when he and three other directors were convicted of insider trading and fraud, and imprisoned. This financial scandal led to the further disintegration of the Guinness family empire and various takeovers, with the business finally being owned by the multinational drinks giant, Diageo. Functions such as cleaning and security were outsourced. The workforce was gradually cut and processes automated, until, in the final years, the post-war workforce of 1,500 was reduced to a dozen workers on each twelve-hour shift. Finally in 2005 the brewery was closed and the massive Art Deco building demolished.

Similar changes affected workplaces and workers' lives throughout the UK. At the end of the 1990s, the *Winners and Losers* project, studying the working lives of young adults aged 24–35 living in Bristol,[36] uncovered clear signs of the development of a low-wage economy, and problems faced by this cohort in settling into any kind of stable career. This was confirmed by Tracy Shildrick, Robert MacDonald, Colin Webster, and Kayleigh Garthwaite in their study of employment in Teesside, which they defined as a 'low-pay, no-pay' economy.[37]

35 T. Strangleman, *Voices of Guinness: An Oral History of the Park Royal Brewery* (Oxford University Press: 2019).

36 ESRC (H. Bradley, S. Fenton, W. Guy and J. West), *Winners and Losers in a Changing Labour Market: Gender, Ethnicity and Young Adults' Employment Strategies.* Grant R000 23 8215, October 1999–April 2002.

37 T. Shildrick, R. MacDonald, C. Webster and K. Garthwaite, *Poverty and Insecurity: Life in Low-Pay, No-Pay Britain* (Policy Press, Bristol: 2012).

Indicatively, the Park Royal workforce was mainly male (coopers, copper-smiths, engineers), though women worked as cleaners and caterers. Indeed, male workers could be considered the major victims of the initial phases of deindustrialization, with very many losing jobs formerly considered secure. The bitterness this engendered can be seen in recent political shifts, whereby those in these damaged communities apparently pinned the blame on migration and the EU rather than rapacious neoliberal capitalism. However, in recent years similar deteriorations at work have hit women harder, as service work in turn has been rationalized, privatized and automated.

Another case which can be seen as paradigmatic is that of care workers. Both domiciliary and residential care services had been previously offered by local councils. But from the 1980s the latter quickly opened up to private provision to cope with the increasing demand caused by an ageing society, increased levels of dementia and other severe conditions, affecting families' ability to handle care of elderly parents in the home. It is estimated that 40% of people over 75 suffer from a long-term and disabling condition. Domiciliary care for such people, however, was still provided by councils, providing secure jobs, tolerable conditions and trade-union protection. In recent decades, particularly as a result of austerity policies, much of this care work was outsourced, leading to worsening conditions and pay for these workers.

Adult social care is a massive industry. Around one-and-a-half million people work within it and 82% of the workforce is female. In addition, large numbers of people work as unpaid carers, around five-and-a-half million according to the Commission on Care (figures in this section are taken from this report).[38] The majority of these are women. Within the residential sector there is a high level of employment of migrant workers, many from the EU; in 2015 over a fifth of this workforce was born outside the UK. In my role as a city councillor, I have visited a number of these homes and seen the work that goes on inside them. The quality of the homes varies (some are very expensive and quite luxurious), but the work is very demanding, especially that with dementia patients and those who are essentially bedbound. As a result there is high turnover among staff and difficulties in recruitment. The high costs charged to families for the residents do not feed down into the pockets of the workers.

The exploitation of the outsourced workers is perhaps worse, although, as discussed by researchers,[39] many of them show very strong attachment to the elders they care for and with whom they build relationships. Working in isolation, they are subject to tight control by their managers, increasingly by electronic monitoring. Paid time spent with each client is strictly limited, though many of those interviewed report spending longer than

---

38 Political Studies Association, Commission on Care, *A New Deal for Care and Carers* (2016), online.

39 Hebson *et al.*, 'Rethinking Job Satisfaction in Care Work', *WES*.

their allocation. The carers must provide their own transport; and they are usually not paid for time spent waiting in their cars between slots. Although local authorities try to bargain for living-wage levels when commissioning companies to take over their services, these are often undercut. According to Sian Moore and Lydia Hayes, 97% of these workers are on zero-hours contracts.[40] A secure job has been thoroughly casualized.

The actual labour of care was described graphically in the account of one young graduate interviewed for a project, *Paired Peers*, carried out by a team of researchers from the University of the West of England (UWE) and elsewhere.[41] Jasmine was a sociology graduate from UWE who had tried hard to gain jobs in the voluntary sector at graduate level but ended up taking low-level care work. Her accounts revealed the demanding nature of this type of work, for which nothing at university had prepared her. This was one of her first assignments:

> I had this woman, the second call, it was like 7.30 in the morning, and she has like fully fledged dementia, completely gone bless her ... she was now back to being like completely childlike. And I was helping her have some yogurt, and she was sat up, she'd been bed bound for 10 years. ... University can't teach you the vulnerability of people. And I was so shocked by that situation. And she was lying there in her bed and I was feeding her yogurt and she was just going 'yah' like screaming in my face 'I want my mum, I want my mum', she was like 90 odd so obviously her mum hadn't been around for years but she was a child again. I put yogurt in her mouth 'oh that's nice' and she's screaming in your face 'you fucking bitch, you fucking piece of shit – ooh that's nice'. And she was smearing her shit all over the walls, and I was, like 'I'm not going back, I can't go back, cannot go back'. But I carried on and from that day onwards I have seen it all, I have been called everything, I've had people slashing their wrists in front of me. So there's nothing that life can't throw at me now.

In her final interview, she described a new job working in a day centre for the disabled which offered her better conditions and meant working as part of a team rather than alone. But funding for the facility was under attack, limiting the range of activities it could provide, and she feared that it might lead to closure and redundancy for her.

---

40 S. Moore and L. Hayes, 'Taking Worker Productivity to a New Level: Electronic Monitoring in Homecare: The (Re)production of Unpaid Labour', *New Technology, Work and Employment* (*NTWE*) 32:2 (2017), pp. 101–14.

41 Leverhulme Trust, *Paired Peers: Phase 2* (H. Bradley, A.-M. Bathmaker, N. Ingram, and R. Waller), 2014–17.

It's very much a respite day centre, as in their parents and their carers get to go shopping that they don't get to do when somebody is … needing constant sort of care really. So I'd say three-quarters of them really need to be there. I'd say a quarter just come as the respite thing just so their parents get a break. But some are completely disabled, you know they're in wheelchairs, they don't have any sort of faculties, the only communication they can sort of achieve is blinking at you. It's pretty sad, it's really eye opening. And then there are some there who have just got sort of a mild learning disability who are fully functioning like members of the community, it's just that they couldn't hold down a job or whatever, things like that. … Salary is £16,500 which for down here was good when I was offered it, but I think every company has just caught up lately and it's not great now. … We are absolutely running out of supplies left, right and centre. It was all slashed last year. I think there's about six services that are like us, are under the same sort of branch and between us, the five of us, they were basically given a million each a year, and now … I don't know what the actual figure is but it's led to everything being absolutely slashed and then getting 17p a month. That's not even a day, it's like what can you do on that? … You see we're running out of supplies, like art's a big thing for people, you know it's therapeutic whatever. We're out of paint and we're running out of paper. They're now drawing on pink paper not plain, and it's whatever we've got lying around really. We just scrape by, we're doing things on a shoestring really.

Care workers can be seen as part of what has been named 'the gig economy'. By analogy with the world of popular music, gig workers are not taken on as permanent workers but are paid to perform a particular task, session or time period of work. Jasmine is part of the millennial generation who are entering this world of deteriorating opportunities and heightened competition for the dwindling numbers of secure, well-paid jobs. Many from this generation get sucked into the gig economy as they struggle to find rewarding work and some degree of security.

Uber and Deliveroo are seen as two organizations epitomizing the gig economy, as discussed by Beynon. Uber and its counterparts attract mainly middle-aged men, often from migrant or minority ethnic backgrounds. Deliveroo targets younger people who need to be fit and strong to transport their meal loads on bikes or, if they are more affluent, on motorcycles.

Harry was one of the UWE graduates in the *Paired Peers* study who had taken on a series of temporary jobs as he was saving money to pay for a master's degree. These included a spell with Deliveroo. His account of the system – at that time only just appearing in Bristol – made clear how exploitative it is. The name and logo are significant. The bikers become human kangaroos, with backpacks instead of pouches.

Most evenings and weekends, yeah, so not quite full time. But I've got a bit of money kind of stashed away and I'm paying cheap rent at the moment, so it's a good way to earn a bit of money. And the pay, it's not a great job for a lot of reasons. It's all commission, so you only get paid per delivery. Because you're not an employee, you're a sub-contractor essentially so you don't get a basic wage, you don't get any benefits or cover. It's really bad employment practice, yeah. But at the moment I'm managing to make about £10 an hour from it. … So you have like an app on your phone and you log in and then you get given jobs. You can just get assigned jobs according to how close you are. It's like Uber but for food delivery. So I don't agree with it as a model to employ people because it's bad, it's really exploitative, but it works for me.

Harry's account is also interesting as it exposes the inequalities of class that mark and mar contemporary Britain:

We're delivering food and it's really aimed at students and you deliver a lot of food to Bristol University students. I can't believe how much money they have that they are ordering this like posh takeaway food and paying £2.50 or whatever for me to deliver it on a bike. And that's actually been quite an alienating thing because I just kind of think 'wow … I could never afford this kind of stuff as a student'. You know I don't feel connected to these students. They obviously inhabit different worlds to what I did when I was there, because I would never have thought to order a £20 meal for delivery for myself.

The growth of the gig economy is clearly facilitated by the lifestyle tastes of those who are able to buy in to a luxury-based, consumerist economy.

The danger of the apparent success of organizations like Uber and Deliveroo, in terms of both being able to recruit vulnerable people as labour and making good profits, is that it sets parameters which other companies may follow in their search for ways to increase profitability. In January 2020 the Morrison supermarket chain announced it was scrapping 3,000 managerial roles, replacing them with 7,000 new roles paid on hourly rates of £9. This exemplifies the way the 'gig economy' is becoming entrenched: secure jobs with reasonable pay and some degree of control and decision-making are being downgraded into part-time positions which may offer 'flexibility' for women struggling to balance paid and unpaid work, but consolidate the experience of low pay and precarity.

All processes of major economic change may lead to alterations in the occupational structure and accompanying possibilities of changes in patterns of segregation. There have been suggestions that deindustriali-zation might mean a shift of men into jobs sex-typed as women's work. There have been minimal shifts of this type; for example, some men, especially from minority ethnic communities, have moved into jobs in cleaning and retail. Younger men may face more competition from their female peers in all sorts of areas. Angela McRobbie, in *The Aftermath of Feminism*, has noted the rise of an ambitious career-oriented type of young women, often from minority ethnic backgrounds, who are challenging male domination in areas such as law and finance within the global economy.[42] In contrast, she also highlights how other young women are inveigled into the burgeoning areas of the sex industry. Despite these developments, the data shows that the pattern of gender segregation has not been dented. As discussed above, women struggle to get on in engineering, the care industry remains female-dominated, while the gig economy organizations Uber and Deliveroo are largely populated by men. The factors shaping gender segregation highlighted by The King's Fund (see above) have not changed in the context of austerity. Indeed, the dual burden faced by mothers has been intensified by the demands of parenting, dealing with household budgeting when the cost of living is spiralling, alongside the pressures of work intensification and the low-wage economy.

IT: technological fix or fixed by technology?

Both care work and food-delivery depend crucially on the use of computerized technology. In 1982, André Gorz's heretical text, *Farewell to the Working Class*,[43] predicted that the drive for capitalist accumulation would involve increased computerization and automation of work processes, meaning that the 'socially necessary time' to produce all the desired goods and services for a nation would be reduced. He pointed to the increasing use of robots in the production of cars, claiming that human labour in many industries would become redundant. While such a scenario could imply – and in fact certainly did – a rise in the number of long-term unemployed people, Gorz's 'post-industrial-socialist' vision of the future proposed a sharing out of work so that everybody had more time to spend on other social activities. This could be seen as a version of the 'leisure society' concept popular in the 1960s and 1970s discussed by Daniel Bell and others.[44] This optimistic view foresaw a society where technological advance would free people from the necessity to labour long hours in boring jobs. The concern then was how people would need to be taught how to use their new-found leisure responsibly.

---

42 A. McRobbie, *The Aftermath of Feminism: Gender, Culture and Social Change* (Sage: 2009).

43 A. Gorz, *Farewell to the Working Class* (Pluto: 1982).

44 D. Bell, *The Coming of Post-Industrial Society* (Basic Books, New York: 1973).

However, debates over technology have always tended to bifurcate between those who see technological advance as a way to enrich work and solve evolving economic and social problems, and those who see it as a way of increasing control, tightening surveillance and maximizing profits. While it is clear that technology can be used beneficially to make life safer and easier (where would we be without our smart phones when our trains or planes are delayed?), digital technology has the ability to monitor and log people's activities. Electronic point-of-sale (EPOS) technology enables supermarkets to analyse individual patterns of consumption and thus target consumers with tailored offers and coupons. Is this a useful function, helping people to save money, or a way to exert pressure to consume more from that particular organization? Certainly it seems that at this conjuncture the prime usages of technological innovation have been to tighten control over workers' activities or to cut labour costs. Two examples illustrate this, care work and retail (see above), both being major employers of working-class female labour.

Moore and Hayes explain how electronic monitoring (EM) has been utilized to tighten management control over the care workers' use of time:

> Time-sheets are replaced by integrated computer-telephone technology to log, analyse, report on and invoice service user visits. ... EM involved workers logging in and out through service-users' telephones, but they may also do so by swiping tags on service-users' files with smart phones or may be tracked through smart phones via GPS [Global Positioning System] technology.[45]

In this way, discretionary use of time can be eliminated or, if it is given, will be unpaid. Workers interviewed by Hayes and Moore spoke of pressure, a decline in the quality of service they could offer, and a sense they were 'working for nothing'. One woman, Gillian, spoke of the system bringing an end to 'human care', as she was expected to 'put drugs in you, whip the hoover around quickly and then get out'. The work thus becomes more standardized, more robotic. Hayes and Moore conclude: 'electronic monitoring is a technological driver for very real degradation of employment and pay'.[46] They calculate that private-sector provision of home care is half the cost of the former public-sector service. The price of care is cheapened at the expense of the care workers' pay, conditions and autonomy.

Another area where technology is having a major impact is retail. As noted, the sector is a major employer of women. Indeed it is one of the largest areas

---

45 Moore and Hayes, 'Taking Worker Productivity to a New Level', *NTWE*, p. 101.

46 L. Hayes and S. Moore, 'Care in a Time of Austerity: the Electronic Monitoring of Homecare Workers' Time', *Gender, Work and Organization* 24:4 (2017), pp. 329–44.

of the economy, with 2.7 million employees: Asda and Sainsbury between them employ over 300,000 people. It is also notorious for its bad conditions. A report commissioned by the Trades Union Congress (TUC) stated that in terms of pay progression it was the worst industry in the UK: 42% of workers in retail had failed to progress over a ten-year period but remained 'marooned' in low-paid work.[47] Young workers were sharing this fate. Median pay in 2018 was £8.42 an hour. In London an estimated 40% of retail workers are paid less than the London Living Wage; only hospitality is worse, an area also noted for the employment of vulnerable people, particularly migrants and young people. The recent move by Morrison to shed managerial posts will compound this situation of low pay and limited progression.

Despite the poor pay, these jobs are popular with women as they can arrange shifts compatible with childcare. However, these very jobs are threatened by the installation of automatic tills. On a recent visit to a local Sainsbury's branch I found a whole new row of these installed alongside the old one, now seventeen in all; only four manned tills were operating. A local mini Marks and Spencer is fully automated. This drive to automation is part of efforts to cut labour costs in the face on online retail threats, especially from Amazon. The Office for National Statistics (ONS) estimates that around two-thirds of cashier jobs are at high risk of being replaced by technology.

Farewell to the working class, again: new formations

These impacts of austerity and neoliberalism, reinforced by technological advance, are mainly felt by working-class people, taking away their jobs, lowering their incomes and pushing their families into in-work poverty. This is part of a significant shift in the experience of class and identity, having its origins in the adoption of neoliberal economic policies in the Thatcher era, and consolidated by the crash of 2007–08.

Having lived and worked in Durham at the time of the 1984–85 miners' strike, like Beynon, in 2004 I wrote a paper entitled 'No More Heroes?' for a conference commemorating its twentieth anniversary. I reflected on that watershed industrial event:

It is possible to see the miners' strike as the last great heroic manifestation of a certain type of class politics which was born with the Industrial Revolution, developed through the 19th century and came to maturity in the first half of the 20th century: a politics that was founded on the

---

47 Trades Union Congress (A. Harrop), *Thousands of Low-Paid Retail Workers Are Getting Stuck, Not Getting On* (TUC: 2018).

collective strength of white, skilled, male manual workers and realised through their unions and their links with the political parties of the left.[48]

Beynon similarly refers to the strike as 'the last throw of the dice'. As he emphasizes, miners had become emblematic of militant collectivism, so "'if the miners couldn't do it what chance do we have?'"[49]

In 2020, after an election when the old mining communities notably and dramatically turned their backs on the parties of the left (ousting ex-miner hero Dennis Skinner from the Bolsover constituency he had represented since 1970) and voted for a Conservative government and for Brexit, these judgements seem prophetic. Though class relations are as potent as ever in shaping the lives of communities and of individuals, the pattern of the old class alliance has been shattered. With deindustrialization, union membership has steadily declined, especially among manual workers; growth has typically been in white-collar areas and among women. The factories where large numbers of employees worked were potent sites of socialization for union membership and Labour voting; few remain. Processes of class decomposition have resulted in the collapse of the 'red wall' of the Labour heartlands. One political commentator reflected on the irony of the contradiction between 'the rise of the most left wing leadership in Labour's history and the low ebb of class struggle'.[50]

This contradiction has been a long time brewing, along with the transformations discussed above. As noted by Graham Bash:

> There are material reasons for this – the weakening of class identity and how vulnerable therefore class is to the myth of national identity – to an English nationalism rooted in the imperial past. This loss of class identity is rooted in the defeats of the last 40 years, the breakdown of working class communities, the shrinking of public services.

It is probably an overstatement to speak of the breakdown of class communities per se, as colleagues have suggested that solidary relations (chats in pubs and shops) prompted the desire to leave the European Union.[51] However, undoubtedly there have been significant processes of class decomposition and re-composition reshaping those communities and fracturing previous class relations in a number of ways. Two are discussed

48 H. Bradley, 'No More Heroes?: Reflections on the 20th Anniversary of the Miners' Strike and the Culture of Opposition' , *WES* 22:2 (2008), pp. 337–49, at p. 338.

49 Beynon, 'After the Long Boom', *HSIR*, p. 199.

50 G. Bash, 'Mourn then Organize', *Labour Briefing*, 19 January 2020.

51 L. Mackenzie, 'Brexit is the only way the working class can change anything', *Guardian*, 15 June 2016.

here: the rise of self-employment and the growth of the 'precariat' as an important element of class configuration.

The impact of deindustrialization and the way this has been heightened by austerity is shown in the rise of self-employment since the crash of 2008, as documented in the Labour Force Survey statistics (ONS). To 2005 the number of self-employed men remained about steady for a decade at something over two-and-a-half million. From 2005 to 2019 it rose from 2,646,512 to 3,317,470. About a quarter of these were employed in construction (880,000), with scientific and technical services the next highest (421,000), followed by transport and storage (300,000). These are the owners of the flotillas of white vans which take to the roads of our cities every day. Such jobs are highly individualized and mainly non-unionized.

Interestingly there has been a similar pattern in women's self-employment. From 1995 to 2005 it hovered around 800,000–900,000, but in 2005 it burst through the million mark, rising to 1,670,952 by 2019. Predictably self-employed women were concentrated in the service sector: health and social care, retail, scientific and technical services. Other services were the largest group, containing the various kinds of 'body work'.

Many of these female small businesses are run by women with children, as a solution to the problem of reconciling paid work and childcare. Businesses can be run from home while children are at nursery and at school. Computerization has enabled many professional women to work in this way, offering advisory services, training and tutoring, web design, editing, and consultancy. The term 'mumpreneurs' was coined to convey how many such enterprises grew out of the actual experience of mothering: childminding and nursery provision, classes for baby and mother, and production and selling of baby clothes and playthings. In Bristol there has been a proliferation of cafes, sandwich bars and niche restaurants, often run by young graduates and providing jobs for other young people. Those without degrees are more likely to be found offering beauty services, hairdressing, sewing or catering from home bases.

Self-employment is notorious for its fragility and the potential for self-exploitation. Many businesses fail in the first couple of years. Others, such as some of the catering enterprises or the various house-maintenance services (plumbing, decorating, carpentry, electrical works, scaffolding), can be extremely profitable. Such self-employed workers can be seen as part of the *petite bourgeoisie*, a class fraction notorious for its individualism and conservatism.[52] Yet culturally many are still rooted within the former working-class communities.

---

52 M. Innanja, 'The Interesting Case of the Petite Bourgeoisie', *Medium*, 30 March 2018. F. Bechhofer and B. Elliott, *The Petite Bourgeoisie: Comparative Studies of the Uneasy Stratum* (Macmillan: 1981).

By contrast, the 'precariat' has been denoted by Guy Standing, its prime chronicler, as the 'new dangerous class'.[53] Standing argues that the growth of the precariat has been a major feature of hypercompetitive neoliberal capitalism from the 1980s. It can be seen as a successor to the 'reserve army of labour' as defined by Karl Marx.[54] Trapped in insecure and temporary work, it differs from the traditional working class by its enforcedly transient engagements with the labour market and the lack of occupational identity as a base for class identity. Moreover, it does not only consist of unskilled labourers, but also has an element of skilled and qualified people forced to rely on short-term and precarious work. Prime examples would be the army of hourly paid lecturers who make up a high proportion of the UK's academic labour force or the many young law graduates employed on temporary contracts as paralegals in city banking. The 'gig economy' is the habitat of the precariat.

Thus the contemporary working class can be seen as more complex and more fragmented, from aspirational well-paid, skilled craftsmen and entrepreneurs at the top (and some moving up into the middle class), down to the long-term unemployed struggling on benefits. As I pointed out in 'No More Heroes?':

> Many elements of the contemporary working-class nexus are not associated with the world of waged labour at all: those dependent on benefit, young folk of the ghettoes and estates hooked in to the 'black economy' or the alternative world of DJs and clubbing, the increasingly numerous early retired, full-time carers (mainly women), the self-employed tradesmen, are all outside the capital/labour relation of appropriation and exploitation as classically described by Marx and Engels. But they are nonetheless the victims of class injustice and inequality. Not all the working class works.[55]

Trade unions and resistance to dehumanization

This recomposition of the working class has clearly impacted on trade-unionism and hastened the decline in union density, since many of these new forms of employment are isolated and non-unionized. Union membership reached a low of 6.23 million in 2016, although there was a slight upturn in cach of the next two years. Union density in 2018 was 23.4%: among male employees it had fallen to 20.7% while rising among women to 26.2%,

---

53 G. Standing, *The Precariat: The New Dangerous Class* (Bloomfield: 2011).

54 K. Marx, *Capital: A Critique of Political Economy, Vol. 1* (1887).

55 Bradley, 'No More Heroes?', *WES*, p. 345.

reflecting the results of deindustrialization. Unionization continues to be much stronger in the public sector at 52.5% than in the private sector, where it has slumped to 13.2%.[56]

However, this does not rule out trade-union resistance to dehumanization and deterioration. The first opposition to austerity came from trade unions organizing major demonstrations in London. The two big celebrations of union tradition, the Dorset festival commemorating the Tolpuddle Martyrs and the Durham Big Meeting or Miners' Gala, continue to draw large crowds and mark the importance of solidary collectivism.

Moreover, there have been stirrings among those in low-paid precarious work, with recent actions by Deliveroo bikers, McDonald's employees, and cleaners employed on the London Underground. As I was writing this piece, it was announced by UNISON that outsourced workers in Bath and north-east Somerset, who had been contracted out to Sirona, were scheduled to be taken back as a council in-house service. In America, Germany, Spain, Poland and the UK, Amazon workers struck for the first time ever in 2019. Amazon warehouse workers – who can be employed either directly or by a labour-supply contractor[57] – were facing speeds of 200–300 orders per hour in twelve-hour shifts. In Britain, GMB officers reported that warehouses were dangerous, causing accidents and broken limbs to workers, many of whom are women and from ethnic minorities: some 600 injuries had been recorded over the three years to 2019. Stuart Applebaum, president of America's retail union, offered a powerful statement condemning the conditions in the company and echoing the theme of dehumanization:

> Testing hundreds of thousands of workers' physical limits as though they were trained triathletes is the wrong approach. Operating at these speeds for this duration means Amazon needs to hire more workers, under more sustainable speeds that don't put workers' lives in jeopardy. Amazon needs to understand that human beings are not robots.[58]

Young organizers have been appointed to work at building union membership among the scattered workers employed by such giant profit-making organizations. This work is highly significant, since, as Beynon suggests, these successful giants establish working practices which are then copied by others across the global economy.

Added to continued strike action by some of the more militant unions, such as the Communication Workers' Union (postal workers) and the Rail,

---

56 Statistics from Department for Business, Energy and Industrial Strategy, May 2019.

57 The identity of the employer is an important factor in the law of industrial action and employment rights.

58 J. Settembre, *World Economic Forum*, 16 July 2019.

Maritime and Transport Union, these movements rebut the idea of workers' apathy. This is despite the fact that legislation removing tort immunity for strikes where ballot participation is below 50% has made it difficult for some unions to take industrial action. This has been the case in the past few years with the University and College Union (UCU), which has had to resort to ballot disaggregation in its recent attempts to mount action over pay claims. For example, the University of Bristol has reached the threshold but the University of the West of England has persistently failed to do so and so cannot participate in the UCU strike action.

Where forces are ranged against traditional forms of worker organization, new forms may emerge. One such form is community unionism, exemplified by the successful growth of ACORN, a powerful organization which evolved to fight against evictions of tenants from the private rented sector in Bristol in 2015 and to expose the shortcomings of slum landlords letting out properties in terrible conditions of damp and decay. ACORN now has many branches across the country, a rapidly expanding membership and is turning its attention to other issues that affect disadvantaged individuals and organizations. On its website it describes itself as

> A community based union of working class people – tenants, workers, residents. We are a member-led campaigning organisation supporting and empowering low-income communities across the country to fight for a better life.

Using techniques of community-based organization and direct action, ACORN has challenged large organizations such as Santander and NatWest banks, forcing them to change their policies on mortgages. It managed to get legislation passed against a variety of dubious fees levied by letting agents, and forced NatWest to drop its policy of forbidding those with its 'buy to let' mortgages from taking on benefit dependants as tenants. It is now turning its attention to campaigning for the re-municipalization of buses in areas with metro-mayors, on the model of Transport for London.[59] ACORN's strength, and that of similar organizations springing up globally, is that it goes beyond a version of being working class rooted only in occupations and sees how work, housing, and community facilities come together to create class-based community identities.

---

59 ACORN the Union: https://acorntheunion.org.uk.

Conclusions: austerity and resistance

Living with capitalism in the twenty-first century is no joke. It has ruined the lives of many people in the UK and around the world, including claims that thousands of deaths have been caused by the policies of austerity. In the UK the worst sufferers have been women, especially lone mothers, migrants, and disabled people. This paper has focused on the way the restructuring of global capitalism on neoliberal principles has affected opportunities for women workers, through the advocacy of the dominance of the market; privatization of former state-run provision (from utilities to prisons and schools); the demolition of the 'post-war consensus' and the welfare state that it created; the stigmatization of welfare claimants, marked by a draconian sanctions regime; an ethos of individual responsibility; and attacks on collectivism through disabling legislation.

In Britain this has widened the gap between rich and poor, increased the proportion of people in in-work poverty, especially women and migrants, led to proliferation of food banks and the spectacle of young people sleeping in shop doorways across our towns and cities. While Conservative welfare policies stress that 'work' is the route out of poverty and benefit dependence, this does not take into account the widespread experience of low pay especially among youth; young graduates interviewed for the *Paired Peers* project often reported annual wages of £12,000–18,000 – no chance of getting a mortgage.

But the lawyers, business owners and financiers who sit in the House of Commons have no experience of the dehumanizing nature of many of the new jobs. What I have highlighted in this article is that, in the last two decades in particular, what Braverman described as the 'degradation of labour' has been taken to new lengths, facilitated by computerized systems. Where people have not been displaced by technology, they have been increasingly controlled by it. The warm human relationships of the Park Royal labour regime are gone, to be replaced by lonely workers in vans, taxis and cars, driven by telephoned directions and apps. It is no surprise that the word 'robot' appears in Beynon's article and has in mine. Human beings are a 'resource' equivalent to physical and technological components of the labour process – robots, cogs in the machine, infinitely replaceable.

In my 'No More Heroes?' paper I stated that every regime of power engenders its own culture of opposition. It can be argued that a new culture of opposition is emerging in a response to the regime of consumer-based neoliberal global capital. One manifestation in Britain has been the political movement which sprung up around the election of Jeremy Corbyn as Labour leader, often referred to as the 'Corbyn surge'. This brought together trade unions, socialist organizations, climate-change activists, minority rights groups, and a generation of young people, especially graduates, deprived of opportunities to build decent lives with secure jobs, homes, and families.

ACORN stands as a classic example of this new movement, which has resonance with others around the globe: the *gilets jaunes* in France, the Bernie Sanders campaign in America, and Podemos in Spain. Whether the radical British movement inside the Labour party will survive the departure of Jeremy Corbyn as leader is debatable, but the campaign for social justice will continue. Demands for an end to the low-wage economy, the restoration of job security, with a continued campaign for gender and ethnic equality at work, must be central to such a movement. Our society must not tolerate the dehumanization of work.

Epilogue

This paper was begun in January 2020. As it approached its final editing, a new actor appeared on the scene: the devastating coronavirus. There can be no doubt that its effects on national economic systems will be drastic and, at least in the short term, transformative; but in March 2020 anybody would be rash to predict the outcome. Two things have become clear, though. First, the vulnerability of the self-employed and workers in the gig economy has been exposed and perhaps more broadly understood by the population. Second, people have seen how many essential workers (nurses, carers, retail assistants, postal workers, drivers, refuse collectors) are among the lowest paid. Just maybe, when the coronavirus pandemic is over, societies will agree that 'low-pay, no-pay' is no longer an acceptable way to manage their economies.

UWE Bristol Business School
Frenchay Campus
Coldharbour Lane
Bristol BS16 1QY

HSIR 41 (2020) 137–67

https://doi.org/10.3828/hsir.2020.41.6

After the Long Boom: The Reconfiguration of Work and Labour in the Public Sector

Bob Carter

Huw Beynon's reflections on the origins and fate of his and Theo Nichols's analysis of *Living with Capitalism: Class Relations in the Modern Factory* are much appreciated.[1] The book succeeded, as did his earlier *Working for Ford*,[2] in melding workers' sharp observations of the nature of work 'in a giant international chemical producer', 'Chemco', 'one of Britain's most progressive manufacturing companies', with a more generalized critique of capitalist production.[3] Its focus, while centring on a single factory, was far removed from plant sociology,[4] instead posing a series of questions on the nature of management and supervision, employer strategy, trade-unionism, and the politics of trust. All these concerns were captured within a framework emphasizing that, notwithstanding the heavy capital investment and the gloss of modern management, capitalism tended to reproduce relations that were essentially similar in some respects, most notably in the continuing generation of unskilled, low-trust, meaningless jobs, as well as new highly skilled occupations.[5] As Beynon notes, Karl Marx and Harry

---

I would like to thank the editors for their advice and assistance.

1 H. Beynon, 'After the Long Boom: Living with Capitalism in the Twenty-First Century', *Historical Studies in Industrial Relations* (*HSIR*) 40 (2019), pp. 187–221; T. Nichols and H. Beynon, *Living with Capitalism: Class Relations in the Modern Factory* (Routledge and Kegan Paul: 1977).
2 H. Beynon, *Working for Ford* (Penguin, Harmondsworth: 1973).
3 Beynon, 'After the Long Boom', *HSIR*, pp. 187–8.
4 Plant sociology analyses the factory in isolation, 'bounded by the factory walls and confined to the present': M. Burawoy, *The Extended Case Study Method* (University of California Press, Oakland, CA: 2009), p. 5.
5 This debate continues; see C. Warhurst, F. Carre, P. Findley, and C. Tilly (eds), *Are Bad Jobs Inevitable? Trends, Determinants and Response to Job Quality in the Twenty-First Century* (Palgrave: 2012).

Braverman were the guides to this world rather than Robert Blauner or John Goldthorpe and his colleagues.[6]

Beynon's article sees *Living with Capitalism* as 'documenting industrial life at the end of an era: an era that would become called "the long boom" or the "golden age of capitalism" and more ubiquitously as "Fordism".'[7] Notwithstanding the terminology, 'the end of an era', he perceives no absolute change in the nature of capitalist social relations before and after. What is presented are accounts and assessments of both continuity of the past within Chemco and features that signalled new practices: older features of capitalism (the preponderance of unskilled work, for instance, and to a lesser extent the recognition and incorporation of trade unions) coexisted with features that appeared novel at the time but portended later more widespread developments (such as the increasing mobility of capital, changes in supervision, and the increasing use in public-sector organizations of management organizational forms and techniques developed in the private sector).

By providing a longer-term view, Beynon is able to reinforce and generalize some of the book's conclusions. The first and obvious one was that technology, under capitalist social relations, did not offer the possibility of better jobs. The work at Chemco also demonstrated that 'participation, team working, job rotation, job enrichment',[8] to all of which the company was committed, proved empty promises. Rather the changes proved, in concert with new management controls and supervisory practices, to be the harbinger of the development of lean manufacturing in auto manufacture,[9] before wider adoption. Chemco also proved to be an example of companies relocating to areas not traditionally associated with manufacturing. Beynon details how, with increasing mobility of capital and the decline of manufacturing, old areas become abandoned, destroying stable local labour markets, and profoundly weakening organized labour in Britain. In this unfolding, the defeat of the 1984–85 miners' strike became a culmination and consolidation of a process of union decline rather than its cause.

This decline of the trade-union movement had a number of sources. The closure and relocation of manufacturing sites was in part a response

6 H. Braverman, *Labor and Monopoly Capital: The Degradation of Work in the Twentieth Century* (Monthly Review Press, New York: 1974); R. Blauner, *Alienation and Freedom: The Factory Worker and His Industry* (University of Chicago Press: 1964); J. H. Goldthorpe, D. Lockwood, F. Bechhoher, and J. Platt, *The Affluent Worker: Industrial Attitudes and Behaviour* (Cambridge University Press: 1968).

7 Beynon, 'After the Long Boom', *HSIR*, p. 187.

8 *Ibid.*, p. 191.

9 J. Womack, D. Jones, and D. Roos, *The Machine that Changed the World* (Macmillan: 1990).

to adverse economic conditions engineered by hostile Conservative administrations. Geoffrey Howe, as Chancellor of the Exchequer (1979–83) in Margaret Thatcher's Conservative government, adopted a sharply deflationary stance in the midst of a recession, causing unemployment to rise to over 12%, a figure only just below that reached in the depression of the 1930s. As Beynon notes, in addition to economic conditions, the unions and workers were on the receiving end of successive legal restrictions and political initiatives to disrupt trade-union and social organization.[10] Little was reversed by subsequent Labour administrations, a judgement supported by Thatcher herself. As Conor Burns reported:

Late in 2002 Lady Thatcher came to Hampshire to speak at a dinner for me. Taking her round at the reception one of the guests asked her what was her greatest achievement. She replied, 'Tony Blair and New Labour. We forced our opponents to change their minds'.[11]

Indeed, under the New Labour government led by Tony Blair (1997–2007) the Conservative legislation was retained and policies antipathetic to trade-union organization and state employees were extended across the public sector. Other features set in train by Conservative reforms also continued, such as the growth in importance of the retail sector and private services. Manufacturing may have declined but, for many factory workers, experiences of drudgery and alienation were mirrored in the new massified warehouses and call centres, work in the latter being graphically described as constituting 'assembly lines in the head'.[12]

This summary inevitably conveys little of the rich content and breadth of Beynon's achievement and this response should be read as an addendum rather than a critique. It seeks to add more on the transformation of work and class relations during the period since the book's publication, through a focus on the significance of state and public-sector employment, as well as the potential for trade-union organization and resistance. Mirroring Beynon's historical approach, the following section examines the fortunes of state and public-sector employment and the consequences for labour in

---

10 For a re-evaluation of Thatcherism using a Poulantzasian framework see C. Leys, 'Thatcherism and British Manufacturing', *New Left Review* 151 (1985), pp. 5–25; and A. Gallas, *The Thatcherite Offensive: A Neo-Poulantzasian Analysis* (Haymarket Books, Chicago, IL: 2016).

11 C. Burns, 'Margaret Thatcher's greatest achievement', *Conservative Home*, 11 April 2008, online.

12 P. Taylor and P. Bain, '"An Assembly Line in the Head": Work and Employee Relations in the Call Centre', *Industrial Relations Journal* (*IRJ*) 30:2 (1999), pp. 101–17.

the move towards what had variously been called a workfare state and a managerial state.[13]

Challenges to the state as a 'model employer'

Living with Capitalism was published at a time of relatively stable public employment, which had increased substantially, from 5.9 million in 1961 to 7.4 million in 1979.[14] The period to 1979 had seen the expansion of nationalized industries (British Steel in 1967 and British Leyland in 1975), as well as further growth in state activities. At the same time, growth was offset by redundancies, particularly in British Coal (formerly the National Coal Board).[15] Just as Beynon characterizes the context for the book as 'the end of an era', so is it possible to discern the beginning of a crisis in the old model of managing public employees.

The idea of the public sector as 'a model employer' developed after the First World War.[16] The general recommendations of the Whitley Committee, aimed at 'securing a permanent improvement in the relations between employers and workmen'[17] via the establishment of joint industrial councils, were largely ignored by private-sector employers. In contrast, the public sector as a whole was to be assigned a particular industrial relations mission – to be a 'model employer' by implementing 'a range of practices which today constitute good management'.[18] This

13 See B. Jessop, 'The Transition to Post-Fordism and the Schumpertarian Workfare State', in R. Burrows and B. Loader (eds), *Towards a Post-Fordist Welfare State* (Routledge: 1994), pp. 13–37; J. Newman and J. Clarke, *The Managerial State: Power, Politics and Ideology in the Remaking of Social Welfare* (Sage: 1997); and G. Dumenil and D. Levy, *Managerial Capitalism: Ownership, Management and the Coming New Mode of Production* (Pluto: 2018).

14 J. Cribb, R. Disney, and L. Sibieta, *The Public Sector Workforce: Past, Present and Future* (Institute for Fiscal Studies: 2014).

15 Until the late 1950s the coal industry employed nearly 700,000. By 1964 that figure had been reduced to 500,000 and the numbers halved again to 250,000 by the time the book was published. For the coal industry's decline, see H. Ritchie, *The Death of UK Coal in Five Charts*: https://ourworldindata.org/death-uk-coal (2019).

16 For a fuller account of the state as a 'model employer' see B. Carter and P. Fairbrother, 'The Transformation of British Public-Sector Industrial Relations: From "Model Employer" to Marketized Relations', *HSIR* 7 (1999), pp. 119–46.

17 Ministry of Reconstruction, Committee on the Relations between Employers and Employed (Whitley), *Final Report*, Cd 9153 (1918), para. 1.

18 Royal Commission on the Civil Service (Priestley), *Report*, Cmnd 9613 (1955), para. 146.

did not necessarily mean that governments paid their employees above the rates of private employers, but that there should be consultation and equity in treatment and processes.

In practice, public-sector industrial relations were far from even and uncontested and it took the need for trade-union co-operation during the Second World War to secure the recognition of the then National Association of Local Government Officers (NALGO) in 1943.[19] With the adoption of Whitleyism as the model by the post-war Labour governments, 1945–51, for industrial relations in the National Health Service (NHS) and some of the newly nationalized industries, the ethos of Whitley became widely accepted in the public sector. Thus, a Treasury statement argued that being a member of an association was not only good for the individual civil servant, but it was also beneficial for the Civil Service as a whole:

> it is hopeless to try to find out the wishes of a scattered unorganised body of civil servants each of whom may express a different view. When they get together in representative associations, the collective wish can be democratically determined and passed on to the 'management' with real force and agreement behind it; the 'management' know where they stand and can act accordingly.[20]

This acceptance of public-sector unions was conditioned by a number of factors. The expansion of the public sector was a result of a popular radicalism that had been engendered by austerity-induced mass privation of the 1930s and the demands and sacrifices of the Second World War. Reconstruction necessitated huge investments that only the state could mobilize. The coal industry was a case in point. Post-war regeneration was predicated on the demand for energy that Britain's fragmented, privately owned and inefficient mines could not provide. Competing demands of labour and capital resulted in the 'post-war settlement', which

---

19 For the National Union of Public Employees (NUPE)'s attempts to win recognition, see B. Fryer and S. Williams, 'Latecomers to Trade-Union Democracy: The Emergence, Growth and Role of Union Stewards in the National Union of Public Employees', *HSIR* 40 (2019), pp. 117–52. Interestingly, they state, 'Once established, the machinery and procedures, at both provincial and national levels, made little provision for the involvement of NUPE's lay members, especially locally, other than to bring forward individual cases and "appeals" for the union's officials to process through the joint machinery', p. 137.

20 Cited in G. S. Bain, *The Growth of White-Collar Unionism* (Clarendon Press, Oxford: 1970), pp. 124–5. This could be conceived as a move towards 'bargained corporatism'; see C. Crouch, *Class Conflict and the Industrial Relations Crisis* (Heinemann: 1977).

comprised a number of key features: nationalization; social welfare; and economic regulation designed to maintain full employment.[21] Nationalization and the growth of social welfare and public administration brought in rationalization and standardization, conditions that encouraged union recognition.[22]

The growth of education, health, and social-welfare occupations meant that the state employed a considerably higher proportion of scientific and professionally qualified staff. The higher concentration gave rise to a style of management that was both bureaucratic and based on professional knowledge. Managers in these occupational areas, in contrast to the private sector, tended to possess relevant professional qualifications and direct experience of practice in the field.[23] Bureaucratic and professional relations, moreover, encouraged particular kinds of trade-union practice. White-collar trade unions could be monopolized by people with more time and resources, such as senior grades in local government and head teachers in education.[24] Even in areas dominated by manual work, national collective bargaining meant that few issues were dealt with at local level, and with Whitleyism encouraging a model that passed interpretation of agreements through a series of stages, the scope for workplace union organization and local industrial action was limited.[25]

By the 1960s, there was a growing concern with Britain's relative economic decline, manifested through the Conservatives' attraction to macro-economic planning, exemplified by the establishment in 1962 of the National Economic Development Council, a tripartite body with representatives from the government, employers and trade unions.[26] The Labour

---

21 B. Jessop, 'The Transformation of the State in Post-War Britain', in R. Scase (ed.), *The State in Western Europe* (St Martin's Press: 1980), pp. 23–93.

22 D. Lockwood, *The Blackcoated Worker: A Study in Class Consciousness* (Allen and Unwin: 1958).

23 P. Armstrong, 'Engineers, Managers and Trust', *Work, Employment and Society (WES)* 1:4 (1987), pp. 421–40.

24 As P. Blyton, N. Nicholson, and G. Ursell, 'Job Status and White Collar Members' Union Activity', *Journal of Occupational Psychology* 55 (1981), pp. 33–45, demonstrated, the occupation of union positions by managerial employees often proved to be an extension of managerial control into the union itself. This phenomenon has implications for trade unions and social class relations at the workplace. The latter is explored in B. Carter, *Capitalism, Class Conflict and the New Middle Class* (Routledge: 2015).

25 The procedures smothered local action and organization, largely limiting critics of Whitleyism to those from the left. See B. White, *Whitleyism or Rank and File Action?* (NALGO Action Group: 1975). There were exceptions, prime among them being the coal industry in which piecework and strong work bonds encouraged local organization and disputes.

26 H. Pemberton, 'Relative Decline and British Economic Policy in the 1960s', *Historical Journal* 47 (2004), pp. 989–1013.

government, 1964–70, increasingly shared a view that the public sector was inefficient and not fitted for the task of modernizing Britain, a task explicitly part of Harold Wilson's government, as Beynon notes.[27]

One attempt to deal with this 'problem' was the Labour government's stimulation of productivity bargaining in public-sector manual work after the creation of the National Board for Prices and Incomes (NBPI) in 1965, and its attempts to limit price and wage increases. Private employers could circumnavigate the restrictions in numerous ways that the highly visible public sector could not. This caused public-sector wage rates to fall behind. Productivity bargaining was offered as the solution: thus began a process of restructuring social relations of work in the public sector so that they increasingly replicated those in the private sector.[28] Ambitions ranged much wider than the introduction of productivity deals, however. In 1967 the NBPI reported a lack of a clear managerial hierarchy in local government employment and complained that 'insufficient attention is given to equipping the officials concerned with the necessary managerial expertise and to encouraging cost consciousness'.[29] Councils were also subject to wider reforms. Four official inquiries – Maud, Mallaby, Redcliffe-Maud, and Bains[30] – collectively reported that, as in business, the need was for 'integration, control from the top, more efficient use of money and labour, forward planning for a bigger impact on the job in hand'.[31]

Alongside the concern with the organizational form and managerial structures of the public sector came pressure to reform the work of professional occupations. Thus the labour process in social work was reorganized following the report of the Seebohm Committee in 1968.[32] Unified social service departments were established which centralized decision-making

27 Beynon, 'After the Long Boom', *HSIR*, p. 188.

28 Fryer and Williams, 'Latecomers to Trade-Union Democracy', *HSIR*, p. 147, referring to the National Board for Prices and Incomes (NBPI), *Report 29, The Pay and Conditions of Manual Workers in Local Authorities, the National Health Service, Gas and Water Supply*, Cmnd 3230 (1967). They note that its solution to low pay and low productivity 'was much greater use of work study, job evaluation, and bonus schemes at local level.'

29 NBPI, *Report 29, The Pay and Conditions of Manual Workers in Local Authorities, the National Health Service, Gas and Water Supply*, Cmnd 3230 (1967), p. 24.

30 Committee on the Management of Local Government (Maud), *Report* (HMSO: 1967); Committee on the Staffing of Local Government (Mallaby), *Report* (HMSO: 1967); Royal Commission on Local Government (Redcliffe-Maud), *Report*, Cmnd 4040 (1969); Study Group on Local Authority Management Structures (Bains), *Report, The New Local Authorities: Management and Structures* (HMSO: 1972).

31 C. Cockburn, *The Local State* (Pluto Press: 1977), p. 13.

32 Committee on Local Authority and Allied Personal Social Services (Seebohm), *Report*, Cmnd 3703 (1968).

within local authorities, moving power from social workers to departmental hierarchies, and from departments to policy-advisory committees. The new structures assumed that:

> Social workers work within technical, administrative and legally-based policies conveyed to them through the Area Team Leader from the Director of Social Services. … These stipulations express prescriptions within which they must work, including the relationship they are expected to employ in performing their tasks and how to develop their roles.[33]

Such organizational changes impacted upon social work practice. The gap between conception and execution widened, making Braverman and labour process theory as relevant to public-sector, professional workers as to manual workers in Chemco. Consequently, for social work:

> the split is about the knowledge of the whole process involved in the work. Some people have to carry organisation and some have to plan it: *the two groups are inevitably split* and do not have cross membership. Thus above team leaders there are very few who *ever meet clients*; below team leaders there are very few people who are structurally allowed to plan or co-ordinate.[34]

Again, it was in the 1960s that rationalization began to take hold on the National Health Service. The 1962 Hospital Plan laid down guidelines for the establishment of large district hospitals. Their development was accompanied by, and further stimulated, changes in organization and management methods:

> specialist officers were created, particularly in the ancillary areas like catering, supplies and purchasing. Management services were streamlined and experienced both a rise in size and status, particularly work study, organisational methods … training and personnel. There

---

33 Conference of Socialist Economists State Group, *Struggle over the State* (Conference of Socialist Economists: 1979), pp. 105–6.

34 D. Gould, cited in S. Bolger, P. Corrigan, J. Booking, and N. Frost, 'Welfare Workers and the Changing British State', in *idem, Towards Socialist Welfare Work* (Palgrave: 1981), p. 67 (original emphasis). It can be argued that this process of separation of conception from execution, central to Braverman's thesis, is equally apparent in academia today.

were the beginnings of an inflow of managers with experience in private industry.[35]

Increasing managerialism eroded the autonomy of the nursing profession, with matrons relegated to a relatively low position in the management hierarchy. With the implementation of the 1966 Salmon Report,[36] the matron was subject to increased control, being now seven steps down in the hierarchy of control, responsibility limited to the co-ordinating and supervising of a divisional unit. There was already some evidence that the matron's managerial role was strengthened albeit within a shrunken area of authority.[37] The corollary of the increased managerial role, at the expense of knowledge and involvement in nursing, was the call for enrolment of non-medical staff to management posts: a reversal of traditions of promotion through an internal labour market.[38]

The restructuring of the matron role portended other changes. Ward sisters, for instance, lost decision-making powers to nurses superior in the hierarchy in three areas – 'determining the rota of work-allocation on the ward; disciplining junior nurses; and perhaps above all training'.[39] Moreover, in spite of the fact that ancillaries were increasingly employed, taking over many of the menial tasks traditionally performed by nurses, the increased division of labour did little to improve nursing. However, it is in the very treatment of ancillaries that the application of capitalist rationality was clearest. Two reports from the NBPI, 1967 and 1971,[40] highlighted their alleged low productivity, and within both were calls for 'clearer allocations of management responsibilities, the wresting of ancillary work from

35 D. Vulliamy and R. Moore, *Whitleyism and Health: The NHS and its Industrial Relations*, *Studies for Trade Unionists* 5:19 (1979), p. 17.

36 Committee on Senior Nursing Staff Structure (Salmon), *Report* (Ministry of Health: 1966).

37 See B. Carter and H. Stevenson, 'Teachers, Workforce Remodelling and the Challenge to Labour Process Analysis', *WES* 26:3 (2012), pp. 481–96, for the implications for class relations, and particularly proletarianization, of more recent, but similar, changes in teaching.

38 For the later changes to public-sector internal labour markets see D. Grimshaw, K. Ward, J. Rubery, and H. Beynon, 'Organisations and the Transformations of the Internal Labour Market', *WES* 15:1 (2001), pp. 25–54.

39 P. Bellaby and P. Oribabor, 'The Growth of Trade Union Consciousness among General Hospital Nurses, Viewed as a Response to "Proletarianisation"', *Sociological Review* 25:4 (1977), pp. 801–22, at p. 811.

40 NBPI, *Report 29, The Pay and Conditions of Manual Workers in Local Authorities; the National Health Service; Gas and Water Supply; idem, Report 166, Pay and Conditions of Service of Ancillary Workers in National Health Service Hospitals*, Cmnd 4644 (1971).

nursing control, tighter job definitions, greater standardisation of methods and equipment, and more centralisation in fewer units'.[41]

Education, unlike other areas of the public sector, had changed throughout the period in ways that were generally supported by its workforce. A series of reports and academic studies – Robbins Report 1963; Plowden Report 1967; Jackson and Marsden; Bernstein[42] – demonstrated how early streaming in primary schools and the tripartite system of grammar, technical and secondary-modern schools, as created by the 1944 (Butler) Education Act, caused a wastage of talent through discarding working-class children. As a result of the Plowden Report, streaming in pre-secondary education lessened considerably and 'child-centred education' became widespread. As to secondary education, supported by teachers, their organizations and influential sections of the population,[43] Labour was committed to expanding comprehensive secondary schools, but, by not compelling local councils to adopt the policy, undermined rather than eliminated the tripartite structure (private schools, as ever, remained untouched). Moreover, streaming by 'ability' was reproduced inside the comprehensives, reinforced by introducing Certificates of Secondary Education (CSEs) alongside the General Certificate of Education (GCE).

If teachers had little fundamental objection to the direction of pedagogy and organization of education, they grew increasingly frustrated by their own terms and conditions. Class sizes remained large, making effective education difficult. However, it was pay that caused the first national teachers' strike in 1969, when a reluctant leadership was pressured by growing rank-and-file agitation to organize a ballot.[44] Teachers had been affected, like other public-sector workers, by the Labour government's incomes policy. As a result:

---

41 Vulliamy and Moore, *Whitleyism and Health*, p. 18.

42 Committee on Higher Education (Robbins), *Report*, Cmnd 2154 (1963); Central Advisory Council for Education (England), *Children and their Primary Schools* (Plowden), *Report* (HMSO: 1967); B. Jackson and D. Marsden, *Education and the Working Class* (rev. edn; Penguin, Harmondsworth: 1966); B. Bernstein, *Class, Codes and Control, Vol. 3: Towards a Theory of Educational Transmissions* (Routledge and Kegan Paul: 1977).

43 B. Simon, *Education and the Social Order: 1940–1990* (Lawrence and Wishart: 1991), pp. 288–9, argued that 'It represented that section of the "new middle class" that rejected private education and instead was determined to shape the national system to its own wishes'. Bernstein, *Class, Codes and Control*, makes a similar point about the importance of middle-class support for child-centred learning.

44 Early in 1969 the National Union of Teachers had accepted an offer that primarily benefited head teachers and other senior grades. Duncan Hallas, a former teacher, gave a coruscating commentary on the decision: 'Survey: Teachers', *International Socialism* (1st series) 36 (1969), pp. 13–14.

In the UK rates of pay of public sector workers were effectively controlled by the incomes policy ... while earnings in the private sector rose rapidly ... The attempt by public sector workers to restore their position relative to private sector earnings is one of the main explanations of the surge in public sector wage rates in the late 1960s.[45]

Richard Hyman, writing contemporaneously of the 'unprecedented' public-sector upsurge, noted that 'Only a few years ago, strike action by teachers – or, more recently, hospital ancillary workers – would have been unthinkable. Other sections of public employees – NALGO and, in 1973, several of the Civil Service unions – have also abandoned their traditional inhibitions against industrial militancy.'[46]

In 1969 the Labour government proposed legislation, based on its *In Place of Strife* White Paper, curbing strikes.[47] Its proposals included the Secretary of State's power to order unions, in certain circumstances, to hold a ballot before an official strike was held; the Secretary of State's power to order a 28-day 'conciliation pause' in certain unconstitutional strikes (in breach of procedure agreements); and an Industrial Board with the power to fine employers, unions or individual strikers for not complying with such orders. The attempt failed due to widespread trade-union opposition and splits within the government and Parliamentary Labour Party, but arguably prepared the ground for passage of the incoming 1970 Conservative government's Industrial Relations Act 1971. Here again, there was widespread trade-union opposition, culminating in industrial action for the release of dockers ('the Pentonville Five') imprisoned for failing to obey a court order restraining them from 'blacking or encouraging others to black lorries entering or leaving' a depot they were picketing. With an unofficial strike movement gathering pace, the Trades Union Congress (TUC) called for a one-day general strike, but the dockers were released after a hasty House of Lords judgment and (unsolicited) representations from the Official Solicitor.[48]

---

45 J. L. Fallick and R. F. Elliott, 'Incomes Policies, Inflation and Relative Pay: An Overview', in *idem* (eds), *Incomes Policies, Inflation and Relative Pay* (Cornell University, New York: 1973), pp. 246–63, at p. 260.

46 R. Hyman, 'Industrial Conflict and the Political Economy: Trends of the Sixties and Prospects for the Seventies', in R. Miliband and J. Saville (eds), *Socialist Register 1973* (Merlin: 1973), pp. 101–52, at pp. 103–4.

47 Department of Employment and Productivity, *In Place of Strife: A Policy for Industrial Relations*, Cmnd 3888 (1969).

48 R. Darlington and D. Lyddon, *Glorious Summer: Class Struggle in Britain, 1972* (Bookmarks: 2001); quotation at p. 159. The Prime Minister's authority was further undermined by the miners' strikes in 1972 and 1974, culminating in the 1974 general election on the theme of 'Who rules Britain?'. The resulting Labour victory made clear the answer was not the Conservatives.

Elected in March 1974, Labour again attempted to secure trade unions' agreement to curb wages (even in the face of rising inflation) by means of the 'Social Contract'. This comprised a succession of pay norms and a pro-labour legislative programme expressly drawing on the Donovan Report.[49] The Trade Union and Labour Relations Act 1974, as amended in 1976, restored the Trade Disputes Act 1906 in wider language to take account of judicial decisions made in the 1960s. Of most relevance here was the right for union lay representatives (including, as a result of the Health and Safety at Work Act 1974, union-appointed safety representatives) to paid time off for training. Legislation encouraged the rapid growth of workplace representatives,[50] but also began the process of formalizing the informal system of industrial relations through greater recognition and integration of lay representatives into unions that Donovan had identified as the cause of much unofficial action.[51]

The first few years of incomes policy saw union co-operation, with the Labour government securing TUC agreement to settlements below the rate of inflation. Following the conditions for an International Monetary Fund loan in 1976, public-spending levels were reduced in 1976–78 by 9.5% in real terms after allowing for inflation,[52] with a number of hospitals closed, and schools, houses and roads deteriorating. As working-class incomes were cumulatively reduced, and tensions rose between the government and trade unions, growing working-class opposition could be seen in rising strike numbers. In the first phase of the incomes policy (1975–76) 3.2 million days were lost through strikes. By stage four (1978), the days lost had risen to 15 million. The following year, with the policy in tatters, 31 million days were lost in what became known as the 'Winter of Discontent'.[53] Although not exclusively a public-sector strike wave, public-sector workers were prominent as NHS and local authority workers struck in large numbers. The subsequent general election of 1979 returned a Conservative government.

---

49 Royal Commission on Trade Unions and Employers' Associations, 1965–68 (Donovan), *Report*, Cmnd 3623 (1968).
50 The speediest growth in the number of full-time senior stewards was in the years 1975–77: *The Times*, 12 July 1975; H. A. Clegg, *The Changing System of Industrial Relations in Great Britain* (Blackwell, Oxford: 1979), pp. 51–3, gives a range of numbers of shop stewards for the years 1959–78.
51 For the Donovan Report's recommendations, see P. Smith, 'Order in British Industrial Relations: From Donovan to Neoliberalism', *HSIR* 31/32 (2011), pp. 115–54.
52 J. Hughes, 'Public Expenditure: The Retreat from Keynes', in K. Coates (ed.), *What Went Wrong: Explaining the Fall of the Labour Government* (Spokesman, Nottingham: 1979), pp. 103–23, at p. 105.
53 For a symposium on the strikes that collectively comprise the 'Winter of Discontent', see *HSIR* 36 (2015), pp. 181–226.

The reconfiguration of the public sector, 1979–2020

As international pressures heightened awareness of Britain's lack of competitiveness, continuing with established arrangements seemed less and less feasible to governments. One sign of this mood change was the reception given to Robert Bacon and Walter Eltis's 1976 book, *Britain's Economic Problem: Too Few Producers*, in which they argued that the public sector was an unproductive burden on the private sector, threatening capital accumulation.[54] While Labour governments from 1964 had initiated reforms in the public sector aimed at making it more efficient and responsive to the needs of British capitalism, the incoming Conservative government decisively changed direction – freeing capital through financial and fiscal deregulation, and reductions in taxes and public expenditure. Collectively, such policies amounted to a major attack on the tenets of the post-war settlement which had underpinned the growth and stability of the public sector. No time needs to be spent examining the Conservative's conscious, and intended, 'creative destruction' of British manufacturing,[55] or the legislation aimed at neutering trade-unionism. Here the concentration is on Conservative policies towards the public-sector work and organization which restricted public-sector employment and reduced its cost by the privatization of public corporations, introduction of 'efficiency' measures, and the use of cash limits to contain pay settlements. With the privatization of the utilities (gas, water, electricity), transport (British Rail, National Bus Company, British Airways), and manufacturing (Rolls-Royce, British Steel), the public-sector headcount fell from over 7 million in 1979 to 5 million in 1997.[56] The proceeds from the sales funded rising unemployment, which in turn depressed wages more generally through expanding the 'reserve army of labour'.[57]

Not only were the cost and relative size of the public sector under scrutiny, however, but also its ethos and form. State policies shifted away from collective provision, welfare justice and rights, towards an emphasis on 'economy, efficiency and effectiveness'. If the term 'model employer'

---

54 R. Bacon and W. Eltis, *Britain's Economic Problem: Too Few Producers* (Macmillan: 1978). For an assessment of its political impact, see B. Mitchell, 'The Bacon–Eltis Intervention: Britain 1976', Modern Monetary Theory blog, (2016), online.

55 Unemployment more than doubled to over 3 million from 1979 to 1983: *ibid*. Manufacturing output fell by 14%: C. Leys, 'Thatcherism and British Manufacturing', *New Left Review* 151 (1985), pp. 5–25; T. Nichols, *The British Worker Question: A New Look at Workers and Productivity in Manufacturing* (Routledge and Kegan Paul: 1986), chs 9 and 10.

56 Office for National Statistics, *Long-Term Trends in UK Employment: 1861 to 2018* (ONS: 2019).

57 See Alan Budd's comment in Beynon, 'After the Long Boom', *HSIR*, p. 197.

retained any currency, it was achieved by mirroring the most advanced initiatives and techniques of the private sector. In areas that remained in public ownership, local authorities and hospitals were compelled to put out specified functions to tender under 'compulsory competitive tender'.[58] Local authorities, for instance, were radically transformed from employers of labour and providers of services to enabling authorities, managing a range of external contracts. According to the public-sector trade union, UNISON, compulsory competitive tendering led to 300,000 manual job losses in the 1980s.[59] The administration and provision that remained in public ownership was organized in fragmented business units.[60] Health, local government, education, welfare and the Civil Service were all subject to parallel changes. Alongside measures promising greater discretion, such as local management of schools, initiatives were developed to test performance and to set targets for change and improvement. This might involve union discussions with local management about how work could be retained in-house. The inevitable result was that unions, while remaining hostile to the principle of tendering, in practice, representing workers in services up for tender (cleaning, catering, portering), appeared complicit at workplace level in decisions to save costs and undermine members' conditions, thereby weakening membership identification with the union.[61]

These trends are best understood as part of what has been widely described as 'new public management' in which policy determination is centralized and enforced through the setting of targets, but managers are allowed some discretion over how to achieve them and are held accountable for their performance. Christopher Pollitt was clear that new public management amounted to the 'injection of an ideological "foreign body" into a sector previously characterized by quite different traditions of thought'.[62] Bureaucratic and administrative relations within workforces were thus transformed into managerially driven ones.[63] The state model

---

58 S. Evans and R. Lewis, 'Labour Clauses: From Voluntarism to Regulation', *Industrial Law Journal* 17:1 (1988), pp. 209–26: 'In the enterprise economy promoted by the Government in the 1980s, labour clauses and, indeed, contract compliance in general, impeded the operation of the free market and impose burdens on employers. Their curtailment is one element of the policy of labour market deregulation', p. 209.

59 UNISON, *Budget Briefing* (UNISON: 1994).

60 D. Foster and P. Scott, 'Competitive Tendering of Public Services and Industrial Relations Policy', *HSIR* 6 (1998), pp. 101–32, at p. 111.

61 See B. Carter and G. Poynter, 'Unions in a Cold Climate: MSF and Unison Experiences in the New Public Sector', *IRJ* 30:5 (1999), pp. 499–513.

62 C. Pollitt, *Managerialism and the Public Services: The Anglo-American Experience* (Blackwell, Oxford: 1993), p. 26.

63 Carter and Fairbrother, 'The Transformation of British Public-Sector Industrial Relations', *HSIR*.

of employment now ignored ideas of equity and standards, and mirrored capitalist organization and techniques. Changes were widespread. The Griffiths Report (1983) introduced general management into the NHS in an attempt to increase control and efficiency, putting managers in conflict with clinical priorities. The NHS and Community Care Act 1990 created an internal market with Health Authorities charged with purchasing services from providers (mostly acute hospitals and those providing care for people with mental health problems and learning difficulties, and older people). Following the 1988 Ibbs Report, the Civil Service was fragmented by the establishment of agencies and executive offices, semi-autonomous managerial structures with discretion to provide services or goods according to proxy market criteria.[64] By 1997, 110 agencies, formally employers with their own bargaining arrangements, had been established; other discrete sections of the Civil Service, including Customs and Excise and the Inland Revenue, were organized on 'Next Steps' lines. This initiative involved 'the separation of the small core of civil servants involved in the policy-making and ministerial support functions of government departments from the vast majority of civil servants, who are involved in the service delivery or executive functions of central government'.[65]

The incorporation of decentralized bodies as separate employers had implications for trade-union organization and strike law.[66] Union representatives were restricted to their new employer only. Workers, used to trade-union coverage, now found themselves without experienced representatives. The consequence was the weakening of the collective organization. The decentralization, fragmentation, and the variation in terms and conditions proceeded alongside a centralization of control from Whitehall. The 1988 Education Reform Act, for instance, enabled Local Management of Schools, thereby 'freeing' schools from local authority control and public accountability.[67] At the same time, a national curriculum was established, and schools were subject to a new central inspection regime, the Office for Standards in Education. The legislation also allowed for City Technology Colleges to be established; these were outside local authority control and funded via a contract with central government. A

---

64 R. Griffiths, *NHS Management Inquiry* (Department of Health and Social Security: 1983); K. Jenkins, K. Caines, and A. Jackson (Efficiency Unit), *Improving Management in Government: The Next Steps: Report to the Prime Minister* (Ibbs Report) (HMSO: 1988).

65 A. Butcher, 'A New Civil Service? The Next Steps Agencies', in R. Pyper and L. Robins (eds), *Governing the UK in the 1990s* (Palgrave: 1995), pp. 61–84, at p. 61.

66 P. Smith, 'Labour under the Law: A New Law of Combination, and Master and Servant, in Twenty-First Century Britain?', *IRJ* 46:5–6 (2015), pp. 345–64.

67 As was also the case with further education colleges.

purchaser–provider split was established in some areas of social services, such as adult social care, with adverts appearing for social care brokers aimed ostensibly at matching clients' needs with appropriate providers: in reality, it matched clients to any available and affordable resource, suitable or otherwise. The effects here, as elsewhere, have been long term:

> the culture of capitalism has colonized the public sector as business thinking and practices have crossed the public–private sector divide and been transplanted into activities such as social work. As a result, social work has shifted to operating in accordance with a 'quasi-business discourse' within which the explicit or implicit assumption is that social work should, as far as possible, function as if it were a commercial business concerned with making profits.[68]

In 1997 New Labour succeeded the Conservatives in government and was equally identified with this mode of management. The term 'New' Labour was first mentioned in 1994 by Blair at the Labour Party conference. The following year, Blair steered amendments to Clause IV of the Labour Party's constitution, effectively jettisoning commitment to nationalization and certainly any conception of socialism.[69] Hugo Young stated: 'It has taken Blair less than a year to prove he's a real leader. A promised land without dogma stretches invitingly before him'.[70] This lack of dogma provided the space for ambiguity. His claim that New Labour's modernization agenda comprised a 'third way' approach, a combination of planning and market-driven strategies, underestimates the continuity with the policies pursued by Thatcher. He was able to boast that Britain had the least regulated labour market in Europe, retaining the anti-union legislation of its predecessor.[71] Simon Jenkins noted that there was no return to high income taxes, no rush to European corporatism, and that privatization was driven into every corner of public services. His verdict was that the consequence of Labour's programme 'was to render Thatcherism irreversible'.[72]

---

68 J. Harris, *The Social Work Business* (Routledge: 2002), p. 5.
69 The clause read: 'To secure for the workers by hand or by brain the full fruits of their industry and the most equitable distribution thereof that may be possible upon the basis of the common ownership of the means of production, distribution and exchange, and the best obtainable system of popular administration and control of each industry or service'.
70 H. Young, 'Marching forward, looking backward', *Guardian*, 1 May 1995.
71 C. Howell, 'Is There a Third way for Industrial Relations?', *British Journal of Industrial Relations* (*BJIR*) 42:1 (2004), pp. 1–22; P. Smith and G. Morton, 'New Labour's Reform of Britain's Employment Law: The Devil is not only in the Detail but in the Values and Policy Too', *BJIR* 39:1 (2001), pp. 119–38.
72 S. Jenkins, *Thatcher and Sons: A Revolution in Three Acts* (Penguin, Harmondsworth: 2007), p. 6.

However, there were some differences. The mantra of 'public sector bad, private sector good', so evident under the Conservatives, ceased,[73] although the government's frustration with the public sector was frequently and strongly voiced. Having called for a 'permanent revolution' in public-service reform to meet the public's 'high expectations', Blair voiced the government's frequent characterization of public-sector unions as conservative forces: 'The danger sometimes is that public service unions and associations get into a competition over who can flag up the most resistance to change'.[74] There were new initiatives, such as the introduction of tuition fees for university undergraduates, initially at £1,000 in 1998 and raised to £3,000 in 2004, but few of the changes introduced by the Conservatives were reversed. Labour accepted that increased financing for state services was needed after a long period of Conservative indifference, but it was made clear that support was tied to reforms of working practices and terms and conditions of work. This led to tensions with public-sector unions. Funding of capital projects and service delivery, via the Private Finance Initiative,[75] wage restraint and restructuring, further reflected continuity with the previous Conservative administrations.

Much of New Labour's policy towards the public sector was expressed under the rubric of 'modernization', a deliberately disarming concept, suggesting technicality and value-neutrality.[76] Many of the proposals could be seen as simply an extension and deepening of new public management. In the NHS, one of the principal beneficiaries of increased spending, 'the government commissioned new entrants from the private sector at premium payments, setting up independent sector treatment centres (ISTCs) that undertook routine diagnostics and elective surgery. Initially, these were said to reduce waiting times but later, "competition in the treatment of NHS patients" was signalled'.[77] There was a growth of demands and targets, and new managerial systems to realize them. Stephen Harrison maintained that one result was 'a medical labour process which embodies many of the specific characteristics of Fordism and ... scientific-bureaucratic

---

73 B. Carter, 'Restructuring State Employment: Labour and Non-Labour in the Capitalist State', *Capital and Class* 63:1 (1997), pp. 65–84.

74 T. Blair, 'Blair sets out EU treaty demands', BBC News 24, 18 June 2007.

75 The Private Finance Initiative was introduced by John Major's government as a mechanism for using private capital for major public-sector infrastructure products. It was enthusiastically continued by New Labour. See 'The Private Finance Initiative (PFI): a brief history and a financial dissection' (2015), online. For the financial consequences of the scheme for hospitals, see D. Gaffney, A. Pollock, D. Price and J. Shaoul, 'PFI in the NHS: Is there an Economic Case?', *BMJ* 319 (1999), pp. 116–19.

76 N. Fairclough, *New Labour, New Language?* (Routledge: 2000).

77 S. Tailby, 'Public Service Restructuring in the UK: The Case of the English National Health Service', *IRJ* 43:5 (2012), pp. 448–64.

medicine'.[78] The failure of general managers to control specialists, who continued to refuse attempts to curtail their autonomy under the cloak of patient needs, was countered by the innovation of 'specifically "clinical governance", a mechanism for controlling the health professions, most obviously Doctors'.[79]

This fate of general managers inside hospitals contrasted to their continued advance in the Department of Health: 'in 2007, there was just one career civil servant among the 32 top officials'.[80] Central control was strengthened by new legislation placing a statutory duty on hospitals for the quality of care, effectively making chief executives responsible for the clinical, as well as the financial performance. The Commission for Healthcare Improvement was charged with conducting a rolling programme of reviews, visiting every hospital trust over a period of three to four years,[81] in much the same way that Ofsted inspected schools, awarding stars according to performance, with poor results leading to sanctions, including mergers or replacement of the managerial and clinical leadership. The 2013 Francis Report, into 400–1,200 excess patient deaths at Mid Staffordshire hospitals between 2005 and 2008, showed the way the pressures affected clinical care and social relations in health. Hospital care had been poor, but was seriously worsened by redundancies and restructuring in early 2006 which cut staffing levels, changed the skill-mix, and subordinated patient care to the financial targets necessary for achieving the goal of 'Foundation Trust' status.[82]

Pressure to change bore down on all layers of staff: 'Ward sisters have been widely re-titled "ward managers" taking on a wide range of management functions, formerly performed by middle managers'.[83] Nurses' roles were extended and, while this extension was portrayed as a positive opportunity for them, in reality it signalled growing workloads and intensification of labour. A reduction of the hours of junior doctors in 1991 increased the pressure on nurses to take over routine work, such

78 S. Harrison, 'New Labour, Modernisation and the Medical Labour Process', *Journal of Social Policy* 31:3 (2002), pp. 465–85, at p. 466.
79 *Ibid.*, p. 472.
80 Tailby, 'Public Service Restructuring in the UK', *IRJ*, p. 452.
81 Hospital Trusts, effectively public corporations, were set up by the National Health Service and Community Care Act 1990. In 2002, the Labour government announced the establishment of foundation trusts, with greater financial autonomy.
82 The Mid Staffordshire Foundation Trust Public Inquiry (Francis), *Report*, Executive Summary, HC 947; 3 Vols, HC 898 (2013). For a review of the issues and responses of trade unions, see B. Carter and R. Kline, 'The Crisis of Public Sector Unionism', *Capital and Class* 41:2 (2017), pp. 217–37.
83 H. Cooke, 'Seagull Management and the Control of Nursing Work', *WES* 20:2 (2006) pp. 223–43.

as inserting intravenous cannulas and certifying expected deaths.[84] They now found themselves being responsible for more 'hands on' management and 'hands on' medical care: '"Hands on" was a widely used term, which denoted routine, low-status work considered suitable for delegation to nurses'.[85] The introduction of the health-care assistant grade had led to greater division of labour and inequality.[86] Further down the hierarchy, facility-management companies continued to grow. As some critics noted:

> Visitors to NHS hospitals today are struck by the way that more and more of their forecourts looked like cramped shopping malls. Cluttered with outlets of W. H. Smiths and café chains, NHS hospitals have become yet another outlet for the fast food industry, adding to the very problems of obesity and heart disease that the NHS exists to combat.[87]

Behind the commerce, enforced efficiency savings meant more outsourcing. Serco, one of the largest companies involved, increased its turnover from £1,202 million in 2006 to £2,587 million in 2011.[88] As functions were turned over to private companies (portering, catering, cleaning, laundry and linen, passenger transport, and some administration), work was intensified and employee conditions worsened,[89] aided by the disruption of trade-union organization and the legal restrictions on industrial action in concert with other groups.[90] In the community care sector, the monthly trade journal, *Community Care Market News*, argued that Labour's policy successor to compulsory competitive tendering, 'Best Value', 'will undoubtedly mean more outsourcing of in-house residential and domiciliary care service'.[91]

The second major beneficiary of Labour's increased spending was education. For teachers, this was accompanied by changes to the labour process. Centralized control was strengthened by the national curriculum and the addition of literacy and numeracy hours. Teachers were now not only instructed what to teach but, especially in the case of literacy, also how to teach. Independence from local authorities was further reinforced

---

84 *Ibid.*, p. 226.

85 *Ibid.*, p. 231.

86 D. Grimshaw, 'Changes in Skills-Mix and Pay Determination among the Nursing Workforce in the UK', *WES* 13:2 (1999), pp. 295–328.

87 A. Pollock, C. Leys, D. Price, D. Rowland, and S. Gnani, *NHS Plc: The Privatisation of Our Health Care* (Verso: 2005), p. 19.

88 I–FM, '15 years of growth and change', online.

89 A. Munro, 'Thirty Years of Hospital Cleaning in England and Scotland: An Opportunity for Better Jobs', in C. Warhurst, F. Carré, P. Findlay, and C. Tilly (eds), *Are Bad Jobs Inevitable? Trends, Determinants and Response to Job Quality in the Twenty-First Century* (Palgrave: 2012), pp. 176–90.

90 See Smith, 'Labour under the Law', *IRJ.*

91 Pollock *et al.*, *NHS Plc: The Privatisation of Our Health* Care, p. 186.

by the growth of Academy and Trust schools, again enhancing head teacher managerialism and accountability. From 2001, when faced with both recruitment and retention crises and the prospect of teacher industrial action over workload, New Labour turned to the idea of workforce remodelling, claiming that standards could be improved and workload reduced by stripping teachers of non-core work and assigning it to teaching assistants and other support workers. In 2003, the government, employers and all but one of the teacher unions, the National Union of Teachers (NUT), signed a national agreement, *Raising Standards and Tackling Workload*.[92]

The agreement identified twenty-five tasks (including collecting dinner money, mounting displays, data entry) that teachers were no longer to perform; guaranteed 10% of teachers' normal timetabled teaching time for planning, preparation and assessment (PPA); and a ceiling of thirty-eight hours per year that a teacher could be required to cover for absent colleagues, with an expectation that over time there would be 'a downward pressure on the burden of cover'.[93] The NUT, the largest classroom teachers' union in England and Wales, refused to sign because of opposition to the use of teaching assistants to take whole classes – a development that undermined the union's desire for teaching to be an all-graduate profession – and because of reservations about the agreement being the centrepiece of a long-term social partnership with the government.

While the 'partnership' unions (National Association of Schoolmasters/ Union of Women Teachers, the Association of Teachers and Lecturers, and Association of School and College Leaders) contrasted their years of marginalization with the new access and influence with ministers, there were dangers in such arrangements. When decisions were reached, all parties had to adhere to confidentiality about positions and compromises, and were bound by the agreement to promote and promulgate the decisions. A consequence was that unions appeared to be the executive arm of the government's strategy, or, as John McIlroy argued, became junior partners in change management.[94] Moreover, there was no indication that the agreement fulfilled its overarching aim of reducing teachers' workloads. Not only were the hours of work of teachers not significantly reduced,[95] but the very restructuring of their jobs gave routine work to poorly paid teaching assistants and other support staff, only to load teachers with

92 B. Carter, H. Stevenson, and R. Passy, *Industrial Relations in Education: Transforming the School Workforce* (Routledge: 2010).

93 Department for Education and Skills (DfES), *Raising Standards and Tackling Workload: A National Agreement* (DfES: 2003), p. 7.

94 J. McIlroy, 'New Labour, New Unions, New Left', *Capital and Class* 24:2 (2000), pp. 11–45.

95 School Teachers' Review Body (STRB), *Teachers' Workloads Diary Survey* (STRB: 2008).

additional expectations. The inspection regime, the tests and the league tables increased the pressure on teachers to perform, and these pressures have been made more effective by the growth and extension of management posts.[96]

Other parts of the public sector were also subjected to changes in ownership, organization and labour processes. Costs were saved, and terms and conditions worsened by further prison privatizations. In the police force, as in teaching and health, there was an expansion of lower grades through the creation of community support officers. From 2004, in Revenue and Customs, tens of thousands of job losses were imposed by the Chancellor of the Exchequer, Gordon Brown. The same year, in direct emulation of private-sector manufacturing, the Gershon review proposed a radical transformation of the labour process through the creation of call centres and large processing centres organized on 'lean production methods'.[97] The work process was deskilled and intensified, and the role of managers transformed from one based on knowledge of taxation, advice-giving and co-ordination, to one that primarily monitored performance against hourly targets.[98] Research reported people crying in the car park at the prospect of the new work regime, of greater levels of illness, and bullying sickness and absence procedures.[99]

Targets were central to government policy.[100] One commentator argued that, in the NHS:

> The Health Commission's finding last week that pursuing targets to the detriment of patient care may have caused the deaths of 400 people at Stafford between 2005 and 2008 simply confirms what we already know. Put abstractly, targets distort judgment, disenfranchise professionals

---

96 Carter *et al.*, *Industrial Relations in Education*, pp. 135–9.

97 B. Carter, A. Danford, D. Howcroft, H. Richardson, A. Smith, and P. Taylor, '"All They Lack Is a Chain": Lean and the New Performance Management in the British Civil Service', *New Technology, Work and Employment* 26:2 (2011), pp. 83–97. P. Gershon, *Releasing Resources to the Front Line: Independent Review of Public Sector Efficiency* (HM Treasury: 2004).

98 B. Carter, A. Danford, D. Howcroft, H. Richardson, A. Smith, and P. Taylor, '"They Can't Be the Buffer Any Longer": Front-Line Managers and Class Relations Under White-Collar Lean Production', *Capital and Class* 38:2 (2014), pp. 323–44.

99 B. Carter, A. Danford, D. Howcroft, H. Richardson, A. Smith, and P. Taylor, '"Stressed Out of My Box": Workers' Experience of Occupational Ill-Health in Lean Clerical Work', *WES* 27:5 (2013), pp. 747–67.

100 Prime Minister Blair established a Delivery Unit in 2001, headed by Michael Barber; see M. Barber, *Instruction to Deliver: Fighting to Transform Britain's Public Services* (Methuen: 2008).

and wreck morale. Put concretely, in services where lives are at stake – as in the NHS or child protection – targets kill.[101]

Where consequences were not so grave, skilled workers were 'disenfranchised' by the narrowing of service provision, game playing and the dilution of public-sector values.[102]

The financial crash of 2008 saw widespread public anger at the feted role of the financial sector. In contrast, the public sector acquired a new status and importance. However, under the Conservative–Liberal Coalition government, 2010–15, this was quickly reversed.[103] Public-sector borrowing had risen steeply because of tax losses and financial support of the banks. Public-sector workers were again seen as a cost:

> Britain is fast becoming two countries, one occupied by workers in the private sector, victims of market forces and the deepening recession and the other by public sector employees, wallowing in the privilege of having their pay and pensions guaranteed by the Government.[104]

Twelve years of unprecedented austerity was imposed. In the initial period, 2010–11 and 2012–15, cuts were targeted mainly on local government, with a 27 per cent cut in the central support that finances the bulk of local services and a 68 per cent cut in the communities' budget that supports social housing'.[105] Education retained almost all of its then current budget in cash terms but suffered a 60% reduction in its capital budget. The NHS was protected against inflation but experienced an 18% reduction in capital spending. The relative protection of health and

---

101 S. Caulkin, *Observer*, 2 March 2009.
102 G. Richards and M. Chegus, 'Does "Deliverology" Deliver?' (2018), online.
103 D. Grimshaw noted that even the governor of the Bank of England had expressed concerns, telling the Treasury Select Committee in 2011 that the billions spent bailing out the banks and the need for public-spending cuts were the fault of the financial services sector: '*The price of this financial crisis is being borne by people who absolutely did not cause it* ... Now is the period when the cost is being paid, I'm surprised that the degree of public anger has not been greater than it has'(original emphasis). D. Grimshaw, 'The Economic Crisis and Policy Change: The Agenda and Consequences of the Cameron Government', *European Work and Research Centre, University of Manchester* (2012), p. 9.
104 N. Tebbit, 'A nation of haves and have-nots', *Daily Mail*, 1 April 2009. For a response see: P. Toynbee, 'Don't blame the public sector for catching the fat cats' virus', *Guardian*, 3 March 2009.
105 A. Hastings, N. Bailey, G. Bramley, M. Gannon, and D. Watkins, *The Cost of the Cuts: The Impact on Local Government and Poorer Communities* (Joseph Rowntree Trust: 2015), online.

education expenditure caused cuts in other areas to be deeper – averaging 19%.[106] Throughout the entire period there were also ongoing cuts in welfare benefits and local authority provision. Women, in particular, were subjected to detrimental changes in pension benefits as the state pension age rose to 65 for women between 2010 and 2018, and then to 66 (2019–20), 67 (2026–28), and 68 (2044–46) for both men and women.[107] The terms of occupational pension schemes were also worsened as retirement ages were raised to match the rising state pension age. Contributions were increased, and accrual rates lowered: workers were faced with the prospect of working longer, paying more and receiving less. Annual public-sector pay increases were frozen or restricted to below inflation. Throughout the period the average nominal wages for government employees had risen under 11% compared to inflation measured by the consumer prices index of over 17%. One prominent welfare specialist considered the welfare cuts to be of such 'exceptional scale, speed and composition and distributional impact' that they amounted to 'a restructuring of the role of government in social provision so far-reaching as to be systemic'.[108]

Changes to work processes continued, such as the expansion of lean production methods into other areas of the Civil Service, for example, the Department for Work and Pensions (DWP).[109] The Health and Social Care Act 2012 was a 'logical extension' of marketization initiated by the internal market set up by the Conservatives in 1989.[110] The Act enhanced the role of general practitioners in commissioning and in doing so, increased competition; created a health-specific economic regulator (Monitor) with a mandate to guard against 'anti-competitive' practices; and proposed moving all NHS trusts to autonomous foundation-trust status. More healthcare services and facilities management were to be purchased from the private sector.[111] The landscape of healthcare provision was to be changed by

---

106 *Ibid.*
107 https://assets.publishing.service.gov.uk/government/uploads/system/uploads/attachment_data/file/310231/spa-timetable.pdf.
108 P. Taylor-Gooby, 'Root and Branch Restructuring to Achieve Major Cuts: The Social Policy Programme of the 2012 UK Coalition Government', *Social Policy and Administration* 46:1 (2012), pp. 61–82, at p. 63.
109 See, for instance, D. Martin, '"Lean" in the UK Civil Service: From the Theory of Improvement to the Varied Realities of Costs Cutting', *La Nouvelle Revue du Travail* 10 (2017), pp. 1–16.
110 J. Le Grand, cited in Tailby, 'Public Service Restructuring in the UK', *IRJ*, p. 449.
111 S. Nickson, 'The Private Sector and the NHS: Not "On the Table", but Already in the Market' (Institute for Government: 2019), online.

competitive innovation through easier entrance to and exit from the market for a range of private and voluntary providers.[112]

The decentralization–centralization paradigm was also apparent in education reforms under Michael Gove, an openly polemical and unpopular Secretary of State for Education between 2010 and 2014. The number of academies – independent, publicly funded schools owned by non-profit-making trusts, outside local authority control – increased. The longer-term trend was for academies to join multi-academy trusts, making any potential privatization more practical and attractive to private capital.[113] In addition, parents and other groups were encouraged to set up publicly funded 'free schools'. Neither academies, nor free schools, have to follow the national curriculum and both provide a mechanism for undermining the power and influence of teachers' unions: they do not have to abide by the national statutory requirements for teachers' pay and conditions, and they can decide teaching hours and the extent of holidays.[114]

Higher education moved further from being regarded as a public good towards an individual investment. Labour had introduced tuition fees in 1999 and increased them in 2004. Following the Browne Report,[115] commissioned by the Labour government, but reporting after it had lost office, the Coalition government raised them to £9,000 in 2011. The removal of the cap on student recruitment created a competitive market. Universities are now businesses with a managerial ethos and dependent on attracting students as 'customers'. The labour process of lecturers has been transformed as

---

112 Virgin Care has been one of the beneficiaries of opening of the market: 'Virgin awarded almost £2bn of NHS contracts in the past five years', *Guardian*, 5 August 2018.

113 By 2012, nine chains consisted of ten or more academies, accounting for some 182 academies that were either open or planned: R. Hill, J. Dunford, N. Parish, S. Rea, and L. Sandals, 'The Growth of Academy Chains: Implications for Leaders and Leadership' (National College for School Leadership: 2012). As of January 2018, the Department for Education had converted 6,996 maintained schools to academies. However, the Department was struggling to convert a sizeable proportion of the underperforming schools it believed would benefit most from academy status: National Audit Office, *Converting Maintained Schools to Academies* (Department for Education: 2018).

114 Since 2012 they have been allowed to employ non-qualified teachers, leading the head of the independent Brighton College to say, in a statement issued by the Department for Education, 'I strongly believe that teachers are born not made and I will actively seek out teachers from all walks of life who have the potential to inspire children. At Brighton College, we have 39 teachers without formal teaching qualifications, including me': 'Academies told they can hire unqualified teachers', *BBC News*, 27 July 2012.

115 Department for Business, Innovation and Skills, *Securing a Sustainable Future for Higher Education: An Independent Review of Higher Education Funding and Student Finance* (Browne) (2010).

they were subjected to metrics on teaching, marking, research and grant-winning. The degradation of work has been accompanied by a huge growth in temporary and part-time, insecure posts,[116] and an attack on the (pre-1992) universities' pension scheme.[117]

Public-sector work and trade unions

Unlike *Living with Capitalism*, there is no standout study of public-sector work to allow a reflection of the continuities and changes of the last forty-five years.[118] Industrial sociology of the period was just that – a focus on industry. It followed the conflict and controversy. Public-sector work was staid and uninteresting, the province of the British constitution-alists and institutional politics, reflected in the pages of the journal *Public Administration*. The working class, not subject to ethnographies, was rendered invisible.[119] Some of this bias still lingers. There are thousands of books on teaching, for instance, but only a handful on teaching as a labour process.[120] Yet many of the issues that Beynon raises have parallels in the public sector. The way that public-sector workers have been treated at work and their conditions degraded are equally worthy of study and documentation. Indeed, when Beynon notes that there is a class war being waged from above, the state has been an actor in that war, as relentless as capital both in general and against its own employees. When he states that 'This invites the question about the other side of the war – those that battle

---

116 According to the University and College Union (UCU), 70% of researchers in 2019 were on fixed-term contracts; 37,000 teaching staff on fixed-term contracts (most on hourly pay); and 71,000 atypical teachers not counted on the main staff record, many on casual contracts. The union estimated that this 'reserve army' of academic labour provided between 25% and 30% of teaching in many universities: *Counting the Costs of Casualisation in Higher Education* (UCU: 2019). For an analysis of proposed cuts in the pension scheme, see D. Leech, 'USS in Crisis? What is really going on? A message for all USS members' (15 September 2017), online.

117 See, for instance, M. Tomlinson, J. Enders, and R. Naidoo, 'The Teaching Excellence Framework: Symbolic Violence and the Measured Market in Higher Education', *Critical Studies in Education* (2018), pp. 1–16; J. Holmwood (ed.), *A Manifesto for the Public University* (Bloomsbury Academic: 2011).

118 The exception was N. Dennis, F. Henriques, and C. Slaughter, *Coal is Our Life* (Eyre and Spottiswoode: 1956).

119 Even to some Marxists concerned with class and the state. See N. Poulantzas, *Classes in Contemporary Capitalism* (Verso: 1975).

120 One exception is the work of Roger Seifert and various co-authors. See, as an example, J. Sinclair, M. Ironside, and R. Seifert, 'Classroom Struggle: Market Oriented Education Reforms and Their Impact on the Teacher Labour Process', *WES* 10:4 (1996), pp. 641–61.

against capital or at least wanting to control its worst excesses',[121] there can be no answer today without considering what has happened to public-sector labour, equally the object of attacks.

There are areas and experiences of work where the parallels do not closely hold. Absent are widespread and obvious examples of a polarity between advanced technology and drudgery in the public sector, although at a more general level the tendency for the separation of conception from execution is replicated in various public-sector sites, from social work to tax collection. The long-term success of Whitleyism in constraining overt conflict, militated against any need for the introduction of participation, but even here the idea of social partnership was floated in both education and the NHS to no visible benefits to workers at local levels. There was some relocation of government offices to the regions, such as the Driver and Vehicle Licensing Agency to Swansea or major Department for Work and Pensions functions to Longbenton in Northumberland, not simply to provide work as part of regional policy but also to avoid overblown property prices and (London weighting allowance) labour costs.[122] Migration of services was constrained by many being inherently local. Hospital services can be concentrated in larger, more distant hospitals, but there are definite limits to their remoteness from potential patients, especially in relation to accident and emergency facilities, and the specialisms that underpin them. Movement of provision, where it has taken place, therefore, has tended to be from public to private ownership.

The primary purpose of contracting out services, such as catering and cleaning, in the NHS is to save money. As the new employer has to provide the same service and make a profit, it is clear that the profit element has to come from either more efficient methods, the costs of labour or material costs. The first element, productivity, involves giving the same workers more work (more wards to clean),[123] thereby increasing the intensity of labour. Second, labour costs can be most easily achieved by cutting the number of staff and paying lower increases than awarded to staff remaining

121 Beynon, 'After the Long Boom', *HSIR*, p. 217.
122 J. N. Marshall, C. Hodgson and D. Bradley, 'Public Sector Relocation and Regional Disparities in Britain', *Environment and Planning C: Government and Policy* 23:6 (2005), pp. 883–906, provide a historical analysis demonstrating that 'relocation of public sector work from London and its environs to the regions has occurred every ten to fifteen years or so, when development pressures increase public sector costs and cause problems for public sector operation close to the capital', p. 885. Such relocation is almost always smaller than intended and never cedes central power of the Civil Service.
123 See Munro, 'Thirty Years of Hospital Cleaning in England and Scotland', pp. 176–90.

with the public employer.[124] Third, material costs can be cut by buying cheaper ones, or using less than traditionally the case (disinfectants for cleaning hospitals, for instance[125]). There are some restrictions on the rights of the new employer to act with freedom on some of these issues, but in practice neither TUPE regulations[126] nor contract compliance have proved long-term safeguards.

The creation of a two-tier workforce through the subcontracting process does not just affect terms and conditions of employment – lack of sick pay, pensions, the same holiday entitlements – but also feelings of dignity and belonging. A recent spate of strikes by outsourced security staff and cleaners at London universities and hospitals have demanded parity of terms but also raised how they feel that they are not respected.[127] More than a transfer of ownership is involved. Teamwork and flexibility are undermined. Cleaners, once able to talk to patients in hospital, an important interaction for nervous, confused patients, now have neither the time, nor the confidence, to tarry. Services are fragmented and identities shrunken. Previous human relations are broken.

The majority of staff have remained in direct public-sector employment, but their work has similarly been transformed. The most obvious change is that ideas of 'a job for life' have been removed and, so far as people have retained jobs, there is a widespread feeling of resentment about the effect of wage restrictions highlighted above. The FDA, the trade union for senior civil servants, issued a report containing accounts from staff 'detailing the effect excessive working hours had on their lives – ranging from soaring blood-pressure levels to nervous breakdowns and depression'.[128] No doubt the pressure on managers was a factor in the treatment of lower grades, 40% of whom reported incidents of bullying or harassment in 2018 – up from 36% in 2017 and 34% in 2016.[129] It is not uncommon to find public-sector staff complaining that their jobs no longer resemble their original ones. Central to the feeling of disillusionment is their inability to provide a good public service: as a report on the NHS recorded, alongside bullying

---

124 D. Grimshaw and M. Carroll, 'Adjusting to the National Minimum Wage: Constraints and Incentives to Change in Six Low-Paying Sectors', *IRJ* 37:1 (2006), pp. 22–47.

125 Contracting out 'resulted in lower cleaning standards as evaluated by patients and higher hospital-associated infection rates as indicated by MRSA rates': S. Elkomy, G. Cookson, and S. Jones, 'Cheap and Dirty: The Effect of Contracting Out Cleaning on Efficiency and Effectiveness', *Public Administration Review* 79:2 (2019), pp. 193–202.

126 Transfer of Undertakings (Protection of Employment) Regulations (1981).

127 See, for example, accounts which foreground justice and dignity with more concrete demands: https://www.uvwunion.org.uk/victories.

128 'People Survey 2018 Analysed', *Civil Service World*, 7 January 2019, online.

129 *Ibid.*

and harassment,[130] 'our people report growing pressure [and] frustration with not having enough time with patients'.[131]

With the indignities and privations visited upon public-sector employees, it might be expected that trade unions would exhibit growth and a new combativity. However, the record of public-sector unions in defending their members is, with some exceptions, a poor one.[132] In areas such as education, health, local government, and welfare, workers have lost considerable control over their work practices in the process of new public management (see above). For too many members the union is a combination of individual representation over disciplinary issues (particularly sickness absence) and ballots for annual pay claims that are poorly supported by a demoralized workforce. With 1.3 million members in health, education and local government, UNISON has a key role in public-sector unionism, but unfortunately exemplifies these problems.[133] For Peter Fairbrother, it was not meant to be like this. From 1994 onwards, he consistently argued that decentralization of management would lead to union renewal – specifically that democratic, participatory and locally-based forms of organization would emerge to counter local managerial decision-making. The thesis was frequently tentative, with renewal always in a process of unfolding, but never quite blooming. In one later instance of this, it is claimed that attempts

---

130 'People report growing pressure, frustration with time allotted to patients, and rising levels of bullying and harassment. Black and Minority Ethnic staff, in particular, report some of the poorest workplace experiences': 2018 National NHS Staff Survey. 'Sickness absence in the NHS runs around 2.3 percentage points higher than in the rest of the economy and around one in eleven of our staff leave the NHS entirely every year. Our NHS Staff Survey provides valuable data that will inform the development of work in this area': NHS, *Interim NHS People Plan* (NHS: 2019), p. 4.

131 *Ibid.*

132 Excluded here are the Fire Brigades Union, the Rail, Maritime and Transport Workers Union, and the Public and Commercial Services Union. In a recent analysis of its effectiveness and the need to organize at the workplace, the National Education Union (NEU) observed that 'Members in schools are struggling in the face of crippling workload, stifling of creativity and punitive policies on pay, sickness etc. It is here that the Union must be seen to make a difference in order for us to be seen as effective in the eyes of members – unless we do this our "big picture" campaigning may come to nothing': *Times Educational Supplement*, 18 December 2019. The NEU was formed in 2017 from a merger of the National Union of Teachers and the Association of Teachers and Lecturers. The latter already had teaching assistants in membership, making possible workplace organization that encompasses all school staff involved in teaching.

133 See G. Looker, 'Union Organising and Full-time Officers: Acquiescence and Resistance', *IRJ* 50:5–6 (2019), pp. 517–31. Gerry Looker writes as a former UNISON regional officer.

to marginalize trade unions 'appear to have provided the impetus for union renewal and revitalisation'.[134] This view has been challenged by showing that new public management has done deep damage to the structures and confidence of organizations and there have been few concerted attempts to build workplace organization. In terms of membership numbers, union density, and effectiveness in gaining higher wages and better conditions, there is little or no evidence of successful union renewal.[135]

As Beynon observes, unions can plead there are mitigating circumstances against this outcome, the legal framework has grown more hostile and other developments have made workers more geographically and socially distant. The legal assault, restricting the scope and substance of industrial action, means the public sector now faces bigger obstacles than most of the private sector. The Trade Union Act 2016 requires not only that at least 50% of the union members entitled to vote must do so in order for the ballot to be valid, but also that in specified public services (health, education of those aged under 17, fire, transport) another threshold requires at least 40% of those balloted to vote yes. As TUC general secretary Frances O'Grady claimed: 'The Conservative Party is not just proposing a few more bureaucratic obstacles that will make life a bit more difficult for trade unions ... they would effectively ban strikes by the back door ... [introducing a] threshold no other ballot in Britain is required to meet and that many would fail ... effectively end[ing] the right to strike in the public sector.'[136]

In his own way, Beynon seems to mirror this pessimism. Referring back to workers' attitudes to unions at Chemco, where union membership was 'virtually compulsory', he notes that, despite clear union presence, workers 'evoked no feelings of the union being *theirs* or that their membership involved them in a trade-union *movement*' (original emphasis). The cause of this alienation was 'a process of bureaucratization associated with a

---

134 P. Fairbrother, J. O'Brien, A. Junor, M. O'Donnell, and G. Williams, *Unions and Globalisation: Governments, Management and the State at Work* (Routledge: 2011), p. 5.

135 For a general assessment see G. Gall, 'The Prospects for Workplace Trade Unionism: Evaluating Fairbrother's Union Renewal Thesis', *Capital and Class* 22:3 (1998), pp. 149–57. For local government, see T. Colling, 'Renewal or Rigor Mortis? Union Responses to Contracting in Local Government', *IRJ* 26:2 (1995), pp. 134–45; and W. Gill-McLure, 'The Politics of Managerial Reform in UK Local Government: A Study of Control, Conflict and Resistance, 1880s to Present', *Labor History* 5:3 (2014), pp. 365–88. For teacher trade-unionism, see B. Carter, 'State Restructuring and Union Renewal: Some Evidence from Teaching', *WES* 18:1 (2004), pp. 137–56. For Civil Service trade-unionism, see B. Carter, A. Danford, D. Howcroft, H. Richardson, A. Smith, and P. Taylor, '"Nothing Gets Done and No One Knows Why": PCs and Workplace Control of Lean in HM Revenue and Customs', *IRJ* 43:5 (2012), pp. 416–32.

136 *BBC News*, 7 September 2014.

corporate form of capitalism in which through the check-off system, contributions to the union emerged as a kind of tax'. He reflects, 'We had not realized just how vulnerable the unions would be to such an attack [of aggressive anti-unionism and the removal of legal immunities] and what would then be needed to regain their previous position'.[137]

The scale of the attacks should not be minimized, but the answer to the question of 'what would be needed' is largely unspoken. It certainly requires unions to look to their own organizations rather than to outside institutions. In order to create collective power, unions need to focus on, and support, workplace organization. There are, in the words of Jane McAlevey, 'no shortcuts'.[138] Workers cannot afford to go into strikes with less than overwhelming support, certainly levels much higher than present legal thresholds. Whether at Chemco all those years ago, or in local government today, the answer is the same: the union cannot win if it does not reflect and represent the vast majority of the workforce.

Despite the seemingly damning assessments of the prospects for unions, there are reasons for envisaging a revitalized trade-union movement, and a central role for public-sector unions in this. The first reason is structural. Health and education services remain important social functions that are both skilled and labour-intensive. There are limits to both labour substitution and their relocation. In the United States, unions in both sectors have demonstrated an ability to utilize their positions to build strong workplace organization and to mobilize large sections of the local community and service users to make gains in the mutual interests of all (safe staffing levels in hospitals, smaller classes, better schools).[139] The second reason is in part conjunctural. One result of the COVID-19 pandemic has been growing recognition of the importance of public-sector work for social reproduction and the fulfilment of basic human needs.[140] Public support, always high for the NHS, has seen thousands of people come out of their houses and flats every Thursday to clap in support of front-line workers. Emotional support for nurses has always been strong among the public but, with widespread

---

137 Beynon, 'After the Long Boom', *HSIR*, pp. 217, 218.

138 J. McAlevey, *No Shortcuts: Organizing for Power in the New Gilded Age* (Oxford University Press: 2016).

139 *Idem*, 'Forging New Class Solidarities: Organizing Hospital Workers', *Socialist Register 2015: Transforming Classes* (Merlin: 2014), pp. 318–35; E. Blanc, *Red State Revolt: The Teachers' Strikes and Working-Class Politics* (Verso: 2019), p. 19; and Economic Policy Institute, 'The Teacher Pay Gap is Wider than Ever' EPI, Washington, DC: 2016). There is evidence that the NEU is taking the experiences of US teacher unionism to reshape its own practice: G. Little, 'If you're in the building, you're in the union: the next steps for the NEU', *Morning Star*, 11 October 2018.

140 See M. Bergfeld and S. Farris, 'The Covid-19 Crisis and the End of the "Low-skilled" Worker', *Spectre* (2020), online.

concern about the absence of appropriate personal protective equipment and deaths of front-line support workers (both inside and outside hospitals), support has widened for those previously dismissed as 'unskilled workers'. The Conservative government, always distrusted on the NHS, has had to rally support for its responses to the pandemic from a daily rostrum decorated with the slogan, 'Protect the NHS'. The National Education Union (NEU) has been central in organizing the provision of education and care for the children of key workers, as well as other vulnerable children, making it clear that it will be reluctant to reinstate some practices (standard assessment tests, base-line assessments) after full return.[141]

What is true for these two core sectors is also the case more generally. Transport and retail food workers, care-home assistants, teachers, and refuse collectors have all been seen in a new light, as essential workers, in contrast to the complete absence of entrepreneurs and hedge-fund managers. For those workers who fall outside the key worker occupations, their status as wage workers has been heightened and reinforced by insecurity, lack of safe working practices, and lay-offs. The task of unions and their members will be to use this new awareness to resist any attempt by the government to recoup its enormous additional expenditure through a new wave of austerity and cuts to public service. In the aftermath of the financial crisis of 2008 the government managed just this. Everyday normality has been challenged so fundamentally that there are signs radical change is welcome.[142] Trade-union leaders, on past performance, are unreliable tribunes: resilient and effective workplace organization will have to be spread to stop a great shift backwards again.

School of Business
University of Leicester
Leicester LE1 7RH

---

141 *Observer*, 3 May 2020.
142 'Coronavirus: Only 9% of Britons want life to return to "normal" once lockdown is over', *Sky News*, 17 April 2020.

https://doi.org/10.3828/hsir.2020.41.7

The Bullock Report and European Experience (1977)

Hugh Clegg

Whatever the shortcomings of the Bullock Committee's terms of reference, the injunction to take account of European experience was not one of them.[1] Almost all the evidence against which proposed schemes for worker directors can be tested and evaluated is drawn from Europe. The Committee therefore did well to follow their instructions in this respect, and to commission Eric Batstone and Paul Davies to summarise and analyse the evidence for them.[2]

Nevertheless the volume and scope of the evidence is limited. Most European countries, including France and Italy, had nothing to offer. The Committee relied mainly on West Germany and Sweden, with occasional references to Holland and Denmark. They might have added Norway, but it cannot add much to the lessons that can be learned from the other two Scandinavian countries. They neglected Yugoslavia, in my view rightly. The Yugoslav workers' councils and management boards consisting entirely of workers' representatives are far removed from the proposals which the Committee were investigating; and evidence drawn from a country ruled by a Communist Party has very uncertain relevance to Western democracies.

This paper by Hugh Clegg was first published in R. Benedictus, C. Bourn, and A. C. Neal (eds), *Industrial Democracy: The Implications of the Bullock Report. Proceedings of a Conference Held at the University of Leicester, 4–5 April 1977* (Department of Adult Education, University of Leicester: 1977), preface by the chairman of the conference, Professor Sir Otto Kahn-Freund. Subject to minor corrections it is reproduced here as in the original; otherwise presentation conforms to this journal's house style. It is reprinted here with the permission of Stephen Clegg. Thanks to Peter Ackers for bringing it to my attention. Paul Smith.

1 *Industrial Democracy* (chair, A. Bullock), Cmnd 7231 (1978).
2 E. Batstone and P. L. Davies, *Industrial Democracy, European Experience*: *Two Research Reports*. Prepared for the Industrial Democracy Committee (HMSO: 1976).

Most of the European experience is as yet brief. In West Germany it goes back to the early post-war years, but the Swedish and Dutch legislation came into operation only in 1973 and the Danish legislation at the beginning of 1974. Moreover the Dutch law did not take full effect until this year.

Finally, the European evidence is limited in content. Equal representation for shareholders and workers has been tried only in the German coal and steel industries where it was originally introduced by the occupation authorities after the war. Last year a new law provided for a different scheme of more or less equal representation in companies with two thousand or more employees outside coal and steel, which comes into operation this year. Thereafter the minority (one-third) representation for workers which at present applies to all companies with more than five hundred employees will continue in companies employing between five hundred and two thousand. Minority representation is also the rule in Sweden and Denmark. Boards must include two worker directors, and this number may be increased in Denmark so long as the worker directors remain in a minority. In Holland directors are co-opted by the existing board, but their names must be approved by both the shareholders' meeting and the works council.

European evidence was used by the majority of the Bullock Committee to support all three of their main proposals: that Britain should not adopt supervisory boards which are the rule in Germany and Holland, but retain single (or 'unitary') boards; that there should be equal representation on the board for shareholders and workers, with additional independent members co-opted by those two groups (the 2X+Y formula); and that trade unions should select the worker directors (the 'single channel').

In West Germany and Holland worker representation applies on the supervisory boards which in turn appoint management boards. Like Britain, Sweden and Denmark have only one board, but Denmark, unlike Britain, does not allow executive managers to serve on the board. The Committee noted that supervisory boards were introduced in Germany long before there was any question of worker directors, whereas if supervisory boards were introduced in Britain it would be to accommodate worker directors, and this would be seen as an attempt to keep worker directors away from the effective management of the enterprise. They also noted in Germany 'the tendency in some companies for the supervisory board, on all but the really major issues, to become a reactive and passive body, meeting three or four times a year to hear reports from management'[3] and, one might add, to draw their very substantial fees.

However, their chief argument against introducing supervisory boards into Britain was that there is in practice little difference between British and German boards:

---

3 Bullock, *Report*, p. 75, para. 9.

Of course there is no British equivalent to the requirement in West German law that companies should have a supervisory and a management board, each with carefully defined powers. But in practice many large British companies and company groups operate a system where the functions of supervision and management are roughly divided between different levels of the organization.[4]

So why bother to introduce the German system into Britain?

It would be facetious to summarise the Committee's argument as saying that supervisory boards are rather feeble institutions and that there is not much difference between supervisory and unitary boards, but there is a serious point to be made. The evidence of Batstone and Davies, and others, is that boards, whether unitary or supervisory, are not normally used to take decisions.[5] They ratify decisions taken elsewhere. Consequently both types of board are mainly supervisory bodies, and there is not much to be said for going to the trouble of replacing the British structure by the German structure.

In presenting their case for equal representation of shareholders and workers the Bullock Committee rely on two reports on worker directors in Europe,[6] the Biedenkopf Report on Western German experience, and the report of the Swedish National Industrial Board on the first three years of worker participation in Sweden.[7] These and other sources indicate that minority representation gives worker directors little or no influence on appointments made by the board; little chance of appointment to the committees which transact much of the board's business; and less information on the company's affairs than they might wish to have. In his paper Paul Davies makes another pertinent point.[8] Where shareholder directors are in a majority they determine what business is to be devolved to managers. If matters do not come to the board they are kept away from the worker directors. In many instances the shareholder directors on supervisory boards are in practice the nominees of the management board and therefore unlikely to probe too meticulously into the conduct of business by the management board.[9] The same point could be made in relation to non-executive directors on many British boards. It does not follow that minority representation is useless. If it is introduced with relatively modest expectations, as it was in Sweden, it may be found to yield

---

4 *Ibid.*, p. 68, para. 27.

5 Batstone and Davies, *Industrial Democracy, European Experience*, pp. 20–1.

6 Bullock, *Report*, pp. 92–8.

7 K. Biedenkopf, *Mitbestimmung in Unternehmen* (1970); Swedish National Industrial Board, *Representation of Employees in Sweden* (1976).

8 Batstone and Davies, *Industrial Democracy, European Experience*, p. 58.

9 *Ibid.*, pp. 57–8.

worthwhile benefits in improved understanding among both managers and workers, and also better-informed decisions. This appears to be the verdict of the Swedish National Industrial Board. But it is a poor instrument for achieving the radical changes in industrial relations and performance that the Bullock Committee were seeking.

When they turned to the Y factor in their formula, the majority of the Bullock Committee distinguished between two ways of achieving parity representation: 'full parity representation (i.e. 50:50 employee and shareholder representation) as in the German coal, iron, and steel industries; or equal representation of employees and shareholders plus the appointment or co-option of a third group of directors', such as they were proposing.[10] They went on to suggest that there were advantages in the second arrangement. But the German coal and steel companies do not have 50:50 representation. An 'eleventh man' is appointed with the consent of both sides. Consequently a board of eleven directors produces a 5+5+1 formula as against 4+4+3 under the Bullock Report's proposals. Is this a major difference? In practice the distinction between the two may be less than this, for the coal and steel legislation in Germany requires each side to select one of their own nominees from outside. Is it not likely that the two sides on a Bullock-type company board might agree that each of them should nominate one of the three independent directors? If so the two arrangements would be almost identical.

The 1976 law in Germany, which applies to companies employing two thousand or more outside the coal and steel industries, provides for boards of 10+10. On the workers' side, three representatives are to be chosen by the trade unions and seven by the works councils. The union do not accept that this is parity representation because one of the works council nominees must be chosen from the senior managers, and they expect him to line up with the shareholders' representatives. In addition the chairman is to be selected from one of the directors nominated by the shareholders, and is to have a casing vote. Nevertheless it is interesting that there was no suggestion of including an independent element, and the reason for this seems to be that the eleventh man in coal and steel companies has turned out to be so much less important than had been expected, because the two sides nearly always agree. The Biedenkopf Report found that 'there was more commitment and co-operation on the board' in these companies than elsewhere where the workers are limited to minority representation.[11] This appears paradoxical, but the explanation is that the managers and the management board do not like to leave decisions to the supervisory board.

---

10 Bullock, *Report*, p. 96, para. 13.
11 *Ibid.*, para. 12.

Recognising the influence which parity representation gives to the worker directors on supervisory boards, they negotiate with them, or with the works council, over contentious issues which are likely to come up at the supervisory board so as to present an agreed solution to the board meeting.[12] Hence the high level of co-operation on the board and the unimportance of the eleventh man. If an independent element turned out to be of so little account in Germany, why should it be a crucial element in the Bullock Report proposals for Britain?

One answer might be that the 2X+Y formula appears to be more politically acceptable than a stark 50:50 arrangement. Another, though certainly not one suggested by the majority of the Committee, could be that the method of selection for worker directors which they proposed would make confrontation more likely than under the German system, so that the independent members would be needed to resolve deadlocks.

The Committee's proposed method of selection was the 'single channel'. Neither the majority nor the minority of the Committee saw a need to spell out the case for an organisation of workers within the company which would be a 'preliminary to representation on the board, encouraging participation below board level and providing the machinery through which employee representatives are appointed and can report back'.[13] The issue for debate was what body should provide this 'substructure' as they called it. They noted that the job was performed by works councils in some Continental countries, and that much of the evidence which they had received argued that Britain should institute similar bodies. The majority held that such councils, 'which represent all employees, whether union members or not',[14] would be inappropriate in Britain, and looked to trade union shop steward organisation in the plant for the substructure. There would then be a 'single channel' within the company for workers to participate in collective bargaining and in the business of the board.

Such an arrangement is not unknown in Europe. The Swedish unions appoint the worker representatives on their company boards. But the majority on the Committee might have noted that the Danish unions, with even greater proportional strength than British unions, are quite content to accept election to the board by all employees whether union members or not. In fact, the senior stewards are almost invariably elected, and it might be confidently expected that the outcome would be much the same if the election of worker directors were conducted in the same way in Britain. In practice the strongest argument for the single channel in Britain is that the unions insist upon it, and no system of worker directors can operate without their consent.

---

12 Commission on Industrial Relations (CIR) Study No. 4, *Worker Participation and Collective Bargaining in Europe* (HMSO: 1974), p. 18.
13 Bullock, *Report*, p. 109, para. 2.
14 *Ibid.*, pp. 109–10.

The majority of the Bullock Committee assumed that the shop steward organisation in Britain could do much the same job in relation to board representation as is performed by the works councils in Germany. There is only one set of functions, but it has to be carried out by different bodies because of the different circumstances of the two countries. The minority take a different view. 'Our own first-hand experience of companies which operate in West Germany', they say, 'leads us to believe that it is the German insistence on effective Works Councils separated from the union negotiating system, representing all employees and given extensive powers, which is one of the key factors in the success of the German system of employee participation'.[15] Although in general I disagree with the minority report a good deal more than with the majority report, nevertheless the minority were undoubtedly right in emphasising works councils as a big factor in employee participation in Germany.

The works councils have two main functions: consultation and co-determination. As consultative bodies they deal with issues similar to those handled by works councils or committees, joint consultative committees and the like in other countries – production issues, investment plans, economic matters – although the obligations on German companies to treat the councils seriously is greater than in most other countries. But the range of issues subject to co-determination – which companies cannot settle without the consent of the works council – is startling. They include working hours, wage payment procedures, holiday arrangements, wage scales, employee housing, productivity bonuses, job arrangements, work environment, production procedures, criteria for job evaluation, reports on efficiency, recruitment and selection standards, training, transfers, redeployment, dismissals, redundancies, close-downs, mergers, new work methods, and production procedures.[16]

At first sight, therefore, the works council appears to have a lot in common with a powerful shop stewards' committee in a well-organised British manufacturing establishment. Both are elected representatives of the workers and both have a decisive say in a wide range of important matters relating to pay, conditions of employment, the organisation of the job, and the deployment of the labour force. But there are differences.

First, the powers of the works councils come from the law. They were not negotiated for them by the unions in agreements with employers, and they certainly were not won by their own efforts in gradually eroding managerial prerogatives in the plant, as is the case with shop stewards in many British undertakings. What the law gives, it can also subject to limitations. The works council is statutorily debarred from calling or organising a strike, and

---

15 Bullock Committee, 'Minority Report', p. 174, para. 17.
16 For the full list see CIR, *Worker Participation and Collective Bargaining in Europe*, p. 24.

this prohibition is generally obeyed. If the council cannot reach agreement with management there are provisions for arbitration.

Secondly, trade unions as such have no status in German plants. Their job is to bargain with employers' associations at national or regional level. The agreements which they reach apply to all the plants in the industry. Except for non-federated firms, and there are few large non-federated undertakings in Germany, there is no plant bargaining by trade unions.

Thirdly, it follows that the works council is not a trade union body. Although the great majority of works councillors are trade union members, they represent all workers and their authority comes from the law, not from the union. By contrast, however independent-minded British shop stewards may be, their power rests ultimately on their positions as trade union representatives. As has often been said before, to most British trade unionists the shop steward *is* the union.

Fourthly, although there are union representatives ('Vertrauensleute': men of trust) in the plant in Germany, and especially in the metal industry, they have little authority. They have no right to negotiate, and if they take up a grievance and cannot settle it at the first instance, it must be handed to the works council. Their main function is to provide a channel of communication between the union and its members. A works councillor may be a union representative as well, but, if so, his powers and duties as a councillor overshadow his union functions.

Fifthly, works councillors are further removed from their constituents than are British shop stewards. Like almost everything else about works councillors, their number is regulated by law. In a plant with four thousand employees the figure is sixteen (1:250), whereas in British manufacturing industry today the figure is something like one steward to thirty or forty workers.

Nevertheless, British stewards and German councillors share one crucial common feature, which offers the outstanding characteristic of industrial relations in their countries. Any explanation of industrial relations in British manufacturing industry must start with the shop stewards – and it is to manufacturing industry that the Bullock Report proposals primarily apply. Similarly, any explanation of German industrial relations has to begin with the works councils. But it does not follow that the two institutions can be expected to play a similar role in relation to worker directors. German works councils, as the minority of the Bullock Committee insist,[17] are a key factor in the success of employee participation in Germany. British shop stewards would no doubt occupy a key role in the operation of a worker-director system if one were instituted in Britain; but given the wide differences

---

17 Bullock, 'Minority Report', p. 174, para. 17.

between works councils and shop stewards, this role might be expected to be very different from that played by the German works council.

The contrast between works councils and shop stewards has little relevance to the majority's decision in favour of the single channel. They had no alternative if their proposals were to be accepted by the unions. But it is very relevant to any forecast of the consequences of applying the majority's recommendations. On this issue Lord Bullock and his colleagues might have hidden behind their terms of reference which bade them accept the need for worker directors. But they did not do so. They argued that their proposals could be the salvation of British industry, and they called on European experience as their witness.

Although there are more modest claims elsewhere in the Report its final conclusions on this issue are bold and unequivocal:[18]

> During our inquiry we found a widespread conviction, which we share, that the problem of Britain as an industrial nation is not a lack of native capacity in its working population so much as a failure to draw out their energies and skill to anything like their full potential. ... if such requirements as we have proposed are carried through, they will release energies and abilities at present frustrated or not used and thereby create a framework which will allow conflicts of interest to be resolved with greater mutual advantage. And we are encouraged in this belief by the success in improving industrial relations which neighbouring countries in Europe, with differing economic and social systems, have had in following this path of development.[19]

Earlier the Report is more specific about 'the neighbouring countries'. Having specifically referred to worker representation on the board in West Germany and Sweden, the majority comment: 'The fact that the West German and Swedish economies, despite differences between the social philosophies of the two countries, have been among the most successful in the world – not least in avoiding the industrial conflict which has cost Britain so dear – has not escaped notice.'[20]

These flights of fancy carry the majority of the Bullock Committee far out of sight of the evidence. It is true, of course, that both West Germany and Sweden have excellent records of economic growth and industrial relations since the war. But it is patently ridiculous to attribute the Swedish record since 1945 to the introduction of worker directors in 1973. Are the majority

---

18 'We tend to agree with those who argue that board level representation will have beneficial effects on the performance of British companies': Bullock, *Report*, p. 50, para. 32.

19 *Ibid.*, p. 160, paras 2–3.

20 *Ibid.*, p. 25, para. 13.

suggesting that Swedish employees worked hard and struck little for nearly thirty years in the hope that their virtue would ultimately be rewarded by minority representation on the board? Nor are their comments much nearer to reality in relation to Germany. The West German experience of worker directors goes back to the early post-war years, but, outside the coal and steel industries, it is experience of a system of minority representation on supervisory boards which the majority of the Committee condemn as largely ineffective in Germany and undesirable in Britain. Their claims might have been less incredible if they had confined their remarks to the coal and steel industries with their parity of representation. But a system applying to those two industries could not account for the enviable performance of the whole West German economy. Moreover, although the coal and steel industries have performed well in post-war Germany, they have not achieved notably better results than other German industries. Consequently, it would seem reasonable to look for the explanation for German post-war achievements in industrial relations in some factor common to the whole of Germany, and not in a factor to be found only in the coal and steel industries.

In reality, such a factor is readily available – the works council. I do not know of any authority on industrial relations in West Germany who does not attach far more importance to works councils than to worker representation on boards in explaining the working of German industrial relations since the war. A different but equally important feature of Swedish industrial relations is at hand to account for Sweden's record since the war – the unique centralization of authority in both the main trade union confederation and in the employers' confederation, along with a high degree of co-operation between these two bodies.

What, then, is the verdict on European experience? What has been achieved by worker representation on boards? Batstone concludes that 'the evidence, largely from Germany, indicates that worker directors have had minimal impact. They have neither brought great rewards of a substantive or symbolic nature to workers nor have they endangered business efficiency or the interests of the shareholders. ... Finally, worker directors have had no important effect on the economy more generally'.[21] This is a verdict I am the more ready to accept in that it agrees with tentative conclusions which I reached almost twenty years ago, and have seen no good reason to revise since then.[22] Batstone also notes that 'where parity representation exists it seems that worker directors have been a factor in improving "democratic" practice within the company',[23] and this conclusion is matched by the Commission on Industrial Relations who report the opinion of the German

---

21 Batstone and Davies, *Industrial Democracy, European Experience*, p. 40.
22 H. A. Clegg, *A New Approach to Industrial Democracy* (Blackwell, Oxford: 1960), ch. 6.
23 Batstone and Davies, *Industrial Democracy, European Experience*, p. 40.

trade unions that parity representation has 'broken down the authoritarian attitudes which were particularly prevalent' in the coal and steel industries.[24] But 'at least part of the credit for ... these changes must be given to the growth of new attitudes among German employers generally, and to full employment. Perhaps the circumstances of post-war German industry would have brought them about without any help from co-determination.'[25]

The final question is: can European experience indicate what is likely to happen in Britain if the majority proposals of the Bullock Committee are embodied in legislation? There seem to be two possible answers. The first assumes that the European systems of worker representation on the board are sufficiently like the Bullock majority proposals to show what effect these would have if they were applied; and the answer then is: very little effect at all. The second assumes that the European evidence is not relevant to the question. The argument for this assumption is that all the Continental experience, outside the West German coal and steel industries, is of minority representation, which is very different from the parity representation proposed for Britain; and the experience of the German coal and steel industries is also irrelevant because it is representation on a supervisory board based on works councils, whereas the Bullock majority proposal is for trade union representation on a unitary board. On this assumption there is no evidence at all in the Bullock Report from which to predict the consequences of implementing the majority proposals. To do so would be to step into the dark.

I tend to accept the second answer, and this leads me to the view that although the Bullock Committee were right to pay attention to the European evidence, because its relevance cannot be judged without examining it, they paid too little attention to investigating the nature of the problem for which board representation is proposed as an answer. In my opinion, European experience is of limited relevance because Britain is not behind European countries in its problem of industrial relations in the enterprise, but ahead of them. This problem stems from what the late Allan Flanders called 'the challenge from below',[26] which is being posed all over the world but more sharply in Britain than anywhere else. The problem is how to organise industrial relations in a situation where management has largely ceased to control the organisation and performance of work. If the Bullock Committee had been willing to forget their terms of reference and their deadline in order to investigate and analyse this problem in depth, they might have emerged with proposals which rested on their analysis and not on European comparisons. But I am fairly confident that if they had matched the problem, it would not be long before other European countries would have been anxious to learn from the British experience.

24 CIR, *Worker Participation and Collective Bargaining in Europe*, p. 22.
25 Clegg, *A New Approach to Industrial Democracy*, p. 56.
26 A. Flanders, *Management and Unions* (Faber and Faber: 1970), p. 112.

Discussion

Michael Gold, University of Edinburgh: How do you account for the upsurge of interest in participation since the 1960s – not just in Britain, but all over Europe – and how do you account for the wave of legislation that has emerged in various European countries since the early 1970s?

Hugh Clegg: I think this may be the first indication that the 'British disease' spreads. Europe, in general, is at the point which the UK was in in 1945, at which time worker participation was out of the question in the UK because of TUC opposition. Of course, we didn't know then that it was ruled out of court right from the start by the trade union movement and by the employers. I don't think, for my own part, that it would have been of much help to us. However, I think if I had to give one reason, it is the beginning of a response – and you can see it in the wave of strikes that followed on from 1968, to the development of interest in shop steward organisations (feeble though they may be), and then a reaction from trade union leaders, from business men, and from governments of 'What might we do about this; let's just put our toes in the water'. Because all the 1970s' legislation – apart from Germany's – was a putting of toes into the water, and the great talk of 'the spectre of participation' which was wandering about Europe at that time, turned out really to be occasioned by something of a leprechaun.

Chairman, Professor Sir Otto Kahn-Freund: I believe there is an additional answer to the question, which refers to France. In France, the great events of 1968 ended with a statute at the end of that year which put the shop stewards and the plant organisation of the trade unions on a statutory basis. This is the direction in which the French drive went, and this is, as Professor Clegg has told us, also happening in Germany, especially in the metal industry with unions' appointment of 'Vertrauensleute' (or 'trust men'). This, I think, is the reality – at least, in part of the European Community. Would you agree?

Hugh Clegg: Yes, I entirely agree with that, and I would also then have to point out that this statute in France, like nearly all statutes saying what should happen in the plant in industrial relations in France, has had virtually no impact whatsoever.

Chairman, Otto Kahn-Freund: No, it hasn't, but it was strenuously demanded.

Hugh Clegg: Yes, I agree.

Dudley Jackson, University of Aston: On this question of the upsurge of interest, it is the case that, if you take 1969 as the dividing line, and compare the annual working days lost through strikes in the period 1969–74 with the previous period, the number of strikes and of working days lost has about doubled. Indeed, in some cases – for example, New Zealand and Canada – the upsurge in strikes occurred before 1968, in 1966–67. It also seems to be the case that in quite a significant number of countries the increase in strikes antedates by a year or two the increase in inflation. The question is, therefore, this: How far is industrial democracy seen in European countries as an attempt to try and do something about an industrial relations problem which is manifesting itself in the form of a higher level of strike activity, and subsequent inflation, helped along by oil price rises, so that industrial unrest has reached a new level?

Hugh Clegg: I think that it is a relevant point. First of all, I don't think that you are really right about past inflation. There may have been a turn upwards before, but if you take the highest year for the number of strikes and the highest year for the number of working days lost in any country that I know of, this peaks after 1970 – sometimes in 1970, sometimes 1971, sometimes 1972 – except, of course, for France and as they don't publish the figures for 1968 in France, that makes it rather difficult to put in the peak on the graph.

That is one point, and the other point which we have always to remember is this: that, yes, strikes doubled in many countries – both the number of strikes and the number of working days lost – but remember the base they were moving from in many cases, including Germany and Sweden. Indeed, even now they haven't got up to the kind of total which Liverpool all by itself would easily exceed. Perhaps I exaggerate a bit there, but they did go up, and this has caused their legislators and trade union leaders a bit of worry. I think it helps to explain the position, but don't let us suppose that such countries have had enormous strike waves – because, of course, most of them haven't.

Chairman, Otto Kahn-Freund: I can't resist the temptation of asking you a question on the strike situation in Germany. We were always told, weren't we, that there are no wildcat strikes in Germany. I am persuaded that this statement is wrong, but the thing that impresses me – and I really want to ask you whether my impression is right – is that the main place where wildcat strikes occurred in Germany was in the 'montan' industries – the only industries in which, since 1951, there has been something which we can call a real system of co-determination. Indeed, as far as I know, there have been more wildcat strikes in the steel industry – that is to say, the industry subject to the present statute of 1951 – than anywhere else in Germany. I wonder whether you can confirm this impression?

Hugh Clegg: I should like to know the source of your information, because remember that West Germany does not produce figures for the numbers of strikes, but only figures for the number of plants on strike. They question whether we are being really honest in drawing our figures from the numbers of strikes. How do you know whether it is one strike or five? So, if steel tends to bring out several plants at a time, then this may affect the statistics. Certainly, the major source, in terms of numbers of wildcat strikes, are the metalworking unions – which fits in with what you were saying.

Gustaf Lindencrona, University of Stockholm: I should like to comment on that question, because I have just been to Germany for about a week, and I put that question there, too. The fact is that there have been no official strikes, but there were some wildcat strikes in 1969.

Nevertheless, these should not, according to our German colleagues, be attributed to co-determination, but to the fact that in that year the unions concluded an agreement on wages which ran for a long period of one-and-a-half or two years. This was too long, but the unions and their members, who wanted a rise in wages, were bound by the agreement. This is the real reason behind these wildcat strikes, and co-determination had nothing to do with them.

May I also take the opportunity to protest at one thing in the Bullock Report, and that is on the value of minority representation. The Bullock Report even cites the German and Swedish experience.[1] I think that the analysis and rejection of minority representation is completely false. Our experience in Sweden, which was mentioned by the speaker,[2] shows first that it has been of considerable value, and we have already spoken today about its value when it comes to disclosure of information. Secondly, where you have strong trade union movements, minority representation also possesses other values. It is not so easy to bypass what this minority says at a board meeting when everybody knows that behind these persons stands a strong trade union movement. You just don't get the experience of these persons on the board saying a lot of things which the majority then passes over. Thirdly – and this is a very important point about minority representation – minority representation is a most valuable first step. It is a kind of experiment, which enables you to introduce the idea of worker or trade union representation without all the fears which a more substantial representation would induce. Such minority representation has been introduced in Sweden, and since its inception it has been shown, for example, that the problem of confidentiality turns out not to be a problem at all. This is

---

1 Bullock, *Report*, pp. 92–4.
2 *Ibid.*, pp. 171, 175, 178.

generally acknowledged. Consequently I think that the Bullock Committee has quite unfairly concluded that minority representation has no value.

Hugh Clegg: First of all, you are, of course, quite right about the major reasons for the outbreak of the unusual figure for wildcat strikes in West Germany in 1969. It was the consequence of the agreement. But please don't be too defensive about the 'montan' industries on this basis. I don't think that anybody in this country could conceivably say that the 'montan' industries' system of co-determination didn't work because they had some strikes. We would all say that they worked wonderfully, if we were going to use the argument that they had so very few strikes, even in 1969; so you don't need to be defensive on that point on behalf of the Germans.

Now, you say that the Bullock Committee has been unfair to minority representation. Well, I could perhaps say that you are unfair to the Bullock Committee and to Davies in that statement, in maintaining that that is what they are saying. I think that they say what you are saying. After all, they must, because they have read the document where the National Swedish Industrial Board says that there are advantages and disadvantages in terms of minority representation on the board. You do get some information, but you don't get all the information which you think you ought to have. They could well have made the point that you made – which I think is an important one for Britain if we ever go down this road – that, with a strong trade union movement behind the workers' representatives, they are in a better position than they otherwise would have been. I think it is all there. Of course, what they are doing is emphasising the points which you say they haven't made at all, or which you don't like very much, and placing very little emphasis on the points which you emphasise – but that, perhaps, is because they are coming to a different conclusion. But if you look for it, it is there in the small print. They haven't been totally unfair.

Alan Neal, University of Leicester: If I can follow up on the Swedish point, I too feel that Batstone has been somewhat unfair to Sweden. This is basically because I feel that he asked the wrong questions, and I think that, in consequence, the Bullock Committee addressed itself to the wrong questions in relation to Sweden. I think that what he should have looked at was the board representation legislation of the experimental 1973 Act – now made permanent – coupled with the moves towards a reform of collective bargaining through legislation which has been in force since the beginning of this year. I think that what one has to see is the development of board representation – minority board representation – in the light of developments at the time. In particular, there was a growing call for information, and it is necessary to see this 1973 legislation in terms of a holding action – as providing a means of getting information and being at the source of information – until the complete reform of collective bargaining had been carried through.

Remember that one is talking about a country where the acceptance of a legal structure for industrial relations has been well established since 1928. Therefore, reform of the structure was not particularly to be attended by the kinds of criticism which might be expected of such a discussion in this country. That being the case, I think that there was an expectation of a coherent whole when the Swedish committee looking into labour reform came to its conclusions, and when legislation was passed on collective bargaining and aspects ancillary to the collective bargaining process, such as the channels of information which now form part of the new Act.

If one looks at the development of board representation in Sweden in this light, perhaps what should have been asked was, 'What role does this minority representation play and what function does it purport to fulfil?' Is it, in fact, seeking to take over a significant role in the bargaining process, or is it merely, as I would suggest, a holding operation? I would suggest that the key to this lies in a piece of legislation which was passed at the same time as the Act making board representation permanent. This was an Act – which the new government has now said that they will put on ice – to allow for representation by means of a form of 'social auditor' on a number of selected boards of limited companies, co-operative associations, and Foundations. This, I think, was clearly intended as an information-gathering measure – a means to information, particularly of a financial nature, about these organisations. I think that if that Act is seen as a parallel – it was passed by Parliament on the same day as the new Board Representation Act – one perhaps gets the key to where the emphasis lies, and I would submit that the emphasis is not on board representation as a means of *influence* but more as a means of *insight*. Perhaps that is the question to which Batstone, and, in consequence, the Bullock Committee, might have addressed themselves in their consideration of minority representation on boards.

Hugh Clegg: I'm not sure that it's worthwhile pushing this question too far. I think the important point here, which everybody recognises, is that the Swedes themselves didn't attach all that much importance to their legislation for representation on the board. They had much more important legislation, which has now been passed, which they thought would make a much bigger, permanent contribution to industrial democracy. They had relatively small expectations and, naturally enough, weren't too disappointed when their expectations didn't prove to be false in that respect. It therefore seems to me fair – and here I am defending the Bullock Committee at last – for the Committee, while assessing the proposal for minority representation in

Britain,[3] to draw attention to the fact that, in Sweden, the official inquiry into the first three years' experience of representation on the board has said that there were these limitations. I think that was perfectly fair. Now you are saying something else. You are saying that if the majority of the Bullock Committee had been prepared to consider minority representation, that they might have said, 'Well, there are some advantages in minority represen-tation which could be helpful to the trade union movement in dealing with questions arising in the board', and, if they had said that, that would have been perfectly true. However, it would have made very little difference to their Report, since, for other more important and quite different reasons, they decided that they must recommend parity representation.

Chairman, Otto Kahn-Freund: Is it possible to consider the situation in Sweden, as the Bullock Report has done, without taking into account, apart from legislation, the inter-industrial agreements on works councils, on disclosure of information, and on a number of other matters? I wonder whether your impression is that this is part of the Swedish experience which the Bullock Report didn't discuss?

Hugh Clegg: I think that is true – just as the Report didn't really discuss the importance of the works councils in Germany. They didn't, in fact, study the industrial relations scene in either country. Rather, they just picked a few bits and said, 'We're going to use these in our report'. That is perfectly true, and the Committee could equally well be criticised for not analysing the elements in the Swedish situation just as they didn't analyse the important elements in the German situation.

Arnold Wagner, Manchester Polytechnic: I think you have answered the first point about which I was going to ask. I have heard it said – albeit from a rather partisan source, from somebody opposed to the majority report – that the methodology of the Bullock Committee, particularly in its research into what was happening in Germany, was, to put it mildly, suspect. It is said that when they visited Germany their minds were pretty well made up, and the Germans they did meet were rather concerned at the attitude which members of the Committee had when they went over there. I wonder whether you know any more about that, over and above what you have already said?

The second point, which also arises out of your comment that the Bullock Report appears to have got it wrong on this score, is of general application. To what extent was the assumption as to whether the Bullock Report's proposals would in any respect be translated into legislation, ever realistic?

---

3 Bullock, *Report*, p. 94, para. 7.

Or to what extent could we say – particularly in the light of the terms of reference under which the Committee set out – that the very preparation of the Report and its whole procedure, the accumulation of the evidence and so on, was itself part of an overall bargaining strategy in relation to what would happen to the question of industrial democracy given the options available?

Hugh Clegg: On the first point, the German visit, these visits aren't serious. I mean, nobody on the Bullock Committee or anywhere else supposes that you can really learn anything serious about Germany or Sweden by going on a junket there for a few days. I must say that we had the same junkets on the Donovan Commission. I didn't go on them. I thought they were a waste of time. I don't know if I was wrong or not. If the members of the Bullock Committee went over to Germany and appeared to have their minds made up, this really doesn't matter because nothing could happen in a period of a week which could seriously help them to make up their minds. They were sensible in choosing other sources of information for those bits of overseas experience which they were actually going to make use of.

I want to say something which I forgot to say earlier, which I think is important. You asked me about the Bullock interpretation of the German element, and there's one thing which I think is very significant in relation to the Y factor, which not many people know. The Bullock Report paid no attention whatsoever to the fact that, in Germany, it has been decided that the Y factor is of no importance because the new legislation has always been based on parity. You can argue whether it is 50:50 or not – of course, it isn't quite 50:50. Indeed, I think the Biedenkopf Commission themselves said that the 'eleventh man' had not turned out to be a very important person because of the negotiations which went on outside the boardroom and because what is going to happen is rarely determined on the board. The 'eleventh man' is not part of day-to-day management, and would only come into the Act at all if there was a serious development on the supervisory board – which is something that very rarely happens.

Now may I move on to your last point, which is a very interesting question indeed. I was very interested to hear what John Edmonds was saying,[4] and I would have added another point to his story. That is, why on earth did the General Council propose to the 1973 TUC Congress that there should be fifty per cent representation? It was then, of course, to be on a supervisory board, but nevertheless it was to be 50:50 boards. My version of the story is this: as you know, at that time Mr Heath was very much an advocate of going into Europe, both in this respect and in others, because he felt

---

4 J. Edmonds, 'The Bullock Committee's Report and Collective Bargaining', Benedictus *et al.* (eds), *Industrial Democracy: The Implications of the Bullock Report*, pp. 4.1–4.25, at p. 4.17.

that, having tried the Industrial Relations Act, and having tried a statutory incomes policy, there must be *some* way of improving British industrial relations, and conceivably this could be it. When it became known by the General Council that Mr Heath was going to propose supervisory boards with one-third representation for workers, Jack Jones said to his colleagues, 'Look, the one thing you cannot do is to say "No". When a Conservative Prime Minister says, "Unions, do you want to go on the board?", you can't say, "No, we reject this, Prime Minister." That's not the way to negotiate, as you know. If the management comes and asks you if you want something, you don't say that you don't want it: you say you want more.' Anyway, he said fifty per cent, and everybody, as John Edmonds said, assured that worker representation would never be implemented , said, 'Yes, let's go for fifty per cent', as a proper reply to this kind of offer from the Conservative government.

Well, that's the beginning of the story. If you want to know about the later part of it, my own belief is that the government have never been serious about these proposals at all, and that they have never intended that there should be legislation. Sometimes they may have got a bit worried, but I think that what they have done all along is to avoid getting themselves into the situation where they are seriously faced with the probability that they would have to negotiate new proposals. So where exactly did the Bullock Report fit into this? For one thing, it was to be ready in a year – but a year, as we know, is a very long time in politics, during which nothing can be done. In fact, the government took eighteen months – because they took six months to set it up, and the Committee took a year to report. That would be my reading of the situation.

Dudley Jackson: You said that you were not going to talk about the Yugoslav experience because it was so totally different. I was always very surprised that the Bullock Committee themselves did not look at Yugoslavia, until it was pointed out to me that their terms of reference limited them to not looking at the public sector – and, of course, everything in Yugoslavia is public sector – so that I can see this as a sort of justification for the Bullock Committee's decision.

On the other hand, if you look at the experience of Yugoslavia – and I have in mind particularly the inflation which they have experienced in Yugoslavia – workers wanting (a) high wage increases, and (b) quite a lot of investment; then, having voted or given themselves these two things, they set out either to quarrel over money or the essential monetary system in Yugoslavia, which is followed by a government credit squeeze, when prices are raised to get the money to pay for the investment. I would have thought that a good old-fashioned government incomes policy or credit control to try to clamp down on these tendencies would have been pertinent to a consideration of what one might land oneself in with a system of worker directors.

I was quite horrified by the closing remarks of Mr Bell last night about how there could be a nice cosy arrangement in a nationalised monopoly industry, where workers and managers simply set about looking for the money from consumers when the pressures became too great. Then you might need consumer interests represented on the board, and I therefore wonder whether the Bullock Committee ought to have looked at Yugoslavia?

Hugh Clegg: I think what you are really telling us is that the Committee ought to have looked at the very different system of worker representation and worker participation in Yugoslavia, and that, if they had, they would have decided that it was no good. That seems to me to not really be proof that they ought to have looked at it.

Dudley Jackson: They might have thought about safeguards or other economic issues.

Hugh Clegg: Of course, if we were going over to what the Yugoslavs have done, we might decide that we needed safeguards. However, what you are saying is that this has some relevance to what has happened elsewhere – and I very much doubt that. Take inflation. Of course, the Yugoslavs themselves say, 'Look at our growth rate. If you could have a growth rate like that, you wouldn't be so bothered about inflation', and that is probably true. But, setting that aside, if you say that the Bullock Committee ought to have taken the Yugoslav experience into account because it is relevant to discuss what happens where you have worker representation of a different kind, then I would say that one should look at the experiences of Sweden, Holland, Denmark, and Germany in this respect, and they are quite different. Whatever else one may say about worker participation in these countries, there is very little reason to say that participation has resulted in raising the rate of inflation to any significant extent. You might say that in Britain we have a different situation, because at the shop floor level we have workers' organisations which are so much more powerful than anything that exists in any of these other countries. You might argue that if they got their toes in the door of the boardrooms they might then behave as works council representatives or management board representatives behave in Yugoslavia. They might, or they might not. The discussion seems to me to be getting to the stage that it was in when I said that if we have that sort of view about what is going to happen in Britain, worker representation is a step in the dark – and I don't think that borrowing a pair of Yugoslav glasses is going to help us very much to see into that dark.

J. L. Worsley, Fisons Ltd: It comes to mind that maybe the Bullock Committee itself was constituted on a 2X+Y basis. Do you think that the Committee itself has shown that this formula does not work, since they obviously haven't come to a satisfactory conclusion themselves?

Hugh Clegg: I think we can conclude that, if you choose people for the board knowing beforehand that they are going to disagree, unless they are all incompetent, they will, when they get to the board, disagree. I don't suppose that, if we had the legislation proposed by the Bullock Report and we did get the two sides choosing their representatives and then co-opting the third side, their prime intention would be to make it impossible for the board ever to come to any decision on the assumption that it would necessarily be split all ways all of the time. I think, in a sense, that the government got in the Bullock Report what they asked for.

Chairman, Otto Kahn-Freund: May I be allowed to say one word, because I cannot resist it? I, personally, was in one hundred per cent agreement with what Professor Clegg said about the German works councils. I think, if I may say so, that he hit the nail absolutely on the head – only he could have said much more, above all, about the fact that the present German Works Council Act of 1972 is an immense improvement on its predecessor and has increased the powers of co-determination very considerably as compared with the position under the previous law. In particular, there is one point which I would like to mention, in addition to the powers which you enumerated. There is, in the later parts of the statute, a special section consisting of various paragraphs which deal with the very problems with which we are concerned here, that is to say, partial closures, restrictions on the undertaking of a transfer of the whole of a plant or essential parts of it, mergers with other plants, fundamental changes in the organisation, and, above all, the introduction of fundamentally new working and production methods. On all of these matters the works council does not just have to be consulted, but the works council and the employer have to agree on something which is called the 'social plan', dealing with redundancies, compensation, and so on. If they do not agree, then, as Professor Clegg has said, there is a kind of arbitration. If I may say so, I would like to associate myself with the remark which Professor Clegg made in his presentation, that the reality of co-determination in West Germany lies here, and not in the representation of the employees and trade unions in the supervisory concept.

https://doi.org/10.3828/hsir.2020.41.8

Reading Hugh Clegg's 'The Bullock Report and European Experience' (1977) in Historical Context

Peter Ackers

Hugh Clegg's riposte (reprinted here) to the 1977 Bullock Report on *Industrial Democracy* was one of seven papers published with additional discussion material from a two-day conference at Leicester University on 4–5 April that year. Other academic contributors were Bill Wedderburn, labour lawyer and member of the Bullock Committee majority, and C. M. Schmitthoff, taking a European Community angle. The trade unions were represented by David Lea (Trades Union Congress, TUC), also a signatory to the Bullock Committee 'main report', and John Edmonds (General and Municipal Workers' Union); the employers by Pat Lowry, former director of the Engineering Employers' Federation, by then director of industrial relations at British Leyland; and J. D. M. Bell, chairman of North West Electricity Board and a former industrial relations academic. All spoke and wrote in a personal capacity. 'Collective bargaining at enterprise level is in its infancy', declared the conference chair, Otto Kahn-Freund in his preface, where he also claimed that 'it is difficult to believe that any major point of view remained unrepresented'.[1]

So, what were the Bullock 'main report' proposals that these papers debated? First, all large companies, over 2,000 employees, should have worker directors on their board. Second, these should be appointed to main

---

1 H. A. Clegg, 'The Bullock Report and European Experience', in R. Benedictus, C. Bourn, and A. C. Neal (eds), *Industrial Democracy: The Implications of the Bullock Report. Proceedings of a Conference Held at the University of Leicester, 4–5 April 1977* (Department of Adult Education, University of Leicester: 1977); *ibid.*, O. Kahn-Freund, 'Preface', p. 1; Department of Trade, Committee of Inquiry on Industrial Democracy (Bullock), *Report*, Cmnd 6706 (1977). For Clegg, see this issue of *Historical Studies in Industrial Relations* (*HSIR*) 41 (2020), pp. 171–90. All page references are to this version.

boards, not supervisory boards as in the German Federal Republic. Third, there should be equal shareholder and worker representation, with a group of independents agreed by the two parties. By contrast, most continental experience was of minority worker representation. Finally, and controversially, these board members should be nominated by workplace trade unions, maintaining the 'single channel' of worker representation through the unions. It is worth registering too the Bullock 'minority report', which suggested possible minority representation on supervisory boards, elected by all employees. Bullock's rationale appeared in chapter 3, 'The Pressures for Change'.[2] These included: the rise of the giant industrial enterprise, raising issues of social responsibility; the decline of deference and increasing employee expectations to have a say; the growth of collective bargaining and a TUC desire to raise this to the level of company decision-making; and the need for Britain to come into line with wider European Economic Community developments.[3]

There are two ways to read Clegg's contribution to the Bullock debate today. First, we need to understand *the context of how things looked at the time*, particularly in industrial relations and labour movement circles. The conference fully expected trade unions and collective bargaining to continue expanding in Britain for the foreseeable future. This was the industrial relations 'spirit of the age', even as the political ground was shifting. There was no expectation that the New Right might soon successfully challenge union power. If political change came, it was expected from a different direction. For Wedderburn, 'looking to the 1980s, the Bullock Report will be seen as a minimum programme for the transition in the direction of a socialisation of the private sector' (p. 1.19).[4]

Clegg's earlier writing on incomes policy was aware of the dangers ahead if the British state could not co-operate with trade unions.[5] Even

2 Bullock, *Report*, pp. 20–5.

3 See M. Gold, 'Worker Directors in the UK and the Limits of Policy Transfer from Europe since the 1970s', *HSIR* 20 (2005), pp. 29–65; J. Phillips, 'UK Business Power and Opposition to the Bullock Committee's 1977 Proposals on Workers Directors', *HSIR* 31/32 (2011), pp. 1–30; A. Williamson, 'The Bullock Report on Industrial Democracy and the Post-War Consensus', *Contemporary British History* 30:1 (2015), pp. 119–49.

4 K. W. Wedderburn, 'Industrial Democracy and Company Law', in Benedictus *et al.* (eds), *Industrial Democracy: Implications from the Bullock Report*, pp. 1.0–1.35. See Royal Commission on Trade Unions and Employers' Associations, 1965–68 (Donovan), *Report*, Cmnd 3623 (1968).

5 H. A. Clegg, *How to Run an Incomes Policy and Why We Made Such a Mess of the Last One* (Heinemann: 1971). See P. Ackers, 'Free Collective Bargaining and Incomes Policy: Learning from Barbara Wootton and Hugh Clegg on Post-War British Industrial Relations and Wage Inequality', *Industrial Relations Journal* 47:5–6 (2016), pp. 234–53.

so, this conference took place at a moment when he hoped the Social Contract incomes policy might work, before the 1978–79 strike wave, particularly in the public sector. Bullock's brief only covered the large-scale private sector. The editors described a 'modern industrial society' (p. v) while, for Clegg, 'Any explanation of industrial relations in British manufacturing must start with the shop stewards – and it is to manufacturing industry that the Bullock Report proposals primarily apply' (p. 5.8). Hence, there was little sense of the growing, feminized service economy or the dramatic post-industrial transition Britain would make in the 1980s.

Clegg's expectation of the European industrial relations future now seems surprising. He foresaw the shop-steward challenge from below, not only continuing in Britain but also spreading to Continental Europe, unravelling the stable, centralized, economically efficient industrial relations systems of Scandinavia and West Germany. 'In my opinion European experience is of limited relevance because Britain is not behind European countries in its problem of industrial relations in the enterprise, but ahead of them' (p. 180). In discussion he mooted the possibility that 'the "British disease" spreads. Europe, in general, is at the point which the UK was in 1945' (p. 181). With hindsight, Clegg failed to grasp the fragility of trade-union power in a voluntarist system, with few legal guarantees. Thus, he claimed in discussion: 'You might say that in Britain we have a different situation, because at the shop floor level we have workers' organisations which are so much more powerful than anything that exists in any of these other countries' (p. 189).

Second, we should read this contribution through the lens of Clegg's *intellectual past*, as a British industrial relations writer and public-policy figure, since there was a consistent theoretical line leading from his early writing. Two concepts were central: industrial democracy and pluralism. Both are open to various interpretations, but Clegg integrated the two, holding to a very consistent perspective throughout his academic career. Clegg's paper refers to *A New Approach to Industrial Democracy*, his last explicit piece on this theme, which he probably felt had settled the post-war debate. His distinctive approach was worked out through dialogue and dispute with the arguments of Sidney and Beatrice Webb, on one side, and G. D. H. Cole, on the other. From the Webbs, he took the description of collective bargaining as a form of *Industrial Democracy*; but they were state socialists who looked forward to a major extension of public ownership. Clegg had left the Communist Party in the late 1940s, becoming intellectually close not only to Allan Flanders and his *Socialist Commentary* group, but to the leading Labour Party social-democratic revisionists, Hugh Gaitskell and Anthony Crosland. His theory of industrial democracy regarded public ownership as irrelevant.[6]

Cole, a Guild Socialist, was critical of the Webbs's bureaucratic approach too but had long seen the solution as 'workers' control' of nationalized organizations. Clegg's first publication, *Labour in Nationalised Industry*, came from a Fabian Research Group initiated by Cole but he rejected the workers' control approach. His research study of the publicly owned London Transport, published the same year, argued that ownership did not change industrial relations. What really mattered were strong trade unions and collective bargaining. This drew Clegg's version of industrial democracy away from both the Webbs and Cole. By 1951, he had further theorized the position that nationalization, even with workers' control, was irrelevant to real industrial democracy, which was adequately defined in practical terms as free trade unions conducting collective bargaining. 'The trade union is thus industry's opposition – an opposition which can never become a government'.[7]

By the 1970s, Clegg preferred the new academic industrial relations language of 'joint regulation' and 'pluralism', but his central idea changed little.[8] This remained *'pressure group democracy ... the industrial parallel of political democracy'.*[9] Shaped by the formative experience of Nazi and Soviet totalitarianism, Clegg's primary pluralist preoccupation was that trade unions should remain strong representative institutions, independent of employers and of the state. With responsible, well-informed collective bargaining there was no need for worker directors. On the Donovan Commission, he supported the majority opposition to recommending even voluntary worker director schemes, against the two union representatives, Lord Collinson and George Woodcock, and Kahn-Freund. One reason

---

6 H. A. Clegg, *A New Approach to Industrial Democracy* (Blackwell, Oxford: 1960); S. and B. Webb, *Industrial Democracy* (Longmans, Green and Co.: 1897); P. Ackers, 'Collective Bargaining as Industrial Democracy: Hugh Clegg and the Political Foundations of British Industrial Relations Pluralism', *British Journal of Industrial Relations (BJIR)* 45:1 (2007), pp. 77–101.

7 H. A. Clegg, *Industrial Democracy and Nationalization: A Study Prepared for the Fabian Society* (Blackwell, Oxford: 1951), p. 22; *idem, Labour in Nationalised Industry: Interim Report of a Fabian Research Group* (Fabian Research Series 141: July 1950); *idem, Labour Relations in London Transport* (Blackwell, Oxford: 1950). For the Webbs, Cole, and Clegg, see P. Ackers, 'An Industrial Relations Perspective on Employee Participation', in A. Wilkinson, P. J. Gollan, M. Marchington, and D. Lewin (eds), *The Oxford Handbook of Participation in Organizations* (Oxford University Press: 2010), pp. 52–75.

8 H. A. Clegg, 'Pluralism in Industrial Relations', *BJIR* 13:3 (1975), pp. 309–16; *idem, The Changing System of Industrial Relations in Great Britain* (Blackwell, Oxford: 1979), 'Theories and Definitions', ch. 11, pp. 444–56.

9 Clegg, *A New Approach*, p. 131.

given in the Donovan Report was that these 'would divert attention from the urgent task of reconstructing company and factory collective bargaining'.[10]

Clearly Clegg's firmly voluntarist and defensive pluralism was not universally held among pluralists, especially those of the second-generation Oxford/Warwick school. Bill McCarthy drafted Labour's 1969 *In Place of Strife* White Paper; while George Bain, Clegg's close colleague and successor as director of the Warwick Industrial Relations Research Unit, signed the Bullock main report.[11] But beyond pluralist theory, it was probably more important to Clegg in 1977 that he regarded worker directors as irrelevant to the urgent, practical task of reforming British industrial relations. Indeed, he remained hopeful for his 1968 Donovan Commission strategy for enlightened management and responsible trade unions.[12] Like John Edmonds in this collection, he thought worker directors would get in the way and confuse the issue.

The Changing System of Industrial Relations in Great Britain repeated Clegg's case against the Bullock proposals, while pressing the argument for collective-bargaining reform. 'By this time, moreover, the reform of plant bargaining recommended by the Donovan report had to a considerable extent been carried through by the spread of plant-wide pay agreements and procedures, although the consequential changes sought by the Commission had been by no means fully realized'. In addition: 'There is therefore a prospect that [incomes] policies may be rather more lasting and successful in the future than in the past'. Moreover, 'Legislation under the social contract has already proved itself more durable than the [1971] Industrial Relations Act … and there is no evidence that a future Conservative government will sweep it away'. In his voluntarist view, the main danger for trade unions lay in accepting more from the law, while wishing to retain their old immunities and autonomy.[13]

Little of Clegg's theoretical case was out in the open in his heavy empirical shelling of the Bullock Committee's research. His target was the 'patently ridiculous' claim for some direct connection between the mere presence

10 Donovan, *Report*, p. 258, para. 1002.
11 P. Ackers, 'McCarthy, William Edward John [Bill], Baron McCarthy (1925–2012), Industrial Relations Scholar and Politician', *Oxford Dictionary of National Biography* online (2016).
12 P. Ackers, 'Game Changer: Hugh Clegg's Role in Drafting the 1968 Donovan Report and Defining the British Industrial Relations Policy-Problem', *HSIR* 35 (2014), pp. 63–88.
13 Clegg, *The Changing System*, pp. 435–6, 382, 434, and, for 'Industrial Democracy', see pp. 438–43; P. Ackers, 'The Changing Systems of British Industrial Relations, 1954–1979: Hugh Clegg and the Warwick Sociological Turn', *BJIR* 49:2 (2011), pp. 306–30. See, too, K. Sisson and W. Brown, 'Industrial Relations in the Private Sector: Donovan Re-visited', in G. Bain (ed.), *Industrial Relations in Britain* (Blackwell, Oxford: 1983).

of worker directors and the low-strike, high-productivity, co-operative industrial relations regime in Sweden. His verdict was devastating: 'These flights of fancy carry the majority of the Bullock Committee far out of sight of the evidence' (p. 178). In discussion, he went further. The Bullock studies of Sweden and Germany neglected crucial national context. 'They didn't, in fact, study the industrial relations scene in either country', while 'nobody on the Bullock Committee or anywhere else supposes that you can really learn anything serious about Germany or Sweden by going on a junket there for a few days' (pp. 186, 187).

From the 1950s, Clegg had tracked Continental European industrial relations developments. He was on especially sharp empirical form in this paper, having not long completed a classic comparative study, *Trade Unionism under Collective Bargaining*. Worker directors could not explain the success of the German and Swedish systems. They were too recent to matter and far less important than German works councils or the central co-ordinating role of the Swedish trade-union confederation, LO. One interesting aspect of Clegg's paper is the importance now conceded to works councils, 'as a big factor in employee participation in Germany' (p. 176), even though they gave workers less power than our shop stewards. 'But it does not follow that the two institutions can be expected to play a similar role in relation to worker directors' (p. 177). Shop-steward organizations were quite different from legally mandated, formally non-union, German works councils and the two should not be conflated.[14] One possible implication is that the German institutional separation between *distributive* collective bargaining and *integrative* workplace participation was crucial.[15] If so, this calls into question Clegg's long-standing scepticism about joint consultation. Equally, institutional separation often required strong national collective bargaining, which, once more, the Donovan Report had dismissed as more or less defunct.[16]

For Clegg in 1977, continental versions of industrial democracy worked where there was already a successful prior industrial relations system, developed through workplace and industry institutional practices over

---

14 H. A. Clegg, *Trade Unionism under Collective Bargaining: A Theory Based on Comparisons of Six Countries* (Blackwell, Oxford: 1976). For a retrospective, see K. Sisson, 'In Praise of Collective Bargaining: The Enduring Significance of Hugh Clegg's *Trade Unionism under Collective Bargaining*', *HSIR* 36 (2015), pp. 137–58.

15 P. Ackers, 'Workplace Participation in Britain, Past, Present, and Future: Academic Social Science Reflections on 40 Years of Industrial Relations Change and Continuity', in S. Berger, L. Pries, and M. Wannoffel (eds), *The Palgrave Handbook of Workers' Participation at Plant Level* (Palgrave: 2019), pp. 557–74.

16 J. Edmonds, 'The Donovan Commission: Were We in the Trade Unions Too Short-Sighted?', *HSIR* 37 (2016), pp. 222–8.

decades. One new, top-level initiative could not create that; nor could you impose corporate co-operation on our different free collective-bargaining system. But why had Britain neglected positive workplace participation institutions for so long? Clegg's answer, which he repeated twice, was British trade-union opposition (notwithstanding recent TUC movement on worker directors). 'In practice the strongest argument for the single channel in Britain is that the unions insist upon it, and no system of worker directors can operate without their consent' (p. 175). In discussion, he added that this was true as far back as 1945, 'at which time worker participation was out of the question in the UK because of TUC opposition' (p. 181).

Clegg's historical realism is understandable in terms of post-war Britain to 1979. The industrial relations system could only be reformed with active trade-union consent, or so it seemed. If the trade unions and employers could not make the collective-bargaining system work, the state could not do it for them. As Clegg understood, British trade unions were not ready for any form of worker participation that challenged collective bargaining. Thus Edmonds concluded another contribution equally critical of Bullock: 'If we are going to extend industrial democracy, we must find our method in the mainstream of British industrial relations. It has to be a method which is consistent with collective bargaining'.[17] The total opposition of employers to the Bullock main report's proposals must also have shaped Clegg's scepticism, following a career-long pursuit of *voluntary* agreements at workplace and state levels.

Clegg's Oxford philosophy tutor, Harry Weldon, had warned against 'the over-simplified doctrine that clever puzzle-solving is a panacea for political difficulties. The position of the statesman and that of the engineer are not analogous.'[18] In Clegg's world, this meant that you cannot simply social-engineer a complex industrial relations problem by top-down institutional tinkering. New institutions must bed down in established industrial relations traditions, so long as organized labour was central to how things work. As Alan Fox saw this, in his surprisingly similar response to Bullock, and later in *History and Heritage*, you should pursue 'methods that work *with* the historical grain' (original emphasis).[19]

---

17 J. Edmonds, 'The Bullock Committee's Report and Collective Bargaining', in Benedictus *et al.* (eds), *Industrial Democracy: The Implications of the Bullock Report*, pp. 4.1–4.25, at p. 4.11.

18 T. D. Weldon, *The Vocabulary of Politics* (Pelican, Harmondsworth: 1953), p. 81.

19 The quotation is from A. Fox, *History and Heritage: The Social Origins of the British Industrial Relations System* (Allen and Unwin: 1985), p. xiii. In *idem*, 'Corporatism and Industrial Democracy: The Social Origins of Present Forms and Methods in Britain and Germany (1977)', *HSIR* 38 (2017), pp. 171–219, at p. 172, he had written: 'certain attempts towards institutional "harmonization" ... may be said to go *with* the grain of one society and *against* the grain of

That need not spell stasis, as Margaret Thatcher (prime minister, 1979–90) grasped in her own way. National traditions are complex, composed of many grains. Once the state and employers had undermined and displaced union power, other 'systems' became possible. Laissez-faire suspicion of the state might lead in different political directions, aiding the transition to an individualist, consumer, service economy. In 1977, this was a possible future that Hugh Clegg did not want to entertain. Looking back now, we might speculate whether either Donovan or Bullock were missed opportunities to change the future course of British industrial relations.[20]

School of Business and Economics
University of Loughborough
Epinal Way, Loughborough LE11 3TU

another' (original emphasis). See also W. Brown, 'Introduction to Alan Fox, "Corporatism and Industrial Democracy"', *HSIR* 38 (2017), pp. 167–70.

20 See P. Ackers, 'Saving Social Democracy? Hugh Clegg and the Post-War Programme to Reform British Workplace Industrial Relations: Too Little, Too Late?', in S. Berger and M. Boldorf (eds), *Social Movement and the Change of Economic Elites in Europe after 1945* (Palgrave: 2018), pp. 257–77.

https://doi.org/10.3828/hsir.2020.41.9

'The Bullock Report and European Experience': What We Can Still Learn about Worker Directors from Hugh Clegg

Michael Gold

There are, perhaps, three aspects of Hugh Clegg's paper, 'The Bullock Report and European Experience',[1] that strike the contemporary reader most forcibly. The first is how *alien* it all seems: the past really does feel like 'a foreign country'.[2] Writing in 1977, Clegg's analysis of the potential role of worker directors appointed to the boards of United Kingdom companies was set against the background of an industrial relations landscape that has long disappeared: a largely white, male working population, employed on generally secure employment contracts in an economy dominated in the private sector by unionized manufacturing companies. Blame for the country's long-term industrial decline was pinned at the time, at least partly, on a fragmented industrial relations system that had led to wage drift, inflationary pressures and poor international competitiveness in consequence.

Trade unions had frustrated all attempts by previous Labour and Conservative governments to introduce statutory incomes policies, so the Labour governments of Harold Wilson and James Callaghan (1974–79) were trying a new approach, the Social Contract. Under this arrangement,

---

1 H. Clegg, 'The Bullock Report and European Experience (1977)', *Historical Studies in Industrial Relations (HSIR)* 41 (2020), pp. 171–90 (page references are to this version); first published in R. Benedictus, C. Bourn, and A. C. Neal (eds), *Industrial Democracy: The Implications of the Bullock Report. Proceedings of a Conference Held at the University of Leicester, 4–5 April 1977* (Department of Adult Education, University of Leicester: 1977), pp. 5–5.24.

2 L. P. Hartley, *The Go-Between* (Penguin, Harmondsworth: 1972 [1953]), p. 7.

unions agreed to voluntary pay restraint in exchange for a wide range of 'social wage' benefits designed to favour working people, including price and rent controls, public transport and housing subsidies, measures to redistribute income and wealth, public control of capital investment, an active labour market policy, the repeal of anti-union legislation enacted by the Conservative government, and – significantly – the 'fostering of industrial democracy'.[3]

Among the measures designed to foster industrial democracy was the Bullock Report,[4] the topic of Clegg's paper delivered less than three months after its publication, which had proposed the introduction of worker directors on the boards of larger private companies in the UK, in line with the practice in certain other successful European economies, notably the Federal Republic of Germany and Sweden. No one at the time had any idea that the world of Bullock and the Social Contract was to be blown apart by the election of the Conservative government of Margaret Thatcher in 1979, which set out to destroy union influence and to restore managerial prerogative at the workplace. Her success in achieving those objectives helps to explain the sense of alienation we have when reading Clegg's paper today.

And yet ... And yet there is a second aspect about this paper which also strikes us, one that is arguably more significant. That is the sense of how *familiar* the central issue is that Clegg is addressing, namely how best to ensure the accountability of businesses to their workforces and other stakeholders. Recent years have witnessed a woeful litany of corporate scandals involving at best neglectful and at worst corrupt boardroom decisions: British Home Stores, which went bankrupt in 2016 with a colossal pension fund deficit; Sports Direct, which was found responsible for 'some appalling working practices'[5] by a parliamentary inquiry in the same year; Carillion, which went into liquidation in 2018 having prioritized dividend payments over its pension liabilities; and GKN, taken over by Melrose, a firm known for asset-stripping and workforce reductions, also in 2018. These scandals, among others, became so infamous that they provoked

---

3 R. Tarling and F. Wilkinson, 'The Social Contract: Post-War Incomes Policies and Their Inflationary Impact', *Cambridge Journal of Economics* 1:4 (1977), pp. 395–414, at p. 395.

4 Committee of Inquiry on Industrial Democracy (Bullock), *Report*, Cmnd 6706 (1977). See A. Williamson, 'The Bullock Report on Industrial Democracy and the Post-War Consensus', *Contemporary British History* 30:1 (2015), pp. 119–49; and J. Phillips, 'UK Business Power and Opposition to the Bullock Committee's 1977 Proposals on Worker Directors', *HSIR* 31/32 (2011), pp. 1–30.

5 *Employment Practices at Sports Direct. Third Report of Session 2016–17 of the Business, Innovation and Skills Committee*, HC219 (House of Commons: 22 July 2016), p. 29, para. 15.

parliamentary inquiries and a certain promise from Theresa May MP as she announced her bid for leadership of the Conservative Party in July 2016:

> The people who run big businesses are supposed to be accountable to outsiders, to non-executive directors ... [but] the scrutiny they provide is just not good enough. So if I'm Prime Minister, we're going to change that system – and we're going to have not just consumers represented on company boards, but employees as well.[6]

Hence, some forty years after the publication of the Labour government's White Paper, *Industrial Democracy* (1978),[7] which had followed the Bullock Report with proposed statutory fall-back rights to board-level employee representation if company-level negotiations on bespoke arrangements failed, the Conservative government under May did indeed take steps to introduce a measure of employee voice into corporate boardrooms. After a Green Paper consultation and a select committee inquiry, it invited the Financial Reporting Council in 2017 to revise its Corporate Governance Code to require companies, on a 'comply or explain' basis, to adopt 'one of three employee engagement mechanisms: a designated non-executive director; a formal employee advisory council; or a director from the workforce'.[8] These provisions came into effect from 1 January 2019.

Clearly these reforms are extremely weak. Indeed, a survey of fifty-seven FTSE all-share companies carried out in spring 2019 revealed that 73% would designate an existing non-executive director to represent employees and 27% would set up a workforce advisory panel, with a 5% overlap of companies combining a non-executive director with a panel. The remainder, a mere 5% (two companies), would opt for a director appointed from the workforce.[9] Nevertheless, the principle had been conceded – and it is a principle to which a future, more radical government could return – that widening the composition of the board of directors is a significant element in securing the fair representation of stakeholders such as employees on the boards of companies, and therefore their potential influence over the earliest stages of decision-making. For the earliest stages of decision-making are critical, as they involve strategic issues such as investments, new products, restructuring and location of operations. At sub-board level,

---

6 T. May, 'Key Excerpts from the Leadership Launch of Britain's Theresa May', Reuters News Agency: 11 July 2016.

7 *Industrial Democracy* (White Paper), Cmnd 7231 (1978).

8 *Corporate Governance Reform: The Government Response to the Green Paper Consultation* (Department for Business, Energy and Industrial Strategy: 2017), Action 7, p. 34.

9 *Employees on Boards: Modernising Governance* (Local Authority Pension Fund Forum: 2019), p. 5.

by which time influence can be exerted merely over the operational aspects of decisions that have already been long taken, it is generally too little and certainly too late.

From this principle of representation there emerges debate over the requirements for a practically effective system of board-level employee representation in the UK. And in this context, Clegg's discussion – of supervisory boards, the minority status of worker directors and single-channel representation through trade unions – suddenly appears rather less alien. For Clegg raises issues that would require resolution by a radical government under any circumstances. Is it reasonable, for example, to place employee directors on unitary boards, or would it be more effective to introduce supervisory boards with an oversight function? European experience is ambivalent in this respect, and the answer depends very much on the historical trajectory of the country under review.[10] To what extent are employee directors at a disadvantage when they are in a minority on the board? In legal terms, in not one of the eighteen of the twenty-seven member states of the European Union (EU) plus Norway that have systems of board-level employee representation can employee representatives outvote shareholder interests on the board, whether unitary or supervisory. In all cases, their success depends on their ability to resolve disputes 'behind the scenes', to delay decisions or to build coalitions of interests over specific issues.[11] And is trade-union membership a significant factor in explaining the influence of employee representation on company boards? Given the minority status of employee representatives across the EU and Norway, then what does seem significant for their success is their training and skills base, as well as their links to other workplace representatives and their deep understanding of employment relations in their own company. All these factors are linked to trade-union membership, which gives them the independence and confidence to deal with the complex issues that arise at board level.[12]

It is noteworthy that such discussion of the practicalities of introducing board-level employee representation into the UK, both today and in the 1970s, continually harks back to European experience. This is hardly

---

10 N. Kluge and M. Gold, 'Board-level Employee Representation: Balancing Interests across the Company', in M. Gold, N. Kluge, and A. Conchon (eds), *'In the Union and on the Board': Experiences of Board-level Employee Representatives across Europe* (European Trade Union Institute, Brussels: 2010), pp. 5–11, at pp. 5–8.

11 *Ibid.*, pp. 9–11.

12 M. Gold, '"Taken on Board": An Evaluation of the Influence of Employee Board-level Representatives on Company Decision-Making across Europe', *European Journal of Industrial Relations (EJIR)* 17:1 (2011), pp. 41–56. See also K. Levinson, 'Employee Representatives on Company Boards in Sweden', *Industrial Relations Journal* 32:3 (2001), pp. 264–74.

surprising given the length of experience that a country such as Germany has had in this respect (though in other countries, such as Sweden, Denmark and the Netherlands, it is much more recent).[13] Nevertheless, it raises the third striking aspect of Clegg's paper, namely, the relevance of *policy transfer theory* to the whole debate. 'Policy transfer', 'lesson-drawing' and 'cross-jurisdictional learning' were not concepts in Clegg's vocabulary at the time,[14] but he was rightly concerned with an issue that could today be identified as central to that area of theory, namely, how relevant European experience actually was for policy-makers in the UK given the contrasting institutions, legal frameworks and cultures between the countries involved.

The choice of worker directors as a key feature of the industrial relations systems in Germany and Sweden would be explained today as a 'dominance effect'.[15] That is, because economic power is spread unevenly between countries, there is a tendency for one or more to take the lead in developing 'more efficient' business and industrial relations practices (such as Fordist mass production in the United States of America in the 1920s or lean production in Japan in the 1950s). Lead societies create dominance effects, or best practices that become global or regional standards, which are subsequently imitated by other societies though generally without the even capacity to do so. Such was the case with worker directors in Germany and Sweden. As Clegg points out, the terms of reference of the Bullock Committee were 'the need for a radical extension of industrial democracy in the control of companies by means of representation on boards of directors' and also explicitly to take into account 'experience in Britain, the EEC and other countries'.[16] The notion of a dominance effect was therefore implicit in the approach adopted by the Committee – though, as noted above, this rang

---

13 J. Waddington and A. Conchon, *Board-Level Employee Representation in Europe: Priorities, Power and Articulation* (Routledge: 2016), pp. 191–219. For an update, see M. Gold and J. Waddington, 'Board-level Employee Representation in Europe: State of Play', *EJIR* 25:3 (2019), pp. 205–18.

14 These concepts became popular in public policy circles in the 1990s. See R. Rose, *Lesson-Drawing in Public Policy* (Chatham House, Chatham, NJ: 1993); E. C. Page, *Future Governance and the Literature on Policy Transfer and Lesson Drawing*, paper prepared for the Economic and Social Research Council (ESRC) Future Governance Programme workshop on policy transfer (Britannia House: 28 January 2000). For an application relating specifically to employment relations, see A. Ferner, P. Almond, and T. Colling, 'Institutional Theory and the Cross-National Transfer of Employment Policy: The Case of "Workforce Diversity" in US Multinationals', *Journal of International Business Studies* 36:3 (2005), pp. 304–21.

15 C. Smith and P. Meiksins, 'System, Society and Dominance Effects in Cross-National Organisational Analysis', *Work, Employment and Society* 9:2 (1995), pp. 241–67.

16 Bullock, *Report*, p. v, para. 1.

some alarm bells for Clegg. To repeat his question: how relevant actually was European experience for policy-makers in the UK?

In the days before any coherent literature on policy transfer, Clegg's analysis is likely to be seen today as partial rather than systematic, and itself raises three sets of questions for the contemporary reader. First, how accurate is his analysis? Is it true, for example, as he suggests, that the introduction of worker directors was intended to bear the brunt of unleashing workers' abilities and improving industrial relations in the UK? He understandably describes these claims as 'flights of fancy' if true (p. 178), but has Clegg understood the objectives behind the Bullock Report correctly? Or has he rather overlooked its context within the Social Contract? Second, what was the role of the European Economic Community (EEC, now the European Union, EU) in promoting worker directors? Clegg failed even to mention, let alone examine, the EEC's draft Fifth Directive on the structure of public limited companies (1972), which was acting as a 'push' factor towards worker directors alongside the 'pull' factors reflected in the Bullock Report.[17] What relevance might the Directive have had on turning an optional measure under the Social Contact into a compulsory one enforceable by the European Court of Justice? And third, the question that leads on from the second, how does more recent research on policy transfer and 'lesson-learning' across national boundaries help to bring Clegg's concerns about the relevance of European experience up to date? Each set of questions is examined separately below.

The Bullock Report and its place in the Social Contract

After its election in October 1974, the Labour government had rapidly enacted measures designed to strengthen collective bargaining and promote the influence of the unions in the formulation of economic and industrial strategy. The objectives of its Alternative Economic Strategy (AES) included economic reflation, public ownership, planning agreements, controls on prices and imports as well as industrial democracy.[18] It reflected the views of the time about the role of tripartite bodies, such as the National Economic Development Council and the Manpower Services Commission, in running economic policy. Nationalization policies, planning agreements,

---

17 Clegg's failure to mention the EEC may be because he wanted to prevent overlap with another speaker's paper dedicated to its influence at the same conference: C. M. Schmitthoff, 'The Bullock Committee and the EEC', in Benedictus *et al.* (eds), *Industrial Democracy: The Implications of the Bullock Report*, pp. 6–6.19.

18 M. Wickham-Jones, *Economic Strategy and the Labour Party: Politics and Policy-Making, 1970–83* (Macmillan: 1996).

sector working parties and the creation of the National Enterprise Board extended the principle of government intervention, but did not create it.[19]

These measures formed the backbone of the Social Contract with the Trades Union Congress (TUC), which dominated the relationships between government, employers and unions over this period.[20] Stuart Holland, one of the minds behind the Alternative Economic Strategy, argued that 'if organized labour intends to secure advances for the working class as a whole, it must use its bargaining power through the Social Contract for dramatic progress towards key features of such a programme [the AES] in one parliament'.[21] It was in this context that certain sections of the labour movement developed an interest in board-level representation in contrast with the period ten years earlier, when the consensus had still emphasized collective bargaining between unions and employers as the principal means of securing influence in industry.[22] Clegg was therefore acting either inaccurately or mischievously when he alleged that the Bullock Report intended worker directors to carry the burden of reforming industrial relations in the UK. The Report, and the subsequent White Paper, were merely pieces in the much larger jigsaw of the Social Contract. Reform was multifaceted and included all the interlocking pieces noted above.

He was on much firmer ground when he declared that he did not know any authority in Germany 'who does not attach far more importance to works councils than to worker representation on boards in explaining the working of German industrial relations since the war' (p. 179), a point supported by Sir Otto Kahn-Freund, who was chairing Clegg's session (p. 190).[23] Indeed, the German system has traditionally – at least until reunification in the early 1990s – kept areas of potential consensus at the workplace (which

---

19 M. Sawyer, 'Industrial Policy', in M. Artis and D. Cobham (eds), *Labour's Economic Policies, 1974–79* (Manchester University Press: 1991), ch. 10.

20 R. Taylor, 'The Rise and Fall of the Social Contract', in A. Seldon and K. Hickson (eds), *New Labour, Old Labour: The Wilson and Callaghan Governments, 1974–79* (Routledge: 2004), pp. 70–104.

21 S. Holland, *The Socialist Challenge* (Quartet Books: 1978), p. 41.

22 J. Elliott, *Conflict or Co-operation? The Growth of Industrial Democracy* (Kogan Page: 1978), p. 205.

23 However, that should not imply that Germans themselves in any way discount the significance of the role played by board-level employee representation in their system of industrial relations. For example, some thirty years later, Angela Merkel, on becoming German Chancellor in 2006, declared that co-determination was an integral part of the country's social market economy and would remain so. See K. Biedenkopf, W. Streeck, and H. Wissman, 'A Core Element of Europe', *Mitbestimmung* 53:8 (2007), pp. 20–5. Clegg might have understood that point better had he bothered to go to Germany on one of – what he dismissed as – 'junkets' organized for the earlier Donovan Commission, of which he had been a member (p. 187).

are dealt with by the works councils) separate from those areas of conflict (which are dealt with by the unions through collective bargaining, generally at sector level). This distinction, and the legal framework within which industrial relations are conducted, has played a significant role in helping to contain strike levels in Germany since 1945. Nevertheless, Clegg did not go far enough in explaining the favourable influences on German economic development, which go well beyond industrial relations to include the role of the banks and the stock market, as well as the relatively concentrated ownership of companies, all of which has contributed to the long-term perspectives of German industry, its focus on 'patient capital' and hence its productivity.[24] The successful transfer of such aspects of the German system into a liberal-market economy like the UK would appear to be vanishingly small, as subsequent developments were to demonstrate.

The role of the EEC in encouraging debate about worker directors

UK accession into the EEC in 1973 focused the attention of the labour movement on the issue of worker directors, and opened up a new area for negotiations in a way unforeseen in the 1960s.[25] One of the aims of the EEC was to harmonize company law between member-states, which meant adoption of the draft Fifth Directive with its controversial provisions for employee representation on supervisory boards. This measure may today be viewed as an instance of 'direct coercive transfer' – that is, one where the EEC attempted to impose transfer on to member-states by means of a directive which is legally binding and enforceable through the European Court of Justice, once adopted by the Council of Ministers.[26]

The Conservative government (1970–74), committed to EEC membership, also apparently supported this Directive. Edward Heath, the Prime Minister, believed that entry into the EEC could help to improve British industrial relations, as Clegg notes (pp. 187–8), and the Commission on Industrial Relations duly produced a report analysing the extent of employee board-level representation across the EEC and its impact on industrial relations.[27] The role of the EEC in promoting

---

24 See M. Gold and I. Artus, 'Employee Participation in Germany: Tensions and Challenges', in S. Johnstone and P. Ackers (eds), *Finding a Voice at Work? New Perspectives on Employment Relations* (Oxford University Press: 2015), ch. 9.

25 M. Gold, 'Worker Directors in the UK and the Limits of Policy Transfer from Europe since the 1970s', *HSIR* 20 (2005), pp. 29–65.

26 D. Dolowitz and D. Marsh, 'Learning from Abroad: The Role of Policy Transfer in Contemporary Policy-Making', *Governance* 13:1 (2000), pp. 5–23.

27 Commission on Industrial Relations, *Worker Participation and Collective Bargaining in Europe*, Study No. 4 (Commission on Industrial Relations: 1974).

industrial democracy was widely acknowledged at the time. For example, the Association of British Chambers of Commerce observed that 'this groundswell of ideas towards greater "industrial democracy" – however defined and understood – has been swept into prominence by the activities of the European Economic Community'.[28]

The views of Jack Jones, then general secretary of the Transport and General Workers' Union (TGWU), are significant here. He noted that part of the Social Contract consisted in a commitment to an Industrial Democracy Act designed to increase workers' control of industry, interest in which had been stimulated by closer contact with the EEC and European trade unions: 'It meant a lot to me personally. From my youthful days I had been associated with the extension of collective bargaining. Now I saw the possibility of elected shop stewards taking their place in the boardrooms of private companies and publicly-owned industries'.[29] Indeed, Clegg reveals in his paper:

> When it became known by the General Council [of the TUC] that Mr Heath was going to propose supervisory boards with one-third representation for workers, Jack Jones said to his colleagues, 'Look, the one thing you cannot do is to say "No". When a Conservative Prime Minister says "Unions, do you want to go on the board?", you can't say "No, we reject this, Prime Minister". That's not the way to negotiate, as you know. If the management comes and asks you if you want something, you don't say that you don't want it: you say you want more.' Anyway, he said fifty percent. (p. 188)

The TUC Annual Congress in 1973 accordingly accepted the TUC's proposals for 50:50 representation on supervisory boards, adding the following year that such appointments would be acceptable only if made through trade-union machinery at company level.[30] It was believed in some quarters that the presence of worker directors on company boards would help to achieve union influence outside the scope of collective bargaining. The principal reason for TUC interest in worker directors lay, therefore, in the appreciation that collective bargaining did have certain limitations which board representation – the chance of which the EEC presented – could possibly overcome:

---

28 *Employee Participation: A Policy Study by Chambers of Commerce of Moves towards Industrial Democracy* (Association of British Chambers of Commerce: 1975), para. 7.

29 J. L. Jones, *Union Man: The Autobiography of Jack Jones* (HarperCollins: 1986), pp. 312–13.

30 *Industrial Democracy*, including supplementary evidence to the Bullock Committee (TUC: 1977), para. 91.

Major decisions on investment, location, closures, takeovers and mergers, and product specialisation of the organisation, are generally taken at levels where collective bargaining does not take place, and indeed are subject matter not really covered by collective bargaining. New forms of control are needed.[31]

Bill Wedderburn, who spoke alongside Clegg at the Leicester conference, also stressed this point in his own presentation.[32] By the mid-1970s, then, considerable pressure had built up around the idea of worker directors, set largely in the context of evidence from overseas. The idea was related to UK entry into the EEC and it was, in British terms, a new departure in industrial democracy. In the context of the Social Contract, it accordingly stimulated new debates which became focused on the deliberations of the Bullock Committee.

Clegg does not address the central issue about how to plug these limitations in collective bargaining other than to comment that minority worker representation on boards is 'a poor instrument for achieving the radical changes in industrial relations and performance that the Bullock Committee were seeking' (p. 174). It is not clear whether he believed that unions simply *cannot* have a say over strategic decisions at board level however important they are for their members' future (because such a move would undermine their principal function, collective bargaining), or whether they *should not* (because otherwise they would lose their independence), or maybe both.

Policy transfer and lesson-drawing

There is some evidence today (contrary to Clegg's opinion) that even minority board-level employee representation does in fact help to protect workers' interests in a variety of ways.[33] Whether or not, neither of the proposals for worker directors examined in this commentary was ever implemented. The 1978 White Paper diluted the Bullock Report in several ways, but was never enacted because the Conservative government of 1979 was fiercely anti-union in its industrial relations policies. The draft Fifth Directive, even though later amended to reflect a wider range of representation models, was eventually withdrawn in 2004. While theories of 'dominance effects' and 'direct coercive transfer' help to explain the

---

31 *Industrial Democracy* (TUC), para. 85.
32 K. W. Wedderburn, 'Industrial Democracy and Company Law', in Benedictus *et al.* (eds), *Industrial Democracy: The Implications of the Bullock Report*, pp. 1–1.35.
33 Gold, 'Taken on Board', *EJIR*.

origins of the proposals for worker directors – through the Bullock Report and the EEC respectively – the question remains why they both failed so miserably in the UK but why the proposals from the Financial Reporting Council were successfully implemented on a 'comply or explain' basis from January 2019.

Contemporary research into policy transfer and cross-jurisdictional learning – which of course long post-dates the work of Clegg – provides a helpful framework for comparing and contrasting the evolution of the debate on worker directors in the UK and in the EEC. 'Policy transfer' has been defined as 'a dynamic whereby knowledge about policies, administrative arrangements or institutions is used across time or space in the development of policies, administrative arrangements and institutions elsewhere'.[34] The literature examines the processes involved in the transfer of policies generally between countries, their content and the rationales involved.[35] While much of the research focuses on cases of successful transfer, Clegg was attempting to explain why he thought the introduction of worker directors would not work, as an example of policy failure. His contribution to the conference reveals the way in which he was groping towards some answers – namely, that policy-makers were not paying sufficient attention to the contexts of the institutions involved, in this case, the role of shop stewards in the UK in contrast to the role of works councils in Germany. The issue is why so many, though not all, influential policy-makers then did believe that worker directors could be introduced successfully into the UK on the basis of continental systems. In this context, it should be noted that one sceptic – Kahn-Freund, who was chairing the conference – had already warned against the misuses of comparative law: he had analysed the failures of the collective aspects of the Industrial Relations Act 1971 largely in terms of its misappropriation of Australian and American models. He had concluded: 'any attempt to use a pattern of law outside the environment of its origin continues to entail the risk of rejection'.[36]

There are two facets to the explanation, which can be couched in today's terminology of policy-transfer theory. The first focuses on the German and Dutch models of board-level employee representation used by the Commission of the EC when drawing up its draft Fifth Directive.

34 D. Stone, 'Learning Lessons and Transferring Policy across Time, Space and Disciplines', *Politics* 19:1 (1999), 51–9, at p. 51.

35 See, for example, Rose, *Lesson-Drawing in Public Policy*; D. Dolowitz and D. Marsh, 'Who Learns What from Whom: A Review of the Policy Transfer Literature', *Political Studies* (1996), pp. 343–57; and M. Evans and J. Davies, 'Understanding Policy Transfer: A Multi-Level, Multi-Disciplinary Perspective', *Public Administration* 77:2 (1999), pp. 361–85.

36 O. Kahn-Freund, 'On Uses and Misuses of Comparative Law', *Modern Law Review* 37:1 (1974), pp. 1–27, at p. 27.

Early versions of the Directive 'owed much to the work of Germans on the Commission's staff'[37] at a time when Germany was extensively admired for its high-wage, high-productivity economy based on industrial consensus (the dominance effect observed above). It had been drafted before UK accession into the EEC in 1973, so it broadly reflected the system of corporate governance of the original six member-states, which corresponded – in the classic terminology of David Soskice – to the co-ordinated market economy model, rather than to the liberal market economy model predominant in the UK, which at that stage was not even considered.[38]

The second facet concerns the practicalities of the proposed transfer from a co-ordinated market economy model into the UK. The 'transfer' was intended by the Labour government as a model for the UK even though the German system, as a co-ordinated market economy, arguably presents the greatest contrasts within Europe with that of the UK as a liberal market economy.[39] Institutional and legal constraints were largely ignored, as Clegg pointed out, even though the 'object' of transfer was an institution firmly embedded into the German industrial relations system.[40] Clegg accordingly focused specifically on the contrasting roles and responsibilities of shop stewards in the UK and works councils in Germany – their different status in law, the lowly status of unions at the German workplace and their differences in accountability, among others (pp. 176–8).[41] He concluded:

> British shop stewards would no doubt occupy a key role in the operation of a worker director system if one were instituted in Britain; but given the wide differences between works councils and shop stewards, this role

37 J. Charkham, *Keeping Good Company: A Study of Corporate Governance in Five Countries* (Oxford University Press: 2000), p. 279.

38 D. Soskice, 'The Institutional Infrastructure for International Competitiveness: A Comparative Analysis of the UK and Germany', in A. B. Atkinson and R. Brunetta (eds), *The Economics of the New Europe* (Macmillan: 1991), pp. 45–66.

39 S. Vitols, 'Varieties of Corporate Governance: Comparing Germany and the UK', in P. A. Hall and D. Soskice (eds), *Varieties of Capitalism: The Institutional Foundations of Comparative Advantage* (Oxford University Press: 2001), pp. 337–60.

40 Dolowitz and Marsh, 'Learning from Abroad', *Governance*, p. 12.

41 His prediction, that other European countries would be 'anxious to learn from the British experience' about the 'challenge from below', has proved without basis. He implies that, because 'management has largely ceased to control the organisation and performance of work' in the UK, it was to do so too in Germany (p. 180). Yet the German works council system, with its durable legal foundation, has arguably, despite challenges, weathered changes in industrial relations over the last forty years far more robustly than shop stewards in the UK voluntarist system. See Gold and Artus, 'Employee Participation'.

might be expected to be very different from that played by the German works council. (p. 177–8)

One of the most significant differences would have been nomination of worker directors. In German companies with between 500 and 2,000 employees, nominations are made by the works council or by 10% of employees (or 100 if this is a smaller number); in larger companies, a proportion is also nominated by the unions, but only a proportion.[42] By contrast, the single-union channel of nominations envisaged in the Bullock Report – for which, as Clegg noted, 'they had no alternative if their proposals were to be accepted by the unions' (p. 178) – would have given a domination to shop stewards' networks, an outcome that may have been welcomed by Jones but was robustly opposed by the employers. The Engineering Employers' Federation (EEF), for example, objected in its evidence to the Bullock Committee to the 'enforced representation of employees on boards of directors' and to 'the appointment of employee directors as nominees of trade unions'.[43] Underlying its objection lay employers' fears of the extension of collective bargaining into the boardroom, a fear unknown in Germany precisely because of its separation of works council and union responsibilities. Pat Lowry, former director of the EEF and in 1977 director of industrial relations at British Leyland, declared at the same conference: 'I certainly find it totally offensive to think that discussions of important items in the boardroom should be based on the "we and you" approach which is the hallmark of collective bargaining.'[44] Such a view would have been – and would be still – inconceivable in Germany.

Meanwhile, actual British experience with board-level employee representation is sparse, though one study of seven private-sector companies with such representation carried out between 1976 and 1979 concluded that the schemes were generally not 'distributive' but rather 'inspired by an incorporative philosophy'.[45] Evidence on its operation overall in the UK suggests patchy outcomes.[46]

42 See ETUI, *National Industrial Relations, Germany: Board-level Represen-tation* (European Trade Union Institute, Brussels: 2020).

43 EEF, *Statement of Evidence to the Bullock Committee of Inquiry on Industrial Democracy* (Engineering Employers' Federation: 1976), paras 1–9.

44 P. Lowry, 'The Bullock Committee's Report and Management', in Benedictus *et al.* (eds), *Industrial Democracy: The Implications of the Bullock Report*, pp. 2–2.24, at p. 2.6.

45 B. Towers, D. Cox, and E. Chell, *Worker Directors in Private Manufacturing Industry in Great Britain*, Research Paper No. 29 (Department of Employment: 1987), p. 31.

46 For a review of evidence on the operation of board-level employee represen-tation in the UK, see Gold, 'Worker Directors in the UK', *HSIR*, pp. 56–61.

The long shadow of Bullock

Though Clegg himself did not attempt to theorize the contrasts between
the UK and Germany as later analysts were to do, it is remarkable that
Alan Fox had done just that in a paper that had gone largely forgotten until
recently. Fox drew a key distinction between forms of 'vertical bonding' in
the processes of industrialization in the two countries. He stated:

> In Britain the rising class of bourgeois entrepreneurs were creatures of
> a society and culture in which feudal and manorial vertical bondings,
> underpinned by paternalist-dependence relations and ideology, had
> been undermined and corroded for a period of two centuries or more. In
> Germany such vertical bonding survived up to the process of industriali-
> zation, which occurred late, quickly and thoroughly, with its 'take-off'
> period in the closing decades of the nineteenth century.[47]

In other words, Fox saw contrasting forms of 'vertical bonding' as a key
distinction between the UK and Germany. In the UK, where it had become
loosened, employers felt little responsibility for their workers, which had
encouraged the development of independent working-class institutions,
notably unions, based on adversarial attitudes towards the bosses. In
Germany, employers felt a greater sense of responsibility, which encouraged
the development of the more consensual relationships that largely endure
to this day. These contrasting attitudes – adversarial and consensual –
underpin much of the contemporary analysis of liberal and co-ordinated
market economies. Fox was clearly ahead of his time.

It remains significant that, faced with a crisis of confidence in the probity
of corporate governance in the UK, May as Prime Minister resorted to
some form or other of board-level employee representation as a possible
solution. The version introduced by the Financial Reporting Council in
2017, as noted earlier, is enforceable only on a 'comply or explain' basis,
and offers companies three anaemic options: a designated non-executive
director, an advisory panel or a director appointed from the workforce.
Early indications suggest a paltry take-up of the director option, which – in
any case – raises none of the challenges of power distribution that concerned
Clegg when analysing the Bullock Report: the role of supervisory boards,
the minority status of worker directors, and single-channel representation through trade unions. However, given Fox's examination of vertical

---

47 A. Fox, 'Corporatism and Industrial Democracy: The Social Origins of
Present Forms and Methods in Britain and Germany (1977)', *HSIR* 38 (2017),
pp. 171–219, at pp. 188–9. Fox develops this argument in relation to the UK (but
not Germany) in his book: A. Fox, *History and Heritage: The Social Origins of
the British Industrial Relations System* (Allen and Unwin: 1985), ch. 2.

bonding, and subsequent research by others into the distinctions between co-ordinated and liberal market economies, the Financial Reporting Council options may be seen as 'a Very British Solution' to the problem of corporate governance: achievable but feeble. Unlike the 1978 White Paper, which was never enacted, they have been successfully introduced by cutting not against but with the historical grain,[48] the grain of the UK national business system which embodies voluntarism, individualism and government non-intervention, not to mention avoidance of union influence.

The discussion comes full circle, and it is now possible to understand better our reactions to Clegg's paper. Initially, and superficially, it seems *alien* as it describes a world of industrial relations long gone. The collectivist solutions proposed by Bullock were overtaken by the election of the Conservative government in 1979. Yet, on a more thoughtful reading, we are struck by the *familiarity* – the enduring nature – of the underlying issues that Bullock was attempting to address, that bubbled up again under the David Cameron (2010–16) and May (2016–19) governments, in the form of scandals, soaring executive pay, worker exploitation, and lack of corporate accountability to broader stakeholders. And then, at the most analytical level, the insights revealed by more recent research into *policy transfer* inform our contemporary understanding of the barriers to Bullock. Clegg was correct when he argued: 'there is no evidence at all in the Bullock Report from which to predict the consequences of implementing the majority proposals' (p. 180). However, while his view was based largely on a recognition of the principal differences between Germany and the UK, ours is based on a deeper and more systematic penetration into the contrasting characteristics between co-ordinated and liberal-market economies. The Financial Reporting Council options, then, undoubtedly reflect the most that would be acceptable to the private sector given the balance of power currently prevailing in the UK.

That said, John McDonnell, then Labour's Shadow Chancellor, announced in September 2018 that under a Labour government 'a third of the seats on company boards will be allocated to workers'. He added that shares would be transferred into an Inclusive Ownership Fund to be managed by workers, to give them 'the same rights as other shareholders to have a say over the direction of their company'.[49] The TUC, which has campaigned to reform corporate governance for many years, also continues to include board-level employee representation among its policies.[50] The

---

48 Fox uses the imagery of imposing change with and against the historical grain in *History and Heritage*, p. xiii.
49 John McDonnell's full speech to Labour Party conference (24 September 2018), p. 3.
50 TUC, *Workers on Board: The Case for Workers' Voice in Corporate Governance* (Trades Union Congress: 2013).

Labour Party lost the general election in December 2019, but these policies demonstrate that Bullock casts a long shadow. If Labour were to win at any time in the future on a platform to introduce worker directors onto the boards of UK companies, its principal challenge would be to learn the lessons from Bullock: that reforming labour relations and corporate governance requires a coherent package of radical policies, certainly, but that they also need to be carefully tailor-made to UK institutions and legal frameworks and not imported from abroad merely on the grounds of their success in their host countries.

School of Business and Management
Royal Holloway, University of London
Egham, Surrey TW20 0EX

https://doi.org/10.3828/hsir.2020.41.10

The Bullock Committee, Industrial Democracy, and the Trade Unions: The Revolution that Never Was

John Edmonds

The Bullock Committee's Report on Industrial Democracy, published in January 1977, was forthright in its ambition: it aimed to transform British industrial relations.[1] Its principal recommendation was that the boards of large companies should be made up of worker and shareholder representatives in equal numbers and that the workers on the board would be nominated by trade unions. The report declared that implementing its recommendations would 'release energies and abilities at present frustrated or not used and thereby create a framework which will allow conflicts of interest to be resolved with greater mutual advantage'.[2]

This transformation never took place. Alan Bullock, the chair of the Committee, was accustomed to success. He had written an acclaimed biography of Adolf Hitler,[3] turned a lowly educational institute into a modern and prestigious Oxford college,[4] and had led an important investigation into the teaching of English.[5] Bullock was a high-minded liberal who believed deeply in the process of building consensus through discussion in committee. But the attempt to find an agreed method of introducing industrial democracy defeated him. The continuous arguments in the

---

1 Committee of Inquiry on Industrial Democracy (Bullock), *Report*, Cmnd 6706 (1977).
2 Bullock, *Report*, p. 160, para. 3.
3 A. Bullock, *Adolf Hitler: A Study in Tyranny* (Odhams: 1952).
4 Against strong opposition from much of Oxford's establishment, St Catherine's Society became St Catherine's College: W. Knapp, 'Bullock, Alan Louis Charles, Baron Bullock (1914–2004), Historian and College Head', *Oxford Dictionary of National Biography* (*ODNB*) (2008), online.
5 Department for Education and Science, Committee of Inquiry (Bullock), *Report: A Language for Life* (HMSO: 1975).

Committee 'strained not only his skill as chairman but his robust health'.[6] An agreed report was not possible. Three members of the Committee representing business interests[7] broke away and wrote a minority report that rejected any attempt to put workers' representatives on the board.

The aftermath was even more disappointing. In an attempt to reduce the opposition to the report, the Labour government's White Paper diluted several of Bullock's recommendations.[8] However, before legislation was tabled, in May 1979 the incoming Conservative government led by Margaret Thatcher declared that the Bullock recommendations would never be enacted.

Formation

From the start, the Bullock Committee seemed dogged by bad luck. It came into existence almost by accident. The Labour government had promised to develop the Social Contract[9] with the trade unions in a manner which gave them a greater influence over industrial affairs. Largely at the insistence of Jack Jones, general secretary of the Transport and General Workers' Union (TGWU) and the most powerful trade-unionist in Britain, the Social Contract included a commitment to develop industrial democracy. As long ago as 1967, Jones had chaired an influential Labour Party group which had called for 'new forms of worker participation'.[10] In his autobiography he said that achieving industrial democracy was a 'lifelong commitment'.[11] Within the Trades Union Congress (TUC), Jones argued strongly in favour of putting workers onto company boards and he expected the government to honour its Social Contract commitment.

According to his colleagues in the TGWU, the strategy of Jones and Len Murray, TUC general secretary, did not involve a committee of inquiry. Their preferred method was to develop a clear trade-union policy on industrial democracy that included the appointment of worker directors in all large companies and then to negotiate an agreement based on this

---

6 Knapp, 'Bullock', *ODNB*.
7 Professor Sir Jack Callard, chairman of ICI and subsequently of British Home Stores; Norman P. Biggs, chairman of Williams and Glyn's Bank; and Barrie Heath, chairman of GKN.
8 White Paper, *Industrial Democracy*, Cmnd 7231 (1978), p. 119.
9 The Social Contract began as an agreement about pay and was developed into a wide-ranging agreement that aimed to give trade unions greater influence over industrial strategy and economic policy.
10 G. Radice, *The Industrial Democrats: Trade Unions in an Uncertain World* (Allen and Unwin: 1978), p. 119.
11 J. L. Jones, *Union Man: The Autobiography of Jack Jones* (HarperCollins: 1986), p. 312.

policy directly with the government.[12] A complication arose when, in order to test the support of Labour MPs for industrial democracy, Giles Radice – Labour MP for Chester-le-Street – submitted a private member's bill. Such bills rarely make much progress as it only requires an objection from one MP to end their life. However, on this occasion, a mistake by the whips meant that no objection was lodged and 250 MPs voted to give Radice's bill a second reading. It went into the committee stage, with Radice playing a leading part.

The Labour government was extremely discomforted and pressed Radice to withdraw the bill. He initially refused and only relented when the government agreed to set up a committee of inquiry.[13] It was an unfortunate start. After all the political manoeuvrings, the establishment of the Bullock Committee looked less like a high-level inquiry into an important policy question than an exercise in damage limitation.

After much discussion, terms of reference were agreed. They included a commitment to recommend an appropriate form of industrial democracy and a requirement that the Committee take due account of forms of employee participation in other European countries. This reference to European practice was helpful to the TUC as the European Economic Community (EEC)'s draft Fifth Directive had commended the appointment of worker representatives to company supervisory boards.

Membership of the Committee was carefully balanced. The three union representatives were Jones, Clive Jenkins (general secretary of the Association of Scientific, Technical and Managerial Staffs, ASTMS), and David Lea (representing the TUC). Each was firmly committed to supporting the appointment of worker directors. There were initially four business representatives, all of whom were expected to express doubts about proposals for worker directors. The two academics, Bill Wedderburn[14] and George Bain, were close to the unions. Bullock as chair was also expected to give general support to the trade-union position.

With this membership, it was no surprise that, thirteen months later, the Bullock majority report gave the trade-union representatives most of what they wanted. It recommended that worker representatives should form part of the boards of large companies, that the number of worker representatives should be equal to the number of shareholder representatives, and that the worker directors should come from the trade unions. Less expected was the uncompromising reaction of the business members of the Committee. Their opposition was anticipated but Bullock believed in consensus and he was disappointed that the business members went as far as to write a minority report. The greater surprise was the ferocity of the attack by

---

12 Private discussion with a TGWU national secretary, 1977.
13 Conversation with Radice, 27 April 2020.
14 Bill Wedderburn and David Lea had drafted Radice's bill.

business leaders that followed publication of the report. This was not the polite disagreement that Bullock might have hoped for; it quickly became a major battle.

Business leaders' offensive

The fierce and vocal opposition of business leaders also startled leaders of the Labour Party. The campaign by many large companies and the organizations representing them was high profile and relentless. John Methven was one of the business representatives originally appointed to the Bullock Committee and during its meetings he had declared his strong opposition to workers on the board. In 1976 he resigned to become director general of the Confederation of British Industry (CBI), where he made opposition to workers on the board the focus of his work: 'Nothing', he told CBI members, 'is more important to the CBI than this'.[15]

Methven set up a committee of CBI grandees to direct the campaign. They aimed to build a formidable political and industrial alliance. Hector Laing of United Biscuits made contact with Thatcher, by now leader of the Conservative Party, to ensure that it would give no support to Bullock. She gave this assurance. With that flank protected, the CBI directed its main attack at the Labour Cabinet. Leading industrialists from Shell, ICI, Courtaulds, GKN, Marks and Spencer, and British Leyland lobbied Cabinet ministers against the report. A constant theme was that industry would withdraw co-operation from the Labour government if attempts were made to implement the worker director proposals. Similar arguments were advanced by the Institute of Directors and by Chambers of Commerce.

At an early meeting with the Prime Minister, James Callaghan, Sir Rowland Wright of ICI told him that his managers were in a state of 'near revolt' at the prospect of the Bullock majority proposals being implemented.[16] A good number of medium-sized companies wrote to their MPs and to ministers to express their opposition. To reinforce its claim that companies were overwhelmingly against the appointment of worker directors, the CBI carried out a survey of its members. Of the 457 companies that replied, two-thirds opposed the Bullock recommendations. The remainder were prepared to accept some minority representation on supervisory boards,

---

15 Letter from CBI to all member companies, 4 March 1977: J. Phillips, 'UK Business Power and Opposition to the Bullock Committee's 1977 Proposals on Worker Directors', *Historical Studies in Industrial Relations* (*HSIR*) 31/32 (2011), pp. 1–30, at p. 21.

16 Meeting in Cabinet Room, 23 February 1977: *ibid.*, p. 20.

with the worker directors elected by all employees, including non-unionists – a much weaker proposal than recommended by Bullock.[17]

In parallel with this attack, business leaders sought to demonstrate that many companies were already providing employees with opportunities to discuss company policy. Unilever and ICI explained their consultation arrangements to the government. There may have been some exaggeration in these presentations. My impression, as a union negotiator at the time, was that the consultation committees rarely discussed company strategy and then only after decisions had already been taken. Nevertheless, this initiative gave business leaders and their political allies the opportunity to claim that effective procedures for worker involvement were already in place and that there was no need for measures as radical as worker directors.

An early objective of the business leaders' offensive was to stop the Labour Cabinet from uniting behind the Bullock majority report. The CBI and its allies noted that Edmund Dell, the Trade Secretary, and Shirley Williams, the Education Secretary, were not very enthusiastic about worker directors. Both were briefed extensively[18] and were offered material to show how seriously consultation with workers was taken in the more progressive companies. These two Cabinet ministers, together with their natural allies, Roy Jenkins, David Owen and Bill Rodgers,[19] gave Methven and the CBI a useful group of 'moderate' insiders who could be fed information in advance of any Cabinet discussion of Bullock.

According to Tony Benn, Callaghan's first inclination was to brush aside the objections of the business leaders: 'They need to get used to a new way of working.'[20] Benn was gratified by this robust approach. However, divisions in the Cabinet, and especially Dell's insistence that the proposals in the minority report should be taken into account and the unexpected insistence by Peter Shore that non-unionists should be included,[21] eventually pushed the Prime Minister into agreeing to an extensive period of consultation.

Callaghan was keen to preserve the industrial democracy initiative because of its place in the Social Contract agreed with the unions. However, Callaghan and the rest of the Cabinet soon became aware that the policy of workers on the board was less popular with trade unions than they had been

---

17 CBI, employment policy committee, 'Employee Participation: A Review', December 1977: Phillips, 'UK Business Power and Opposition to the Bullock Committee', *HSIR*, p. 9.

18 Conversation with Radice, 27 April 2020. In 1976 Radice had been Shirley Williams's Parliamentary Private Secretary.

19 Jenkins, Owen, Rodgers, and Williams left the Labour Party in 1981 to form the Social Democratic Party, which Dell then joined.

20 T. Benn, *Against the Tide: Diaries, 1973–76* (Hutchinson: 1989), p. 690.

21 Conversation with Radice, 27 April 2020.

led to believe. Opposition from the business leaders had, of course, been anticipated but Callaghan expected the committed support of the unions. He did not get it. The great tragedy of the industrial democracy initiative of 1977 was that the TUC had not done the planning and communication work which was necessary to prepare the union movement for what amounted to a radical change in policy.

Independence or participation

The extent of the change should not be underestimated. The trade-union approach to board membership had been decided in the 1940s. When the transport and energy industries were nationalized by the Labour government elected in 1945, with Clement Attlee as Prime Minister, the trade unions debated whether they should become involved in the management of these companies or remain independent of management. After much soul-searching, the TUC decided to endorse the policy which had been developed in the TUC's post-war reconstruction report five years earlier. The report to the Congress in 1949 was emphatic and was carried by a large majority. The trade-union movement, it declared, 'should retain its complete independence of the executive and employing authority. ... Only thus can unions exert their power of independent criticism and perform, without divided loyalties, their primary functions of maintaining and advancing the working conditions of workpeople.'[22]

Hence, trade unions chose independence rather than participation in management decision-making. Although both the 1944 and the 1949 reports related specifically to the nationalized industries, the principle was applied to all companies in all sectors of the economy. The commitment to independence meant that trade unions focused on strong workplace representation and effective collective bargaining. Union structures were designed to deliver those objectives. By the time the Bullock Committee was appointed, this had been the pattern of trade-union activity for more than a quarter of a century.

The first indication of any appetite for change had come in the TUC's evidence to the Royal Commission on Trade Unions and Employers' Associations (Donovan Commission) in 1967, which suggested that workers might be appointed to some boards on an experimental basis. Otto Kahn-Freund, a member of the Commission, was very surprised when he read that part of the TUC evidence: 'I thought, I can't be awake. This can't be true. This is a complete change of position.'[23]

---

22 Trades Union Congress (TUC), Annual Report 1949, p. 213.
23 J. Edmonds, 'The Bullock Committee's Report and Collective Bargaining', in R. Benedictus, C. Bourn and A. C. Neal (eds), *Industrial Democracy: The*

In 1973, after several failed attempts to reform industrial relations, Edward Heath, the Conservative Prime Minister, surprised TUC representatives by indicating that he was favourably disposed to the suggestion in the EEC's draft Fifth Directive which commended minority worker representation on company supervisory boards. According to Hugh Clegg, Jones responded to Heath in a manner familiar to trade-union negotiators:

> Jack Jones said to his colleagues ... 'When a Conservative Prime Minister says, "Unions, do you want to go on the board", you can't say, "No, we reject this, Prime Minister". That's not the way to negotiate. ... If the management comes and asks you if you want something, you don't say that you don't want it: you say you want more.'[24]

The TUC did exactly that. It told Heath that minority worker representation on company boards was not acceptable. The TUC wanted 50%.

That claim went into an interim report laid before delegates at the TUC's Congress in September 1973.[25] Although support for the appointment of worker directors represented such a radical change, the report generated little interest. Given the political context, it was difficult to take the issue seriously. No one really believed that a Conservative government would agree to workers filling half the seats on company boards. In any event the trade-union movement had bigger things to worry about. The oppressive Industrial Relations Act 1971 was in force and a statutory incomes policy was restricting pay negotiations.

In 1974, the political situation changed very quickly. The Conservatives did badly in the February general election; Heath's attempt to form a coalition with the Liberals failed and Labour was able to form a minority government. Ideas about worker directors which had seemed laughable when proposed by Heath now became the stuff of real-life politics. The trade unions had a promise in principle from Labour to promote industrial democracy but detail was lacking. 1974 became a moment of decision for the TUC. Perhaps it was the right time to forget about striking negotiating

---

Implications of the Bullock Report. Proceedings of a Conference Held at the University of Leicester, 4–5 April 1977 (Department of Adult Education, University of Leicester: 1977), pp. 4.1–4.25, at p. 4.19. Kahn-Freund chaired the conference and commented frequently. Some experimentation took place in the British Steel Corporation and later in the Post Office. For steel, see P. Brannen, E. Batstone, D. Fatchett, and P. White, *The Worker Directors: A Sociology of Participation* (Hutchinson: 1976).

24 H. A. Clegg, 'The Bullock Report and European Experience', in Benedictus *et al.* (eds), *Industrial Democracy: The Implications of the Bullock Report*, reprinted in *HSIR* 41 (2020), pp. 171–90, at p. 188.

25 TUC, Annual Report 1973, Annex C: Supplementary Report B, 'Industrial Democracy', pp. 384–422.

postures and start thinking deeply about the changes that were needed and, in particular, the implications for trade unions of appointing worker directors to the boards of big companies.

The TUC report

Unfortunately there is no evidence that any such fundamental analysis ever took place. The TUC administrative machine set about turning the interim report which had been nodded through the 1973 Congress into a final report.[26] Its message was unequivocal. The TUC wanted workers on the boards of big companies, it wanted the unions to select those worker representatives, and it insisted that the number of worker representatives on the board should be equal to the number of shareholder representatives. There was little suggestion that appointing workers to the board might create problems for trade unions. According to the TUC's final report, worker directors would increase the power and influence of trade unions and could readily co-exist with the trade unions' traditional commitment to collective bargaining.

Some unions were less convinced and began to ask questions. Would the change have to take place in every major company, even where the workers showed no interest? How would worker directors decide their policy? And crucially, how would collective bargaining be affected in companies with workers on the board? The TUC responses were reassuring in tone but lacking in detail. As a result, several unions decided to submit motions to the Annual TUC Congress reaffirming the movement's commitment to collective bargaining as the principal method for improving the pay, conditions and influence of union members. The composite motion which was debated at the 1974 Congress insisted

> that the best way to strengthen industrial democracy is to strengthen and extend the area of collective bargaining ... Congress rejects the mandatory imposition of supervisory boards with worker directors, and calls for a more flexible approach giving statutory backing to the right to negotiate on ... major issues, but relating the control more directly to collective bargaining machinery.[27]

At first sight it is difficult to reconcile the terms of this motion with the commitment to worker directors contained in the TUC's final report.

---

26 TUC, Annual Report 1974, Annex B: Supplementary Report B, 'Industrial Democracy', pp. 292–330.
27 *Ibid.*, Composite Motion 17, p. 557; original motions, p. 567; debate on pp. 523–30.

Nevertheless, Murray told delegates that the report and the motion were, in fact, compatible. Although many union delegates were still unconvinced, they wanted to avoid a public row which might embarrass a minority Labour government. Murray's verbal gymnastics were accepted and both the report and motion were carried by votes of the delegates. To many people inside and outside the hall, it seemed to be a classic case of the trade-union movement facing both ways.

Murray was subsequently pressed to explain how the TUC's evidence to the Bullock Committee would be framed. The fear of some unions was that the TUC might rely on the report and ignore the terms of the motion. Murray's response was that the TUC evidence would reflect the nuances of trade-union opinion. And it is fair to record that the TUC evidence did indeed emphasize the importance of collective bargaining.[28] Nevertheless, taken as a whole, the evidence made far too little of the range of opinion in the trade-union movement and implied a unanimity which did not exist.

This outcome was convenient to the Bullock Committee which decided to accept the TUC evidence as the authentic voice of the trade-union movement. As a result the Committee did not seek evidence from individual unions and, although six unions sent in submissions, they were not invited to give oral evidence. Bullock explained this decision by declaring the Committee's faith in the authority of the TUC evidence: 'we know that the TUC is speaking for a large number of affiliated unions who have not felt it necessary to submit evidence on their own account.'[29] It is difficult to avoid the conclusion that, in failing to investigate trade unions' reservations about the appointment of worker directors, the Bullock Committee was guilty of a failure of process.

By deciding not to explore the views of unions more carefully, the Committee certainly simplified its work but it also ensured that the reception to its report was far more mixed than the chair might have expected. Once the three business representatives decided to produce a minority report, Bullock knew that the reaction from the CBI and the Institute of Directors would be antagonistic. But he must have been surprised at the lack of warmth shown by so many trade-unionists. After all, Lord Watkinson, CBI president, had labelled the Bullock proposals as a 'power-grab by the unions'.[30] When the report was published it seemed that many trade-

---

28 TUC, *Industrial Democracy* (TUC: 1977), containing the TUC's 1974 'Statement of Policy' and the 'Supplementary Note of Evidence to the Bullock Committee 1976' (approved by the TUC General Council in March 1976 and subsequently endorsed by the September 1976 TUC). The Supplementary Note can also be found in TUC, Annual Report 1976, pp. 321–5.

29 Bullock, *Report*, p. 26, para. 2.

30 Lord Watkinson, CBI president, to C. A. Shillingham, Coca-Cola senior vice-president, 24 February 1977: Phillips, 'UK Business Power and

unionists were less interested in grabbing the power associated with board membership than Bullock had been led to believe.

Worker directors and collective bargaining

At various times the trade-union members of the Bullock Committee were pressed to consider the problems that the appointment of worker directors might cause for trade unions. During its meetings, Jones was insistent that worker participation in board decision-making would not damage unions' ability to negotiate better pay and conditions. He argued that negotiations took place with company management while the worker directors would be concerned with the company's overall strategy.[31] In Jones's view, they could exist side by side, without conflict and without significant overlap.

To say the least, Jones's view was optimistic. A discussion about company strategy will certainly involve decisions about labour costs and how they might change. Once that figure is set, it will inevitably have a strong effect on what is offered at the negotiating table. If offers on pay and conditions based on that figure are rejected by union negotiators, company representatives are very likely to mention that the worker directors had signed off the strategy that had set the limit. Of course, it is theoretically possible for company boards to avoid setting a figure for labour costs until negotiations are complete but that would very likely lead to the worker directors coming under pressure from the union negotiators to support union claims at board meetings. None of this suggests that the strategic questions decided by the board and the process of collective bargaining can be kept separate.

More serious problems would arise if a company decides to close an office or a plant. The normal reaction of union members is to call on their union to oppose the closure. That opens up questions about the role of the worker directors. Was the closure discussed in the board and, if so, why did the worker directors not block it? And if the worker directors say it was not discussed, union members will want to know why and will ask what they are going to do about it.

Whatever the truth of the matter, the worker directors are likely to be held at least partly responsible for the bad news. That will risk bringing the union negotiators and the unions' executive committees, which by now might be mounting a campaign to oppose the closure, into conflict with the worker directors. As was recognized in the TUC's 1949 decision, the involvement of workers in company decision-making puts them in a

---

Opposition to the Bullock Committee', *HSIR*, p. 21.
31 Bullock Committee minutes, 22 December 1976: *ibid.*, p. 16.

compromised and vulnerable position. There is a real danger that, when difficult issues arise, the worker directors would become scapegoats, distrusted by union members and pinpointed by management as having been party to unpopular decisions.

These problems are serious, but with goodwill and some important changes in union structure their effect might be mitigated. Unfortunately between 1974 and 1977 there was no determined attempt to identify potential problems and to find workable solutions. On one side were those union leaders, such as Murray and the three trade-union representatives on the Bullock Committee, who suggested that the difficulties were inconsequential; on the other side were those such as Frank Chappell, general secretary of the Electrical, Electronic, Telecommunications and Plumbing Union, who was against worker directors on political grounds, and committed negotiators like David Basnett, general secretary of the General and Municipal Workers' Union, who believed that the trade unions should forget worker directors and build on what already existed.[32]

End of Bullock

The effect of the business leaders' offensive and the splits in the trade-union movement was that industrial democracy stopped being a cause for celebration in the Labour Party and became a political difficulty which had to be managed. During the months of consultation that Callaghan had agreed, little common ground was found. Radice, who had tabled the private member's bill in 1975, feared that his initiative and the Bullock Report would lead nowhere.[33] So he proposed a series of compromises, many of which were accepted by Callaghan and formed the basis of a White Paper.[34] The right to board-level representation for workers in big companies was confirmed but it would be introduced in stages. At first a joint union committee would be established and after three or four years the committee could claim the right to board membership for workers on the higher of a two-tier board structure. The most important change was that, to start with, workers would only make up a third of the board rather than the 50% claimed by the TUC. Non-unionists might also be included if they formed what was called 'a homogenous group' and appealed successfully to a newly created regulatory body.

The White Paper was not well received. Every group seemed to have objections, and legislation based on the White Paper would have struggled to get through the House of Commons. However, that was never tested.

---

32 Private conversation with David Basnett, July 1977.
33 Radice, *The Industrial Democrats*, pp. 134–5.
34 White Paper, *Industrial Democracy*.

During the winter of 1978–79 the government tried to enforce a pay norm below the rate of inflation and, after a series of high-profile strikes, Labour lost a vote of no confidence in the House of Commons and the Conservatives won the May 1979 general election. That ended any political discussion of the Bullock recommendations.

Whatever the short-term relief felt by some union negotiators at the failure of the proposal to introduce worker directors, in the longer term the outcome of the argument over the Bullock Report proved profoundly unsatisfactory to the trade-union movement. In its first sentence, the White Paper had boldly stated that 'In a democratic society, democracy does not stop at the factory gate or the office door.'[35] This optimistic sentence was mistaken. Forty years later, the anomaly of autocratic power in British business has still not been corrected. After the bruising struggles of the 1970s, industrial democracy disappeared from Britain's political agenda. Eleven general elections have been held since the Bullock Committee reported, and putting workers on company boards has not been a significant campaign issue in any of them.[36]

Inadequacy of collective bargaining

During the 1980s the trade-union movement relied on collective bargaining to defend its members and to improve their lives. However, in an increasingly neoliberal economy, with a public sector greatly diminished and with employment in manufacturing industry shrinking every year, they lost millions of members, forfeiting industrial strength and political influence. In reality, collective bargaining had never been very effective in helping members with little negotiating power. Soon after I became GMB general secretary, I recall one union official sadly commenting on the limited reach of collective bargaining: 'Even when trade unions had twelve million members, it was no fun being a kitchen porter in a hotel which would not talk to trade unions.'[37]

Moreover, collective-bargaining strength has never proved effective in stopping even heavily unionized companies from reducing their workforce or closing down workplaces. In the 1970s a widespread and certainly exaggerated perception of trade-union power had tended to conceal the

---

35 Bullock, *Report,* para. 1.
36 Even the 1979 Labour Party manifesto was cautious: 'We will establish an industrial democracy commission to stimulate and monitor schemes of industrial democracy in the private sector and nationalised industries.' It was almost as if the Bullock Committee had never existed.
37 Private conversation with GMB official, 1986.

many limitations of collective bargaining. But the economic and political changes of the 1980s exposed them in full.

Some of these gaps can be filled by legislation. During the heyday of trade-union power, such unions as the TGWU and the Amalgamated Engineering Union insisted that the law should stay out of industrial relations. Slowly, as the limitations of collective bargaining came to be more widely recognized, unions have accepted that the law can be an ally as well as a threat. Nowadays, much trade-union campaigning is directed at achieving improvements in legal rights, including the minimum wage.

But, as the trade-unionists on both sides recognized in the 1970s, creating industrial democracy requires a change in the balance of power. Company strategy remains a managerial prerogative. Employees may be informed; they may be asked for their views; they may even be permitted to put questions to senior managers. However, whether the consultation with employees is extensive or non-existent, in the end it is the senior managers acting alone who take the decisions.

There is some political recognition that the current balance of power is not ideal, but this is coupled with a notable reluctance to get to grips with the issue. When Theresa May became Conservative leader, her acceptance speech contained a hint that employees might be represented on the board.[38] But that gentle suggestion was not pursued. In its 2019 general election manifesto, the Labour Party proposed that employee be part-owners of their companies. Part-ownership can easily be taken to imply some represen- tation on the board but this was not spelt out in the manifesto.[39]

The TUC maintains a long-standing commitment to industrial democracy but is similarly reluctant to adopt it as a high-profile issue. This is unfortunate because greater democracy will not be achieved until the trade-union movement develops and promotes a coherent policy. Ironically this is now much easier than it was in the 1970s.

A new policy

Forty years ago, the trade-union movement would not agree to non-unionists being given any representational rights in companies. In its rapid survey of practice in other European countries,[40] the Bullock Committee took a look

---

38 11 July 2016.

39 'We will give workers a stake in the companies they work for – and a share of the profits they help create – by requiring large companies to set up Inclusive Ownership Funds (IOFs). Up to 10% of a company will be owned collectively by employees': *Labour Party Manifesto 2019.*

40 Clegg dismissed the overseas visits made by the Bullock Committee as 'junkets': Clegg, 'The Bullock Report and European Experience' (1977), *HSIR*, p. 187.

at German works councils but would not recommend them as a possible model for Britain because members of works councils are elected by all employees rather than by trade-unionists. This was a great pity because, as Clegg and many others have remarked, works councils are an impressive part of the German industrial relations system and of great value to German workers.

Works councils cannot organize a strike and cannot negotiate pay increases, matters which are dealt with elsewhere. But they have substantial rights guaranteed by law, including consultation rights on economic and financial matters and a long list of important co-determination rights on issues ranging from salary scales and shift patterns, to methods of work, dismissals and redundancy. Amazing as it may seem to anyone accustomed to the arbitrary behaviour of some British managers, German companies cannot conclude such matters without the consent of the works councils.

Importing works councils into Britain would not be painless. There is an obvious trade-off. Are British trade unions prepared to give up their policy of excluding non-unionists from decision-making and accepting a limit on local bargaining in return for a range of rights far greater than those which exist in most British workplaces? In the 1970s trade unions had reason to hesitate; there was still the possibility that strong shop stewards' committees might achieve the best of both worlds. But in the 2020s the choice is more straightforward. Because trade unions are weaker, most members have only a forlorn hope of winning by local negotiation the power and influence which German workers are guaranteed by law. Nowadays the balance of advantage is decisively in favour of adopting the German system. As a first step towards industrial democracy, British unions should campaign for the creation of elected bodies on the model of works councils.

The significant legal rights of works councils limit decisions that management can make without consultation and agreement. But by their nature a works council cannot have much effect on a company strategy decided at board level. To achieve anything close to industrial democracy, the issue of board representation has to be addressed.

In order to gain TUC support, the Bullock Committee had to accept the demand for 50% worker representation on the board. At a meeting with Callaghan, Murray and Jones explained that they wanted a major transfer of power which only 50% representation would deliver.[41] This was an understandable negotiating position in the 1970s but, even then, the leap from having no workers on the board to parity with shareholder represent-atives looked very ambitious. Nowadays, with weaker trade unions and, after four decades when the neoliberals have successfully established the

---

41 Meeting, 4 May 1977: Phillips, 'UK Business Power and Opposition to the Bullock Committee', *HSIR*, p. 26.

primacy of shareholder rights, a demand for 50% worker representation on the board might be regarded as unrealistic.

Fortunately, the choice is not just between parity and no representation at all. Even minority board representation would give workers and their unions useful information about the state of the company and about management intentions. If worker representatives probe intelligently, they will uncover many of the company secrets and will get much earlier notice of troublesome matters than if they decide to remain on the outside.

The Bullock Committee rejected the proposal that union members could mandate the worker directors.[42] The Committee wanted to avoid the threat of a deadlock on the board but that decision was a mistake. Telling union members that they cannot decide on the policies which their representatives should pursue at board level would have fatally undermined the credibility of worker directors.

An alternative plan began to be developed in the White Paper which was given less attention than it deserved. The proposal was that a supervisory board should be created, and should include a minority of worker directors, 'in close touch with employees and their unions'.[43] Minority representation removes Bullock's objection to mandating, and opens other opportunities. Once mandating is allowed, worker directors can promote the wishes of their members on the supervisory board in a forthright manner. Managers would, of course, be able to use their majority on the board to outvote the worker directors, but that would mean taking sole responsibility for the outcome. Worker representatives could not be blamed for unpopular decisions and it would be difficult to use policies decided by the supervisory board to deny claims made by union negotiators.

Under this arrangement, unions would be able to promote interlocking policies on the supervisory board and during negotiations. This coherence would be reinforced if there were some overlap of membership between the supervisory board and the union negotiating team. The Bullock Committee decided that only company employees could be worker representatives. That was also a mistake. Filling all or most of the worker director seats with full-time officials would certainly be foolish but the presence of even a single official from the negotiating team on the supervisory board would encourage worker directors to take due account of the union's negotiating priorities.

The final decision is whether the worker representatives on the supervisory board should be elected by all employees or only by trade-unionists. There are strong arguments for an exclusively trade-union approach. Trade-union membership gives worker directors independence

---

42 Bullock, *Report*, p. 85, para. 40.
43 White Paper, *Industrial Democracy*, para. 25.

and a system of accountability that keeps them in touch with employees, and provides sources of expertise which enable them to develop robust arguments.

Unfortunately a contrary argument is easy to make. Nowadays trade unions have too few members in many private companies to claim the democratic legitimacy to speak on behalf of all employees. Nevertheless, giving trade unions no effective influence is liable to have unfortunate results. Supervisory boards in non-union companies might well become like many existing consultative arrangements where more time seems to be spent eating lunch than scrutinizing management proposals.

The best available compromise might be to include all employees in the election process but give trade unions the responsibility for triggering the new system. With this approach, an election of worker directors would not take place until a trade union with members in that company makes a formal application.

This is a final compromise in a policy which some will say is already too half-hearted. The justification for this approach is sad but obvious. If the issue of industrial democracy is to be restored to the political agenda, trade unions need to make proposals which both appeal to people at work and avoid the questioning of their motives as was common in 1977, when the Bullock Report was described as a 'power grab by the unions'.[44] In the 2020s there should be no doubt that a campaign for industrial democracy aims to benefit most people in Britain by reducing the autocratic power of management and giving all employees greater control of their working lives.

---

44 Lord Watkinson to Shillingham, 24 February 1977: Phillips, 'UK Business Power and Opposition to the Bullock Committee', *HSIR*, p. 21.

https://doi.org/10.3828/hsir.2020.41.11

Backwards in Time? Reflections of an Industrial Relations Officer in the Coventry and District Engineering Employers' Association, 1977–1979

Neil Ritson

Introduction: Mobil, Essex and Coventry

After graduating in psychology my first job was at the Mobil Oil Company Ltd in London and Essex. Mobil was one of four American oil companies which invested in the United Kingdom post-war and so competed with BP, Shell and Burmah. Esso had engendered a sea change in industrial relations with its 1960 productivity agreements, as analysed by Allan Flanders in his seminal book,[1] followed by Mobil, written up in a book called *New-Look Industrial Relations*,[2] and these cascaded through the rest of the industry, and more widely in the UK following government pay-restraint policies. These allowed for increases in earnings so long as they were supported by increased productivity.

After first working as employee relations adviser at Mobil's London head office, I was promoted to work at its Coryton refinery in Essex. Here I was responsible for relations with the production division's general union, the Transport and General Workers' Union (TGWU); the maintenance division's six craft unions organized in the Joint Crafts Union Negotiating Committee; and some thirteen external contractors' trade unions.[3] The last

---

1 A. Flanders, *The Fawley Productivity Agreements: A Case Study of Management and Collective Bargaining* (Faber and Faber: 1964).

2 F. W. Oldfield, *New-Look Industrial Relations* (Mason Reed: 1966).

3 Mobil recognized six major craft unions: the Electrical, Electronic, Telecommunications and Plumbing Union; the Amalgamated Society of Boilermakers,

were covered by the Coryton Site Agreement which copied the national agreement of the Engineering Employers' Federation (EEF), the so-called 'Black Book'.

I was impressed with the ways in which these agreements worked: negotiations with trade unions took place daily, and fortnightly consultation sessions were also held to 'clear the air' and listen to their grievances and ideas. Mobil was a first-names company, with 'single status' – a single canteen, no overtime pay, a single pension plan – but there was still a division as between blue- and white-collar staff – the former on fixed salary grades; the latter with additional 'merit' pay. Both were paid monthly by bank transfer and the blue-collar unions were recognized, with a de facto closed-shop and 'check-off' system of monthly union subscriptions deducted at source.

Around Mobil's refinery were other process plants (Shell, Van den Berg and Jurgens, Portland Cement) and also Ford's Dagenham car plant and its Basildon tractor plant. Light engineering was represented by firms such as Kodak and Yardley. As the area was only some thirty miles from London, new developments post-war had encouraged displaced families from London's devastated East End to move to Basildon, Laindon, Pitsea, Canvey Island, and Southend. The labour market was tight, and trade-union attitudes from the London metropolitan area were exacerbated by the moves to this new and, at first, almost barren land.

Mobil management sent me on a course at the Coventry Management Training Centre in Leamington Spa, run by the Coventry and District Engineering Employers' Association (CDEEA), to learn about the new suite of employee relations law introduced by the Labour government elected in 1974.[4] The difference from Essex was stark: the setting of Woodland Grange, the restaurant at the Blackdown Hotel, and the spa town itself was inspiring. The week-long course, with guest lecturer Olga Aikin, provided intellectual stimulation.

When later I saw an advertisement in *Personnel Management* for an industrial relations officer at the CDEEA, I was immediately interested

---

Shipwrights, Blacksmiths and Structural Workers; the Amalgamated Union of Engineering Workers (AUEW) – the Engineering Section, representing mechanical trades, and the Construction Section, representing trades such as crane drivers, scaffolders, and riggers; and the National Union of Sheet Metal Workers, Coppersmiths, Heating and Domestic Engineers representing welders. Also recognized was the Transport and General Workers' Union (TGWU) representing semi-skilled production workers and manual workers in maintenance.

4 Health and Safety at Work Act 1974, Trade Union and Labour Relations Act 1974 (as amended in 1976), Employment Protection Act 1975, Sex Discrimination Act 1975, Race Relations Act 1976. See M. Davies and M. Freedland, *Labour Legislation and Public Policy: A Contemporary History* (Clarendon Press, Oxford: 1993), ch. 8.

– more in leaving Essex than leaving Mobil. After the interview, I had a letter thanking me for my application but regrettably not appointing me. A week or so later I received a phone call from the deputy director asking if I was still interested as there had been another resignation. Later, he told me that he had persuaded the director to appoint me as I was 'so modern' – perhaps a reference to my productivity bargaining at Mobil and its relevance to the 1968 agreement to allow it in the EEF. I accepted the offer of an appointment as an industrial relations officer with slightly more pay, a company car and an opportunity to develop my career.

Coventry and its industrial district provided at first a similar outlook to Mobil and Essex – Rolls-Royce (formerly Bristol Siddeley), General Electric Company (GEC); the factories of the British Leyland Motor Corporation Ltd – Triumph Motors, Jaguar-Daimler, Morris Motors, Alvis, Coventry Climax; suppliers such as Brico, Coventry Radiator, Dunlop, Lucas, Motor Panels, Sterling Metals; and machine-tool makers such as Alfred Herbert, Coventry Tool and Gauge, and Webster and Bennett; other large companies such as Massey-Ferguson, Chrysler (formerly Rootes), and Automotive Products (in Leamington).[5] This impression, as it turned out, was naive, and completely incorrect.

Coventry and District Engineering Employers' Association

From 1977 to 1979 I worked as an industrial relations officer at the CDEEA, when it was, as it had been for very many years, a major force in industrial relations in the locality. Few studies of employers' associations have been based on empirical research; most have derived their analyses from secondary data and other studies.[6] Hugh Clegg noted that

---

5 Case studies of industrial relations in three Coventry engineering companies can be found in M. Terry and P. K. Edwards (eds), *Shopfloor Politics and Job Controls: The Post-War Engineering Industry* (Blackwell, Oxford: 1988). S. Tolliday, 'High Tide and After: Coventry's Engineering Workers and Shopfloor Bargaining, 1945–80', in B. Lancaster and T. Mason (eds), *Life and Labour in a Twentieth Century City: The Experience of Coventry* (Cryfield Press, Coventry: 1986), pp. 204–43, gives an overview, with case studies of Standard, Rootes, Jaguar, and Alfred Herbert. Also see H. A. Turner, G. Clack, and G. Roberts, *Labour Relations in the Motor Industry: A Study of Industrial Unrest and an International Comparison* (Allen and Unwin: 1967); and D. Lyddon, 'The Car Industry, 1945–79: Shop Stewards and Workplace Unionism', in C. Wrigley (ed.), *A History of British Industrial Relations, 1939–1979* (Edward Elgar, Cheltenham: 1996), pp. 186–211.

6 E. Wigham, *The Power to Manage: A History of the Engineering Employers' Federation* (Macmillan: 1973), is a national history. R. Croucher, 'The Coventry Toolroom Agreement, 1941–1972, Part 1: Origins and Operation',

'Employers' associations can easily preserve secrecy, and they have little incentive to do otherwise.'[7] This paper, in utilizing an auto-ethnographic model of participant observation (where I was a member of the organization analysed),[8] offers insights into the little known or acknowledged norms, values, and behaviours that impacted on how the CDEEA operated in the 1970s.

From 1977 to 1979 I worked as an industrial relations officer at the CDEEA, when it was, as it had been for very many years, a major force in industrial relations in the locality. The role of the industrial relations executives and officers at the CDEEA was to give advice; represent firms at industrial tribunals, and at arbitration and conciliation hearings; and chair 'conferences', that is negotiations, between the signatory trade unions and the management of the member firms in the district. Some 200 firms were members of the CDEEA in the 1970s, though it was dominated by a small number of major companies. There were eight officers in total who administered the employers responses under the procedural agreement. A separate division operated as Coventry Management Training Centre and I was one of a small team of three staff, chosen for our apparent outgoing personalities as much as our expertise, who led training at the Coventry Management Training Centre on one-week courses; the topics covered were Complete Employment Law, Industrial Relations, and Negotiating Techniques.[9] The centre was a highly professional and well-organized operation, with experienced and friendly staff who had developed courses based on their specialism, including a specific group on training and consultancy in occupational health and safety. We also conducted in-plant training at member firms' premises on various topical issues, usually employment law.

Historical Studies in Industrial Relations (HSIR) 8 (1999), pp. 1–41, and *idem*, 'Part 2: Abolition', *HSIR* 9 (2000), pp. 37–70, are essential reading for industrial relations in the Coventry engineering industry. R. Hyman, *Disputes Procedures in Action: A Study of the Engineering Industry Disputes Procedure in Coventry* (Heinemann: 1972) covers the late 1960s along with some case studies from 1970; this predates the withdrawal of the unions from the national procedure agreement in 1971 and the new agreement of 1976 with only one stage of procedure external to the factory. See also, more generally, A. McKinlay, 'The Paradoxes of British Employer Organization', *HSIR* 31/32 (2011), pp. 89–113.

7 H. A. Clegg, 'Employers', in A. Flanders and H. A. Clegg (eds), *The System of Industrial Relations in Great Britain: Its History, Law and Institutions* (Blackwell, Oxford: 1954), pp. 197–251, at p. 201.

8 P. Atkinson and M. Hammersley, 'Ethnography and Participant Observation', in N. K. Denzin and Y. S. Lincoln (eds), *The Sage Handbook of Qualitative Research* (Sage, Thousand Oaks, CA: 1994), pp. 248–61; J. P. Spradley, *Participant Observation* (Harcourt College Publishers, Orlando, FL: 1980), pp. 58–62.

9 I was also sent to Belfast to teach for the Northern Ireland Training Board.

In addition we undertook research projects such as creating an algorithm for member firms in line with the government's pay-restraint policies and the EEF national negotiations, advisory work for non-member clients, and surveys of member firms on government initiatives such as the Short-Time Working Compensation Bill, and the White Paper on Industrial Democracy.[10] These were sent to the EEF, edited if necessary and forwarded to government.

We also handled industrial tribunals, advised on legislation, and conducted arbitration and conciliation claims. These included individual dismissal cases with local officers of the Advisory, Conciliation and Arbitration Service (which had only recently been established in 1975 as an independent statutory body), and collective cases to the Central Arbitration Committee (CAC) under Schedule 11 of the Employment Protection Act 1975 and under the Fair Wages Resolution (FWR). These allowed trade unions within a firm (the FWR was limited to government contractors) to claim additional pay increases if their rates of pay were unfavourable as compared to relevant district wages. In some cases, member firms were sympathetic to such claims so as to prevent the loss of critical staff. After one such case, the GEC industrial relations director sent a letter to Alan Berry, CDEEA director, congratulating me on the outcome of a CAC hearing which 'could not have been better from the company's point of view'.[11] This represented a wage increase for technicians stymied under the government's pay policy. Taken up by the Association of Scientific, Technical and Managerial Staffs (ASTMS), it had the support of the company which was concerned about staff turnover in a critical area.

Perhaps the most important role of CDEEA staff was to chair conferences for member firms under the Procedure for the Avoidance of Disputes. It allowed for domestic conferences (negotiations) at the workplace; if a 'failure to agree' was recorded, the issue could be referred by the instigating party – usually the trade unions but sometimes the employer – to an 'external conference' between the full-time officers of the relevant unions and an officer of the CDEEA. A failure to agree at this level could be followed by official industrial action by either party – a lockout of the workers by the employer or industrial action by the trade unions.

An industrial relations officer chaired the conferences but in some of the larger firms the industrial relations manager or production manager might take that lead role, and the association staff member would act as secretary. Conferences were usually held at 10.00 am or 2.30 pm at the offices of the member firm. For staff trade unions there was a further stage in the procedure, held at the CDEEA's offices. These negotiations consisted of

---

10 Short-Time Working Compensation Bill [Bill 116], 1978–79; White Paper, *Industrial Democracy*, Cmnd 7231 (1978).

11 The letter is in my files.

234 HISTORICAL STUDIES IN INDUSTRIAL RELATIONS 41

a very wide variety of issues – safety, dismissals, the annual pay round, piecework, equal pay. They involved both manual and staff trade unions, but predominantly the former.

When a trade union sent a formal reference in the procedure to the CDEEA, the conference was set up by the appropriate administrator. The letter to the employer and the relevant trade unions confirmed the conference details, including the exact wording of the reference and a copy would be given to the nominated association officer. This was not done by the hierarchy, with regard to experience or other factors, but by the administrator, whose decision was simply pragmatic as to who was available. This meant sometimes an awkward scheduling and in one month I chaired three or four annual pay conferences at Coventry Climax, each covering a different group of staff. It then was convenient for the company's personnel manager (or whatever title the post-holder was given) to claim any failure to agree was based on my lack of expertise rather than the company's low offers. Apparently, this was not an unusual problem, but staff simply took it as part and parcel of the role.

In either role, the CDEEA representative would take and write up the official notes. Such were the number of conferences each week that we were issued with small cassette recorders to use to dictate the draft of the official minutes immediately afterwards, adding our recollection to the notes taken where appropriate. These were then typed and sent back to the firms for record purposes. There were usually no notes to accompany the reference, which was at first quite alarming. The reasons apparently were that the officer would be briefed by the employer before the conference or during the usual adjournment after the trade unions had delivered the reference's justification. Thus, the conferences were quite predictable, though of course not always conducted in a rational manner: one official of the Amalgamated Union of Engineering Workers (AUEW) in particular was prone to emotional outbursts.

The format would follow a standard pattern of trade-union submission, adjournment, employer response, back-and-forth argument, further adjournments, summary. Sometimes the reference would be referred back to the domestic level if there were overall agreement, but detail needed to be reconsidered. Otherwise, there would be an agreement reached or a failure to agree as the end of procedure, thus allowing the unions to invoke industrial action or the company to lock out the affected employees – sending them dismissal letters – something which hardly ever occurred. Most of the conferences I chaired, according to notes I made at the time, ended in a failure to agree. It was obvious there was little preparation to engage the unions. The management team was usually not well known beforehand, and introductions took most of the time. The idea was to listen to the union case, and then adjourn to think up a response. No one referred to the fact that the claim had already gone through the domestic stage.

The Director, A. P. Berry, was a powerful figure at the national level of the EEF and locally. He was a member of the Manpower Services Commission, the Industrial Tribunals panel, the West Midlands Economic Planning Council, and chairman of governors of Lanchester Polytechnic (now Coventry University). He had authored several publications published by the CDEEA.[12]

As a powerful employers' organization in a vital industry the CDEEA was an important constituent of the EEF which represented the sector to government. Berry had had the strong support of Conservative ministers and civil servants at the Department of Employment when in 1972 he had led the successful campaign by the CDEEA to abolish the Coventry Toolroom Agreement, which had determined wages for skilled engineering workers in the area since 1940.[13] This relationship was rekindled in 1979 after the election of the Conservative government under Margaret Thatcher as Prime Minister. Her personal private secretary, Adam Butler, was literally sent to Coventry to meet the CDEEA's management board at the Davenport Road headquarters. (I was present at the meeting, taking notes.) Butler, the son of the former Conservative politician, 'Rab' Butler, was an Eton-educated, Oxford graduate in his mid-forties and clearly held views similar to Thatcher. In his opening comments, based on the Conservative manifesto, he sketched out what he thought was a strict divide between socialist and communist forces and the employers' power to manage. In this he was supported by Berry and several senior managers (who referred to the manual employees of the member firms as 'the troops'). Butler's main thrust was to enquire if the government, in 'taking the unions on', would be supported by Coventry employers. Around the table sat ten or twelve major employer representatives – chief executive officers, chairmen and directors; the general effect was for them to look at their feet. They were perhaps fearful of a similar reaction by workers to the last Conservative government's Industrial Relations Act 1971.[14] One board member, from a minor refitting site on a distant aerodrome in Bitteswell, part of British

12 CDEEA, *Wage Drift, Work Measurements and Systems of Payment* (CDEEA, Coventry: 1968); A. P. Berry, *Workers' Participation: The European Experience* (CDEEA, Coventry: 1974); *idem*, 'Labour Relations in Japan', *Industrial and Commercial Training* 11:3 (1979), pp. 114–16.

13 Croucher, 'The Coventry Toolroom Agreement, Part 1', *HSIR*, and 'Part 2', *HSIR*.

14 On 18 March 1971 Coventry engineering workers left work in their thousands to join a huge demonstration in the Precinct against the Industrial Relations Bill. For the Joseph Langston case at Chrysler Ryton, Coventry, see B. Weekes, M. Mellish, L. Dickens, and J. Lloyd, *Industrial Relations and the Limits of Law: The Industrial Effects of the Industrial Relations Act, 1971* (Blackwell, Oxford: 1975), pp. 58–61. For the Industrial Relations Act 1971, see Davies and Freedland, *Labour Legislation and Public Policy*, ch. 7.

Aerospace, expressed his support for action but was ignored. Another commented 'but these are our people, we employed them, trained them … they make our products'. Butler was aghast and seemed not to understand. He asked if Renold was an American firm (maybe hinting that would be understandable: was he thinking of J. J. Reynold the tobacco company?), but of course it was not. In the event the EEF only moved to support legislation to restrict and regulate trade unions and industrial action after the 1983 general election when – in the aftermath of the Falklands War and the split in the Labour Party – Thatcher was returned with a robust majority, and mass unemployment had severely weakened trade unions.

Personal reflections

At the outset, as a newcomer to Coventry, I was soon alerted to the CDEEA's specific ethos which was based on Coventry's industrial history. This had not been obvious at the interview but was hinted at in the subsequent offer letter. Though the salary was higher than at Mobil, and a company car was provided, the letter was oddly phrased in that holiday had to be taken in 'Coventry Holiday Fortnight' and 'Coventry September Week'. What were they? When? Were all staff going to be absent at the same time? What about all the staff at member firms? Was it like 'Wakes Weeks' in the Lancashire cotton mills? Would Coventry then be deserted? It turned out only to be a directive for association staff. This was a foretaste of the unusual, the different culture in Coventry and the CDEEA which I had later to reflect on. For example, in the wider city, many factories had not been replaced or refurbished post-1945, and were Edwardian brick construction. I never knew about the newer 'shadow' factories, built as part of the rearmament programme just before the outbreak of the Second World War. Lucas's building still bore the faint painted zigzag camouflage stripes from that period, which had not been removed.

Early in my post I was seconded to GEC's main factory (in Stoke, an area of Coventry) for a month to accustom me to the local scene. My first impressions were not good: the facilities were meagre, often conferences were held in the manual workers' canteen, with 'noises off', poor-quality furniture, and even dirty. The factory offices had walls which were not plastered but painted eau de Nil. Asked about how I was getting on by the chief executive officer, I mentioned that the general environment might discourage the trade unions from conciliating, as they might feel they were being put down. He laughed at my apparent naivety: 'Painting walls doesn't bring profits'. GEC managers were conservatively dressed. The senior industrial relations manager, a former shop steward, had sticking plaster over the bridge of his glasses, slicked-back black hair and wore both belt and braces on his trousers. His boss was a small, neat man, a former RAF pilot, with a pleasant but steely attitude.

The CDEEA's office was located in a spacious building in its own grounds in a shady, quiet avenue, Davenport Road, opposite Bishop's House (the residence of the Bishop of Coventry). Offices were shared, two or three industrial relations officers in each, located each side of the main entrance, fronted by a small reception window. Each desk was not only provided with a phone and cardex diary system, but with a large leather-tooled cigarette box. Inside were three compartments: two were separately filled with untipped and tipped cigarettes and a central compartment held matches and pipe cleaners. These were supposed to be offered to visitors but of course the staff who smoked occasionally dipped into it. Upstairs were the offices of the deputy director and his secretary, and at the rear the small kitchen and dining room. At the front of the building was the director's large office which was equipped with a drinks' cabinet, sofas and lounge chairs, and an en-suite toilet, shower, and his exercise bike. At the rear of his office there was a sliding door which led to the large panelled boardroom.

The fact that the CDEEA had a distinct culture was highlighted from the beginning in the different lunch times of the association as against those of the member firms, whose day started earlier, and whose lunch hour in general was 12.30–1.00 pm or 1.30 pm, whereas the association's ran from 1.00 to 2.00 pm, but we assembled a 12.30 pm. I heard several complaints from member firms about this: we were out of reach from 12.30 to 2.00 pm each day, and they finished about 4.00 pm while we worked till 5.00 pm. There was also a very useful meeting of the team on Friday afternoons when the director was briefed on what had happened during the week. This was held in the director's large first-floor office, attended by the secretary and his deputy. One afternoon, the deputy had made the error of talking too much and the director asked him to open the window, 'and John', he intoned, 'close it after you'. There was no teamwork as such. We were all strong individuals – each lunchtime witnessed a battle of egos, trading 'war stories', clever remarks and in-jokes. Later, in one of my MBA assignments on metaphors, I described the association as 'a nest of vipers' or 'a snake pit'. The origin of these labels was the lack of support, backbiting, and competition to do down a rival in front of the director.

On the very first day of my employment I had arrived at about 8.30 am at the Davenport Road entrance, and was taken to Parkside garage to collect my company car: I had chosen a blue Triumph Dolomite (a sports saloon, made at the BL Triumph factory, Canley, Coventry). I returned, excited and looking forward to my new career. In the entrance lobby was a large-bodied, tall, greying man of some six feet berating a woman struggling with a sheaf of files. My emotions kicked in: I felt scared and on the left I saw my name on a side door. I fled inside, and approached an older man sitting at the desk on the left (who turned out to be the senior industrial relations officer) and asked, 'Who the hell was that?' He replied: 'The director.' 'Thank God', I said, 'he won't be here often.' 'Oh no, he's here every day' came the reply.[15] I knew I had made a mistake in coming here, straight away. No one at Mobil, my former employer, would have bullied staff in public – or in private. No one. Thus, by accident, I had met the CDEEA's director. Worse was to come, for instance later that week I was informed by the receptionist/telephonist to limit my external phone calls, as 'they are giving you enough rope to hang yourself'. I explained to her that I needed to use the phone to sell my house in Essex – to contact the solicitor, estate agents, purchasers – but she just shrugged, 'I told you anyway'. Similarly, within a week of arriving, I was accused by Berry of being 'challenging'; I said, 'yes I'd been asking questions as I was new to the procedures'!

As I was looking for a house, the director's personal assistant suggested Southam, the small town where she lived, but I preferred city life. Indeed, I fancied one of the plush apartments just down the road from the association offices. 'Oh, no', she countered, 'if you live locally, he'll want you to stay after work to accompany his drinking; the secretary often has to do that'. So I bought a house in Leamington Spa, ten miles away.

Berry was addressed either as 'director' – a strange salutation – or 'Mr Berry' (I never heard anyone call him 'Alan' except some of the CDEEA board members). According to the senior industrial relations officer, Berry was a barrister, educated at Oxford University, and now in his sixties, who apparently had been headhunted from the West of England Engineering Employers' Association to be appointed CDEEA director in 1963. Berry had in turn appointed an old colleague, Roger Farrance, as his deputy in 1968. He had set up the Coventry Management Training Centre, derided by many member firms that had paid for it as 'Berry's Folly', which apparently he found very amusing as it became so successful a business. Berry was collected each day from his house in Leamington by his chauffer in a Jaguar XJ6 and taken to the Davenport Road offices or to meetings. In the evenings he was taken home as at official functions he had often drunk alcohol so would not have been able to drive himself.

The internal telephone directory was interesting: all the men were listed as 'Mr' with their surname and all the women were listed with only their first names. The female administrative staff addressed us as 'Mr' in public but used our first names in any one-to-one communication. I felt instantly ill at ease as Mobil was a first-names-only company.

---

15 This is a reconstruction. I have rehearsed this scene several times while discussing it with colleagues at the CDEEA and ex-colleagues at Mobil. It haunts me.

The association adopted a strict daily routine: conferences began at 10.00 am and finished hopefully around 12 noon. Lunch was compulsory. There was no opportunity to take a walk after a conference or meet friends and family. The ritual began at 12.30 pm with a round of drinks from a cabinet in the director's room. We were monitored to ensure no one avoided alcohol, and after the first round he announced, 'the second half'. The dining room was catered for by a gourmet chef and a waitress. Each day a full meal was served, and wine was served if there was a visitor for lunch. The director preferred red wine at 'room temperature' and the wine waiter – we all took turns – had to warm the bottle up in the kitchen to ensure it was not cold. He despised Spanish wine and so on one occasion the deputy director exchanged a bottle of claret for one of Rioja. Berry did not notice the difference: it was a puerile practical joke but one which ensured sniggers after lunch.

Amazingly, we all had to eat the same food. I tried to change this to my former diet of a salad, but the director challenged me with 'On a diet, Neil? Losing weight?' Later that day I was summoned to the office of the deputy director who told me he had a message from the director that I was to eat the same meal as everyone else, so demonstrating teamwork. I thought this was just a suggestion, but he indicated that if I did not toe the line, I would have to find another job!

The secretary was a former army officer with legal training; the deputy also had no relevant experience in industrial relations. The administrative staff all reported as a group to the secretary. The two accountant clerks and the conference organizer constituted a small unit with, and, in the larger space, a line of three audio typists who transferred the notes of the conferences and meetings into minutes on tape. As they were not answerable to us, this created issues of allegiance and co-operation with the industrial relations 'team'.

The 'team', as the director referred to us, were a disparate bunch, but all male. Perhaps the major irritant was the former Royal Air Force staff officer who had been initially appointed as a deputy secretary and had no relevant industrial relations experience. Apart from myself, having worked at an American oil company, there were two officers from local engineering companies, an industrial relations officer in the car industry, and two others who had been recently appointed – one a former metallurgist, and the other a former car industry graduate who had been a personnel manager from the coffee factory of Maxwell House in Banbury. Another appointed during my tenure was from Flavel (a manufacturer of central heating boilers in Leamington). The senior industrial relations officer was an avuncular figure, a nice guy, clever like a fox, old in years and an old-style negotiator. He had several sayings which he frequently trotted out: 'Everything is negotiable' and 'Industrial relations today is about how many angels can dance on an equal pay packet' and, best of all, 'Don't worry, I've been insulted by experts' – a phrase I still find useful.

The sole industrial relations executive was a brusque former personnel manager who held forth on subjects on every available occasion but was very experienced, confident, and took some major industrial tribunal claims such as a series of equal pay claims which were highly political, involving hundreds of female employees. He had been, rather ironically, 'sent to Coventry' by the director for the six previous months and he eventually left; we had a sad valediction at a deserted Coach and Horses pub on the Kenpass Highway. Another executive left in 1977, and the deputy director left in 1979. This seemed to reflect a high level of staff turnover. There was an atmosphere of negativity. This was revealed in different ways: company cars were monitored for dirt and, if seen driving too fast or in a way that otherwise engendered the displeasure of the director, the offender would be counselled accordingly. However, when I became very ill with bronchitis he sent round his chauffeur with the Jaguar, and I was whisked up to my parents' house in Cumbria for rehabilitation. As an example of its employment relations practices, after some months the director opened the door to my shared office and leaned in, holding a small card to his chest: 'Neil: 5971? 6345.' He then left. Perplexed, I looked at my office colleague: 'What was that?' 'That was your appraisal'. The numbers were my current and enhanced salary.

Overall, the office was well organized, with lists of tasks for major events such as seminars, tribunal procedures, and so on: in this way, it was rather like the Army, I was told.[16] Thus it was a 'difficult' place to work, and before he resigned, the deputy director told me he had been disappointed not to promote me to an industrial relations executive and that he had 'failed to protect me from the director'. What a statement! Eventually the CDEEA's culture 'got' to me. There was no formal training, or informal or other discussions about industrial relations generally, or anything, really, such as the currency of everyday politics or economics. I was just another functionary, another brick in the wall. I resigned in 1979 to join Urwick Orr, the well-respected firm of management consultants which had restructured Ford's job grades by its 'profile' method of job evaluation.

The member firms

After chairing a number of such conferences I became aware that the aim was not to listen and conciliate on claims but simply to counter them.

---

16 'The Birmingham Association was more like an officer's mess than a modern office': McKinlay, 'The Paradoxes of British Employer Organization', *HSIR*, p. 106.

Employees were not seen as part of the company. The company was the directors, senior management and perhaps a few middle managers who had been there many years and been accepted by that hierarchy. The culture of the association and member firms' senior managers was an 'officer class' where 'the troops' were not seen as part of 'the firm' – necessary but annoying elements of mass production. Even skill was derided.[17] At a conference at Webster and Bennett we were hosted by the managing director in his huge oak-panelled office complete with coal fire and a large fireplace screen. After the usual brief conversation about the dispute (piecework and safety) he said we should see the work on the shop floor. The assistant then got up and went to the wall, pushing apart the oak panels next to the fire, and we then walked straight through onto the shop floor, like a scene in a James Bond film.

One of the most hard-line companies in negotiations was GEC.[18] Its industrial relations director who had sent the letter to Berry congratulating me (see above) also wrote regarding the forthcoming annual negotiations to say that the company would prefer any other officer but myself because I 'did not put the company's case strongly enough'. This meant that I was not supposed to modify the approach taken by the managers. A subsequent discussion with Berry revealed that the association's policy was 'not to push the member firms forward but simply to represent their [narrow] interests'. In contrast, in my accepting the view of one company, Rotherham (a small specialized instrument and clockmaker) whose managing director refused to pay mandatory national rates, the AUEW officer wrote to Berry complaining that I, and two other industrial relations officers, did not accept them as being mandatory.

GEC's policy reflected its year-long production system for manufacturing telephone exchanges; this meant it could absorb even a prolonged strike as lost production could be made up afterwards by overtime or by employing additional labour-only contractors. Car and component companies did not have this option. Working days lost in strikes or even strike days did not automatically align with production losses, if any![19]

Many of the occupants of the important management positions were offering what were essentially lay solutions to complex managerial problems. One example was a conference at Standard Triumph on job evaluation. The industrial relations manager, a former engineer, asserted

---

17 See R. P. Dore, *British Factory, Japanese Factory: The Origins of National Diversity in Industrial Relations* (University of California Press, Berkeley, CA: 1973), p. 54.

18 Croucher, 'The Coventry Toolroom Agreement, Part 2', *HSIR*, p. 44.

19 J. F. Peck, S. Bowden, and A. McKinlay, *The British Motor Industry* (St Martin's Press: 1995); D. Barnes and E. Reid, *Governments and Trade Unions: The British Experience 1964–79* (Heinemann: 1980).

that job evaluation was about how 'hard' a job was. I pointed out that this was subjective, and the usual definition was 'value to the company' which was more easily objectified. He and his assistant just laughed. He had no qualifications in industrial relations nor had his assistant, who had been an 'administrative apprentice' in the past, a common way of recruiting and training staff. However, the approach relied on internal knowledge instead of a more objective assessment such as an external diploma in management studies, available at the local polytechnic.

This impression of a lack of professionalism was exacerbated by frequent cases of managerial excess. At a conference at Webster and Bennet I was genially hosted by the managing director in his huge oak-panelled office complete with coal fire and a large fireplace screen. After the usual brief conversation about the dispute (piecework and safety) he said I should see the work on shop floor. The assistant then got up and went to the wall, pushing apart the oak panels next to the fire, and we then walked through straight onto the shop floor. Its opulence and the contrasting example of technology was like a scene in a James Bond film.

An example of managerial indifference and laxity was the Jaguar axle dispute which dragged on for weeks. The operators had complained about safety: the large rear-axle assembly was very heavy as it comprised the cage, the differential and inboard brakes, but there was no jig to lift it into position under the body shell. While clearly a safety matter, possibly a fatal accident in waiting, it was ignored until a new industrial relations manager arrived from a different factory. Another example at Jaguar was the problem of high levels of grease which were applied to car bodies arriving from the Castle Bromwich factory in Birmingham. With no protective clothing, operatives were supposed to clean these off with a rag and then wash them down prior to painting. A new industrial relations manager became incensed as the evidence from the union side was presented. At the end he apologized to those present at the conference and referred the issue back for domestic discussions. This was a highly irregular and concessionary approach: the new manager had once been a shop steward in the garage and was appointed presumably to smooth over relations as the company was suffering economically.

Other incidents revealed a very conservative attitude. I arrived to look over the cause of a dispute at the Alvis, Holyhead Road, works, where small tanks were manufactured. As I walked around the works I needed a toilet. There was a painted sign on the brickwork so I wandered over, but my host told me it was only for the hourly paid, and I should go to the office block, where there were toilets for the monthly paid (cheque and bank transfer). Arriving at reception I was advised to use the directors' toilets and was given the key to a rather lavish set of rooms. So, three sets of toilets!

Multi-unionism was a perennial issue. I had arrived at a large conference venue at BL's Triumph Canley site where the office, part of the original factory, was referred to as Ivy Cottage. In the room were assembled several smartly dressed full-time union officials seated at the table; behind them, standing in line, were a large number of men in long, brown work coats. Rather surprised, I asked the Triumph managers who they were. I was introduced to the union officials, whom I met for the first but not the last time, and the shop stewards of the various unions. The TGWU and AUEW I knew, whereas the National Society of Metal Mechanics and the National Union of Vehicle Builders were new to me. But why were officers and shop stewards of the Furniture, Timber and Allied Trades Union there? Of course, they represented the joiners and carpenters who in 1977 worked in the trim shop, cutting, shaping and fitting wooden rails to Triumph car doors and windows! There was no joint shop stewards' committee presence in the form of a convener, and so each union official, backed by his appropriate steward, gave separate presentations. Needless to say, these union presentations lasted more than an hour, and after the standard adjournment, the conference had to be reconvened to allow time for the management reply as I was due at GEC in the afternoon. The argument over differentials was confused with the separate payment systems including overtime opportunities and various piecework earnings. The final outcome was a failure to agree across all of the unions' claims.[20]

'Unconstitutional action', that is industrial action taken outside procedure and without the authority of the trade union, was a major point of discussion with the CDEEA director at his weekly Friday meetings and there existed a short position paper written by him. While this seemed to excite the director, I found it perfectly normal behaviour as Mobil had no procedural agreement and short stoppages – 'downers' – were quite frequent and appeared a normal factor of production. However, these were unconstitutional stoppages before the procedure had been exhausted. The problem with the procedure, as I saw it, was that it was administered by the employers whose managers had an incentive to delay. This was not an unusual situation in industrial relations.[21] With the exception of the Coventry Toolroom Agreement dispute, the CDEEA did not get involved in the course of industrial action; this was the responsibility of member firms. I had arrived just after the British Leyland toolmakers' strike of

---

20 I was then out of the picture and unsure as to what happened thereafter.

21 At Mobil I had avoided the scaffolding shop steward as any meeting would be detrimental; if we failed to agree he could then call a shop meeting and possibly invoke industrial action. If I agreed to his claim then he would have won, and the maintenance work would be delayed by yet another demarcation. So, the only course of action was not to have the meeting.

February–March 1977,[22] which was hardly mentioned. I had to look it up to find the date. The burgeoning national problems at British Leyland were outside the association's remit.

In these research areas I was regarded if not as an expert then at least as competent since I had enjoyed similar roles at Mobil. This refers to the rather limited experience and expertise of colleagues who had not developed these skills at member firms, being tied to piecework as a reward system which, it was believed, meant that the management of productivity was set up accordingly and no great changes were anticipated. This was despite the fact that larger firms were moving away from piecework and several were attempting productivity bargaining. As Mobil had been at the forefront of this movement I assumed that was the reason for my appointment. This was wrong: I was a functionary, like the others.

Conclusion: industrial relations in Coventry engineering

Whatever the exogenous issues in the UK economy at the time, and the way in which these debouched into engineering in general and Coventry in particular with a tight labour market and soft product markets, the industrial relations expertise that might have attenuated the problems was lacking. Not only was this the case at the grassroots level but the history of the member firms militated against evolution. Jaguar's founder, Sir William Lyons, spent time and money renovating Wappenbury Hall, Sir John Black left a legacy at Standard Triumph, Lord Nuffield at Morris, the Rootes brothers at the Humber and Ryton works, with founders' names and culture attached to most of the member firms. These were exacerbated by the elevation to very senior positions of an engineering cadre based on long service rather than wider experience. The arrival at British Leyland in late 1977 of Michael Edwardes, a South African, from Chloride was a rare example of a new entrant to the industry at the senior level.

After 1945, and as the 1950s progressed, the employment situation in many regions of the UK was challenging from the management point of view as regards the commitment, productivity and sheer 'bloody-mindedness' of shop-floor employees. With the exception perhaps of the West Country, managers could attest to difficulties in motivation, engagement, and low productivity: not only the structural factors such as demarcation between trades and an overtime-creation culture, but also in terms of a lack of pride in their employment, and a hostile, defensive

---

22 See H. Scullion, 'The Skilled Revolt against General Unionism: The Case of the BL Toolroom Committee', *Industrial Relations Journal* 12:3 (1981), pp. 15–27.

attitude. The Coventrian possessed 'a defiant ... assertion of self-respect that is typical of the West Midlands as it is of industrial mid- and north Britain in general'.[23]

Partly this undeveloped state of industrial relations was also due to the abrogation of direct labour management under the dominant pay system of piecework. Instead of new methods of working, enhanced rewards and co-operative teamwork, management was unusually reticent as to the way which piecework distorted internal supply chains and unbalanced line efficiency. This was a historical nicety, as 'entrenched during the long years of management dominance and weak union organization, the men and women on production lines [who] were under permanent pressure from the "rate fixer" [whose] job was to constantly retime their work and thus ensure the piece rate could ... be reduced, so that men [sic] would have to work even harder to make the same money. Workers were permanently tired.'[24]

As workplace union organization developed, workers became adept at turning the piecework system to their advantage or at least mitigating its impact on them.[25] As well as obvious disadvantages such as difficulties scheduling the disparate efforts of the various jobs, piecework became costly for companies. Much excess work-in-progress was created, which tied up capital. Alvis managers had tried to buy out the piecework system. Numerous industrial engineers were employed to measure new work methods and equipment: often they would look up specific arm/hand movements in a book of 'synthetics' assembled from books of individual motions. These stopwatch experts then evaluated effort on a scale 80–100–120 – slow, normal, fast. These efforts were time-consuming and erratic, which led to disputes over remeasurement and payment levels. Unfortunately, the financial or works accounting system at Alvis had not kept pace with the booking of work. My research revealed that hundreds of pieceworkers had hidden, or rather retained, previous work 'in the back of the book' in case of strikes or other lack of work caused a drop in earnings: they could then book the work in the accounts department and be reimbursed. At a conference, the company revealed that the cost of buying back work would have been ruinously expensive and so the proposed change was dropped. Thus the practical problems of moving to a 'more rational' system were simply too great; though British Leyland did move to measured-day work, it still proved problematic.

Managers at all levels, and the leaders of employers' associations, were unprepared for the new industrial relations. For the EEF, the 'decade from

23 F. Taylor, *Coventry: Thursday 14 November 1940* (Bloomsbury: 2015), p. 248.
24 *Ibid.*, p. 249.
25 For piecework pay systems in Coventry see W. Brown, *Piecework Bargaining* (Heinemann: 1973).

1948 to 1957 was the most frustrating in [its] history'.[26] Within the CDEEA, there was a lack of specific industrial relations experience and expertise. This reflected the comments of Arthur Marsh regarding the disparate backgrounds of employers' association staff. Moreover, they noted that the employers' association role relieved a member firm's industrial relations staff of the opportunity to develop their training and skills.[27] Alan Gladstone also noted 'the availability of an array of services ... [provided by an association] may be partly responsible for the sometimes undeveloped state of personnel administration in labour relations functions in particular enterprises'.[28] In Coventry, this can be related to the recruitment of former military officers as managers in engineering. Indeed, a former CDEEA colleague described the management cadre as an 'officer class' – we industrial relations officers did not fit in, did not count, were seen only as apparatchiks, there to hit the unions on the head during conferences, as the formal letter from GEC (see above) evidences.

The CDEEA lost membership over the 1980s as the engineering industry contracted as a result of high interest rates, a high pound-sterling exchange rate, and increased competition (especially by European companies). In addition, employers moved to company bargaining.[29] In 1984 the CDEEA merged with the West Midlands Engineering Employers' Association, which in turn moved to an advisory role, extending its services to other sectors (such as further education colleges after their incorporation as separate bodies in 1994).

This paper illustrates an overriding culture of traditional engineering in an industrial setting, Coventry, known for its own specific social and economic history. The comparison with Mobil perhaps illustrates the widespread effect of the different production system on attributes, as well as systems. I hope this account will encourage more research on the role of

---

26 Wigham, *The Power to Manage*, p. 160.

27 A. I. Marsh, *Industrial Relations in Engineering* (Pergamon Press, Oxford: 1965); *idem*, 'The Contribution of Employers' Associations', in B. Towers, T. G. Whittingham, and A. W. Gottschalk (eds), *Bargaining for Change* (Allen and Unwin: 1972), pp. 84–99.

28 A. Gladstone, 'Employers' Associations and Industrial Relations: Functions and Services', in J. P. Windmuller and A. Gladstone (eds), *Employers' Associations and Industrial Relations: A Comparative Study* (Oxford University Press: 1984), pp. 24–43, at p. 31. Mobil had been very different. Despite engineers dominating most managerial positions, even within industrial relations, and the refinery being located in a tight labour market in the wider London area, its culture and production system were oriented to accepting change, even if this was achievable only over a longer term.

29 See K. Sisson and W. Brown, 'Industrial Relations in the Private Sector: Donovan Re-visited', in G. S. Bain (ed.), *Industrial Relations in Britain* (Blackwell, Oxford: 1983), ch. 6.

employers' association officials given their centrality to much of twentieth-century British industrial relations.

Faculty of Agribusiness and Commerce
University of Lincoln
Lincoln 7647
Canterbury, New Zealand

HSIR 41 (2020) 249–60

https://doi.org/10.3828/hsir.2020.41.12

Then and Now: Vulnerable Workers, Industrial Action, and the Law in the 1970s and Today

Alan Tuckman

S. Groves and V. Merritt, *Trico: A Victory to Remember* (Lawrence and Wishart: 2018), 268pp., hbk £25.00, ISBN 978-1-912064-87-8.

S. Anitha and R. Pearson, *Striking Women: Struggles and Strategies of South Asian Women Workers from Grunwick to Gate Gourmet* (Lawrence and Wishart: 2018), 232pp., pbk £18.00, ISBN 978-1-912064-86-1.

At a time when strikes are on the verge of disappearance, at least according to official figures, interest in them seems increasingly rare. But at any hint of the spectre of industrial militancy, talk of unwarranted withdrawal of labour, mass picketing, and 'bringing the country to its knees' soon re-emerges. Images are presented of men raising their hands at mass meetings in favour of a walkout; presented as 'a world to which we must not return'. Labour's announcement in its 2019 election manifesto of plans to replace Conservative trade-union legislation was greeted by the *Sun* – reminding readers that it had first coined the label 'Winter of Discontent' in 1978 – as heralding 'a red riot … to paralyse Britain'.[1] The *Mail Online* reported that John McDonnell, the Shadow Chancellor of the Exchequer, 'refused to rule out restoring the punishing secondary striking rights which crippled Britain's public services in the 1970s'.[2] The *Daily Telegraph* has even asked if the COVID-19 pandemic might prove to be the winter of

---

1 A. Mathews, 'RED RIOT Labour to Paralyse Britain with "Winter of Discontent"', *Sun*, 22 November 2019.

2 J. Elsom, 'Labour Reveals "Winter of Discontent" Strike Plan That Would Paralyse Britain', *Mail Online*, 22 November 2019; see also P. Evens and J. Collingridge, 'Are We Facing Another Winter of Discontent?', *Sunday Times*, 10 November 2019.

discontent for this generation.[3] This review analyses three strikes – the origins of each dispute, their external support and the importance of picketing – and assesses the impact of trade-union legislation on industrial action.

While the disputes of the winter of 1978–79 have received considerable attention recently,[4] there is little that challenges the mythology of individual strikes of the 1970s or the impact of subsequent trade-union legislation on workers' ability to defend their interests at work. These two books are exceptions, challenging the conventional image of strikers as they explore three strikes and the workers involved in them: Trico Folberth and Grunwick in the mid-1970s; and Gate Gourmet in 2005, some thirty years later. All three strikes were in west London, involving 'vulnerable' workers finally taking action to challenge real and long-standing grievances when other means of resolution seemed exhausted, by staging largely spontaneous action. But each action occurred in the context of a divided workforce fractured by divisive action. Trade-union legislation since 1980, and unemployment and precarious employment, have exacerbated such divisions and enhanced the capacity for employers to control the workforce, as exemplified at Gate Gourmet.

Largely drawing upon the voice of workers involved, the books focus on the motivations that underlie the actions rather than any 'mindless militancy'. In each case there was clear injustice and discrimination, which was challenged by the largely female workforce. The lives and background of the Grunwick and Gate Gourmet strikers is the focus of Sundari Anitha and Ruth Pearson's analysis, which challenges the stereotypes of South Asian women to question any view of their homogeneity. The Gujarati women at Grunwick, migrants from India and some expelled from East Africa, were educated and had experience of employment before migration, but often suffered downward social mobility with the move to the United Kingdom. The Punjabi women at Gate Gourmet, from a less affluent background and less likely to have had paid work in India, had longer experience of employment in the UK. However, once settled in employment both groups had 'commonalities in their experience' (*Striking Women*, pp. 62–3).

The detail of the disputes is not the central consideration of Anitha and Pearson's account, which is concerned with why Grunwick, rather than other strikes involving South Asian women – such as at Mansfield

---

3 T. Welsh, 'Covid-19 Could Be Our Winter of Discontent, but Shift the Country Left', *Daily Telegraph*, 15 March 2020.

4 T. Martin López, *The Winter of Discontent: Myth, Memory, and History* (Liverpool University Press: 2014); J. Shepherd, *Crisis? What Crisis? The Callaghan Government and the British 'Winter of Discontent'* (Manchester University Press: 2015); 'Symposium: The Winter of Discontent', *Historical Studies in Industrial Relations* (*HSIR*) 36 (2015), pp. 181–226.

Hosiery and Imperial Typewriters, both before Grunwick – has become embedded in the folk memory of the labour movement. This focus provides valuable insights into the strikers' background and extends the analysis of Grunwick and Asian women workers found earlier in work by Amrit Wilson.[5] While the Grunwick plant has been demolished to make way for housing, the strike and picket are celebrated in a mural at Dollis Hill underground station that adjoins the site, and the events of the strike have recently been the subject of a touring play.[6] The Trico strike did receive considerable support at the time, particularly from sections of the women's movement, but another recent account refers to it as 'the forgotten strike'.[7] The initial action by Gate Gourmet workers, mistakenly referred to in some accounts as a sit-in,[8] might not have constituted a strike. Dismissed workers did strike afterwards, with British Airways (BA) baggage handlers coming out in sympathy. These actions stopped BA flights from Heathrow for two days, but had been 'outlawed' under Conservative legislation enacted in the years after Trico and Grunwick.

Sally Groves and Vernon Merritt's goal is to document the Trico strike before ephemeral material and the memory of the participants were lost. Both were participants in the 21-week strike across the long, hot summer of 1976 and give a graphic story of the dispute, drawing from accounts of other workers involved. It is important to remember, at its fiftieth anniversary, that the Equal Pay Act (EqPA) 1970 did not resolve pay inequality without recourse to industrial action. While equal pay is more often associated with the women sewing machinists at Ford, whose dispute gave ammunition to Barbara Castle in promoting new legislation (*Trico*, pp. 198–9),[9] the Act was only fully implemented in 1975. This was intended to allow adequate

---

5 A. Wilson, *Finding a Voice: Asian Women in Britain* (Virago: 2018 [1985]).

6 *We Are the Lions Mr Manager*, Townsend Theatre Company.

7 G. Stevenson, 'The Forgotten Strike: Equality, Gender and Class in the Trico Equal Pay Strike', *Labour History Review* 81:2 (2016), pp. 141–68. The Trico strike was also the subject of a play, *Out on the Costa Del Trico*, performed at various trade-union and similar venues by the Women's Theatre Group in 1977–78.

8 R. Hattersley, 'Comment & Analysis: The Storm Troopers Have to Be Curbed: The Heathrow Strike Highlights the Plight of Contract Employees', *Guardian*, 15 August 2005; D. Murray and R. Singh, 'Flying With BA? Then Pack Your Own Sandwiches', (London) *Evening Standard*, 10 August 2005; D. Reece, 'BA Left Running on Empty after Caterers' Strike', *Independent*, 11 August 2005.

9 See also S. Cohen, *Notoriously Militant: The Story of a Union Branch* (Merlin Press: 2013); H. Friedman and S. Meredeen, *The Dynamics of Industrial Conflict: Lessons from Ford* (Croom Helm: 1980).

time for working arrangements to be changed to conform to the Act.[10] The Trico strike was the first to involve the Act. It gained considerable external support, particularly from the recently emergent women's movement. It is against this background that the authors lead us to evaluate a strike called by a minority of the workforce after a show of hands at a mass meeting outside the factory.

The 1970–74 Conservative government of Edward Heath had unsuccessfully tried to control trade unions through its Industrial Relations Act (IR Act) 1971; by the time of the Trico and Grunwick strikes this had been repealed by Labour's Trade Union and Labour Relations Act 1974 (as amended in 1976). This essentially returned the regulation of strikes to the 'golden formula' of the Trade Disputes Act of 1906. Under this, action 'in contemplation or furtherance of a trade dispute' was given tort immunity and unions were not liable in civil action against them for damages caused by the industrial action;[11] dismissed strikers could, in some circumstances, claim unfair dismissal. The interpretation of what constituted a 'trade dispute' remained wide, including secondary action broadened to suppliers, contractors and other companies beyond the immediate employer of workers in dispute. Neoliberals, such as Friedrich Hayek,[12] railed against these immunities which they argued put unions above the law. They also argued that much of the behaviour of trade unions constituted intimidation of their membership as much as of employers. This intimidation was reflected in strikes, often started as spontaneous walkouts or after a show of hands at a mass meeting, and by picketing as a feature of the strike.[13]

I

In the wake of the implementation of the EqPA, the Amalgamated Union of Engineering Workers[14] had been in ongoing negotiations over two years

---

10 See P. Davies and M. Freedland, *Labour Legislation and Public Policy: A Contemporary History* (Clarendon Press, Oxford: 1993), pp. 211–20.

11 See J. Saville, 'The Trade Disputes Act of 1906', *HSIR* 1 (1996), pp. 11–45; K. Ewing (ed.), *The Right to Strike: From the Trade Disputes Act 1906 to a Trade Union Freedom Bill 2006* (Institute of Employment Rights, Liverpool: 2006).

12 F. A. Hayek, *A Tiger by the Tail* (Institute of Economic Affairs: 1972); see also, *idem*, 'Trade Union Immunity under the Law' (Hayek Letter) [Revoke Privileges Granted by Trade Disputes Act, 1906], *The Times*, 21 July 1977.

13 See A. Tuckman, *Kettling the Unions? A Guide to the 2016 Trade Union Act* (Spokesman, Nottingham: 2018); Lord Wedderburn, 'Freedom of Association and Philosophies of Labour Law', *Industrial Law Journal* 18:1 (1989), pp. 1–38.

14 Now, after several amalgamations, a constituent of Unite the Union.

with the Trico management to address inequality between men and women's pay. As with many workplaces at the time, Trico had segregated men and women: women worked the day shifts, earning on average 80% of the rate for men on 'a complex piecework formula' (*Trico*, p. 15). Much of the differential was justified in terms of men's potentially greater flexibility because of their capacity to work night shifts. The impasse in the negotiations was aggravated when, in the aftermath of some work moving to a new factory in Northampton, five male workers were redeployed to the day shift, although still being paid a higher rate than the women they worked alongside.

A mass meeting on 24 May 1976, held in a park behind the Trico factory, heard of the breakdown of negotiations. Women refused to return to work although most of the men had drifted back before this final item on the agenda. Initially the strike consisted of around 400 women and 20 men. A further 150 men joined the strike when it was made official by the union in June. However, around 1,000 workers, including those in the offices, remained at work. Picketing continued throughout the summer, blockading stock within the plant. When the strikers introduced all-night pickets at the end of June, management attempted to run the blockade with a convoy of trucks. Groves and Merritt's book conveys the importance of the picket in frustrating management's attempts to move goods.

The story of the strike is punctuated with first-person narratives by participants, one of the lengthier being from Groves herself, describing the 'battle of Trico gates' when six pickets attempted to stop a convoy of trucks supported by coachloads of police. In scenes that were to be repeated only a few weeks later a few miles away at Grunwick:

> The strikers were horrified by the blatant police collusion with the company's American gangster-style tactics. A little while back they would never have believed that Trico would be employing strike-breaking mercenary convoys of highly-paid scabs to charge through their picket lines. They would never have believed that the police would drag peaceful pickets away, preventing them from even speaking to the drivers, as they believed to be their right. (*ibid.*, p. 96)

After the lorries had left, Groves and Merritt followed them across London to their destination at the Trico Northampton plant (*ibid.*, pp. 86–7).

With increased publicity the Trico strike mobilized external support from trade unions and the women's movement, specifically from the Working Women's Charter, which had been initiated by London Trades Councils two years before. Brent Trades Council – and its secretary Jack Dromey – also played an important role in developing support across London, as it would later in the Grunwick dispute (*ibid.*, p. 98). Collections held locally raised large amounts of money. Strikers also embarked on a speaking tour, with the book highlighting one meeting in Glasgow when they met Jimmy Reid from the Upper Clyde Shipbuilders' work-in (of 1971–72).

Trico's attempt at resolution was through appeal to an industrial tribunal.[15] The union refused to participate as tribunals' interpretation of 'equal pay for equal work', the initial requirement of the EqPA, had favoured employers. In the first six months' operation of the Act, industrial tribunals rejected seventy-nine applications, upholding only thirty-one – a failure of 72% (*ibid.*, p. 105). The authors give a number of illustrations, such as the claim by Rowntree management, upheld by the tribunal, that wrapping Black Magic chocolates was work for women and paid less than wrapping Kit Kats done by men. Most of the management successes revolved around men being 'flexible' and, as in the final tribunal decision in the Trico case, while there was no difference between the work being carried out by the men and women – indeed they were working alongside one another – that the men had worked nights demonstrated a difference. Like other examples, the management intent was not to raise women's wage to that of men but gradually to ease men from these positions to accommodate a race to the bottom with cheap labour.[16]

As the dispute continued through the summer, things seemed to get more difficult for the strikers: support and donations continued, but positions appeared more entrenched. Trico attempted to withhold all holiday pay from the workforce and, in September, it announced the layoff of 445 men and 77 women from its two plants. The continuing wrangle about equal pay was clearly hitting the company. Its major customers, the car companies, were finding alternative suppliers for windscreen wipers. Strikers were to remain outside the Trico gates until 18 October when a return to work was agreed with a 'common operating rate' to be paid 'throughout the payment-by-results area, regardless of sex' (*ibid.*, p. 155). As a result the women earned £6.50 per week more.

II

Before the Trico strike had ended, workers at Grunwick had staged their much better remembered walkout from the photo-processing works in Dollis Hill, just a few miles away. In events that are well documented,[17] on 12 August two workers had walked out from the Grunwick post room

---

15 Later renamed as Employment Tribunals.
16 The main loophole in the EqPA 1970, which allowed such anomalies between men and women's pay to continue, was ended in 1983 with the introduction of the comparison of 'work of equal value'.
17 J. Rogaly, *Grunwick* (Penguin, Harmondsworth: 1977); J. Dromey and G. Taylor, *Grunwick: The Workers' Story* (Lawrence and Wishart: 1978; 2nd

after an argument about sorting crates of outgoing mail. Later that Friday afternoon they were joined by Jayaben Desai who had also walked out after refusing to work overtime. The two young men and Mrs Desai decided to talk to other workers about conditions at Grunwick, later approaching a Citizens' Advice Bureau, then Brent Trades Council, about joining a trade union. The workers had simply left the factory and, only afterwards, in discussions at the gate, did they begin to organize, joined by others from the plant. There had been an attempt at trade-union recognition a few years earlier when some members of the Transport and General Workers' Union (TGWU)[18] were made redundant, but this time the workers joined the Association of Professional, Executive, Clerical and Computer Staff (APEX).[19] Not all Grunwick workers had joined the strike, with Mrs Desai and 137 strikers dismissed in September from a workforce of 429. With 140 students working as temps during the busy summer period,[20] the proportion continuing work, as against striking, became contentious. This division became central in the intransigence of the owner in his refusal to engage with any arbitration, frustrating attempts by the Advisory, Conciliation and Arbitration Service (ACAS) to facilitate a solution.

As the strike continued, each side mobilized support. On the workers' side, the pickets were joined by other trade-unionists and allies. The Union of Post Office Workers[21] 'blacked' (refused to handle) Grunwick mail (the company was heavily dependent on postage for delivery and return of processed film in the pre-digital age). Threatened by an injunction and legal action, the blacking was called off after Grunwick claimed it would co-operate with ACAS in finding a solution to the strike. When this co-operation failed to materialize, the blacking was reimposed, unofficially, by workers at the Cricklewood sorting office even when the Post Office threatened to stop paying them.[22] To combat this, Grunwick was assisted by the National Association for Freedom,[23] an anti-union pressure group, which smuggled the mail out of the plant to be posted around London.

In June 1977, ten months after the walkout, mass picketing was called for the streets outside Grunwick's two sites in Willesden. Picketing drew support from across the country, including coaches of miners. Arthur Scargill, president of the Yorkshire Area of the National Union of Mineworkers, was among the many arrested as the police tried to push back

edn, 2016) gives the union account; G. Ward, *Fort Grunwick* (Temple Smith: 1977), the employer's account.

18 Now, after amalgamation with Amicus, a constituent of Unite the Union.

19 Now a section of the GMB.

20 Dromey and Taylor, *Grunwick* (1978), p. 15.

21 Now the Communication Workers Union.

22 Dromey and Taylor, *Grunwick* (1978), pp. 141–2.

23 Later The Freedom Association.

the pickets so that buses full of workers could enter through the gates. With Grunwick's rejection of any proposed settlement, including a proposal for trade-union recognition by the Scarman Court of Inquiry,[24] picketing became more desperate. While the Grunwick strike committee wanted to continue this action it was losing support from APEX and the Trades Union Congress (TUC). Mrs Desai and some other strikers staged a hunger strike outside Congress House, TUC headquarters, seeking support for wider sympathy action from other unions but this did not materialize. The strike was called off on 14 July 1978.

III

The Gate Gourmet strike occurred only a few miles away but some thirty years later and in a very different legal context for workers and trade unions. While the development of the Trico and, particularly, the Grunwick strikes were a symptom of the weakness of the workers against a determined employer, they were taken up by the emergent Thatcherite right as symbolic of over-powerful trade unions and a working class out of control.[25] The Conservative government of Margaret Thatcher, after its election in 1979, set about a programme of trade-union and employment legislation. After the Heath government's attempt at comprehensive reform with the 1971 IR Act,[26] essentially made unworkable by union opposition, the Thatcher government initiated a 'salami slicing' of trade-union rights and immunities through a series of Acts of Parliament: six were enacted by Conservative governments, 1979–97, and subsequently largely adopted by New Labour governments, 1997–2010.[27]

---

24 Court of Inquiry (Scarman), *Report*, Cmnd 6922 (1977), completed before the end of the dispute.

25 See Institute of Economic Affairs (IEA) (ed.), *Trade Unions: Public Goods or Public 'Bads'?* (IEA: 1978); K. Joseph, *Solving the Union Problem Is the Key to Britain's Recovery* (Centre for Policy Studies: 1979); J. Burton, *The Trojan Horse: Union Power in British Politics* (Adam Smith Institute: 1979).

26 B. Weekes, M. Mellish, L. Dickens, and J. Lloyd, *Industrial Relations and the Limits of Law: The Industrial Effects of the Industrial Relations Act, 1971* (Blackwell, Oxford: 1975).

27 Employment Act (EA) 1980, EA 1982, Trade Union Act 1984, EA 1988, EA 1990, Trade Union Reform and Employment Rights Act 1993. Labour government legislation: Employment Relations Act (ERA) 1999, EA 2002, ERA 2004, and later extended by David Cameron's Conservative government in the Trade Union Act 2016. The legislation is brought together in the Trade Union and Labour Relations (Consolidation) Act 1992, as amended. See Tuckman, *Kettling the Unions*; L. Dickens and M. Hall, 'The State: Labour Law and Industrial Relations', in P. Edwards (ed.), *Industrial Relations: Theory*

Taken as a whole, the legislation included the requirement for unions, in order to retain tort immunity, to hold a postal ballot of the workers called upon to strike, with a majority voting in support, and the loss of tort immunity from industrial action outside the primary employer (inhibiting 'secondary' action), and other restrictions. Unions were thus laid open to injunctions (stopping strikes) and financially liable for damages (and legal costs) for 'unlawful' action. Workers dismissed for being on unofficial strike had no recourse to unfair dismissal; workers on official strike, from April 2000, had a period of 'protected industrial action' during which dismissal would be deemed unfair. Lawful picketing was confined to the workers' place of work (rather than the employer as a whole), while a Code of Practice limited the number of pickets to six workers.[28]

Gate Gourmet was a product of government privatization, marketization and competitive tendering. Initially the BA in-flight caterer, Gate Gourmet, had been sold to a Swiss Air catering subsidiary, which had in turn been sold to the Texas Pacific Finance Group, a private-equity company. The essence of private equity is to purchase companies cheaply, restructure them, and then sell them on. This is usually at the expense of the terms and conditions of employees. Roy Hattersley MP (former Labour Party deputy leader) characterized such firms as 'the storm troopers of the competitive economy, the advance guard of market capitalism who only win contracts by cutting costs to the bone. The cost that is easiest to cut is labour.'[29] The workforce at Gate Gourmet consisted largely of women from the Punjab. Anitha and Pearson emphasize the experience of these women in the type of work at Gate Gourmet, and their traditions of trade-unionism. From the time of the takeover, Texas Pacific had been in negotiations with the TGWU, the union which represented the workers, trying to change the workers' conditions of service which largely dated from the period of BA, and to reduce labour costs by £14 million by cutting 600 from the workforce.[30]

During this period minor disputes had erupted – management claimed a total of seven 'illegal [i.e. unofficial] strikes' – when workers deployed their own customary action: 'assembling at the canteen as well as the informal mechanisms of collective negotiations with the management ... [This was a practice] developed at Gate Gourmet through years of experience

---

and *Practice in Britain* (Blackwell, Oxford: 1995), pp. 124–56; P. Smith, 'New Labour and the Commonsense of Neoliberalism: Trade Unionism, Collective Bargaining, and Workers' Rights', *Industrial Relations Journal* 40:4 (2009), pp. 337–55.

28 Lord Wedderburn, *The Worker and the Law* (3rd edn; Penguin, Harmondsworth: 1986).

29 Hattersley, 'Comment & Analysis', *Guardian*.

30 Reece, 'BA Left Running on Empty after Caterers' Strike', *Independent*. M. Tran, 'Gate Gourmet Dispute Escalates', *Guardian*, 9 January 2005.

of union membership and organisation' (*Striking Women*, p. 158).[31] The company had developed a strategy to counter this:[32] on 10 August 2005, workers arrived to find managers already at work, with security guards in the building, and agency workers in place on the food line. Instead of starting their shift, the workers gathered in the canteen, their normal reaction, awaiting some resolution through negotiation between their shop stewards and management. There is controversy about subsequent events. Many accounts talk of this as a sit-in,[33] the then Gate Gourmet vice-president, HR (Europe), claiming that the workers 'barricaded themselves in and refused to leave'.[34] The workers' accounts shed light on these events.

Management was intent on replacing the South Asian women workers with Eastern European agency workers on lower pay and worse conditions.[35] When they congregated in the canteen the workers were instructed to return to work or be sacked. Shop stewards told them to stay put until the issue of the agency workers, who were already taking their places on the line, was resolved. When workers refused to return their identity cards and leave the plant, as instructed by managers, they were detained by security within the canteen for seven hours (*ibid.*, p. 156). Dismissal notices were later issued to 813 workers, many of whom had not been involved in the shift blockaded in the canteen, but all were labelled 'troublemakers' and accused of unlawful action.

The strikes that followed stopped flights from Heathrow, when BA baggage handlers and others took sympathy action. None of this was preceded by a postal ballot, clearly ruled out by the immediacy of the dispute that provoked it but, because of this (that is, the strikes were unofficial), the TGWU had to repudiate the actions, otherwise it would be liable for damages.[36] In all, 130 Gate Gourmet workers were dismissed without compensation, 411 paid the equivalent of their redundancy entitlement, and only 272 reinstated. Almost all of these dismissals were later upheld by employment tribunals to be 'fair' because the workers were deemed to be on unofficial strike. But eighteen workers were eventually found unfairly

---

31 Management claimed there had been 'seven illegal strikes in three years': HR Director Europe, 'Dispute Was Last Straw for Half of HR at Gate Gourmet', *Personnel Today*, 28 February 2006.
32 There was a rebuttal by the company of a leaked document indicating a plan to replace workers drawn up before the dispute; M. Costello, 'Gate Gourmet Hits Out at "Lunacy" of Strike Claim', *The Times*, 15 August 2005.
33 'New BA Strike Threat as Talks Break Down', (London) *Evening Standard*, 17 August 2005; Hattersley, 'Comment & Analysis', *Guardian*.
34 Cited in 'Dispute Was Last Straw for Half of HR at Gate Gourmet', *Personnel Today*.
35 This was denied by Gate Gourmet; *ibid.*
36 J. Hendy and G. Gall, 'British Trade Union Rights Today and the Trade Union Freedom Bill', in Ewing (ed.), *The Right to Strike*, pp. 247–75.

dismissed; most had been 'off work sick, on holiday, or on compassionate leave' at the time, and the convener was found to have been in the canteen 'at the request of the management' (*ibid.*, pp. 173–4).

IV

These books try, in different ways, to represent the voices of strikers. One seeks to preserve the memories of those at Trico, along with various ephemera relevant to it. The other, while offering considerable insights into the strikes through the interviews with strikers, is more focused on the background and cultural heritage they brought to it. Both tell a story not of mindless militancy of the stereotype constructed of the period, of traditional male manual workers walking out over trivial grievances; these were workers subject to discrimination, arbitrary management, and injustice, using the limited power available to them when all else seemed to fail. More than four decades after the Trico strike and, as Groves and Merritt discuss in their closing chapter, with the gender pay gap still at almost 20% (*Trico*, p. 209), there are still drawn-out attempts to rectify such discrimination. In 2019 women working for Glasgow City Council finally won a twelve-year dispute by strike action, after having tried 14,000 tribunal claims over job evaluation that entrenched gender divisions.[37] Recent research by law firm DLA Piper indicates that, fifty years after the EqPA, there are still 29,000 complaints annually to employment tribunals about equal pay.[38] Although such discrimination and injustice remains, the number of strikes has withered. Workers are far more likely to take the option first taken at Grunwick, to just walk off the job rather than collectively resist.[39]

But despite the justice and legitimacy of the grievances at Trico and at Grunwick, the walkouts, the strikes, and the picketing would now be even less protected after subsequent legislation. If the workers' union did not formally repudiate the action, it could be subject to an injunction (disobedience of which would lead to a hefty fine and possible sequestration of funds) and be liable for damages with costs; even with union repudiation of their action, dismissed unofficial strikers have no claim for unfair dismissal. This was the story of the Gate Gourmet dispute and the secondary action by BA ground staff.

Each of the strikes attracted support from others, most dramatically those joining the pickets at Grunwick. Mass picketing became a feature of

---

37 L. Brooks, 'Women Win 12-Year Equal Pay Battle with Glasgow City Council', *Guardian*, 17 January 2019.

38 S. Goodley, '29,000 Claims a Year despite 50 Years since Equal Pay Act', *Guardian*, 24 May 2020.

39 A. Perkins, 'Collective Failure', *Guardian*, 22 April 2006.

some later strikes, such as by print-workers at Wapping in 1986–87 and, of course, during the miners' strike of 1984–85. While similar support has continued, such as in the recent strikes (2018 and 2019–20) by university lecturers, this is no longer anywhere near the scale of mass mobilization of these earlier disputes. From 1980, spaces for workers' collectivity and solidarity were closing. Rights in the form of unions' tort immunities, which had created space for workers to fight for their interests against unilateral action by management, were progressively narrowed. Lawful industrial action was increasingly restricted, regulated, and formalized; even more so was the space for the expression of solidarity. What legislation has done is close these spaces while not resolving any of the underlying grievances; indeed, economic changes have acted to greatly expand the latter.

A new trade-unionism is appearing among cleaners and other agency workers, not just taking industrial action but using picketing as a carnival of collectivism and solidarity. This style has also been adopted recently by university staff, a previously privileged group of workers whose pay and conditions have been degraded over many years. Even in the burgeoning zero-hours economy, where the 'independent self-employed' appear to have no employer from which to withdraw labour, spaces are appearing. Controlled by the discipline of the apps used by Uber, Deliveroo, and various other platforms, such workers have found space on social media to organize protest and stoppages. The pages of the web and of Facebook are perhaps accumulating the sources for accounts of this new form of worker protest taking shape in the world of precarious employment.[40]

Business School
Keele University
Keele ST5 5BG

---

40 See H. Bradley, 'Crisis at Work: Gender, Class and the Dehumanization of Jobs', *HSIR* 41, pp. 111–37; *Notes from Below*, online; and C. Cant, *Riding for Deliveroo: Resistance in the New Economy* (Polity Press, Cambridge: 2020).

https://doi.org/10.3828/hsir.2020.41.13

Extended Review

Roger Seifert and Tom Sibley

Anthony Carew, *American Labour's Cold War Abroad: From Deep Freeze to Détente, 1945–1970* (AU Press, Edmonton: 2018), 528pp., hbk £45, ISBN 978-1-77199-211-4.

This lengthy and scholarly study provides a detailed account of the machinations surrounding the splits within and between national and international trade-union centres in the Cold War years of 1945–70. Its main focus is American governments' use of above-board and below-the-belt means to generate divisions along so-called ideological grounds – communists versus the 'free world' – among a range of trade-union leaders, aided and abetted by a variety of characters from the world of politics and espionage. Indeed, at times it reads like a James Bond novel with villains and heroes, corruption of the flesh and of the wallet, and with high stakes and low morals.

Readers should beware. This book is not true to its title. Rather, it tells the story of the efforts of the United States secret services, encouraged by the US State Department, to corrupt or destroy all the progressive trends in labour movements during the early years of the Cold War, using anti-communism as the pretext. The book centres on the activities of Jay Lovestone and Irvine Brown, nominally unelected union officials linked with the American Federation of Labor (AFL) but whose real masters were the Central Intelligence Agency (CIA) and associated US giant multinational companies. Long before Lovestone and Brown came onto the scene, the AFL was an unwavering opponent of the Left (in particular, communists) both at home and abroad. Lovestone and Brown were given full rein to sharpen this focus without challenge from within what passed as democratic structures in the AFL. Rank-and-file members had no say in these developments which were often characterized by attacks on the World Federation of Trade Unions (WFTU, the united world trade-union centre until 1949, from which the AFL excluded itself on the grounds of anti-communism). After the formation, in 1949, of the International

Confederation of Free Trade Unions (ICFTU), with an anti-communist constitution, the AFL, although a founding member, constantly accused the European affiliates of being soft on communism.

The attention to detail and the concentration on certain individuals and institutions illustrates the strengths and weaknesses of the politically committed labour historian: a mixture of mastery of infighting and sectarian casuistry with a lack of context and perspective. This book would be hard going for those previously unaware of what was happening, and harder work still for readers under the age of 60! At times it seeks to score too many debating points and to become so intricate as to lose the plot. At the end of each chapter there is some attempt to draw the storyline together and send us on our way, but that is a poor substitute for a more cogent analysis of these events.

Anthony Carew's arguments are based on a number of contentious premises. For example, he trots out a well-trodden trope that the search for universal labour unity was doomed to failure given the fundamental differences in the objectives and approaches of the main WFTU affiliates. He posits that the American unions in the period under review were free agents, independent of state interference and fundamentally anti-colonialist. He seems to believe that their record on colonialism was exemplary (p. 168), a position, as we will argue, far from reality. Indeed Carew writes as if neo-colonialism did not (and does not) exist. Therefore, in his eyes it is a concept that cannot be used as an explanation for the brutal policies used by the United States of America with the full support of the AFL. In many parts of the world, where national liberation movements and progressive governments were quashed in the name of anti-communism, millions died and millions more were maimed and injured (in particular in Guatemala, Indonesia, Vietnam, and Chile).

The basic question being addressed is did the European trade-union leaders jump of their own accord into the damaging anti-Soviet positions or were they pushed by US money and the Marshall Plan? While Carew remains unclear on this point, others have decided they jumped.[1]

The first three chapters cover the determinant years from 1945 to 1950. Here was the first flush of victory over the horrific brutality of the Nazis and their fascist allies. The Soviets were our comrades and this was reflected in both words and deeds of unity across the labour movement with the birth of the WFTU – a formal bridge, as Carew explains, between the communist and non-communist worlds. While this raised an eyebrow

---

1 R. Saville, 'Politics and the Labour Movement in the Early Cold War', *Our History Journal: Journal of the History Group of the Communist Party* 15 (1990), pp. 20–35, at p. 33; P. Weiler, 'The United States, International Labor, and the Cold War: The Breakup of the World Federation of Trade Unions', *Diplomatic History* (*Dip. Hist.*) 5:1 (1981), pp. 1–22.

among Walter Citrine's followers in the British Trades Union Congress (TUC),[2] it was the embittered and forceful Lovestone who was alarmed and dismayed. It triggered a full frontal initiative by the Americans; Brown was sent to Europe to sow sedition and discontent among the winnable anti-communists. Carew spends much time explaining the Lovestone–Brown bond and joint ventures. He sees them as the conduits through which flowed CIA money and dark arts.

The scene shifts to Brown's work among labourites in western and northern Europe. A tireless meddler and fixer appears to be Carew's view of Brown. They seek him here and they seek him there, but the elusive Brown with his shadowy backers is credited with engineering the split in the WFTU and helping to found the ICFTU. The CIA-backed AFL is portrayed as the arch-splitter as intrigue upon intrigue is dissected and painstakingly explored.

Stories of undermining local trade-union bodies in Finland, France, Australia and Italy add flavour to the splits within splits and the tactical cross purposes that dominated confused American handlers along with their conflicted European counterparts. Secrets wrapped up in the flow of dollars and favours have been unearthed by Carew's diligence, but to the neglect of class struggle and orthodox analysis of trade unions as job-preservers and wage-bargainers. Whatever the outcomes from the national and international politics of schism, jobs and livelihoods needed to be protected. Carew at times drifts into a turn of phrase and analytical miasma that seems to place, for example, the TUC general secretary at the centre of British trade-unionism. He seems uninterested in the sentiments and actions of workplace union activists, and unperturbed by shop-steward power, strike action, and the wages' movement.

His defence is that the book is about the export of Cold War imperatives from the US movement in the shape of the AFL – and later the merged AFL–CIO (Congress of Industrial Organizations) – to European, African, and Asian union leaders and organizations. But the success or failure of such an enterprise was largely about the acceptance by rank and file of the relevance of such incursions, rather than who bribed whom, with what, and why. Indeed Carew fails to explain the origins of the American trade-union movement with its craft and industrial base and conflicts. With figures such as Samuel Gompers, the AFL was formed in 1886, and by 1894 it began the annual exchange of delegates with the TUC. There remained an uneasy truce between craft and industrial unionism until supporters of the latter split to form the CIO in 1938. Such background information rooted in both

---

2 Walter Citrine was general secretary of the Trades Union Congress, 1926–46; president of the International Federation of Trade Unions (the 'Amsterdam International'), 1928–45; and president of the World Federation of Trade Unions, 1945–46.

the economism of the American unions and the pro-capitalist stance of their leaders would have helped explain the pattern of future AFL and CIO activities and relations.[3]

In the UK, the 1950s saw the start of thirteen years of Conservative government (1951–64). This was important for the American anti-communist crusade since it considered the TUC pivotal to its cause. But having an anti-working-class party in power does not mean a compliant trade-union movement, whatever some union leaders said and did. The next two chapters deal with unfolding events throughout the 1950s. The rival American trade-union centres, the CIO and AFL, according to Carew, were equally anti-communist: the CIO tended to play the right-wing social-democratic card of 'neither Standard Oil nor Stalin' (p. 107), as Walter Reuther (CIO president, 1952–55) said; in contrast the AFL was unconditionally theocratic in its anti-communist stance.

The Reuther brothers (Walter and Victor)[4] had a long-standing rift with Lovestone and became increasingly concerned that the Marshall Plan was being used to favour employers at the expense of European workers' pay and conditions. Meanwhile, the CIA and Brown were seeking to further exploit splits in the French and Italian communist trade-union groups. Using a combination of funds, the poor administration of Marshall Aid, and secret surveillance, the American union centres became entwined in the job of weakening communist influence and driving wedges between the various European tendencies.

As Carew recognizes, Walter Reuther was just as committed to an anti-communist strategy as his more robust associates in the AFL. He happily took CIA money to support the CIO's attempts to divide western European unions (particularly in France and Italy) along political lines and to bolster State Department attempts to foster the Marshall Plan objectives to hold down wages and to introduce 'speed-up' productivity deals. Peter Weiler explains that the Marshall Plan was used to repaint the Americans as the saviours of the working class and the Soviets as abusing their position to undermine the movement for their own ends. As he noted, 'Ultimately, the Marshall Plan revealed that the existence of the WFTU depended on the configuration of international politics. Once the wartime détente ended and a new configuration came into being, its demise was inevitable.'[5]

Carew's apparent respect for the AFL mirrors that of Citrine, Ernest Bevin, Arthur Deakin, Jack Jones, and Hugh Scanlon, despite that organization's

3 B. Wallace, 'The United States of America', in *idem*, *World Labour Comes of Age* (Lawrence and Wishart: 1945), pp. 37–41.

4 Victor Reuther worked for the United Automobile Workers (UAW), eventually becoming its international director.

5 Weiler, 'The United States, International Labor, and the Cold War', *Dip. Hist.*, p. 22.

record in class terms on almost everything.[6] This was particularly evident in its lack of support for racial equality (and all other equality issues) and its enthusiastic endorsement of US foreign policy objectives – encompassing the 1954 regime change in Guatemala accompanied by the murder and imprisonment of thousands of trade-unionists, the failed invasion of Cuba at the Bay of Pigs in 1961, the Vietnam War, and the murder of Chilean president Salvador Allende in 1973. Lovestone and Brown are credited by Carew with too much influence. The dominant right-wing, social-democratic trend in the west European labour movement found American dollars helpful but not decisive in its drive to defeat communists – even when the price for this was to provoke labour movement splits and divisions in many European centres, leaving international labour weaker than it was in 1945–49.

It is about at this point in the book that Carew's apparent lack of a theoretical framework within which to debate trade-unionism becomes a worry. Whether within and between the AFL and CIO, or the Confédération Générale du Travail and the TUC, or the WFTU and ICFTU – what is their purpose and what about the workers? Carew's account then becomes a superstructural set of fantastic tales not rooted in everyday struggles and without the context of the rebuilding of post-war capitalism. The European version of this was fighting colonial wars, fending off liberation movements, and coming to terms with the might of US corporations. These are not woven into the fabric of Carew's analysis.

In Greece, for example, 'The TUC leaders, including Walter Citrine, Victor Tewson and Victor Feather not only sabotaged the democratically elected Greek trade union movement … [but did so] in conjunction with employers' representatives, the political right and even pro-fascists.'[7] This naturally formed the basis for TUC attacks on the WFTU as its leaders sided with American corporations in Europe to counter communist

---

6 For Citrine, see n. 2 above. Ernest Bevin, Arthur Deakin, and Jack Jones were Transport and General Workers' Union general secretaries, in 1922–40, 1940–55, and 1969–78, respectively; Deakin followed Citrine as WFTU president, 1946–49. Hugh Scanlon was president of the Amalgamated Engineering Union (and its successors), 1967–79.

7 Saville, 'Politics and the Labour Movement', *Our History*, p. 31. Vincent Tewson was TUC assistant general secretary, 1931–46, TUC general secretary, 1946–60, and ICFTU president, 1951–53. Bevin, when Labour foreign secretary, 1945–51, encouraged the TUC to send Victor Feather (who had joined the TUC in 1937) on missions to Europe 'to help rebuild and redesign post-war European trade unions'; Feather became TUC assistant secretary (no. 3 in the hierarchy) in 1947, then assistant general secretary in 1960, and was general secretary, 1969–73: G. Goodman, 'Feather, Victor Grayson Hardie, Baron Feather (1908–1976)', *Oxford Dictionary of National Biography* (2011), online.

influence in their own backyard. Infiltrating and sponsoring training for trade-unionists has long been seen as a vital part of winning hearts and minds to the cause. Communists understood that and focused on union education as a means of influence, and so the AFL acting on behalf of the CIA sought to counter-attack in like manner. In the early 1950s the ICFTU embarked on such a strategy, but it was soon undone by a combination of failing to meet required expectations as in France (p. 123) and a lack of coherent and consistent approach. Its links with the Ford Foundation, for example, channelled funds from the CIA through the CIO into other fronts. But overall, the European trade-unionists seemed uninterested in the source of the money and deeply unappreciative of their sponsors.

The direction of the anti-communist 'divide-and-rule' tactics took another twist with the death of Stalin in March 1953. The Americans appeared to be confused by the loss of their hate figure. They had panicked in the face of the communist takeover of China, and were disheartened by what they saw, according to Carew, as the half-hearted anti-communism of the TUC. The shocking compliance, however, with events closer to home in South America was more revealing than all the bluff words about democracy. In Guatemala there was murder and torture by the CIA and its local agents. Those killed included union leaders opposed to the United Fruit Company's ruthless search for land. As was reported at the time, 'George Meany, AFL president,[8] daring to call this democracy, has urged the US Government to "exercise all the influence and pressure in its power"' to support the clamp down. Further, 'no worker can remain indifferent to the despicable crime at present being committed in Guatemala. The military Junta which has seized power has immediately struck at the workers of Guatemala. 45 trade unionists … have been shot, after being brutally tortured'.[9] Carew is silent on such matters.

The AFL and CIO moved closer together on domestic issues and were able to co-operate more meaningfully on the world stage, especially against the growing peace movement. Again Carew's insistence on seeing the world through the eyes of a handful of powerful men – women are noticeably absent both from centre stage and Carew's account (a point he notes in passing, p. 132) – fails to explain why the AFL and CIO merged in 1955 (p. 144) and fails to locate this development alongside the new AFL–CIO joint ventures abroad.

By the mid-1950s, shorn of its radical wing (expelled communist-led unions had about 25% of its membership), the CIO leadership, directed by Walter Reuther, moved sharply to the right. The political differences with the AFL were narrowed on the AFL's terms. This and the CIO's underlying

---

8 George Meany was a leading official of the AFL for many years, before becoming president in 1952, and then AFL–CIO president, 1955–79.

9 *Journal of the National Confederation of Peasants of Guatemala*, reprinted in *World Trade Union Movement Monthly* 12 (August 1954), pp. 16–17.

financial difficulties threw the once powerful and radical CIO into the arms of the AFL which, under Meany's leadership, had begun to clean up some of the long-standing corrupt and reactionary practices that characterized the operations of many of its affiliates, including the need to tackle widespread racial discrimination in its ranks – if only in words. Under Reuther's leadership the merger was agreed in 1955, very much on AFL terms. Again Carew fails to discuss the internal politics and pressures of the American unions, and thereby sacrifices an important analytical aspect that helps understand the shifts in policy.

Carew refers to the merger as a 'wedding without a honeymoon' and relates how it did nothing to clarify AFL–CIO interference in the trade-union movements around the world. A combination of 'de-Stalinization' with an upsurge in anti-colonialism movements meant that the crude and clandestine anti-communism of the early 1950s was no longer appropriate. From the development of a so-called non-aligned bloc (Tito, Jawaharial Nehru, and Kwame Nkrumah) to uprisings in Hungary and Poland in 1956, the world order was shifting without, as yet, disintegrating. Meanwhile, Carew continues with his Agatha-Christie-like detection of motives and opportunities for his main cast of characters.

The rise of the Atlantic Alliance (p. 162) is linked with a rather clumsy and superficial attempt to take the reader through the intricacies of revolt and revolution throughout Africa and parts of Asia. In our view, Carew does not get it. His lack of depth and careless approach to complex and important events in Algeria and Kenya, let alone India, diminishes the struggles that took place and their part in his thesis. Meanwhile, the ICFTU seemed to be withering on too many vines. Carew senses that the powerful grouping of the AFL–CIO no longer had to live through its creature, the ICFTU. Indeed it was a case of 'fools rush in' and endlessly tiresome plots and palace coups and *coups de main* that revolved around a handful of middle-aged, white men seeking to outmanoeuvre each other for control of the ICFTU (p. 185), in order to reinstate a series of failed polices born in 1948 and no longer useful ten years later. Carew sums this up: 'Here the lack of urgency with which the ICFTU approached the requirement to build its organization in Africa proved fatal' (p. 189). But why?

The book enters its final phase of developments in the 1960s. By now Carew, along with the leadership of the ICFTU, is running out of steam. His detailed account of machinations within the American trade-union movement, and with its task of exporting counter-revolution, is not really sustainable without being grounded in the political economy of class struggle in all its forms. He finds it increasingly difficult to navigate the murky waters of the individual contests by office holders, would-be office holders, and institutional power plays. The ICFTU's leaders sought a pragmatic form of anti-communism that would provide a realistic chance of influencing union policy; but Meany at the AFL–CIO was not content with what was seen as lukewarm posturing. This became an immediate issue when dealing with African national liberation movements. Neither Carew's protagonists nor Carew himself seem to have a serious grasp of these insurgencies. The book provides yet more detail on the musical chairs being played in high office within the ICFTU, and all of the scheming seems a long way away from the harsh really existing struggles of trade-unionists fighting colonial powers and their would-be puppets.

By 1962 Carew's version of John le Carré's *Smiley's People* – with Lovestone, Brown, Reuther, and Meany – came to a head in the ICFTU's Berlin conference (p. 211). Strategic and tactical differences remained unresolved; much appears to have come to crisis point over the fate of the ICFTU general secretary, Omer Becu (1960–67). This personification of differences was, according to Carew, a vital aspect of the search for a foothold inside the anti-colonial movements to ward off Soviet influence. This became more important with the arrival of George Woodcock as TUC general secretary (1960–69) because, despite his anti-communism, his largely ineffective leadership meant that the official central arm of British trade unions was a worthless ally for AFL–CIO adventurism. Woodcock tended to side with UK foreign policy in seeking to keep Africa coloured 'pink', and therefore was unhelpful towards American efforts to usurp the old empire with its new star-spangled version.

By 1965 the very splits that the ICFTU was set up to exploit among various world trade-union groupings were visited upon its own host. The ubiquitous Brown, according to Carew, went about setting his own agenda and following his own AFL–CIO path irrespective of the knowledge or wishes of the ICFTU leadership. This was most evident again in sub-Saharan Africa and increasingly in South Vietnam (pp. 225–7). Brown and Meany believed they could finally take over the ICFTU machine once and for all and, with Lovestone's support, this *folie à trois* continued to fantasize about the importance of their roles (pp. 229–30).

The final chapters of Carew's book deal with the strange death of formal institutional efforts to split the trade-union movements throughout Africa, Asia, and Europe. Little is said about South America or even about union politics in the USA itself. As we approach the pivotal years of 1967–68, Carew's enthusiasm for detailed accounts of shadow battles overwhelms his ability to explain to the reader how real changes in workers' attitudes and behaviour influenced the outcomes of the planned coups by the American union leaders. By now the AFL–CIO was drawing back from funding the ICFTU and its exploits, but the mantle of anti-communism was taken up by the United Automobile Workers (UAW) through its Free World Labour Defence Fund (p. 241). There is a telling mention by Carew that the funds were available because the UAW had not spent its own massive strike fund. Unfortunately, Carew fails to delve deeper into this link between anti-communist business unionism inside the USA and its ability to export trouble overseas. He also fails to follow this up in terms of the challenge to the American automobile industry from European and Japanese manufacturers, and the use of UAW funds to hinder such expansion and competition.

The main difference in approach was that the UAW leadership sought to disguise its friendly donations as being worker-to-worker (almost comradely) support rather than the previous top-down, over-controlled programme. By directly involving some of its own (handpicked) activists to travel abroad and by helping, for example, striking French miners (p. 242), the Americans in this phase sought influence through good deeds on the ground. As Carew notes, 'the UAW's key strategic focus was to help the non-communist labour movement become a more effective representative of the worker vis-à-vis employers' (p. 244). Under the short-lived John F. Kennedy administration (1961–63), Walter Reuther (UAW president, 1946–70) promoted the Italian centre-left, among others, with political support from the US government. This was nothing more nor less than a recognition of the realities facing trade-unionists in Europe and parts of South Asia as they were confronted with *revanchist* employers, shifting skills and labour markets, and the resurgent communist movement. It was not a brilliant *coup d'état* as Carew would have us believe, but a pragmatic response to the new realities. None of this disguised the anti-communist interference in the affairs of others, and nothing reduced the counterproductive nature of taking the American dollar along with the American politics.

This approach through the UAW came up against the dogma of Lovestone and the refusal to accept the lingering death of the ICFTU. By the mid-1960s the UAW's apparent social-democratic credentials were at odds with the remaining clandestine work of the CIA through its own preferred fronts inside the AFL–CIO and the ICFTU. There is not enough reflection here on the relative success and failures of the competing strategies, and more needed to be said about the apparent contradiction of the Reuther brothers' centre-left leanings and their interference in the trade-union movements across the globe. On the Vietnam War, Walter Reuther remained equivocal. Aware that a good number of his members opposed the anti-war movement, he procrastinated and refused to give it his endorsement, let alone support. Instead he declared that he agreed that 'the war was wrong but he could not openly campaign', saying that 'it was no time to split the union on this kind of ideological issue'. And during the 1950s Carew shows that Brown, on the AFL's behalf, floated a proposition to help build the South Vietnamese anti-communist union federation as a paramilitary force to defend the country against the communist threat.[10]

---

10 See N. Lichtenstein, *Walter Reuther: The Most Dangerous Man in Detroit* (University of Illinois Press, Urbana, IL: 1997), p. 421.

The extent to which the leadership of central parts of the US trade-union movement were out of step with world developments (the start of détente) and the aspirations of trade-unionists worldwide, became increasingly clear. Whether when dealing in France and Germany, Yugoslavia or Ghana, Korea or India, the Americans could not ditch their habits of using blood money and bullying to seek influence over other union leaders. The Vietnam War was lost on the battlefields of peasant land – just as the ideological war on union purpose was being lost by the Americans on the battlefields of strikes, political association with national liberation movements, and the newly found socialist revival.

Carew passes by such developments. He spills over into the anti-Sovietism that he seeks to depict and thereby loses the analytical edge needed to dissect the strangely out-of-touch methods of his American protagonists. So while Brown was still plying his trade across Africa, at times accompanied by high-ranking US government leaders (pp. 286–7), the ICFTU was falling away to be replaced by direct American interference. This was plain to see from Nigeria to the Congo, and from Togo to Kenya; the stylized pan-Africanism peddled by the ICFTU was a sham. But the wider and deeper US influence in Africa was more sinister than anything offered by the trade-union movements' splits and rivalries. Here were indeed the foundations of murder and corruption on a large scale, backed by the US, endorsed by the retreating European powers, and underwritten by the CIA through fronts such as the ICFTU. This tragic story of unfolding misery, starvation, and eventually catastrophic state failures is not told by Carew. He is too intent on informing us about the wrangles inside the movement.

We are told again about the ins and outs of replacing the ICFTU leadership, who backed whom and why (p. 299). The same characters reappear with Lovestone snapping at Meany's heels over the latest ICFTU leadership contest that was about to fall apart, with the Americans finally leaving their creature to its fate. These men, now out of their time, refused to accept the legitimacy of efforts to reduce the threat of nuclear war, despised the peace movement, raged against any co-operation with communists, and showed their true colours as zealots without morality, and as fanatics without a fan base. With the abrupt end of the Prague Spring in August 1968 came mixed signals: Meany, through the AFL–CIO, thought it vindicated his staunch anti-communism and would stem the tide of détente; the WFTU backed the Czech trade unions in their opposition to Soviet intervention (p. 307). Rather than stepping back into the old Cold War posturing, the opposite happened – the move to find common ground across the left divide grew stronger and there began the long road from Sovietism to a post-Stalinist Soviet communism. In all of this Carew appears to share the anti-Soviet sentiments of the far-left and the near-left. This makes it harder for him to come to terms with real developments, so he tends to hide behind his wall of detailed personal interactions to the detriment of sending the reader a clear message about the incompetent meddling of American trade unions in international affairs.

Back in the USA the UAW was ready to split from the AFL–CIO (leaving in 1968, but reaffiliating in 1981). Such typically vain moves provide the lie of any slogans associated with either 'unity' or 'class interests'. Carew explains the pain this caused in the ICFTU (pp. 314–16), and the whys and wherefores of the AFL–CIO's final departure from the ICFTU – the child biting the hand that fed it. The lies and deceits that had become the everyday world of the ICFTU even shocked the retiring Woodcock at the TUC. This was itself based on the UAW's attempt to affiliate in its own right to the ICFTU. The Reuther brothers' plan to bypass the AFL–CIO in this manner found few friends in Europe. As Carew points out, 'The ICFTU was of steadily diminishing relevance in Meany's scheme of things, and during the 1960s the AFL–CIO's international effort was increasingly made through the regional auxiliary bodies' (p. 320).

This was a recipe for constant discord. As encouraged by the US State Department, the AFL promoted American state policies and sought to undermine the ICFTU's attempts to encourage a social-democratic approach to trade-union development across the globe, based on the creation of strong national unions and, where possible, industry agreements, as well as links with national governments. Such an approach was strongly favoured by the British Foreign Office and the TUC, but often ineptly applied.

In all of this there is no mention in the book of America's own backyard – nothing on Brazil and Mexico, Chile or Peru. But the importance of South and Central America in this saga should be clear – that USA workers' relative prosperity and moderation was in part predicated on the violent exploitation of their southern neighbours, and thereby allowed some of their leaders to engage in the expensive and self-indulgent forays into foreign trade-unionism. We have mentioned the tragedy in Guatemala; to that can be added the bloody consequences of the Meany–CIA collaborations in El Salvador and Haiti. As has been argued by Paul Buhle, 'Again and again, the fusion of corporate, CIA, State Department, AFL, and then AFL–CIO enterprises, along with satellites like International Rescue Committee and (much later) Freedom House, vigorously supported and hailed numerous terror regimes.'[11]

In 1969 the AFL–CIO began the formal disentanglement from the main body of ICFTU (leaving that year and not rejoining until 1984). The TUC, now under the leadership of the passively acquiescent Feather, and Force Ouvrière in France seemed to be the only main blocs interested in keeping the Americans inside the tent. Carew provides a detailed and painstaking

---

11 P. Buhle, *Taking Care of Business: Samuel Gompers, George Meany, Lane Kirkland, and the Tragedy of American Labor* (Monthly Review Press, New York: 1999), p. 145.

account of the divorce ('au revoir becomes adieu'), with accounts of endless meetings, references to serial minutes, and use of public and private statements from the main runners and riders. The extent, at times desperate and bizarre, to which sections of the ICFTU went to keep the AFL–CIO on board was a sign of the need for both their dollars and their networks. In itself that is the fate of all puppets, when the puppetmaster lets the strings flop into a tangled mess of lifeless inaction. So it was with ICFTU.

Inside the UAW and AFL–CIO, leaders' sins came back to haunt them – secret meetings, lies and distortions, corruption of others, enemies within, dangerous liaisons with the CIA and the FBI (Federal Bureau of Investigation), and essentially 'Oh, what a tangled web we weave when first we practise to deceive'. Meany and Walter Reuther, Feather and Harm Buiter, had all deceived their members and others in the name of the greater good of anti-communism. When such habits were used against each other they were 'shocked' at such duplicity. The story Carew tells, and his telling of it, sound an oddly old-fashioned chord. Middle-aged, white men in suits deciding the fate of others, turning their backs on their own working-class members, playing the patsy to the more powerful forces of capital, and ultimately sounding and acting like shadow boxers in a failing light. With the death of Walter Reuther (1970) and the decline of Meany, the AFL–CIO's fight over the ICFTU dimmed. Carew summarizes: 'The AFL–CIO had broken with the ICFTU ... simply because its key affiliates gave insufficient support to the fundamental purposes of the ICFTU as they and the Americans had understood them in the past' (p. 340).

Carew concludes with an assessment of the AFL–CIO's role in sowing disunity and dissent among union leaders across the globe (p. 341): from the aspirations of 'unity is strength' inside the WFTU to the damaging infighting and undermining of the high tide of the ICFTU. The sham of support for 'free trade unionism' was increasingly exposed as American union leaders supported far-right regimes in South America and Africa. But this reality of posing as a democratic defender of the workers was always a con trick, although at times Carew seems to believe there was something more sincere under the surface. He does succeed in taking us back to the bitterness and fanaticism of the Cold War, and even convinces us of the importance of the trade-union movement within the wider and deeper political economy of nations. But he ends not with a bang but a whimper, seeming to side with Solidarność in Poland as the embodiment of the AFL–CIO's definition of 'free trade unionism'.

To claim as Carew does, without supporting evidence and argument, that the AFL's vision of pure and simple trade-unionism was influential in the development of the Polish trade-union federation Solidarność is nonsense. The AFL and Solidarność had but one thing in common – both fiercely anti-communist. But Solidarność ideologically owed more to the Pope and the Catholic Church than to the AFL's notion of free trade-unionism.

Within three years of its establishment as a legal entity, its leadership determined to form a political party. Far from distancing itself from the state, Solidarność became a leading force in the state before falling apart into warring factions.

American Labour's Cold War Abroad is a worthy testament to Carew's years of scholarly research and publication. He has performed a great service by uncovering and piecing together the intricate story of the international trade-union institutions and their American puppet-masters from 1945 to 1970. He has sustained his argument, marshalled an enormous array of information, and delivered a fascinating account of one of the more significant intrigues of the Cold War years. Its readership, though, will be limited to those concerned with such American meddling and institutional history. For an account of trade-unionism during the Cold War that is rooted in class, class struggle, and an analysis of the balance of class forces, we will have to look elsewhere.

Roger Seifert
Emeritus Professor
Wolverhampton University
Wolverhampton
WV1 1AD
r.v.seifert@outlook.com

https://doi.org/10.3828/hsir.2020.41.14

Book Reviews

Kim Moody, *Tramps and Trade Union Travelers: Internal Migration and Organized Labor in Gilded Age America, 1870–1900* (Haymarket Books, Chicago: 2019), ix+255pp., pbk £15.99, ISBN 978-1-60846-755-6.

There was a time when historians hunted high and wide for the 'American Character', the essential gene that distinguished the upstart republic from its Old World antecedents. Largely forgotten now is the contribution of the Yale scholar George W. Pierson. 'What made and kept us different', he wrote in a widely discussed 1962 essay, 'was not just the wildness of the North American continent, nor its vast empty spaces, nor even its wealth of resources, powerful as must have been those influences. No. It was, first of all, the M-factor: the factor of movement, migration, mobility.' Pierson's argument was both an extension and a critique of Frederick Jackson Turner's frontier thesis, which argued that the constantly receding area of free land explained American uniqueness. Turner, he suggested, 'half sensed the power that was in migration, but then imprisoned this giant in the rough homespun of the vanishing pioneers'.[1]

In his valuable new book, Kim Moody makes no reference to Pierson's work (although he does discuss Turner) and, in truth, there is little reason for him to do so. United in their belief that internal migration has been undervalued as a component of America's past, the two men are separated by a cultural and intellectual chasm as well as by generation. Pierson had no interest in class, or in labour and social history for that matter, and would have had little empathy with the explorations of industrial organization and resistance undertaken here, or, even less likely, the author's Marxism. But, in his essay, Pierson identifies migration as a 'disintegrator', a word Moody might well be inclined to accept. *Tramps and Trade Union Travelers* studies the impact of internal migration during a critical period of American industrial and political development, the last three decades of the nineteenth century, when economic output reached new levels and the nation struggled to deal with the consequences. Pursuing arguments about exceptionalism requires a degree of comparative analysis, and the author, a veteran writer and activist, is well fitted to the task. American-born, but now domiciled in the United Kingdom, Moody owes a particular debt to E. P. Thompson whose understanding of class and pioneering work on early English radicalism he exploits to transparent and beneficial effect. The book began life as a doctoral dissertation at the University of Nottingham; supervision sessions must have been lively affairs on the evidence provided here.

The questions that Pierson asked over half a century ago now seem anachronistic; by contrast, Moody's resonate strongly with contemporary concerns. 'While no work of history can supply simple answers to the problems of another era', he writes, 'an understanding of how the forces of immigration and internal migration affected the efforts to build labour organizations in a prior age of new technology and geographic mobility has central relevance to today's world of work and conflict' (p. 182). Moody sets out his historiographical and methodological stall in a lengthy introduction which evaluates traditional understandings of American exceptionalism. His aim in the book is to explain the relative weakness of trade unions and working-class politics in the late nineteenth-century United States when compared to those in European economic powerhouses, Britain and Germany. The factors usually cited include the impact of state power; gender, race and ethnicity; and the opposition of established political interests, notably urban political machines. While Moody concedes that all of these contributed to labour's industrial and political fragility, the 'missing' factor, in his view, is geographic mobility. His purpose is not to dismiss or demote these 'recognized and plausible causes' of labour's weakness, 'but to introduce the dynamics of internal migration into our understanding of the unevenness of class formation and organization in the Gilded Age' (p. 21).

He first explores class consciousness, how it formed and how it was perceived. Its absence among workers, asserted or implied in so many texts, was a key element in American exceptionalism. Following Thompson's definition of class as relational, rooted in experience, he identifies class consciousness in Gilded Age America as embodying, first, 'a general identity of wageworkers as a class in formation' and, second, 'the perception of the emerging capitalist class or employers as different and opposed to the interests of the working class' (p. 28). He especially highlights the role of the labour press as a major shaper of class ideas. In the mid-1880s, anything from 400 to 800 labour newspapers were in circulation, with a potential readership of two to four million. By challenging the received wisdom of the mainstream press, these papers formed an impressive network helping to create and sustain a working-class culture of opposition that proved vital to resisting capitalist demands. Moody rejects the narrative that portrays 'pure and simple' craft unionism as coming to dominate organized labour after 1886, and points out that 'by some of the most common measures of class consciousness, most of the 1890s were even more divided by class and class conflict' (p. 49). In 1894, over half a million workers came out on strike, more than in any previously documented year. There was further mass mobilization of labour in the opening years of the new century, adding force to his point that, although class consciousness may have changed shape, it had far from evaporated.

Having established the pervasiveness of class consciousness, the book next investigates the missing ingredient in labour's inability to sustain effective organizational momentum: internal migration. It is a given that nineteenth-century America saw extensive movement from country to city, from farm to factory, but Moody demonstrates that this was only part of a much wider mobility. During the thirty-year period covered by the study, over seven-and-a-half million people, many of them recent immigrants, moved from one state to another. There was also extensive intrastate migration. This vast movement reflected the high turnover and irregular employment integral to the rise of industrial capitalism. In a revealing comparison, he shows that American migration rates were over five times those of England and Wales, a fact attributable to the different stages of industrialization and urbanization on the two sides of the Atlantic. In America, the high degree of mobility resulted from a number of factors, including the sheer size of the country. But, above all, it was the relentless, unpredictable dynamics of capital accumulation that Moody considers key. Workers, who now increasingly formed a permanent class of wage earners, were pushed and pulled across America's vast spaces as it experienced 'rapid and turbulent' industrialization (p. 87). In a companion chapter, the author fleshes out the theoretical and statistical bones of this story of movement. Constant migration may well have passed by historians; it certainly caught the attention of contemporaries, often to negative effect. Nineteen states passed laws between 1876 and 1886 to discourage those without work; many more states would follow. The tramp has been a familiar figure in American popular culture, but there was nothing aimless or romantic about workers following the frontiers of economic development. Moody includes fascinating detail here about tramping and the use of travelling cards which gained transient workers access to local unions. There are also exemplary sketches of individual trades, some of which, like those connected to the railroads and the telegraph, one obviously associates with mobility, while others – printers, machinists, iron moulders and cigar makers – less so. In addition to these skilled migrants were the vast numbers of semi- and unskilled workers and labourers, the very sort that middle-class observers dismissed as tramps and vagrants, but who were vital to industrialization's march.

Moody's last two chapters confront head-on the dramatic history of organized labour in the 1880s and 1890s and the failure of independent working-class politics to make permanent inroads into America's two-party domain. The story is mostly a familiar one, from the Knights of Labour's rise and sudden collapse in 1886 to the abortive farmer-labour initiatives of the following decade. In retelling it, the author is adamant that internal migration was the missing factor in explaining the numerical and organizational weaknesses that caused the overall failure. In 1886–87, a 'perfect storm' of migration occurred as labour organizations were undermined by the 'sheer volatility' of economic growth (p. 123); and, in the decade that followed, labour's incessant mobility continued to be decisive in trade-unionism's halting progress. Not until the final years of the century, when big business achieved relative organizational and geographic stability, did union growth and self-confidence resume. In his final chapter, Moody reviews the arguments regarding the failure of independent political action, insisting again that the problem 'was not one of consciousness, but of organization that was repeatedly undermined by the massive movement of people in the turbulence of rapid and uneven industrialization' (p. 154). Among mobility's negative effects was its role in workers' ability to vote. With so much of the attention on voter participation in late nineteenth-century America focused on black disfranchisement, it is good to be reminded of how restricted the suffrage had become for the nation's working class overall.

Moody is sensitive to the many elements, including racial and ethnic division, which contributed to the fragility of organized labour in the Gilded Age, and if he is not clear about their relative weight, the lucidity and directness of his argument provide ample compensation. His solution to the conundrum of labour's political failure is necessarily speculative, but that is no bad thing; and, if it does nothing else, his book will encourage other scholars to revisit this far from settled ground. In his conclusion, Moody acknowledges how recent work in labour and social history has enriched our understanding of the working-class experience, but makes the telling point that while post-Civil War African-American migration has been extensively investigated, the wider mobility has gone largely unnoticed, or at least unintegrated into wider analytic frameworks. In sum, this is a resourceful, well-written, and thoroughly recommendable study. Clear in its objectives and crafted from a strong research base, it more than deserves its place on the labour and industrial history bookshelf.

Martin Crawford
Keele University

Note

1 G. W. Pierson, 'The M-Factor in American History', *American Quarterly* 14 (Summer 1962), pp. 275–89, at p. 278.

Jim Phillips, *Scottish Coal Miners in the Twentieth Century* (Edinburgh University Press: 2019), xi+316pp., hbk £85, ISBN 978-1-4744-5231-1.

The Scottish miners are surely one of the most studied groups of workers in British labour historiography. Robin Page Arnot's *History of the Scottish Miners* (1955) devoted significant attention to the first half of the twentieth century, although within the framework of an uncritical and politically sympathetic official union history. My own two-volume *The Scottish Miners* (2000), examining the industry, its communities and trade unions, stretched from 1874 to 1939,[1] and studies with John McIlroy in this journal and elsewhere pushed that terminal date to 1945.[2] Rob Duncan's *The Mineworkers* (2005) provided an accessible overview of the Scottish coalfields from the eighteenth to the twentieth centuries which synthesized secondary literature and primary research, although treatment of the recent past was inevitably limited.[3] Jim Phillips himself has already added to our knowledge of the coal industry and its workers through a series of articles and an impressive monograph on the 1984–85 miners' strike in Scotland.[4] This successfully married 'high politics' with an industrial 'history from below' of individual collieries and settlements to explore the complex relationship between industrial and community structures and the agency of politicians, National Coal Board (NCB) managers, union leaders and local activists. Is there any necessity, then, for a further study? On the evidence of the book under review then the answer is emphatically in the affirmative.

Given the balance of the existing literature, Phillips concentrates on developments from the 1920s, with a particular focus on the nationalized industry between the 1940s and 1980s. He has assembled data from an impressive array of sources, including oral history collections and his own interviews, official publications, the national and labour press, and ephemeral publications. His excavation of the extensive NCB documentation in both the National Archives, Kew, and the National Records of Scotland, in conjunction with the National Union of Mineworkers Scottish Area (NUMSA) and local branch minutes, is exemplary; his bibliography of the secondary literature is extensive (although I found curious the omission of reference to Roy Church and Quentin Outram's important work on coalfield strikes, which holds particular significance for the extraordinarily high strike rate in Scotland).[5]

The volume of empirical detail from these diverse materials is daunting, but Phillips imposes order on it through a series of analytical devices. Taking inspiration from the injunctions of Ayrshire's Barony Colliery banner to 'Legislate, Educate, Organise', he loosely structures his book around these three themes. He relates them to the attempts to minimize economic insecurity in a market economy outlined by Mike Savage in his examination of Preston's cotton workers through strategies of mutualism, economism and statism.[6] The miners' unions and political representatives are characterized as articulating 'the central linkage between economic security and political voice' (p. 3). He draws on the notion of a distinctive 'popular moral economy' (a concept that he has more fully elaborated elsewhere) evolving from the 1940s which informed trade-union and political strategies. The inheritance of the insecurities from the period of private industry led to an insistence under nationalization, in the context of negotiation within the NCB's corporatist, consensual framework, that collieries and the employment opportunities they provided were social as well as economic resources: 'pit closures and job losses had to be negotiated with union representatives rather than imposed by NCB management; and the loss of pits and employment could only be accepted where communal as well as economic security was guaranteed' (pp. 143–4). And he borrows Paul Blyton and Peter Turnbull's concepts of the extent, location and scope of employee involvement to suggest how the ambitions of union goals moved from the workplace to the macroeconomic level.[7]

The opening chapter summarizes changes in ownership and employment, encapsulated in a table (p. 31) describing a Scottish mining workforce of 126,000 in 1925, which had fallen to 77,000 by nationalization in 1947, rising to 86,000 a decade later, but falling again to 36,000 in 1967 and 21,000 in 1977. By 1987 it was 6,000. This restructuring involved internal migration from the west to the eastern mining areas of Scotland and outflows of miners to English coalfields. It was also compensated to a degree by new industries so that coal jobs were in effect traded for jobs in other sectors. Migration carried implications for housing and the nature of mining communities.

Phillips adopts a novel threefold typology to exemplify these long-term changes and which he uses to categorize the twenty-one Scottish mines in 1977: 'village pits' were established in the 1900s, their smaller workforces utilizing semi-mechanized coal cutting and based around a solidaristic community; 'new mines' in the 1930s, with greater mechanization and miners travelling short distances to work; and large 'cosmopolitan collieries' opened in the 1960s by the NCB, employing fully mechanized power loading, with workers commuting up to fifteen miles daily. He later inventively links this structural schema to sociological generations within the miners' unions. The 'Village Pit generation', born in the 1890s, aspired to the economic security offered by nationalization; the 'New Mine generation', born in the 1920s, came to perceive problems with the nationalized industry and exercised greater vigilance on pit closures; the 'Cosmopolitan Colliery generation', born in the 1950s, encountered falling real wages and a management offensive that reversed previously negotiated procedures underpinning economic security.

These generations were personified by the leaders of NUMSA: the first by Abe Moffat (born 1896), the second by Moffat's protégé, Michael McGahey (born 1925), and Lawrence Daly (born 1924), all representatives of the Communist Party ascendancy within the union from the 1920s onwards. The third was embodied in a new cohort of younger miners. Although the average age of the workforce initially increased under nation-alization – from 40.5 years old in 1957 to 44.2 in 1973/74, it then markedly reversed, so much so that by March 1984 almost one-fifth of the workforce was under 25 years old. The differential reaction of these generations to job loss and closures structures detailed chapters on the experience of the Second World War, on wages and redundancies in the 1960s and 1970s, and the campaign for jobs and communities in the 1980s. These are intersected by an intermission on 'Miners and the Scottish Nation'. This chapter addresses the role which NUMSA played in the Communist Party-supported campaign within the Scottish labour movement for 'Home Rule' as a political response to deindustrialization and which ultimately contributed to securing the devolution settlement of 1999.

The final substantive chapter deals with the gathering crisis which culminated in the strike of 1984–85, the appointment of the hard-line NCB area director, Albert Wheeler, and the Thatcherite violation of the fundamental tenets of the miners' moral economy. In a telling observation earlier in his text, Phillips notes that Prime Minister Margaret Thatcher's personal copy of the 1944 White Paper on *Employment Policy* had the paragraphs on the need for workers to accept the inevitability of economic change and occupational mobility underlined in both red and blue pencil (p. 4). Given his previous monograph on the dispute – one that can be read with profit in tandem with the volume under review – Phillips provides a summary of the strike which was particularly bitter in Scotland given the greater incidence of victimization of arrested miners, irrespective of guilt or innocence. He responds to critiques of that study which echoed the common criticisms of the National Union of Mineworkers (NUM) strategy focusing on the lack of a national ballot, the threat to labour movement solidarity induced by picketing of steelworks, and the suggestion that a more flexible negotiating stance might have brought greater success. His case, which he makes persuasively, is that a national ballot would probably not have secured the required 55% majority, a result that would not have led to those on strike returning to work but rather an equally ragged and divisive retreat. Even if it had secured the necessary majority, the strike would still not have been solid in the English Midlands and elsewhere. He finds the charge of isolation exaggerated. Crucially, he points to the government papers released in 2014 of which his critics were unaware and which he reported on in this journal that same year.[8] They underscored the Cabinet's determination to secure total victory which no amount of compromise on the part of the NUM leadership could have countered.

This is an impeccably researched and conceptually ambitious study. As always, there are quibbles. The focus on long-term historical processes suggests there is still scope for more detailed study of how the Communist Party operated in the Scottish coalfields, one of its few British bastions, in the post-war era. If the politics of the popular front and wartime alliances helped inform the strategy of 'broad left unity' pursued by the Moffats (Abe and brother Alex) and McGahey, it was done on their terms, with rival Labour Party activists such as Eric Clark or Alex Eadie acquiescing in being sidelined in safe parliamentary seats. More work might also usefully address the extent and role of Orangeism and religious sectarianism in the coalfields, which continue to scar former mining areas to the present day and which Phillips alludes to in his description of two images by the documentary photographer, Milton Rogovin: the first depicts a group of miners in familiarly iconic pit helmets and NCB donkey jackets; in the second, one of the group is pictured at home with his family in front of portraits of the Queen (Elizabeth II) and William of Orange, his arm tattooed with the red hand of Ulster. The suggestion that the miners' moral economy appealed to Orange, Green and Red adherents may be true, so far as it goes, but is not the whole story nor entirely convincing.

Phillips's concluding reflections contain insights into the way mining has been memorialized in Scotland and essay brief assessment of the political traditions which remain implanted in the former coalfields, evidenced by support for Labour in the general elections of 1987 and 1992. In a curious chronological reversal, he notes the European referendum of 2016, with former Scottish mining areas all recording majorities for 'Remain', then proceeds to the 2014 independence referendum where many such areas registered support for 'Yes'. The elephant in that particular room is the subsequent collapse of the Labour vote (in 2015) with one Westminster MP and a third-placed rump of MSPs in Holyrood about whom the adjective 'mediocre' would be overgenerous. When the history of the rise of the Scottish National Party in the twenty-first century comes to be written – its membership now dwarfs that of the Labour Party in Scotland by a factor of 10 – then the deindustrialization of the mining areas and destruction of their communities will surely loom large. Phillips's account constitutes a major starting point for such a project.

Alan Campbell
University of Liverpool

Notes

1 A. Campbell, *The Scottish Miners,1874–1939, Vol. 1: Industry, Work and Community*; *Vol. 2: Trade Unions and Politics* (Ashgate, Aldershot: 2000); see review by Bill Knox in *Historical Studies in Industrial Relations* (*HSIR*) 12 (2001), pp. 148–54.

2 See, for example, J. McIlroy and A. Campbell, 'Beyond Betteshanger: Order 1305 in the Scottish Coalfields during the Second World War, Part 1: Politics, Prosecutions and Protest', *HSIR* 15 (2003), pp. 27–72, and 'Part 2: The Cardowan Story', *HSIR* 16 (2003), pp. 39–80.

3 R. Duncan, *The Mineworkers* (Birlinn, Edinburgh: 2005).

4 J. Phillips, *Collieries, Communities and the Miners' Strike in Scotland, 1984–85* (Manchester University Press: 2012).

5 R. Church and Q. Outram, *Strikes and Solidarity: Coalfield Conflict in Britain 1889–1966* (Cambridge University Press: 1998); see the review essays by A. Campbell, 'Exploring Miners' Militancy, 1889–1966: I', *HSIR* 7 (1999), pp. 147–63, and P. Edwards, 'Exploring Miners' Militancy, 1889–1966: II', *HSIR* 7 (1999), pp. 165–75.

6 M. Savage, *The Dynamics of Working-Class Politics: The Labour Movement in Preston, 1880–1940* (Cambridge University Press: 1987).

7 P. Blyton and P. Turnbull, *The Dynamics of Employee Relations* (3rd edn; Palgrave Macmillan, Basingstoke: 2004).

8 J. Phillips, 'Containing, Isolating, and Defeating the Miners: The UK Cabinet Ministerial Group on Coal and the Three Phases of the 1984–85 Strike', *HSIR* 35 (2014), pp. 117–41.

Andrew Brady, *Unions and Employment in a Market Economy: Strategy, Influence and Power in Contemporary Britain* (Routledge, Abingdon: 2019), xv+209pp., hbk £120.00, e-book £40.49, ISBN 978-1-13848-98-75.

This is a valuable, engaging and intriguing book. Its *value* lies in Andrew Brady's focus on the various ways in which British trade-union leaders have been able to influence or even shape the employment and industrial relations policies of the Labour Party, and of recent Labour governments, under different economic, political and social conditions; and, by learning from this experience, how unions may be able to do so more effectively in the future. The book is *engaging* by virtue of its approach and methods of inquiry: first, in its central analysis of four contrasting instances of recent Labour government policies and, second, in its deployment of extensive verbatim quotation from interviews conducted by the author with some twenty-six senior trade-union leaders and national politicians closely involved in the design, development or implementation of the policies reviewed. The data reported in the book are *intriguing* in the insights they give into the complex interplay of formal and informal relations, and into the linkages between the range of institutional arrangements, varying ideologies and shifting dynamics of interpersonal contacts that frame the various mechanisms, machinations and manoeuvres, which lie behind the policy negotiations and outcomes described.

However, the substance of the research reported in the book is also both daunting and ambitious. This can be seen simply by considering the scope and complexity of the four instances of policy chosen for exploration: the Social Contract (1974–79), the National Minimum Wage (1998), the Employment Relations Act 1999, and the 'Warwick Agreement' (2004). Not least of the challenges faced by the study is the author's quite proper determination to 'chart the ability of trade unions to influence employment relations regulation through political action in two structurally different contexts' (p. xiii): these he denotes respectively as '*collective laissez faireism*' and '*liberal market*'. The first he describes as having been 'enabled by an interventionist state' (p. xiv) which promoted an inclusive approach to unions in the management of the economy. By contrast, the second, the liberal market economy, typically favoured first by Margaret Thatcher's governments of the 1980s and not entirely reversed by subsequent Labour governments, where increasingly marginalized and weakened unions were confronted by a succession of 'decollectivist, deregulatory and privatisation policies' (p. xiv) and a drive towards the individualization of employment relations. So far, this is largely familiar territory: but the enormous challenge that the author sets himself, in centring his attention on what he terms 'the locus of leadership' (p. xiv) of UK trade unions, is convincingly to demonstrate that, even in these extremely straightened circumstances, it has been possible for union leaders 'to meaningfully shape the employment relations framework' (p. 6), thus repudiating simplistic assumptions that structural conditions alone determine outcomes in the sphere of industrial relations.

One naturally wonders what innovative perspectives or new evidence Brady can adduce in the shadow particularly of such authoritative, detailed and sophisticated studies of Labour Party–trade union relations by Lewis Minkin,[1] and other studies of contemporary United Kingdom trade-unionism and industrial relations. But, to his credit, he provides insights through four 'case studies' in four main ways: by reference to, and, where appropriate, citation from relevant scholarship (the extent of which he appears to be admirably aware of); through judicious quotation from his twenty-six interviews with actors who were often directly involved in the events described, or close to them; by the selective use of extracts from key documents, biographical accounts and the official records of meetings; and by the development and deployment of a group of conceptual categorizations intended to differentiate the various circumstances and relative degrees of success (or otherwise) of the four episodes under review.

Thus, in the early and mid-1970s, following the era of so-called '*collective laissez-faireism*', the Trade Union–Labour Party Liaison

Committee is depicted as constituting the appropriate mechanism and 'channel' for trade-union leaders to help shape the policy that resulted in the Social Contract, incorporating as it did both representatives of the Trades Union Congress (TUC) and unions that were not affiliates of the Labour Party. Irrespective of the ultimate breakdown of the Social Contract and the conflagrations of the 'Winter of Discontent', Brady is at pains to underline the palpable gains secured for both the unions and the then Labour government, achieved through a political dialogue combining formal and informal relations, fostered by the operation of the Liaison Committee.

After the Conservative governments' progressive adoption throughout the 1980s and 1990s of neoliberal, punitive socio-economic policies, increasingly restrictive labour legislation and the successive defeats inflicted on organized labour – steelworkers, miners, seafarers, Fleet Street printers – the Labour government, elected in May 1997, came to power furnished with a slew of transformative organizational and ideological shifts of its own, in part responses to the emergent dominance of neoliberal thinking and practice, which signalled changed relations with the UK trade-union movement in an era of 'growing union–party detachment' (p. 64). With the demise of the Liaison Committee, informal processes became pivotal, replacing formal structures and figuring first as a 'Contact Group' between leading members of the TUC General Council and Labour Shadow Cabinet, although even these sorts of links were steadily eroded by Tony Blair and replaced by irregular bilateral discussions which underlined significant differences in unions' priorities. This trend towards distancing and greater informality was consolidated under the Blair-led government. Brady bluntly records that 'trade union actors intimately involved in the transition from formal to informal processes through successive Labour leaders all emphasise the centralisation of power and detachment which emerged under Blair's leadership' (p. 71). Alongside this, and the production of the pre-election report, *Labour into Power: A Framework for Partnership*, the core notion of *'social partnership'* came to underpin an approach which Brady characterizes as *'regulated individualism'*, with greater emphasis on 'supply side initiatives such as skills, training and flexibility in the labour market' (p. 79). As well as the trade unions, employers and their representative organizations were also included as key members of this new approach to the determination of government employment and industrial relations policies. Such was the context for the introduction of the National Minimum Wage.

As Brady reports, the genesis and implementation of Labour Party and Labour government policy regarding a National Minimum Wage was 'historically one of the most contentious policy issues and vociferously opposed by powerful sections in the trade union movement' (p. 79). There were four main considerations in play: first, and most importantly, the question of whether or not unions should endorse the very principle of a statutory national minimum wage (a fierce battle and eventually successful campaign was largely fought out in the 1970s and 1980s, championed by Rodney Bickerstaffe as general secretary of the National Union of Public Employees, 1982–93); second, the level and scope of any proposed intervention, including which groups of workers, companies and sectors should be embraced by the proposed measure; third, the intended system of overseeing the scheme – matters such as how best to review its operation and impact, together with questions of methods of enforcement, up-rating and so on; and fourth, the potentially wider economic effects on such diverse matters as inflation (a major concern for employers' representatives who lobbied hard with predictions of dire consequences), traditional wage differentials (an anxiety especially for those unions chiefly representing skilled, higher-paid, and craft workers – particularly in manufacturing industries), and progress towards equal pay, and the implications especially for low-paid women and part-time workers.

In the absence of any established, authoritative, and inclusive institutions or well-oiled structures through which to address such sensitive and potentially divisive issues, the run-up to the newly elected Labour government's National Minimum Wage Bill in November 1997 was bound to underline semi-open conflicts of opinion and preference between and inside different unions, within the Labour Party, between the parliamentary party and the leadership, and even among ministers responsible for different elements of the government's programme. In such circumstances, informality, individual political preferences, personal alliances and a cat's cradle of shifting interactions in seeking resolution of these tricky issues were inevitable and, in any case, were the pattern of union–government relations favoured at the time by the Labour leadership. For their part, union leaders looked for such support as they could muster among favourably inclined ministers and union-sponsored Labour MPs, even though the latter had no formal role in the party's decision-making processes.

The consequent vagaries, struggles and vicissitudes surrounding the introduction of the National Minimum Wage, including the establishment of the Low Pay Commission, are briefly but usefully tracked by the author in the limited space that he affords himself and are colourfully illustrated by some well-chosen quotations from his interviewees, including the cool assessment by the lead specialist adviser in Downing Street (Jon Cruddas) that all the ensuing battles and toing and froing in defence of the ground-breaking initiative were simply 'the product of normal negotiations' (p. 99). Finally, whatever disappointments some union leaders expressed about the eventual level and scope of the National Minimum Wage, and the observation by some academic commentators that its final form illustrated the unions' relative weakness at the time, the verdict of the then TUC general secretary, John Monks, surely deserves acknowledgement: namely that the very establishment of a statutory minimum wage amounted to a significant 'milestone in twentieth-century industrial relations' (p. 92).

The experience of their discussions with the Labour government over low pay was confirmed for union leaders by the limited progress and eventual outcome of the negotiations prior to the Employment Relations Act 1999: the lack of co-ordinated union strategy facilitated the government's clear preference for individual rather than collective rights. Although the policy atmosphere was decidedly more benign than under the previous Tory governments, some of the union leaders interpreted the Blair government's stance on the issue of the legitimacy of unions' role in the shaping of public policy as amounting to little more than studied neutrality: unions had to demonstrate their value, utility and worth to their members, employers and the public at large. Rather than a concern with promoting trade-unionism as an institution, this was predominantly an era of what the author typifies as '*regulated individualism*' in which opportunities for collective decision-making and resolutions were diminished. Moreover, the retirement of prominent union leaders, with their close personal relationships, contributed to the fragmentation of co-ordinated action. As far as possible, those looking to strengthen the union case for a reformed legal framework sought to mobilize support from union-sponsored MPs and the Trade Union and Labour Party Liaison Organisation (TULO) which in 1994 had replaced Trade Unions for Labour (TUFL). This was a period, between 1997 and 2001, typified by relatively dilute union influence on government policy which Brady characterizes as one of '*group contestation*'. Some union leaders identified the corresponding absence of a co-ordinated strategy as both a consequence and cause of the government's increasing tendency towards a manipulative approach in its dealings with unions. Consequently, on the union leaders' side, around the time of the 2000 National Policy Forum, there emerged a '*collective adversarial*' strategy against the Labour government's perceived perspective. This emergent view encapsulated increased criticism of the then Labour government's approach, increased scepticism about its direction, and some serious consideration of selective disaffiliation from the Labour Party.

A combination of factors thus led to a reorientation of union efforts to influence government policy, most notably in the shaping of the so-called 'Warwick Agreement' of 2004. In addition to union disappointment at what had so far been secured from the government, there were deep structural changes to contend with, including widespread industrial and occupational restructuring, the pervasive effects on employment of globalization, a continued decline in membership density, major mergers resulting in the formation of the 'Big Four' unions – AMICUS, GMB, Transport and General Workers' Union (later Unite), and UNISON (and closer relationships between their newly elected leaders) – and the changed composition of the organized labour movement (away from manual, manufacturing and private industry). It was these shared understandings of the new generation of union leaders, assisted in part by a reconfiguration of TULO, and their desire for a more co-ordinated approach to seeking to influence government policy that resulted in the much more successful Warwick Agreement, incorporating a range of measures not only in respect of 'fairness at work', but also with agreed commitments on pensions, the operation of public services, the future of manufacturing, and actions to deal with such diverse challenges as domestic violence, older-age unemployment, rip-off credit agencies, and the future of the Royal Mail.

Admittedly, the new, concerted focus on Labour Party parliamentary politics was secured somewhat at the expense of excluding both the TUC and unaffiliated unions from the core discussions. Even so, all of this, Brady maintains, demonstrates that, even in the undoubtedly straightened and structurally uncongenial circumstances faced by UK unions, concerted, co-ordinated, and ideologically aligned union leadership can exercise decisive influence over a Labour government that is willing to listen. Duly co-operative human agency, in the form of determined leadership, can still prevail, despite the limitations inherent in harsh economic realities, lower trade-union membership and density, and reduced collective-bargaining coverage.

Within the context of what is a most useful and well-organized study, it is hardly surprising that there remain some flaws, none of them serious enough to vitiate the overall value of this book. First, the narrative too often betrays its apparent origins as a doctoral thesis. Thus, although the multiple scholarly references in the text and at the end of every chapter are impressive, the arguments that they purport to either support or refute are insufficiently spelt out, and the concepts are inadequately elaborated. In fairness, each of these weaknesses may be the result of a shortage of space or simply overzealous editing. Second, the author's understandable desire to place the study and events it analyses in an internationally comparative context, by 'book-ending' the study with a brief consideration of the 'varieties of capitalism' perspective, does not really work: it is both too condensed and, in any case, does not figure sufficiently in the rest of the book's analysis. Nor is it really necessary. Third, although the interviews and oral evidence are illuminating, they still manifest some well-known methodological drawbacks: they constitute essentially retrospective testimony, some of it from actors who were not even involved in the action being considered; all have a point to make or a position to justify or defend; and finally, oral evidence of this rich kind is inevitably selective – normally to support a given point of view or some analytical interpretation, and so requires more validating triangulation than is marshalled here. Fourth, the author's focus on union leaders necessarily masks a vast undertow of manoeuvrings, debates and differences both within and between different unions that at least needs referencing, if only in passing; if you like, the attitudes and behaviour of the unions' members are missing and are given no role at all in the dramas described.

Fifth, there is a lack of definitional or analytical clarification of what the author understands by the respective terms of 'leadership' and 'a market economy', given not only that these two concepts are both central to the book's main argument but are also each deeply contested notions, especially in self-identified 'democratic' organizations, such as trade unions. Sixth, there is some confusion around the precise status of the various concepts deployed by the author to differentiate the character of the four instances of policy formation covered by the study: sometimes they refer to the unions' or their leaders' perspectives, sometimes they summarize the government's preferred approach, and sometimes they are intended to describe the outcomes of the actions or relationships described. Seventh, and this is a minor quibble, the book's title is somewhat misleading; it is only about one dimension among many of union 'power' and not really about 'employment' but about policies towards industrial relations, unions' status, and related issues. Finally, this excellent study merits a more robust set of conclusions than the author rather modestly offers; such an engaging and relevant account of trade-union leaders' influence on the policies of Labour governments deserves more elaborate exposition. None of these criticisms, however, detract from Brady's valuable contribution to analysing the relationship between trade unions and Labour governments.

R. H. (Bob) Fryer

Note

1 L. Minkin, *The Contentious Alliance: Trade Unions and the Labour Party* (Edinburgh University Press: 1991); *idem, The Blair Supremacy: A Study in the Politics of Labour's Party Management* (Manchester University Press: 2014).

https://doi.org/10.3828/hsir.2020.41.15

Abstracts

'A Great Number of … Women'?: The Changing Involvement of Female Workers in Master and Servant Cases in England, 1685–1860 (pp. 1–35)
Madeleine Chartrand

Between the late seventeenth and mid-nineteenth centuries in England, female workers' involvement in employment disputes that were summarily adjudicated by Justices of the Peace (magistrates) under master and servant law decreased. Women's diminishing work opportunities in arable agriculture after the late eighteenth century likely contributed to this downward trend. However, female textile workers were a notable exception, as manufacturers and magistrates used employment law to coerce greater productivity from them. Master and servant prosecutions both reflected changes in women's occupational patterns and served as a means to exploit a feminized textile labour force that was crucial to industrialization and to our interpretation of its nature and causes.

Time, Tea Breaks, and the Frontier of Control in UK Workplaces (pp. 37–64)
Martin Upchurch

A by-product of the intensification and reorganization of work over the last four decades has been a squeeze and sometimes elimination of paid rest breaks – lunch breaks, tea (or coffee) breaks, as well as individual toilet breaks. This paper explores the history of such breaks in Britain, covering whims, fads and changes in management ideologies and practices as they apply to time discipline and patterns of resistance seen through the lens of the 'frontier of control'. More recent developments have seen a partial return to the 'paid break', running against the dominant trend of cutbacks in breaks or conversion from paid to unpaid breaks. Traditional battles over the 'frontier of control' on the line or in the office will persist as pressures on time continue through processes of both temporal flexibility and density.

After the 1910 Eight-Week Lockout: 'Flächentarifvertrag' *in the German Construction Industry* (pp. 65–84) Jörn Janssen

The greatest industrial dispute before the First World War in Germany, a national lockout in the construction industry, lasting eight weeks and involving up to 245,000 workers, ended with a defeat of the German Construction Employers' Federation – Deutscher Arbeitgeberbund für das Baugewerbe – on 18 June 1910 after a tripartite process of arbitration. This industrial dispute about a new national framework contract – *Flächentarifvertrag* – on collective employment relations and bargaining in the construction industry heralded a new stage in labour–capital relations. It led to a substantial unification and concentration of workers' organizations and divided the employer's organization, benefiting, on the one hand, the sectoral labour unions to the detriment of local unions, and, on the other, the joint-stock corporations to the detriment of smaller, individually owned companies.

Cash Wages, the Truck Acts, and the 1960 Payment of Wages Act (pp. 85–108) Christopher Frank

From the mid-1950s until the early 1960s, there was an ongoing tussle between British employers and the Trades Union Congress (TUC) over whether to repeal the (1831–96) Truck Acts which established the right of manual workers to be paid in cash ('coin of the realm') and regulated employers' ability to fine them or take deductions from their wages. Many employers advocated repeal, insisting that truck legislation was ill-suited to the modern economy, interfered with freedom to contract, and impeded more efficient forms of paying wages. Organized labour, through the TUC, countered that these laws protected workers from arbitrary deductions and prevented employers from imposing unpopular methods of paying wages (such as by cheque or bank transfer). This dispute resulted in the minor reform of the 1960 Payment of Wages Act.

The (1959–61) Karmel Committee, which studied the contemporary operation of the Truck Acts, recommended repeal, though keeping some protection, but there was disagreement about who should be covered and what should be protected. The TUC, near the apex of its power, had proved the efficacy of the law and, given the inability to reach consensus, the government eventually dropped the subject for a generation.

Crisis at Work: Gender, Class, and the Dehumanization of Jobs (pp. 109–35)
Harriet Bradley

Drawing on Huw Beynon's paper in *HSIR* 40 (2019), this article surveys the position of women in the UK labour market over the last fifty years. It suggests that many of the developments Beynon describes are relevant to women's employment, but with the added twist that women's position in the labour market and society is structured by their responsibility within the total social organization of labour for reproductive labour. Despite increased women's employment, gender segregation, both horizontal and vertical, is obstinately persistent, especially in working-class occupations. Two of these occupations, care work and retail, are used to illustrate how increasing precarity of jobs combined with technologies of control have brought about a dehumanization of work. It is concluded that the restructuring of global capitalism on neoliberal principles has negatively affected opportunities for women workers.

After the Long Boom: The Reconfiguration of Work and Labour in the Public Sector (pp. 137–67) Bob Carter

This response to Huw Beynon's paper, 'After the Long Boom: Living with Capitalism in the Twenty-First Century' in *HSIR* 40 (2019), offers a parallel analysis of the fortunes of labour in the public sector. Among Beynon's central observations, drawing on Karl Marx and Harry Braverman, was the continued reproduction of 'unskilled' and degraded labour. A parallel process, de-professionalizing occupations through the separation of conception and execution, has been a feature of the almost continual restructuring of state and local authority organizations and their work practices since the 1960s. This has accelerated in the era of governments committed to neoliberal values and policies. Despite public-sector trade unions having been largely conservative and defensive in their values and practice, a number of factors, both structural and conjunctural, have compelled them to face this new reality and make them the most likely organizations to challenge the expanding reach of neoliberalism. Recognizing these factors provides a possible remedy to the implied pessimism that follows the largely private-sector focus of Beynon's contribution.

The Bullock Report and European Experience (1977) (pp. 169–88) Hugh Clegg

Whatever the shortcomings of the Bullock Committee's terms of reference, the injunction to take account of European experience was not one of them. The volume and scope of the evidence is, however, limited: equal representation for shareholders and workers has been tried only in the German coal and steel industries where it was introduced by the occupation authorities after the Second World War. Most European countries, including France and Italy, have nothing to offer. The Committee relied mainly on West Germany and Sweden, with occasional references to Holland and Denmark. Continental versions of industrial democracy worked where an industrial relations system already existed, developed through workplace and industry institutional practices over decades. Nevertheless, the Committee's majority report used European evidence to support its three main proposals. Worker directors are irrelevant to the task of reforming British industrial relations. European experience is of limited relevance because Britain is not behind European countries in its problem of industrial relations in the enterprise, but ahead of them in what the late Allan Flanders called 'the challenge from below', which is being posed all over the world but more sharply in Britain than anywhere else.

Reading Hugh Clegg's 'The Bullock Report and European Experience' (1977) *in Historical Context* (pp. 189–96) Peter Ackers

Hugh Clegg's riposte to the 1977 Bullock Report on Industrial Democracy was one of seven papers published from a conference on the subject in April that year. His contribution has to be seen against his long-standing views (expressed, for example, in 1951 and 1960) on industrial democracy which he saw in practical terms as free trade unions conducting collective bargaining. On the Donovan Commission (1965–68), he supported the majority opposition to recommending even voluntary schemes for worker directors. In 1977 he regarded worker directors as irrelevant to the urgent, practical task of reforming British industrial relations. For Clegg, continental versions of industrial democracy worked where there was already a successful prior industrial relations system, developed through workplace and industry institutional practices over decades. One new, top-level initiative could not create that.

'The Bullock Report and European Experience': What We Can Still Learn about Worker Directors from Hugh Clegg (pp. 197–212) Michael Gold

Hugh Clegg's paper, 'The Bullock Report and European Experience', written in 1977, analyses the role of worker directors appointed to the boards of UK companies, a move which formed part of the then Labour government's Social Contract with the trade unions designed to stem the country's long-term industrial decline. My commentary argues that three aspects of the paper are likely to strike the contemporary reader most forcibly. Initially it seems *alien* as it describes a world of collectivist industrial relations that was erased by the Conservative government elected in 1979. Yet on closer reading its main theme – reforming corporate accountability – emerges as all too *familiar*, as worker exploitation and other corporate scandals have continued largely unchecked to the present. And we may reflect that more recent research into *policy transfer* has improved our contemporary understanding of the barriers to corporate governance reform since the 1970s. Clegg correctly cautioned against attempting to import institutions from countries such as Germany into the UK, a view that has since been refined by analysis of the contrasts between co-ordinated and liberal market economies. Reforming corporate governance requires tailor-made policies, not those transferred merely on grounds of success in their original host countries.

The Bullock Committee, Industrial Democracy, and the Trade Unions: The Revolution that Never Was (pp. 213–28) John Edmonds

The report of the Bullock Committee on Industrial Democracy aimed to transform British industrial relations by instituting worker directors on the board of large companies. This transformation never took place. A minority report by the three committee members representing business interests opposed putting workers' representatives on the board. The aftermath was even more disappointing: the Labour government's White Paper diluted several of Bullock's recommendations but before legislation could be tabled, in May 1979, the incoming Conservative government led by Margaret Thatcher declared that the Bullock recommendations would never be enacted.

The goal of industrial democracy is to reduce the autocratic power of management and give all employees greater control of their working lives. Given the weakness of trade unions today, it is time to look again at statutory works councils in Germany and representation of a minority of worker directors on the board, both elected by all employees. This would

give workers and their unions information about the state of the company
and about management intentions.

---

*Backwards in Time? Reflections of an Industrial Relations Officer in the
Coventry and District Engineering Employers' Association, 1977–1979*
(pp. 229–47) Neil Ritson

The paper presents an auto-ethnographic account of a personal socio-
psychological 'journey' from work in a modern 'progressive' oil company
in south-eastern England to the engineering industry in the Coventry
district. The role of the association in industrial relations, in which the
author was involved, is described in a series of vignettes. The paper
presents detailed observations regarding the extant culture of that area
and industrial relations in the companies represented by the Coventry and
District Engineering Employers' Association from the point of view of a
quasi-independent but participant observer.

---

*Then and Now: Vulnerable Workers, Industrial Action, and the Law in the
1970s and Today* (pp. 249–60) Alan Tuckman

With the much vaunted 'withering of the strike', a mythology of past
militancy appears to have taken root; militant men taking to the picket
line on the flimsiest of pretexts. This stereotype is challenged through
exploring two accounts of three strikes, Trico and Grunwick in 1976,
and, following the raft of 'salami slicing' legislation kettling workers and
trade unions, the dispute at Gate Gourmet in 2005. These were acts of
desperation by vulnerable workers. Each book highlights the heterogeneity
of race and gender, and in some cases how this served to divide workers.
The attack on existing conditions and the increased use of agency workers,
the issues challenged by Gate Gourmet workers, and continued disputes
concerning equal pay, as with the Trico strike, indicate the limited power of
organized labour today in the context of the persistence, if not escalation,
of employment grievances.

Printed and bound by CPI Group (UK) Ltd, Croydon, CR0 4YY

23/04/2025

14660994-0001